ITALY 1636

Italy 1636 is one of the most closely-researched and detailed books on the operation of early modern armies anywhere, and is explicitly inspired by neo-Darwinian thinking wherein human beings are evolved animals equipped with a wide variety of innate predispositions. Taking the French and Savoyard invasion of Spanish Lombardy in 1636 as its specific example, it begins with the recruitment of the soldiers, the care and feeding of the armies and their horses, the impact of the invasion on civilians in the path of their advance, and the manner in which generals conducted their campaign in response to the information at their disposal. The next section describes the unfolding of the long and stubborn battle of Tornavento, where Spanish, German, and Italian soldiers stormed the French in their entrench-ments. The book describes in unprecedented detail the tactics of both the infantry and the cavalry, and validates the effectiveness of Spanish methods in the 1630s. The account focuses on the motivations of soldiers to fight, and how they reacted to the stress of combat. Gregory Hanlon arrives at surprising conclusions on the conditions under which they were ready to kill their adversaries, and when they were content to intimidate them into retiring. The volume concludes by examining the penchant for looting of the soldiery in the aftermath of battle, the methods of treating wounded soldiers in the Milan hospital, the horrific consequences of hygienic breakdown in the French camp, and the strategic failure of the invasion in the aftermath of battle. This in turn underscores the surprising resilience of Spanish policies and Spanish arms in Europe. In describing with painstaking detail the invasion of 1636, Hanlon explores the universal features of human behaviour and psychology as they relate to violence and war.

Gregory Hanlon is a French-trained behavioural historian of the early modern period. He has written books on religious history in France, rural history in Italy, and three books on the involvement of Italy and Italians in the great wars of the early modern era. All this work is directly influenced by the social and behavioural sciences, from psychology, to anthropology and sociology, to primatology and human ethology. These sciences enhance our understanding of humans everywhere as evolved, thinking animals, packed with natural dispositions.

'Gregory Hanlon, a noted connoisseur of both the military and the Italian history of Early Modernity, [has] presented [a] masterpiece of contemporary "operational history" or "histoire bataille."'

Sven Externbrink, *Francia-Recensio*

'It will certainly be of interest to political and military historians with a special interest in the Thirty Years War, Italian states and France.'

Nina Lamal, *European History Quarterly*

'This is an exciting book that, at times, has a polemical quality; mostly it is full of rich, careful analysis.'

Bruce Vandervort, *Journal of Military History*

Italy 1636

Cemetery of Armies

GREGORY HANLON

OXFORD
UNIVERSITY PRESS

OXFORD
UNIVERSITY PRESS

Great Clarendon Street, Oxford, OX2 6DP,
United Kingdom

Oxford University Press is a department of the University of Oxford.
It furthers the University's objective of excellence in research, scholarship,
and education by publishing worldwide. Oxford is a registered trade mark of
Oxford University Press in the UK and in certain other countries

First published 2016
First published in paperback 2018

Impression: 2

Published in the United States of America by Oxford University Press
198 Madison Avenue, New York, NY 10016, United States of America

British Library Cataloguing in Publication Data
Data available

Library of Congress Cataloging in Publication Data
Data available

ISBN 978–0–19–873824–4 (Hbk.)
ISBN 978–0–19–873825–1 (Pbk.)

Printed and bound by
CPI Group (UK) Ltd, Croydon, CR0 4YY

à mes maîtres

Acknowledgements

A mere dilettante in military history, I have benefited from the counsel of a variety of persons more expert than myself in fields that pertain to this study of a particular campaign of the Thirty Years' War in Italy. The entire description of the battle echoes the wise advice of Malcolm Wanklyn of the University of Wolverhampton, but the continental tactics are rooted in the work of Czech historian Pavel Hrnčirik, relayed first to me by Giovanni Cerino Badone. The sounding board for knowledge of the Spanish army and its officer corps has been Fernando Gonzalez Leon in the United States, and for the Neapolitans, AngelAntonio Spagnoletti in Bari. The advice of Giovanni Vittorio Signorotto to look for important neglected documentation in Florence proved entirely sound. I heartily thank the director of the Archivio di Stato of Florence, dott.ssa Carla Zarrilli, for trying to track a battlefield sketch of Tornavento, and Giampiero Brunelli in Rome for elucidating a published source for me. Paragraphs based in animal ethology were helped greatly by my Dalhousie University colleague Simon Gadbois, giving more context to the human psychology behind the military institution of which Marco Costa at the University of Bologna is the principal inspiration. Local historians, Franco Bertolli in Lombardy, Mario Zannoni and Giuseppe Bertini in Parma, and Alberto Menziani in Modena, have pointed me to key archival sources. Portions of this work have been presented to research seminars for valuable feedback, at the University of Pavìa for Mario Rizzo and his colleagues, Paris IV-Sorbonne for Denis Crouzet, the Ecole des Hautes Etudes de Sciences Sociales in Paris, for Robert Descimon, and the University of Grenoble for Gilles Bertrand, Giuliano Ferretti, and Stéphane Gal. To all of them my heartfelt thanks.

Contents

List of Illustrations

List of Maps

Introduction
The Thirty Years' War in Italy

Ne pas 'croire'...ne porter aucun jugement moral. Ne pas s'étonner. Ne pas s'emporter.

(Marcel Mauss, *Manuel d'Ethnographie* (1926), 6)

Of all the genres of written history, the oldest one *celebrates* the armed encounter of men in opposing armies on a battlefield: it has always been the 'grand genre de narration historique'.[1] There are good reasons for this, for the people who participated in wars understood that they were important events worth committing to institutional memory. Battles built and destroyed polities and swept away civilizations. A decisive battle is the midwife of History, goes the saying. Early scribes exulted in the slaughter of enemies and acclaimed these triumphs of kings as glorious accomplishments. Glory, in the sense of an expression of power worth remembering, remains a word almost synonymous with martial prowess. Official commemorations today are more muted than in the past, but the possibility of war still looms on the horizon of every human society.[2] Given its salience throughout time, understanding armed conflict and organized human aggression should be high on the list of problems in all the social sciences. War would not exist if there were not good reasons to wage it, that is, that the perceived benefits of it outweighed its obvious drawbacks.[3] Few states today have come into being without armed strife in the past, and today's two hundred sovereign states are but the residue of a vast number of others, large and small, extinguished by conquest.[4] Even peaceful states today all rely, at bottom, on the threat and occasional employment of armed force against recalcitrant or belligerent people in order to protect lives and property of the others. Governments will employ coercion, if they must, to levy taxes for all their functions. Whenever necessary, or even merely opportune, states marshal and expand the same armed forces to counter foreign threats or to smite their enemies pre-emptively. Despite its costs and its risks, many people still today glorify war and consider it a viable option, under certain conditions. It remains a *natural* mechanism for resolving disputes, a human universal in every era

---

[1] Olivier Chaline, 'La bataille comme objet de l'histoire', *Francia*, 32/2 (2005), 1–14.
[2] John Keegan, *A History of Warfare* (New York, 1993), 3.   [3] Ibid. 59.
[4] Robert Wright, *Nonzero: The Logic of Human Destiny* (New York, 2000), 54–64.

of history, and it was not at all peculiar to the period and place that will be the focus of this book.[5]

War is a fact of life rooted in the normal logic of human behaviour. Its roots are older than humanity itself, as primatologists know.[6] Any behaviour manifested everywhere by a species must therefore possess an adaptive basis for its practitioners. Our behavioural repertoire contains traits that are normally quiescent, even over generations, but which can be triggered in certain circumstances.[7] It remains with us expressed in more benign activities, wherever competition between teams draws supporters and spectators. Both human children (overwhelmingly males) and chimpanzees indulge in mock fighting and invent play weapons of every description.[8] Violence has multiple roots in human drives, only one of which is instrumental for predatory ends. First and foremost, violence is implicit in the Golden Rule; it keeps others within bounds on threat of revenge. Primate species, and humans among them, engage continually with each other and invest effort and resources in order to extract recognition and help from those they live with. Disappointment triggers a keen desire—a deep-rooted passion—to retaliate. This violent reaction is innate and universal, not learned.[9] Throughout time, human groups defend themselves against aggression or spoliation and populations everywhere rise up against rulers whose actions they think are unfair. A common origin of war is a keen desire for moralistic revenge, to even the score for perceived wrongs.[10] To echo Frans de Waal, aggression is something you should not wish to eradicate, for it makes social life possible.[11]

Humans are not egalitarian, anywhere: aggression in males results from the drive for status, supremacy, or dominance over rivals, which yields benefits in access to more females. Prehistoric men with no use for land or gold cultivated war in order to build large kin alliances, expressed in multiple wives and abundant offspring. These were markers of status and tangible proof of success.[12] Our willingness to cooperate with others for our individual advantage magnifies the repercussion of violence many times when we form coalitions around leaders. Our friendship with X, and his kin, will compel us to take a dim view of Y, or at least our need for X outweighs our need for or fear of Y—for now.[13] Coalition-building entails some

[5] Frank Tallett and D. J. B. Trim, 'An Overview of Change and Continuity in Late-Medieval and Early Modern Warfare', in F. Tallett and D. J. B. Trim (eds), *European Warfare 1350–1750* (Cambridge, 2010), 22.

[6] Michael P. Ghiglieri, *The Dark Side of Man: Tracing the Origins of Male Violence* (Cambridge, MA, 2000), 171–5.

[7] Steven Pinker, *The Better Angels of our Nature: The Decline of Violence and its Causes* (London and New York, 2011), 488.

[8] Marvin Zuckerman, *Sensation Seeking and Risky Behavior* (Washington, DC, 2007), 87.

[9] Marco Costa, *Psicologia militare: Elementi di psicologia per gli appartenenti alle forze armate* (Milan, 2003), 42.

[10] Pinker, *Better Angels*, 508–43.

[11] Frans B. M. de Waal, 'Morality and its Relation to Primate Social Instincts', in Henrik Høgh-Olesen (ed.), *Human Morality and Sociality: Evolutionary and Comparative Perspectives* (Basingstoke and New York, 2010), 31–57.

[12] Napoleon A. Chagnon, *Noble Savages: My life among Two Dangerous Tribes—the Yanomamö and the Anthropologists* (New York and London, 2013), 49–54.

[13] Costa, *Psicologia militare*, 39–42.

important cognitive requirements. Evolutionary psychologists stress how the ability to distinguish between cooperators and defectors enables us to mete out both rewards and punishment to our peers and rivals.[14] It also entails long-term planning: we can feign friendliness and contain our desire for attack or riposte until a more propitious moment arrives. Wars past and present erupt because the initiator believes it is opportune to strike a potential enemy pre-emptively. These practices, charted by Chagnon for primitive societies in Amazonia, are still operant in the twenty-first century.[15] We do not need to assume that all states are always locked in a competitive battle for hegemony, as Alan James phrases it; in every period these political entities have coexisted. But periodically their respective interests seem incompatible; at that moment, the military option tempts one or both sides.[16] One single warlike group is enough to force many others to defend themselves from spoliation.[17] Since the recourse to arms belongs to the human cognitive and behavioural repertoire, it is not excessively difficult to recruit people to voluntarily submit to its rigours, and some people, again almost exclusively males, actively seek it out. Although war is less widespread today than in the past, we will not see its complete disappearance any time soon. Whenever a modern state gives up control over part of its territory—on any continent—competitive young men with weapons immediately fill the void.

Given the universality of war, rooted in the competition and bonding of men, we must study it squarely as a value-free phenomenon. A condemnation of war as universally *evil in principle* perhaps has merits on ethical grounds (although I doubt it), but this rigid stance cannot help us understand human behaviour either then or now. Mainstream academic historians have for at least a century considered anathema military history in general and battle history in particular, often deploring the interest in military affairs as intellectually unhealthy and crypto-militarist. This scorn is something to be deplored, for people who mock the field tend to be blind to its ongoing importance.[18] This intellectual aversion to such a universal phenomenon is not just a defect among historians. In anthropology too, notwithstanding war's centrality in the existence of many of the societies fieldworkers studied at close quarters, an interest in the problem developed only recently.[19] In the general public, on the other hand, impervious to arcane currents of cultural history, the appetite for the thick description of war and battle among the reading public has never lapsed. Battle history, together with the growing

[14] John Tooby and Leda Cosmides, 'The Evolution of War and its Cognitive Foundations', *Institute for Evolutionary Studies Technical Report 88–1* (1988), 2.

[15] Chagnon, *Noble Savages*, 220–2, 314–27.

[16] Alan James, 'Rethinking the Peace of Westphalia: Toward a Theory of Early-Modern Warfare', in Jonathan Davies (ed.), *Aspects of Violence in Renaissance Europe* (Farnham and Burlington, VT, 2013), 107–26.

[17] Ghiglieri, *Dark Side*, 191–2.

[18] Peter Paret, 'The Annales School and the History of War', *Journal of Military History*, 73, 2009, 1289–94; Lucien Febvre called military history obsolete back in 1920, but he was not the first, Chaline, 'La bataille', 3.

[19] Keegan, *History of Warfare*, 102; the illusion of the noble savage still has considerable hold on modern anthropology, as related by Chagnon.

phenomenon of military re-enactment, seek to provide a vicarious and bloodless experience of the real thing.[20]

The revolution in historical investigation originating in France after the Second World War deliberately turned its back on a rich legacy of military historical scholarship in order to give priority to other problems and explore in particular the great rural majority of the population that scholars had neglected. It was not long before social historians of this *Annales* school began to mine army archives too in novel ways, for that generation actively sought to widen historical perspectives by adopting the methods of other social sciences. André Corvisier almost single-handedly invented the study of the army rank and file, by transcribing the files of hundreds of thousands of individual soldiers into early computer programmes, and then by examining the machinery of army administration in war and peace over almost a century.[21] Philippe Contamine rejuvenated late medieval military history by placing endemic war in its social context.[22] Geoffrey Parker's ground-breaking work on the Spanish army of Flanders, which made the connection between the details of recruitment and logistics and military success or failure, appeared not long after.[23] A German business historian, Fritz Redlich, simultaneously opened a third axis of research, into the role of private enterprise in waging war during the seventeenth century. He showed how colonels formed little business consortia in order to recruit, equip, and maintain soldiers in the field in the hopes of reimbursement or some similar reward from the various warlords who granted them commissions.[24] Younger scholars quickly emulated these studies in Europe and America to the point where the bibliography today is considerable in all three areas, with a great deal of cross-fertilization.

Military historians steeped in the literature of battles protested that the authors moving in new directions were missing the main point: that armies existed to fight, and that those who would analyse the dynamics of great power politics could not understand them from the sociology of armies and logistical matters alone.[25] But drum-and-trumpet history of the popular sort was not considered a genre worthy of a serious modern historian until the publication of John Keegan's *The Face of Battle* in 1976. That author brilliantly reconstructed the predicaments and the psychology of the combatants inasmuch as these could be surmised from the sources, which were principally literary. He and some of his most influential peers, while armed with doctorates, did not follow a typical university *cursus*. Keegan, Christopher Duffy, David Chandler, and Paddy Griffith all taught at the prestigious British army's officers' academy at Sandhurst. Their students were professional officers destined for leadership positions in the armed forces. Interestingly

---

[20] Richard Holmes, *Acts of War*, 2nd edn (London, 2003), 4–5.

[21] André Corvisier, *L'armée française de la fin du XVIIe siècle au ministère de Choiseul: Le soldat* (Paris, 1964); Corvisier also published the first synthesis of such studies, *Armées et sociétés en Europe de 1494 à 1789* (Paris, 1976).

[22] Philippe Contamine, *Guerre, Etat et société à la fin du Moyen Age* (Paris, 1972).

[23] Geoffrey Parker, *The Army of Flanders and the Spanish Road (1567–1659)* (Cambridge, 1972).

[24] Fritz Redlich, *The German Military Enterpriser and his Work Force* (Wiesbaden, 1964).

[25] Dennis E Showalter, 'A Modest Plea for Drums and Trumpets', *Military Affairs*, 39 (1975), 71–4.

enough, the instructors' extra-curricular activities fed their passion for battle history. David Chandler was a pioneer military re-enactor, a pastime which has flourished and expanded since. Paddy Griffith designed tabletop war games, first for the military college itself, and then commercially for private enthusiasts. American historians of early modern battles, Brent Nosworthy and William P. Guthrie, were likewise war-game designers in the late 1960s and 1970s when this activity was popular in English-speaking countries. This observation in not intended to deride them or diminish the value of their work, quite the contrary. This playful approach to military history underpins considerable research into the details of weapons and tactical systems that governed the mechanics of battle. There is something in militaria that sparks men's imaginations.[26] This is surely no artefact. In all the societies studied to date, men and principally young men wage war, and they constitute most of the victims of violence too. If women and children appear among the victims, they usually figure as some sort of 'collateral damage' inflicted off the battlefield.[27]

Only in recent years have early modernists with university berths re-examined the accounts of battles rendered famous by centuries of celebration. This time their works are more often rooted in a fair-minded spirit that takes pains to consult sources generated by all the belligerents. The approach is not everywhere the same, owing in part to enduring academic traditions in different countries. John Lynn's work sets combat into a broad intellectual framework, which is common in America where the Great Books Tradition, rooted in nineteenth-century idealism, is never far away. Britain's civil war inspired generations of scholars and has resulted in a copious literature on almost every aspect of the conflict, dwarfing the study of other wars. In France the revival of battle history is still very modest and confines itself largely to the reigns of Louis XIV and Napoleon; André Corvisier made it more respectable in his late career at the Sorbonne, where Olivier Chaline and Hervé Drévillon teach today.

Building on that background, this book examines how leaders conducted war in 1636, how the soldiers—volunteers in their great majority—fought it, and how the civilians caught in the path of armies reacted to their predicament. It focuses on what was by European standards a minor battle in a secondary theatre of the Thirty Years' War, but its ultimate aim is much broader. The general public still conceives of Europe's first Great War as a period of endemic conflict waged on a vast scale that had its epicentre in Central Europe. Not all of it fits conveniently into the German narrative, however, for it engulfed most European states for longer or shorter periods. Spain committed vast resources to the struggle for practically the entire duration of the war and even beyond, from 1620 to 1659 (and it fought vainly against breakaway Portugal until 1667). The war provoked that great empire's relentless decline, slower and more fitful than once thought, but which was real enough.[28] The Italian theatre is usually absent from general accounts of

[26] Holmes, *Acts of War*, 16.   [27] Costa, *Psicologia militare*, 58–70.
[28] On the slow decline of the Spanish imperial system, Robert Stradling, *Europe and the Decline of Spain: A Study of the Spanish System 1580–1720* (London and Boston, 1981); and Stradling, *Philip IV and the Government of Spain, 1621–1665* (Cambridge and New York, 1988).

the Thirty Years' War, like those of Peter H. Wilson and Geoffrey Parker.[29] Sometimes historians include the fateful campaigns of the Mantuan Succession (1629–30) because they drew the German Imperial army down into Lombardy to remove the incipient French threat. This interlude gave the Protestants some crucial breathing space and allowed Gustavus Adolphus to pick up the fallen Protestant torch, which led to the further internationalization of the conflict. The Italian theatre was more than a minor detail in the broader tableau of the war, however. Campaigns pitting French and Savoyard armies against the Spanish-led forces and their German auxiliaries in Italy lasted almost a quarter-century. Yet this theatre interests neither the French, nor the German, nor even the Spanish historians to this day. For the French, Italy was 'the cemetery of armies', where their designs for conquest or domination always came undone. Still more, this endless war (beginning in 1625, erupting again in 1628–30, and then raging uninterrupted between 1635 and 1659) resulted in no obvious advantage for either side. Italian historiography is slender too, despite the fact that the contest, which at various times implicated every part of the peninsula, constituted the single most important event in the country's history between the Council of Trent and the French Revolution. Italian academic historians, with a few important exceptions, wilfully ignore the war, because it does not fit the local framework in which they operate. More generally, Italians *avoid* military history, for it has associations with an unsavoury Fascist past. It is acceptable to study defeats like Novara, Custoza, Adua, Caporetto, and El Alamein, for colleagues in a competitive and often cut-throat environment cannot then accuse an incautious historian of cultivating dangerous martial instincts. Italian historians who constitute the exceptions, and whose works are of generally high calibre, focus on army administration and finance of a single participant, and tend to reduce the campaign narratives to a minimum.[30]

Campaigns of movement, siege, and attrition wore down much of North-Central Italy for decades. Battles, in contrast, were infrequent events, and never matched those of the German or Low Countries theatres in scale or decisiveness, with the single exception of the siege and battle of Turin in 1706. Most of the armed encounters on Italian soil were 'actions', or engagements committing fewer than 10,000 men on each side, and usually many fewer. None of them destroyed the capacity of the loser to continue the war or permitted the victor to occupy whole provinces. Tornavento, examined here, was the largest event between the day of Pavia in 1525 and the contest of La Marsaglia in Piedmont in 1693, but neither side numbered much more than 15,000 combatants. Our battle's decisiveness emerged only in hindsight, in a negative way: it prevented a French conquest of Milan and Spanish Lombardy, the key to the entire peninsula. Contemporaries could not know in advance that it would be the sole set-piece battle in a quarter-century of continuous campaigning.

---

[29] Peter H. Wilson, *The Thirty Years War: Europe's Tragedy* (London, 2009); Geoffrey Parker et al., *The Thirty Years War* (London, 1984).

[30] A few of the more salient students of this period are Guido Candiani and Luciano Pezzolo (Venice), Davide Maffi (Milan), Mario Rizzo (Pavia), and Carla Sodini (Florence).

If the rare Italian battles were comparatively small-scale and indecisive, why bother studying one at all? First and foremost, battles tested a state's ability to resist foreign conquest. Contemporaries were well aware of the likely consequences of success and failure on the field. The long day's outcome at Tornavento vindicated the Governor of Milan's confidence in the ability of Spain to confront its adversaries and it confirmed his impression that he could count on the willingness of the Lombards themselves to resist the Franco-Savoyard invaders. These are important conclusions in the political history both of Italy and of the Spanish empire. The presence of Tuscan and Modenese contingents assisting Spain and the watchful apprehension of neighbouring states, like the republics of Genoa and Venice and the Papal States, teach us something too about the dynamics of Italian territorial entities before the peninsula's political unification. The campaign leading up to the battle also sheds light on the ambitious policies of France's chief minister Cardinal Richelieu, which historians usually study from the perspective of French interests alone. By denying the legitimacy of the interests of France's few Italian allies, the powerful minister destined his schemes to fail.

But there are other, more general lessons too we can draw from the campaign of 1636. The operations teach us about the ability of armies to function in hostile territory. The art of war in the mid-seventeenth century teaches us a great deal about early modern economic limitations, which prevented armies from achieving decisive results quickly. Strategy demanded that armies seize bulk resources from the zone of operations, but the enemy did not make it easy for them. The contest of Tornavento also serves as a window to observe the mechanics of combat in the crucial decade of the 1630s, which historians consider to be a turning point, from hand-to-hand affrays with pikes and swords to lengthy firefights. The sources shed light on important problems relative to combat at that time, and some aspects of combat throughout time. We can assess the behaviour of the soldiers too, who were subject to considerable *natural* inhibitions towards killing other people face to face. Both before and after the fight, campaigning unfolded in a framework of discomfort, lax sanitation, and rampant disease. And finally, war inflicted terrible hardship and loss of life among civilians, both those living in the combat zone and the harried refugees who reached protective spaces. Even though shared rules of engagement with enemy combatants and civilians mitigated war's savagery, the conflict still inflicted death on a large scale. These phenomena still hold true today.

The sources tend to be laconic to a fault, alas!, for the rank and file of European armies did not write letters home with the frequency or fluency of their descendants in the Napoleonic era. The advent of popular letter-writing and a cheap postal service lay far in the future. South European soldiers were more generally unlettered than their contemporaries in Germany, northern France, the Low Countries, and England. Even for the literate minority, committing experience to paper while the memory was fresh did not correspond to the vagabond lifestyle of soldiers. As for the officers, most of the senior ones were at some level courtiers, given to rivalry and self-censorship. Scholars have disinterred from the archives only a few accounts of the action penned by officers below commanding general. Other accounts are scarce too. A diligent search of over one hundred volumes of manuscript catalogues covering all of Italy uncovered exactly one (anonymous) account of the battle of Tornavento, and precious few other references to battles and sieges of the Thirty Years' War. In the 1630s, there was apparently no large public avid for news and descriptions of battles taking place on Italian territory. Bombastic printed accounts of battles dating from the era took the form of propaganda pamphlets. Fortunately however, the three published accounts (two French and one Spanish) prove to be remarkably concordant. We also possess an invaluable summary of the day's fighting by the diplomat-administrator Michel Particelli d'Hémery. While not a combatant properly speaking, it fell to him to find money and supplies for the French army, and to keep the lines of communication open between King Louis XIII and Cardinal Richelieu on the one hand, and Duke Victor-Amadeus of Savoy on the other. His continuous dispatches to Paris are refreshing in their frankness. The Spanish materials are fewer in number, and contain few details on the stages of the combat. The supreme commander Leganés confined his description of the fighting to the Council of State in Madrid to four or five lines of text. The lone Italian anonymous account emanating from the Habsburg army is one of the most detailed and valuable we possess, but it too ignores the manner men fought.

Malcolm Wanklyn writes that the narrative historian's traditional role has been to use the traces of the past to recount what happened in past centuries and then proceed to explain it. These analytical descriptions must conform to the laws of logic in terms of evidence and argument, and must 'take cognizance' of narratives already in existence.[31] The principal difficulty of writing battle history lays in the lumpy nature of the evidence. Eyewitnesses placed the emphasis on what they considered worth remembering, while ignoring common practice, and leaving the carnage only implicit.[32] Historians who write books describing strategy are more numerous than those who examine the procedures of battle and the routine of campaigning. Even where first-hand accounts exist, battles remain difficult phenomena to study in their particulars. Witnesses often assumed that their audience was familiar with the mechanics of warfare, and so neglected to spell it out for them.[33] It remains difficult to establish an accurate narrative of the battle of 22 June 1636 that plots the most significant events in chronological order, even though there is little from the several accounts that is contradictory. Multiple eyewitness accounts are not in themselves a remedy against contradictory or incomplete observation, for the persons present on the ground would have had only a partial and limited view of the combat. Even senior officers present in the command tent the night before the event, when they laid their plans, had much difficulty following the ebb and flow of battle beyond the sector they commanded.

We should not exaggerate the gaps in the evidence, for a number of newly discovered sources sharpen our image considerably. One obvious text neglected until now is the report of the battle published in the *Gazette de France* just a few weeks

[31] Malcolm Wanklyn, *Decisive Battles of the English Civil Wars: Myth and Reality* (Barnsley, 2006), 7–8.

[32] Brent Nosworthy, *The Anatomy of Victory: Battle Tactics 1689–1763* (New York, 1990), p. xi.

[33] Olivier Chaline, *La bataille de la Montagne Blanche (8 novembre 1620): Un mystique chez les guerriers* (Paris, 1999), 13.

later. It is more detailed (and more tendentious) than Victor-Amadeus's original dispatch to the King and Cardinal Richelieu because the Count Palluau, one of the heroes of the day's fighting, embellished the event more fully at court.[34] An anonymous Italian manuscript from the Spanish side has been hiding in Bologna; it is so full of detail confirmed by various other sources that we can conclude that, if the writer was not directly an eyewitness, he was very well-informed. It contains no information on the aftermath of the campaign and therefore appears to have been written immediately after the event.[35] Several reports sent back to Florence by the colonel of the Tuscan contingent in the Spanish order of battle have been completely unnoticed until now. The Tuscan ambassador Pandolfini in Milan interviewed other participants in order to send a fuller picture to Grand Duke Ferdinando II, and crowned these several dispatches with the transcription of a captured private account of the battle penned by one of the French colonels to a friend in Provence.[36] No doubt other private correspondence will contain other eyewitness experiences of Tornavento, but historians in archives across Europe will uncover these only gradually.

Apart from the manuscript accounts drafted by people who were present on the field, we possess two fairly detailed narratives of the battle and campaign by a pair of remarkable historians, neither of whom were in the French or Spanish allegiance at the time they wrote. Girolamo Brusoni, a Venetian libertine monk (1614–86) produced the most detailed relation around twenty years after the event, as part of his history of the Italian wars.[37] Galeazzo Gualdo Priorato (1606–1678) published a lengthy and impressively impartial account of the wars between 1630 and 1640, which is informed by a soldier's experience almost unmatched in Europe. A native of Vicenza (a subject city of the neutral Venetian Republic), he was perhaps unique among Italian soldiers in having served with German Protestant armies in Germany, as well as with the Dutch army of Frederick of Nassau, the French royal army at La Rochelle, the Imperial army of Count Wallenstein both in Germany and in Italy during the Mantuan war, and the Swedish army following the death of Gustavus Adolphus! He haunted the courts of German princes during the darkest years of the great war. In later years he attached himself to the entourage of Cardinal Mazarin and became a naturalized French subject, then moved to Vienna to serve the Holy Roman Emperor Leopold I, before finally retiring to his native city in old age. His account of Tornavento appeared only five years after the event. Gualdo Priorato, like other diligent historians of that remarkable generation, actively sought out eyewitnesses to the events he described in the pages of his book. This author of the high baroque era wrote with candour and directness in both content and style and displayed—not least of his many virtues—a desire for what we would

---

[34] *Gazette de France 1636*, no. 99; the battle unfolds over about ten pages, making it one of the fullest relations of the event. Victor-Amedeus appears to have been the author of the dispatch, but the messenger purportedly added variations to it that were not to the Duke of Savoy's advantage. Archivio di Stato Torino, Materie politiche interne: lettere ministri, Francia 34, 15 July 1636.

[35] Biblioteca Universitaria Bologna, Ms 473, Misc.H, n.15.

[36] Archivio di Stato Firenze, *Mediceo del Principato* 3176, 3180, 3258.

[37] Girolamo Brusoni, *Delle Historie memorabili, contiene le Guerre d'Italia de'nostri tempi* (Venice, 1656), 29–39.

call impartiality.[38] That impartiality is lacking in another valuable account also published five short years after the action by the Milanese priest and bishop of Tortona Giovanni Francesco Fossati.[39] Most historians of the period wrote about Tornavento in their accounts of the Italian wars, but not as accurately as these three. Some writers just repeated what they read in other accounts.[40] Finally, there exists a published anonymous engraving from the period, available on the internet, that purports to display the battlefield and the armies arrayed on it.[41] But its scale is such that its author just represented Spanish forces by conventional symbols, and left the French troops and their entrenchments virtually invisible. There are several other significant distortions in the image that render it unreliable in its details, but one comprehends the stakes of the fighting easily enough. In addition to accounts of the battle, we have three precious chronicles compiled by people living close by, who experienced first-hand the devastation inflicted by the Franco-Savoyard invasion. Giovanni Battista Lupi, parish priest of Busto Arsizio, a scant twelve kilometres from the battlefield, recorded the most detailed of these. Two other contemporaries living even closer to the site of the combat left additional texts, transcribed and published with some important contextual information provided by Franco Bertolli and Umberto Colombo.[42]

The modern historiography is very slender, for until very recently Italian and foreign scholars considered the whole period of Spanish ascendancy to be one of unrelieved decadence and therefore unworthy of attention. The soldier-scholar Edouard Hardy Perini in the early twentieth century wrote of the battle from the perspective of the French sources and ignored the Spanish and Italian ones.[43] Gian Domenico Oltrona Visconti wrote from the Spanish perspective while ignoring most of the French literature. This local historian speculates on the positions of the French entrenchments on which so much of the narrative hinges. Based on his work, the amateur military historian Pierre Picouet designed and uploaded to his website a series of elegant maps.[44] A very recent short book on the battle and campaign (80 pages, including the abundant illustrations), written by the journalist Luca Cristini and the commerce professor Giuseppe Pogliani, seems destined for a popular market of military buffs. The authors examined no other sources save the

[38] Galeazzo Gualdo Priorato, *An History of the late Warres and other State affaires of the best part of Christendom* (London, 1648 for the English tr. of the original Italian work of 1641), 354–61, but one would be amply repaid to look also at the author's address to the reader. On this generation of 'realist' historians and their liberty of tone, see Brendan Dooley, 'Snatching Victory from the Jaws of Defeat: History and Imagination in Baroque Italy', *The Seventeenth Century*, 15, 2000, 90–115.

[39] Ábbate Giovanni Fossati, *Memorie historiche delle guerre d'Italia del secolo presente* (Milan, 1640), 167–73.

[40] Daniel Ménager, 'Le récit de bataille', in D. Bohler and C. Magnien Simonin (eds), *Ecritures de l'histoire (XIVe–XVIe siècles)* (Geneva, 2005), 339–49.

[41] <http://www.fmboschetto.it/Lonate_Pozzolo/battaglia_di_Tornavento.htm>. I wish to thank Dr Boschetto for replying to my inquiries, and for transmitting crucial information on local history.

[42] Franco Bertolli and Umberto Colombo, *La peste del 1630 a Busto Arsizio* (Busto Arsizio, 1990).

[43] Edouard Hardy de Perini, *Batailles françaises* (Chateauroux and Paris, 1894–1906), iii. 204–20.

[44] Pierre Picouet, see <http://www.reocities.com/aow1617/TornaventoFr.html>: Bataille de Tornavento 22 June 1636.

earlier work by Oltrona Visconti and the French pamphlet published at the time of the battle (available online), together with excerpts from Girolamo Brusoni. They confine their discussion of the battle itself to a few paragraphs.[45]

One might hope to understand the battle better by studying the terrain on which it was fought. Unfortunately, this site is located in one of the most intensively developed regions of Europe, a mere two kilometres from Malpensa international airport. Just east of where the French raised their earthworks, the Fascist regime established a military airfield with its fortified bunkers, now covered with forest. On the north side of the battlefield sits a modern helicopter factory. An express highway serving the airport and a gravel pit of important dimensions sit astride the axis of the Spanish army's approach, utterly obliterating the original features of the landscape. Below the crest of the heights overlooking the Ticino river there lay three canals, the unused and empty Canale Villoresi dating from the late nineteenth century following the trace of the old Panperduto ditch, a large hydro-electric and irrigation canal along the valley bottom where part of the battle took place, and next to it the vestiges of the original 'naviglio' that made the site so important. The distortion of almost four centuries of development is partly compensated by the survival of a careful irrigation project map dating from the eighteenth century, which pinpoints the levees on the heath and allows one to accurately fix the initial French positions. In addition to the Panperduto channel, whose course is still discernible from satellite views today, the irrigation map depicts and even measures the smaller ditch, the Fosso della Cerca, running north–south about 300 metres east of the hamlet.[46] Most of the battlefield sits in the Ticino valley nature park, with its bicycle paths and walkways for hikers. But no panels tell tourists that this was where the battle of Tornavento took place. Today it remains, like so many other Italian battlefields, a 'lieu d'oubli'.

Altogether this disparate material makes it possible to reconstruct a general narrative of the battle, much more detailed than any before it. Unlike so many other contests, the opposing sources agree on a great deal: on the location, the relative size and consistency of each army, the timetable of the operations, and the duration of the fighting. However, nobody thought to discuss tactics explicitly, still less the sentiments of soldiers undergoing the ordeal. So we must proceed by assumptions derived from the flow of the combat, something Wanklyn labels 'inherent military probability'.[47] Other battles of the era that have been better studied permit some points of comparison, previous ones like Breitenfeld (1631), Lützen (1632), and Nördlingen (1634) in Germany where some of the officers present at Tornavento had fought, and subsequent combats like Wittstock (1636)

---

[45] Luca Cristini and Giuseppe Pogliani, *La battaglia di Tornavento del 1636 e la guerra dei 30 anni in Italia* (Milan, 2011); I have published elsewhere a survey of these works and an introduction to the sources generally, Gregory Hanlon, 'Sources for a Battle: Tornavento (1636)', in Alessandro Buono and Gianclaudio Civale (eds), *Battaglie: L'Evento, l'individuo, la memoria* (Palermo, 2014), 39–58.

[46] Archivio di Stato Milano, Miscellanea Mappe e Disegni, arruotolate 110: '*Topografia per l'irrigazione delle Brughiere di Somma, Carlo Migliavacca ingegnere, 14 giugno 1777*'.

[47] Wanklyn, *Decisive Battles*, 30.

and Rocroi (1643) where the same Spanish tactics employed in Italy contributed to catastrophic failure.[48]

Some theoretical literature likewise sheds light on the recorded behaviour of the soldiers at Tornavento, first and foremost the writings of Charles Ardant du Picq, who was the first person to study combat scientifically in the 1860s.[49] This French officer, himself killed in battle in 1870, introduced an element of timelessness into the study of war that helps this analysis considerably. If one can resume his approach in a single formula, it would be that 'les siècles n'ont pas changé la nature humaine'. Both soldiers and social scientists have explored the realm of combat in recent years, now that the combatants themselves are more literate. American army psychologists and sociologists followed troops in combat in the Second World War and made some startling discoveries concerning the motivations and behaviour of men emerging from the ordeal, discussed in S. L. A. Marshall's little book, *Men Against fire*. The close-order combat of Tornavento and Ardant du Picq is a thing of the past, but the American social scientist echoes the French colonel in emphasizing that combat and its peculiar mechanisms are part of the human behavioural repertory.[50] In the wake of Marshall and John Keegan, a number of authors are looking at old sources with new questions and sensibilities. Keegan astutely included in his bibliography some of the emerging literature in the new discipline of human and animal ethology, like Konrad Lorenz and the evolutionary anthropologist Lionel Tiger. Keegan's later book *A History of Warfare* expanded that literature and introduced the neurochemistry of aggression. The second edition of Gwynne Dyer's popular book *War* also attempts to better understand the phenomenon by a sweeping survey of the behavioural sciences.[51] Men are not merely cultural beings fashioned by their education and their experiences; they remain evolved animals packed with emotions and universal instincts that channel their behaviour in important ways on the battlefield and away from it. The most compelling recent work in this 'postcultural' vein is by the Marines psychologist Colonel Dave Grossman, whose writings on combat and killing enable us to sketch something about the human ethology of combat in order to better understand how the contest unfolded on that terrible day in 1636.[52] Humans have experienced conflict since prehistory. An empirical historian explaining a problem in

---

[48] The German battles are recounted according to the most recent literature by William P. Guthrie, *Battles of the Thirty Years War: From White Mountain to Nördlingen* (Westport, CT, and London, 2002); and Guthrie, *The Later Thirty Years War* (Westport, CT, and London, 2003); for Rocroi, see Laurent Henninger, *Rocroi 1643* (Paris, 1993).

[49] Charles Ardant du Picq, *Etudes sur le combat: Combat antique et combat moderne* (Paris, 2004; repr. of the 1904 edn); for a modern appraisal of his work, see Stéphane Audoin-Rouzeau, 'Vers une anthropologie historique de la violence de combat au XIXe siècle: Relire Ardant du Picq?', *Revue d'histoire du XIXe siècle*, 30 (2005), 85–97.

[50] S. L. A. Marshall, *Men Against Fire* (New York, 1947 [sic: publ. 1967?]).

[51] Keegan, *History of Warfare*, 79–84; Gwynne Dyer, *War*, 2nd edn (Toronto, 2004).

[52] Dave Grossman, *On Killing: The Psychological Cost of Learning to Kill in War and Society* (Boston, 1995); *On Combat: The Psychology and Physiology of Deadly Conflict in War and Peace* (Mascoutah, IL, 2004).

historical time must leave the distant origins of these traits in the background, and concentrate on the period and place under examination. War in the seventeenth century was not characterized by unmitigated savagery. Officers and ranks observed rules of engagement with enemy combatants and with civilians, rules whose human logic and necessity we can apprehend with close study. We will catch continual glimpses of these rules in the chapters that follow.

1

Cardinal Richelieu's War

The Thirty Years' War raged year after year in Germany as a brutal civil war between the Imperial Catholic House of Austria (the Habsburg sovereign of the Holy Roman Empire) and its Catholic allies on the one hand, and a shifting coalition of insubordinate German Protestant princes on the other. The war erupted in 1618 when the Protestant subjects of the Emperor in Bohemia reneged on a previous decision to elect Ferdinand as successor to the throne upon the death of Emperor Matthias, his uncle, fearing his militant Catholicism and his well-known intention to curtail Protestantism in his realms. The Estates of Bohemia elected as King of Bohemia in his stead the Calvinist elector Palatine Frederick. Protestant armies from Bohemia, Germany, Hungary, and Transylvania were initially successful in 1619, driving the Habsburg heir from Vienna. Emperor Ferdinand II only survived the challenge because Europe's single most powerful monarch, King Philip IV of Spain, was his cousin and natural ally. Animated by the same militant Catholicism, both branches of the House of Austria lent their support to each other at critical moments during their respective wars, though without ever adopting a single overarching policy. It was not excluded that the Spanish and the German crowns might one day be reunited under a single head, as they had been under Emperor Charles V (1517–55).[1] Spanish, Walloon, and Italian troops dispatched from Flanders and Italy joined the Emperor's army and the Bavarian allies, and crushed the anti-Habsburg rebellion at the battle of White Mountain outside Prague on 8 November 1620. For its part, Spain had waged a seemingly endless war against the young Dutch Republic, which had risen up against Spanish rule in the 1560s and broke away completely in the early 1570s to create an independent state dominated by Calvinist Protestants. Spain and the Dutch rebels arranged a twelve-year truce in 1609 after decades of fighting left the region split into halves, the Flemish-speaking United Provinces in the north and an incipient bilingual and Catholic 'Belgium' to the south. Hoping to achieve a more advantageous final outcome, both sides wished to renew hostilities in 1621.

For years after the great war's outbreak in 1618, the king of France Louis XIII and his chief minister Cardinal Richelieu plotted to end the Habsburg preponderance in Europe. France constituted the most powerful and populous single state in

---

[1] Jean Bérenger, 'La collaboration militaire austro-espagnole aux XVIe–XVIIe siècles', *L'Espagne et ses guerres: De la fin de la Reconquête aux guerres d'Indépendance* (Paris, 2004), 11–33.

Europe, but it was forced to retreat from an active hegemonic role by its own wars of religion. These first flared up in the early 1560s and only the conversion to Catholicism by the Calvinist King Henri IV in 1593 brought a precarious end to them. Henri IV and the Catholic elites sealed peace with the religious minority by an edict granting official status for Protestants (the Edict of Nantes) in 1598. Such a policy of *official* toleration was extremely rare in Europe and was substantially more liberal than the de facto toleration of the large Catholic minority in the Netherlands, or of Jews and Christians in the Ottoman Empire. The Edict of Nantes did not enjoy a broad consensus within the kingdom, for it left scores of fortresses in the hands of the Calvinist lobby. After presiding over a decade of rapid economic recovery, Henri planned to unite the kingdom even more by launching a great offensive war against Spain with the aid of German Protestants. By the treaty of Brussol on 10 April 1610, France proposed to conquer the Habsburg Duchy of Milan with the aid of Duke Charles-Emanuel of Savoy and confer the spoils on Savoy and Mantua.[2] King Henri's assassination by an isolated fanatic in Paris on 14 May aborted the project. The eldest of his two legitimate sons, Louis XIII, was a mere lad of 8. The queen regent Maria de'Medici lacked the authority to unite the kingdom's fractious senior aristocracy, the Grands.[3] It was all she could do to prevent a new outbreak of religious war in France, especially after she married the young king to the daughter of the king of Spain, Anne of Austria in 1615 (i.e. of the House of Austria, the Habsburgs). As soon as he assumed full command of his kingdom in 1620, Louis himself unleashed a renewal of the religious struggles in France, with the aim of disarming the Protestants and depriving them of the means of waging war from behind the modernized ramparts of their towns (Fig. 1.1). The military chief of the Protestant forces scattered across the kingdom, Duke Henri de Rohan, led small and very mobile armies back and forth across hundreds of kilometres in southern and western France to rescue towns and to animate the resistance, but with diminishing strength.

During these wars, the insecure and socially awkward Louis came to rely on a clever appointee of his mother, Armand Jean DuPlessis, bishop of Luçon, promoted Cardinal Richelieu, who moved to the forefront of the royal councillors to become chief minister in 1624 (Fig. 1.2). Richelieu wished to confiscate completely the military assets of the Protestants, while respecting their right to practise their religion openly. The cardinal's strategy enjoyed wide support in a kingdom that was about 95 per cent Catholic and where Catholic institutions were waxing stronger with each passing year. The climax of these wars was the protracted and cruel siege of La Rochelle from July 1627 to November 1628. French siege methods had fallen behind other European nations, so the great Protestant fortress port had to be blockaded, the supporting English fleet driven off, and the city starved into submission. But Richelieu finally prevailed. Sporadic Protestant resistance in

---

[2] Giuliano Ferretti, 'Au nom du droit (de conquête): La politique italienne de la France au XVIIe siècle', *La pierre et l'écrit: Revue d'histoire et du patrimoine en Dauphiné*, 23 (2012), 101–25.

[3] For an good overview of this turbulent period in French history, Joël Cornette, *Histoire de la France: L'affirmation de l'Etat absolu 1515–1652* (Paris, 1994); and Yves-Marie Bercé, *The Birth of Absolutism: A History of France 1598–1661* (London and New York, 1996; 1st publ. 1992).

Petrus Daret Sculpsit   1643   LP 20. 8²

† 1643.

Ce grand Roy , dont voicy l'adorable visage ,
Vainqueur de ce bas Monde au Ciel est remonté.
A genoux donc Mortels ! que tout luy rende hommage,
Ou redoutez sa foudre , ou loüez sa bonté.

Louis XIII, Roi de France en 1610, né en 1601.

Fig. 1.1. Louis XIII, king of France 1610–43, depicted in his armour, extolled as a saintly figure. A 'roi de guerre', the timid monarch committed France to foreign adventure and expansion for most of his reign.

Jean Armand du plessis Cardinal duc de Richelieu

+ 1642.

Petrus Daret Scul. et ex Cu. privil

Fig. 1.2. Armand DuPlessis, Cardinal de Richelieu, chief minister of state for Louis XIII from 1624 until his death in 1642. The Cardinal's policy of all-out war against the Habsburgs of Spain and Austria was perhaps the salvation of European Protestantism.

mountainous southern France flickered out the following year and the Peace of Alès finally pacified the kingdom in 1629.[4]

The pacification of the realm and disarming the Protestants were not Richelieu's ultimate goal, however. He wished to exploit the great turmoil of his Habsburg neighbours and expand France's territories at their expense, replacing the 'Austrian' pre-eminence in Europe with a Bourbon one. This policy of war with Catholic Spain and Germany just when the combined Habsburg monarchies seemed capable of defeating the Protestants outright proved much less popular with the French public. The Florentine queen mother Maria de'Medici echoed vehemently these dissenting voices at court. A direct frontal assault on the champions of Catholic Europe was out of the question in the incendiary religious climate of the 1620s. In 1625, Richelieu adopted an indirect approach, by arming and assisting the neighbouring duchy of Savoy's attempt to conquer the Republic of Genoa, an

---

[4] Victor-Lucien Tapié, *La France de Louis XIII et Richelieu* (Paris, 1967), 168–99.

important ally of the Spanish monarchy, both the principal source of loans and a vital conduit for supplies and reinforcements between Spain and Germany. Timely Spanish and Imperial intervention foiled the invasion and resulted in the Franco-Spanish Peace of Monzon of 1626 that restored the status quo ante, though the Savoyards skirmished with the Genoese for years thereafter. Duke Charles-Emanuel sought to engineer a coup in the great port in 1628, but news of it leaked and the republic's patricians executed the plot's ringleaders in a rare show of unity.[5]

Not long before, the problem of dynastic succession to the small north Italian duchy of Mantua had escalated into a major confrontation between French and Habsburg alliances. The new duke Charles de Nevers, who belonged to the French branch of the house of Gonzaga, seized the recently vacant throne surreptitiously in January 1628 without obtaining the prior approval of the Habsburg Holy Roman Emperor. The two disconnected portions of his states, Monferrato on the upper Po, and the duchy of Mantua proper on the lower Po river, both straddled the Habsburg lines of communication in Northern Italy. The Spanish first minister Olivares would not stand by while a French client seized such strategic lands, and he instructed his chief functionary in Northern Italy, the Governor of Milan, to lay siege to Casale, a great stronghold on the Po, while Charles-Emanuel of Savoy occupied other parts of the Monferrato. Louis XIII and Richelieu suddenly appeared in March 1629 with a French army, forcing Savoy to withdraw from the Spanish alliance, and relieved Casale with French reinforcements. Then Louis withdrew to quell a Protestant uprising in Northern Languedoc.

Olivares instructed Ambrogio Spinola to recommence the siege of Casale Monferrato in the summer of 1629, in the teeth of fierce resistance from the Marshal Toiras in command of a mostly French garrison. Having practically vanquished the Protestant opponents in the Empire, Ferdinand II sent a large German Imperial army to lay siege to the capital Mantua in September 1629. Following the Peace of Alès, Louis XIII and Richelieu crossed the Alps again in December 1629, and a French army under Marshal Créquy seized the Savoyard fortress of Pinerolo on the edge of the Po valley. Spinola's siege continued through the winter and into the spring and summer of 1630, with little success. On the other hand, the Imperials routed the Venetians, who were timidly assisting the Mantuans, at Valleggio in May 1630, then stormed Mantua itself and sacked it in July, capturing Charles of Nevers. French and Spanish forces measured each other warily in Piedmont, until papal diplomacy under a young captain, Giulio Mazzarini, achieved a ceasefire that led to a general peace granting Imperial approval for Duke Charles of Mantua. Louis and Richelieu returned over the Alps to Lyon, where the king lay dangerously ill for some weeks.[6] Richelieu pushed the king to consider a general war with the House of Austria, in the face of fierce resistance from the queen mother who tried to have the cardinal removed from power. She advocated either a domestic policy of prolonged peace and internal reforms or a bellicose

    [5] Thomas Allison Kirk, *Genoa and the Sea: Policy and Power in an Early Modern Maritime Republic, 1559–1684* (Baltimore, 2005), 103–4.
    [6] Gregory Hanlon, *The Twilight of a Military Tradition: Italian Aristocrats and European Conflicts, 1560–1800* (London and New York, 1998), 111–16.

foreign policy that guaranteed Catholic victory over Protestants. The king hesitated between the two opposing visions until 10 November 1630, when he finally decided on full-scale war with Spain, with 'reasons of state' prevailing over religious fervour.[7]

Rather than rushing to war with a kingdom still licking its wounds from internal strife, Richelieu preferred to continue subsidizing the Protestant armies struggling against the Spanish and German Habsburgs. He approved the long-standing policy that encouraged French military aristocrats to serve in Dutch, German Protestant, and Swedish armies, where they could keep abreast of military innovations. The Dutch halted the early progress of the Spaniards in the Low Countries by the late 1620s, and embarked on a successful adventure of seizing with their navy Spanish and Portuguese colonies around the world (for Portugal comprised one of the many kingdoms under Spanish direction). The Mantuan Succession War was a serious distraction to both branches of the Habsburgs, forcing them to divert precious resources to Italy. In the meantime, the Protestant powers acquired a second wind, fuelled with French money. When Gustavus Adolphus, the king of Sweden, smashed the German Catholic forces in Saxony in 1631, it looked like Richelieu's indirect approach would lead to complete success. However, Emperor Ferdinand II brought his best general out of retirement. Albrecht Count Wallenstein, who had been sidelined for his excessive ambition, fought the king of Sweden to a draw in two battles, and Gustavus Adolphus died at the second of these, the bloody combat of Lützen on 16 November 1632. Still the Swedes (enjoying substantial French subsidies) would not withdraw from the war, which continued inconclusively in 1633. The following year, the 'Swedish' army (comprised largely of north German Protestants and Scots) determined to attack the Imperials besieging the town of Nördlingen in Franconia, and persisted in their plan even after they learned that a sizeable contingent of Spanish and Italian troops en route to the Spanish Low Countries had joined the besiegers. The fruitless repeat assaults on the Spanish and Neapolitan positions on 15 September 1634 turned into a complete disaster for the Protestants, for the combined Catholic army chased their attackers as they withdrew and massacred many as they fled. The Imperials and Spaniards almost completely destroyed the coalition army in its rout.[8] Many of the warring German princes made their peace with the Emperor in the weeks following the battle, and only considerable French subsidies kept the Swedes and the hardline Protestant princes in the war.[9]

After the dismal failure of the indirect approach, Louis XIII and Richelieu resolved at the end of 1634 that France must intervene everywhere against the

---

[7] Bercé, *Birth of Absolutism*, 117–28; an old article has lost none of its pertinence, Georges Pagès, 'Autour du "grand orage": Richelieu et Marillac', *Revue Historique*, 179 (1937), 63–97.

[8] For the surprising scale of Scots participation in the German war, Steve Murdoch and Alexia Grosjean, *Alexander Leslie and the Scottish Generals of the Thirty Years' War 1618–1648* (London, 2014).

[9] William P. Guthrie, *Battles of the Thirty Years War: from White Mountain to Nördlingen* (Westport, CT, and London, 2002), 264–71; the most detailed and up-to-date account is that of Peter Engerisser and Pavel Hrnčiřik, *Nördlingen 1634: Die Schlacht bei Nördlingen—Wendepunkt des Dreissigjährigen Krieges* (Weissenstadt, 2009), 185–94.

House of Austria with all its strength. The cardinal justified this war policy in France via the pamphlets of a team of talented propagandists, who claimed that the kingdom was menaced with encirclement by the Habsburgs, from Spain in the south, to Spanish Burgundy and Imperial Germany in the east, to the Spanish Netherlands in the north. One of Richelieu's apologists, the jurist Besian d'Arroy argued that Louis inherited the legacy of Charlemagne and would be fully in his rights to claim the entire Carolingian dominion that would include all of Germany, Italy, and Spain itself. Moreover, the king of France's rights were eternal and could never be extinguished by treaty. Any territory that France had relinquished under duress in the past (such as Milan or Flanders) must be redeemed and 'reunited' with the kingdom.[10] At the very least, the king and the cardinal wished to annex to France the Spanish Netherlands (most of which spoke French as the native tongue), as well as the Spanish Franche Comté of Burgundy and Lorraine, both French-speaking autonomous states within the Holy Roman Empire. Yet another French-speaking territory in the Empire vulnerable to French conquest was Savoy in the Alps, the dynastic seat of the House of Savoy, which transferred its capital from Chambéry to Italian-speaking Turin in Piedmont in the 1560s.

Cardinal Richelieu intended to push France's borders outward in all directions. In order to disarm potential adversaries, Richelieu proclaimed abroad that France was not interested in making conquests in Italy, but this was likely disingenuous. France never relinquished its fifteenth-century claim to the rich duchy of Milan, which it held briefly in the early sixteenth century, but lost to the Habsburg emperor Charles V after a spectacular defeat at Pavìa in 1525. Along with Milan (which at its height included Bergamo, Brescia and the Valtellina, Parma and Piacenza), French kings claimed Genoa, its subject lands extending along the Ligurian coast, and its island colony of Corsica. Louis XIII had never renounced the claim the French crown enjoyed over the kingdoms of Naples and Sicily either, the target of repeated failed invasions in the first half of the sixteenth century. The reconquest of Milan probably figured at the top of the list of strategic objectives once Cardinal Richelieu decided to commit France to full-scale war against Spain in 1635. Richelieu drew from the history of the previous century that, while French armies might win victories in Italy, it proved difficult to maintain its conquests.[11] The cardinal and his advisers believed that there still existed in Italy a pervasive anti-Spanish sentiment that France could exploit to its advantage. To this end, Richelieu worked to detach most of the half-dozen leading Italian princes and republics from their traditional alliance with Madrid and Vienna (Map 1). In his correspondence with Italian princes, like that which he maintained with their German homologues, he pretended that they were *sovereign* states free to ally with France even against the wishes of their ultimate suzerains, the Emperor and the Pope. France would therefore act as a 'liberator' in Italy, and everywhere French

---

[10] Joël Cornette, *Le roi de guerre: Essai sur la souveraineté dans la France du Grand Siècle* (Paris, 2000), 128–41.

[11] Ferretti, 'Au nom du droit (de conquête)', 106.

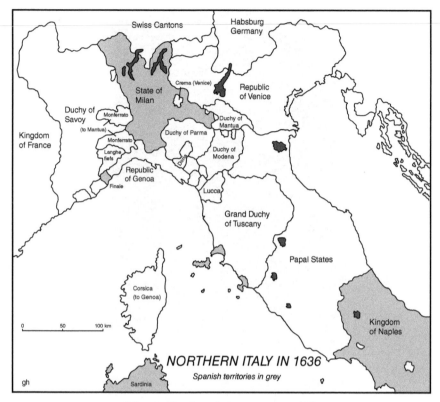

Map 1. Northern Italian states in 1636.

armies ejected the Spanish, he promised that the conquered territories would be awarded to its Italian allies.[12]

Louis XIII, a timid man who shunned the public, felt most comfortable in his role as France's chief soldier. He was an authentic 'roi de guerre' in Joël Cornette's phrase, who enjoyed the company of his senior officers and even delighted in the rigours of campaigning in open country—for kings never truly roughed it. So, pressed by the cardinal to choose definitively between a policy of full-scale war against the Catholic powers (even as the ally and saviour of the Protestant cause), on the one hand, and one of prolonged peace and reform under the direction of devout Catholic ministers, he chose the former, more controversial path, and protected the cardinal from his many domestic enemies. This war against the Catholic House of Austria polarized the French political class, however, and the general population especially resented the relentless tax increases that preparing for it entailed. The king

[12] Gabriel de Mun, *Richelieu et la Maison de Savoie: L'ambassade de Particelli d'Hémery en Piémont* (Paris, 1907), 27; Sven Externbrink, "'Le Cœur du Monde" et la "liberté d'Italie": Aspects de la politique italienne de Richelieu 1624–1642', *Revue d'Histoire Diplomatique*, 114 (2000), 181–208; Françoise Hildesheimer, 'Guerre et paix selon Richelieu', in Lucien Bély (ed.), *L'Europe des traités de Westphalie: Esprit de la diplomatie et diplomatie de l'esprit* (Paris, 2000), 31–55.

D. GASPAR DE GVZMAN DVX SANLVCARI
MAYORIS, COMES DE OLIVARES.

Olivarès, (Don gaspard de Gusman, Duc d')
premier Ministre de philippe IV.
+ 1643.

Fig. 1.3. Don Gaspar de Guzman, Count Duke of Olivares, valido or chief minister of King Philip IV of Spain from 1621 to his dismissal in 1643. Partisan of a policy of preservation of Spanish territories, his Union of Arms attempted to raise resources equitably across his master's vast dominions. It failed, accelerating Spain's military decline.

left the administrative details of diplomacy and war to his chief minister, who had been raised as a youth to serve in the army before he entered the church out of family interests. The king admired Richelieu's focus and his ability, and remained faithful to him until the prelate's death in 1642. Neither the cardinal nor the king could foresee that the war they provoked would last a quarter-century.

Richelieu's worthy adversary was the 'valido' or chief minister of the king of Spain, the Count-Duke of Olivares (Fig. 1.3). He and King Philip IV felt that the realms under their direction were vast enough and saw no advantage in their extension, but they had every right to retain them. In Olivares's view, this policy of 'conservation' could only be achieved by credible deterrence, that is, by inflicting sharp defeat on any challenger.[13] Spain's Italian dominions (Milan,

---

[13] J. H. Elliott, 'Managing Decline: Olivares and the Grand Strategy of Imperial Spain', in Paul Kennedy (ed.), *Grand Strategies in War and Peace* (New Haven and London, 1991), 87–104.

Naples, Sicily, and Sardinia), which together comprised about 40 per cent of the peninsula's population, contributed men, ships, horses, and money to every theatre of war from 1621 onward, and constituted, together with Castile, the font of the great empire's military capacity. The duchy of Milan shielded the other Spanish territories for it could not be by-passed by French invaders. Moreover, Milan and its window to the sea, Genoa, allowed the easy passage of Spanish and Italian reinforcements through the Alpine passes to the Spanish Netherlands (modern Belgium). On three occasions, in 1620, 1633, and 1634, troops levied and equipped in Lombardy assisted the king's Austrian cousin Ferdinand II in Germany.

Olivares's bellicose outlook led him to be more rigid than was necessary with the upstart Duke of Mantua in 1628, for he was certain that ejecting him would not be difficult. It was Spain's great misfortune that its most renowned general, the Genoese Ambrogio Spìnola, was unable to capture the citadel of Casale Monferrato in 1629–30, defended stubbornly by a French garrison under the able Marshal Toiras (Fig. 1.4). This garrison reduced the Duke of Mantua Charles Gonzaga to the status of a French puppet unable to pursue an independent foreign policy.[14]

IO . DE SAINCT BONNET
D . A TOIRAS
FRANCIÆ MARE SCALLVS.

Fig. 1.4. Jean de Saint-Bonnet de Toiras, one of France's most talented field marshals, but mistrusted by Richelieu. He served as confidant and military adviser to the Duke of Savoy until his death at Fontaneto on 14 June 1636.

[14] David Parrott, 'The Utility of Fortifications in Early Modern Europe: Italian Princes and their Citadels, 1540–1640', *War in History*, 7/2 (2000), 127–53.

During an operation to come to the relief of the threatened fortress in 1630, the French Marshal Créquy seized the important stronghold of Pinerolo from the Duke of Savoy (an ally of Spain). The fortress commanded the access to an Alpine pass and opened a secure route for French armies into Northern Italy. Spain would never consent to a definitive peace with France as long as this fortress remained in the latter's hands. Richelieu pretended to give it up in a brokered peace settling the Mantuan succession in 1631, but French soldiers hidden in the bowels of the fortress overpowered the new Savoyard garrison as soon as the Imperial supervisory force marched away. Richelieu signed the Peace of Cherasco with Duke Victor-Amadeus of Savoy the same year by which France compensated the disappointed duke for its loss with a few villages in the Monferrato belonging to the hapless Duke Charles of Mantua. There were secret clauses in the treaty that showed that Savoy was very much the loser in the bargain, such as the perpetual sale of Pinerolo to France. The aim of the secret clauses was to hide from the public, and from Spain, the intention of France to pursue its warlike policies in Italy.[15] This stealthy approach did not fool Olivares for an instant, for he realized that France would launch an offensive war against Spain at an opportune moment, and that it was necessary to take precautions against it.[16]

After 1630, Richelieu embarked on a policy of disarming the neighbouring secondary powers by multiplying fortified bridgeheads or 'portes' to serve as bases for future expansion, and to pin down Spanish forces in multiple locations. France had long intimidated its potential enemies by establishing powerful fortified bases beyond its borders.[17] He began first in Lorraine, where the duke was hostile to the cardinal and gave refuge to his enemies. In 1632 French troops occupied the principal fortresses, dismantled others, and erected new ones in order to render powerless Duke Charles, who was a prince of the Empire and an ally of the House of Austria.[18] Louis XIII and Richelieu fully intended to incorporate the duchy as a French province, administered from Metz, despite the hostility of the population.[19] The following year, the French army occupied much of Alsace too, on the pretext of protecting it from the ravages of Swedish and Imperial armies. The cardinal next intended to disarm Savoy, whose new duke Victor-Amadeus had married Princess Marie-Christine, sister of Louis XIII. Everyone understood that the seizure of Pinerolo and its retention were clear signs that France intended to invade Italy. Pinerolo secured the Alpine passes, while Casale Monferrato served as an advanced base in the direction of France's ally Mantua and the friendly Venetian Republic. It looked possible for France to extend its control clear across Northern Italy, especially if it could add to the chain some powerful fortresses in the hands of an eager ally, the young Duke of

[15] Ferretti, 'Au nom du droit (de conquête)', 115.

[16] Robert Stradling, 'Olivares and the Origins of the Franco-Spanish War, 1627–1635', *English Historical Review* (1986), 68–94.

[17] Gaston Zeller, 'Saluces, Pignerol et Strasbourg: La politique des frontières au temps de la prépondérance espagnole', *Revue Historique*, 193 (1942–3), 97–110.

[18] Stéphane Gaber, *La Lorraine meurtrie*, 2nd edn (Nancy, 1991); Philippe Martin, *Une guerre de Trente Ans en Lorraine, 1631–1661* (Metz, 2002).

[19] Marie-Catherine Vignal Souleyreau, *Richelieu et la Lorraine* (Paris, 2004), 181.

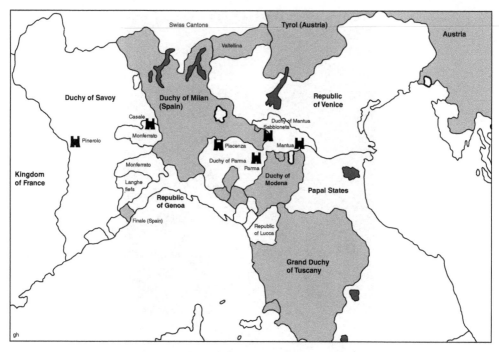

Map 2. French forward fortresses in 1635.

Parma, Odoardo Farnese. In anticipation of joining the French alliance against Spain, this prince began hiring French and Italian soldiers to garrison his two capitals, Parma and Piacenza, and a smaller fortress, Sabbioneta, over which he obtained temporary custody in the aftermath of the Mantua Succession war. With these bases in hand, Richelieu would call upon other Italian princes to join France in order to restore Italian 'liberty' (Map 2).

Duke Odoardo Farnese, only 19 years old when Richelieu contacted him to join his alliance, was from his earliest years a boy who dreamt of 'opening the path of glory with his sword'. He ardently hoped that the great wars of his time would continue so that he might reap his share of renown. His chief minister, Count Fabio Scotti, persuaded him that Spain's pre-eminence was drawing to a close, and that it would be opportune to abandon the traditional Habsburg alliance (which prevented the expansion of any Italian state at the expense of another) and join France. Odoardo welcomed with open arms and clamorous demonstrations of military potential a diplomatic mission by the Marshal Créquy at the end of 1632. Olivares did not try to mollify him with territorial or symbolic concessions, and so in early 1633 Odoardo began to enlist mercenaries hoping for war at the earliest opportunity.[20] Odoardo held his duchy as a vassal of the Pope, however, who did

[20] AGS Estado 3673, Consulta of 24 May and 14 July 1631; Odoardo's misadventure is related in my book, *The Hero of Italy: Odoardo Farnese, Duke of Parma, his Soldiers and his Subjects in the Thirty Years' War* (Oxford and New York, 2014).

Fig. 1.5. Maffeo Barberini, Pope Urban VIII (reigned 1623–44): Partisan of total Catholic victory in the Thirty Years' War, the Supreme Pontiff raised Rome's military profile and tried to ensure the continuation of the status quo in Italy.

not approve of his plans, so he sought Cardinal Richelieu's support in order to minimize Rome's interference.

Pope Urban VIII Barberini deplored the tensions between Catholic powers just as the House of Austria was prevailing against the Protestants, but he too doubted the ability of Spain to retain its Italian possessions. Even if he would not join a French alliance, the Pope was more favourably disposed to Paris than his predecessors (Fig. 1.5).[21] He thought that the equilibrium of power between France and Spain was the best guarantee for the autonomy of the minor Italian states. Urban VIII proposed a defensive league of Italian states under papal leadership, and dispatched his ablest diplomat Giulio Mazzarini to Paris in 1634 to argue its merits, but the future Cardinal Jules Mazarin was notoriously pro-French and quickly became Richelieu's willing instrument. French emissaries also made approaches to the young Grand Duke Ferdinando II de'Medici in Florence, and Duke Francesco I d'Este in

---

[21] Auguste Leman, *Urbain VIII et la rivalité de la France et de la Maison d'Autriche de 1631 à 1635* (Paris and Lille, 1919), 312; Jacques Humbert, *Le Maréchal de Créquy, gendre de Lesdiguières (1573–1638)* (Paris, 1962), 190–9.

Modena, both of whom were Odoardo's brothers-in-law. Having failed to seize the Genoese Republic by force, the cardinal sought to bring the state into the French orbit by establishing a permanent embassy there, without success, however.[22]

Paris set great store by an alliance with the only consistently anti-Habsburg state in the peninsula, the Republic of Venice. The aristocratic republic, with some two million subjects and substantial commercial and industrial capital, possessed more military assets than any other Italian territory.[23] In the first decades of the century, Venice had been on the threshold of war with the papacy and with Spain, and ardently wished for French aid that was not forthcoming.[24] It waged its own war with the Holy Roman Empire in 1617 in order to protect its shipping from Uskok corsairs in the north-eastern Adriatic Sea, and came perilously close to a full-blown naval war with Spain in 1618. It relied on the Valtellina as a corridor for the Dutch and German Protestant soldiers it employed in its armies, and so mobilized after 1620 to restore the valley to the Grison League. Its failure to reconquer the valley in 1626, and above all, the miserable performance of its troops assisting Mantua in 1629–30, inoculated the cautious patricians against a new military adventure.[25] The Venetian ambassador in Paris in 1634 underwent intense pressure from Cardinal Richelieu to take the lead of an anti-Spanish alliance in Italy and attack Spanish Lombardy from the east.[26] The republic considered that a French conquest of Milan (Fig. 1.6) would only whet the appetites of Italian princes for more territory, and introduce permanent instability. Richelieu sent emissaries on a tour of Italian capitals in the spring of 1634 in order to reiterate promises that France would not keep any territories it captured from Spain in the coming war. Most Italian states had legitimate grievances against Spain and Olivares's policies, and they would not have regretted a decline of Spanish power, but Philip IV of Spain was to be preferred to Louis XIII and the wily cardinal. They invoked the fable of Aesop in which the lion hunted large prey with the help of smaller animals, only to reward them by devouring each in turn.[27]

The indispensable participant in any French alliance in Northern Italy would have to be the Duke of Savoy, for two compelling reasons. First, the duchy could hinder French access to Northern Italy by pinching off the arteries leading across the Alps. And second, Piedmont and Savoy were large and populous enough, with over a million people, to maintain a sizeable army without French assistance. Before the great plague of 1630, Charles-Emmanuel I (reigned 1580–1630) was able to mobilize, albeit briefly, a mercenary army of almost 30,000 men.[28] The

[22] Ferretti, 'Au nom du droit (de conquête)', 108.

[23] Peter January and Michael Knapton, 'The Demands Made on Venetian Terraferma Society for Defence in the Early Seventeenth Century', *Ateneo Veneto*, 194 (2007), 25–115.

[24] Gaetano Cozzi, 'La Repubblica di Venezia e il Regno di Francia tra Cinquecento e Seicento: Fiducia e sfiducia', in Alberto Tenenti (ed.), *Venezia e Parigi* (Milan, 1989), 113–44.

[25] Stefano Andretta, *La Repubblica inquieta: Venezia nel Seicento tra Italia e Europa* (Rome, 2000), 45–61.

[26] Ibid. 85.

[27] *Memoires de François de Paule de Clermont, Marquis de Montglat* (Amsterdam, 1727), i. 115.

[28] Stéphane Gal, *Charles-Emmanuel de Savoie: La politique du précipice* (Paris, 2012), is a flattering recent biography of the energetic duke, certain to please the Piedmontese. For troop numbers, 118–20.

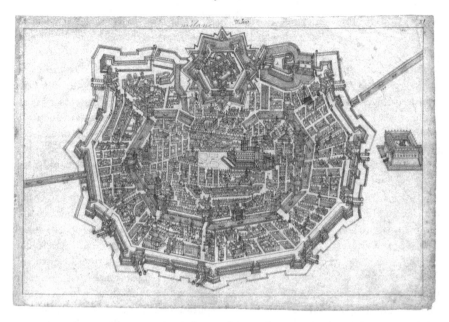

Fig. 1.6. Milan, *c.*1600: An industrial powerhouse of over 120,000 inhabitants until the terrible plague of 1630, the city and its powerful citadel dominated most of Northern Italy and blocked French expansion.

Savoy dynasty was one of the most ambitious and bellicose in all of Europe and Duke Charles Emanuel I had tried to conquer, at different periods, Dauphiné and Provence in France, Genoa and the Ligurian riviera, the Mantuan Monferrato and Protestant Geneva. Under his son Victor-Amadeus (Fig. 1.7), Savoyard ambition still fixated on the acquisition of royal status, and territories to match. In exchange for consenting to the heartrending loss of Pinerolo the duke obtained from Louis XIII the 'royal treatment'. This meant that France recognized his title of 'Royal Highness' in any correspondence, and accorded his state diplomatic precedence over territories under mere dukes. The royal duke promised to join the anti-Spanish alliance on condition that France should award him conspicuous territories taken from the Habsburgs and their allies. At the very least, Victor-Amadeus expected to receive all the duchy of Milan east of the Ticino river, and the district of Alessandria south of the Po, along with the Mantuan Monferrato. Richelieu also promised that France would help him conquer the neutral Republic of Genoa within three years, although he likely had no intention of keeping it. In fact, Louis XIII and Richelieu remained vague as to which territories would be assigned to their allies, in order to retain ultimate control of the agenda.[29] When assessing the true aims of French policy, it is perhaps a mistake to make a literal

---

[29] Anna Blum, *La Diplomatie de la France en Italie du Nord au temps de Richelieu et de Mazarin* (Paris, 2014), 47.

VICTOR AMEDEE DVC DE SAVOYE
ET PRINCE DE PIEDMONT ✝ 1637

B. Moncornet ex cũ Avec Privilegie. ✝ 1637.

Savoie (Victor Amedée 1er Duc de) fils de
Charles Emmanuel, né en 1587.
✝ 1637.

Fig. 1.7. Balthasar Moncornet, Victor-Amadeus, Duke of Savoy 1630–7: The duke's predicament was to avoid being despoiled by his French ally while simultaneously besting the Spanish army. Hence the cautious advance and long periods of indecision.

interpretation of the clauses in the multiple treaties Cardinal Richelieu established with his Italian allies, for the duplicitous minister was always quick to make new demands for each concession he obtained.

Victor-Amadeus's younger brothers, Prince Tommaso and Cardinal Maurizio and his sister Margherita, dowager duchess of Mantua, warned him not to believe French promises. French kings had seized Savoy and Piedmont without any serious legal claim and ruled them from 1536 to 1559 as French provinces, and the memory of that subjection was still keen.[30] Cardinal Maurizio, the most popular of the duke's several siblings, sponsored a literary academy in Turin, the Accademia dei Desiosi, whose prominent members reflected his anti-Bourbon views. Prince Tommaso evolved to adopt an anti-French position in the aftermath of the War of

[30] Ibid. 56.

the Mantuan Succession. He was brother-in-law of the Comte de Soissons, a French Prince of the Blood and mortal enemy of Cardinal Richelieu. Prince Tommaso attended the French court at Lyon during the summer of 1632, where he gradually understood Cardinal Richelieu's ultimate design to subjugate all of France's neighbours.[31] Richelieu was tricking Victor-Amadeus into carrying the burden of the war in Italy, he claimed, only so that France could concentrate its forces in the Spanish Low Countries near Paris. Any concession of territory by the cardinal in Italy he could easily rescind in the future. Prince Tommaso thought the moment opportune for Savoy to renew the Spanish alliance and to save itself from imminent peril.

Cardinal Richelieu's most effective ally at the court of Turin was the imperious duchess Marie-Christine, whose two sisters were queens of Spain and England. The duke yielded to the naked threat of being treated like the Duke of Lorraine if he refused to cooperate.[32] Victor-Amadeus tried to negotiate better conditions with the French ambassadors in Turin, the soldier César de Choiseul, comte du Plessis-Praslin (1602–75), and the civilian administrator Michel Particelli d'Hémery (1596–1650) (Fig. 1.8).[33] The negotiations of 1634 and 1635 revolved around the use of the royal title for the duke and duchess. Richelieu then proposed exchanging mountainous Savoy for territory the allies would conquer in the rich duchy of Milan and the Monferrato. The cardinal never established the exact delineation of territories to be conceded to Victor-Amadeus, however. In order to avoid being devoured by the French lion, the duke obtained supreme command over the French army that was to operate in Italy, on condition that he work alongside the Marshal Créquy, another of Richelieu's clients. The two were not on amicable terms, but the general was a major power in nearby Dauphiné where a good portion of the troops were recruited and supplied. At the last minute, as the duchy began filling with French soldiers for the coming campaign, Richelieu made new demands, such as the transfer to France of an important zone in the Piedmontese plain at the foot of the Alps, in order to support the army in Italy. He followed this with yet another demand that the duke transfer ultimate sovereignty of Savoy from the Emperor to the king of France. These last conditions the duke refused outright, and Richelieu was forced to retreat in order to achieve the treaty signed at Rivoli near Turin on 11 June 1635.[34] The cardinal would return to these demands at a more opportune moment, in order to annex to France most or all of the Savoyard patrimony.[35]

It was not easy to entrap the House of Savoy. In 1634, Prince Tommaso left for Brussels to take up the post of Captain-General of the Spanish army of Flanders,

[31] C. E. Patrucco, 'L'Antifrancesismo in Piemonte sotto il regno di Vittorio Amedeo I', *Bollettino Storico-Bibliografico Subalpino*, 2–3 (1896), 158–74.

[32] Gabriel de Mun, *Richelieu et la maison de Savoie: L'ambassade de Particelli d'Hémery en Piémont* (Paris, 1907), 46.

[33] *Memoires du Maréchal Du Plessis*, in J. Michaud and J. Poujoulat (eds), *Memoires pour servir à l'histoire de France depuis le XIIIe siècle jusqu'à la fin du XVIIIe siècle*, vii (Paris, 1838), 358; Mun, *Richelieu et la maison de Savoie*, 27–30.

[34] Humbert, *Le Maréchal de Créquy*, 207–9.

[35] Ferretti, 'Au nom du droit (de conquête)', 115–16.

MESSIRE MICHEL PARTICELLI CHEVALLIÉ
Seigneur Demery, de Thore et de Tanlay, Conseiller du Roy
en ses Conseils Controlleur General de ses finances, &c
B Moncornet. excudit cum privilegio.

LP 20 - 101[3]

(1630).

Contrôleur général des Finances.

Fig. 1.8. Michel Particelli d'Hémery, French ambassador to Turin and a former army intendant entrusted with finding men, money, and supplies for the French army in Italy, while maintaining the relationship with the Dukes of Savoy and of Parma. His pessimistic reports to Cardinal Richelieu betray a realistic vision of Italian politics in the era of Spanish ascendancy.

that is, the senior field commander in the theatre.[36] Prince Maurizio embraced his ecclesiastical vocation in earnest and moved to Rome where he served as 'cardinal protector' for the Habsburg Holy Roman Emperor. No historian has ever found an incriminating document proving that the Duke of Savoy intended to play both sides simultaneously, but contemporaries certainly believed it. French diplomats asked as much in their dispatches to Paris. In July 1635 Victor-Amadeus explained

---

[36] Paolo Negri, 'La casa di Savoia alla vigilia del quarto periodo della Guerra dei Trent'Anni', *Bollettino Storico-Bibliografico Subalpino*, 14 (1910), 141–61.

to the ambassador of his brother-in-law the Duke of Modena that he was compelled to ally with Louis XIII, but that he was deliberately stalling for time. He made sure that Spain's ambassador Francisco de Melo in Milan was informed of developments so that Olivares could make defensive preparations.[37]

Other signs equally filled the French with foreboding. France expected Victor-Amadeus to furnish the artillery for the army in Italy, in order to avoid hauling the heavy tubes over the Alps, but he provided only about a dozen guns, a number woefully inadequate for a siege of any importance. He also forbade his subjects on pain of death from selling foodstuffs or fodder to the French troops and established something of an embargo around Pinerolo, which was France's most important magazine of military stores in the theatre. Rather than open operations against Spain in the spring (France declared war on the House of Austria early in May 1635), the duke delayed the onset of campaigning until late in the summer. We can well understand the dismay of the French officers that the commander-in-chief of their army might betray them. Duke Charles of Mantua was also an unwilling ally, bitter that France should use its territory to compensate Savoy.[38] The latter maintained his resident in Milan in order to facilitate communication with Madrid.

From 1634 the Spanish knew that Northern Italy would soon be the target of a French invasion, but even engaged as they were in the war against the Dutch Republic and in support of their German cousins, Philip IV and Olivares did not wish to make any major concessions, and one may doubt whether any concessions would have satisfied Cardinal Richelieu, who was confident that the balance of power had shifted towards France. The hard-working and frugal Spanish favourite, who enjoyed the complete confidence of the king, remained convinced that a bellicose policy was the best one.[39] If the French military strategy multiplied the offensive bases beyond its frontiers, Spain articulated its defence around specific strategic regions that protected others further away. In Italy, Milan served this function, protecting Naples and Southern Italy from invasion. It sufficed to place garrisons in the city's great citadel and in the subject towns nearby, and to hold securely the Apennine passes towards the Ligurian and Tuscan coasts by which reinforcements could arrive by sea from Spain or Southern Italy.

---

[37] Gianvittorio Signorotto, 'Modena e il mito della sovranità eroica', in Elena Fumagalli and Giovanni Vittorio Signorotto (eds), *La Corte estense nel primo Seicento: Diplomazia e mecenatismo artistico* (Rome, 2012), 11–50, 26. Signorotto cites two remarkable letters in the Imperial archive in Vienna, HHS It-KS, cart.12, letters to the resident of the Duke of Modena, 4 Aug. 1635, and to the Emperor, 9 Sept. Nevertheless he opines that this declaration of reluctance was disingenuous and macchiavellian, for Savoy had predatory intentions; Giovanni Vittorio Signorotto, 'Milan et l'ennemi savoyard dans la première moitié du XVIIe siècle', in Giuliano Ferretti (ed.), *De Paris à Turin: Christine de France, duchesse de Savoie* (Paris, 2014), 35–58.

[38] *Memoires du Maréchal Du Plessis* (Paris, 1838), 358.

[39] Miguel Angel Ochoa Brun, 'La diplomatie espagnole dans la première moitié du XVIIe siècle', in Bély (ed.), *L'Europe des traités de Westphalie*, 537–54; Robert A. Stradling, *Europe and the Decline of Spain* (London, 1981), 103; on the bond between King Philip and Olivares, J. H. Elliott, 'Staying in Power: The Count-Duke of Olivares', in J. H. Elliott and L. W. B. Brockliss (eds), *The World of the Favourite* (New Haven and London, 1999), 112–22.

The Catholic King and his chief ministers adhered to a century-old political strategy of rewarding leading families for their active support with social recognition and other forms of conspicuous recompense. Ever since Charles V assumed the ducal title over Milan in 1535, Spanish monarchs took pains to respect the dignity and the jurisdiction of the institutions in place, leaving them in the hands of urban patricians. In the eyes of Lombard dignitaries, *somebody* had to be king. Kings of France were likely to be more invasive and less respectful of the established order, and their toleration of Protestants offended Italian sensibilities. The dukes of Savoy were certain to deprive them of all political autonomy and subject Milan to the court in Turin.[40] In contrast to past generations of patriotic Italians who deplored the Catholic legacy of foreign kings, modern historians tend to emphasize the pragmatism and flexibility of successive Spanish monarchs and their viceroys, who actively courted powerful people with this policy of rewards (*mercedes*). Milanese and Lombard notables who performed loyal service received in exchange fiefs and titles in Northern Italy or the kingdom of Naples. Philip IV offered gratifications and advantages on a truly imperial scale, making Milanese aristocrats viceroys of Spanish provinces or admitting them to membership in the international Order of the Golden Fleece. Even under tremendous financial stress, Spanish ministers avoided lodging troops on the estates of important dignitaries and paid special regard towards the Catholic Church's autonomy and immunities.[41] In Southern Italy similarly, Neapolitan, Sicilian, and Sardinian elites saw the Habsburg kings as the legitimate heirs of the medieval Aragonese dynasty, and they considered the Spanish language and customs as more compatible with their own than the French ones.[42] So Spain's defence of its subject territories in Italy was rooted in the monarchy's collaboration with the dominant classes.[43] Nor were Spain's traditional allies or satellite states neglected, for Habsburg princes had long guaranteed their territorial integrity through the good offices of the Governor of Milan. When Cardinal Ferdinand, King Philip IV's younger brother and heir passed through Milan in May 1633, the regional princes and even delegates of the Republic of Venice flocked there to pay their respects.[44] The Catholic King also discreetly extended his royal 'protection' to Duke Francesco of Modena, in recognition of three generations of service of the house of Este to the Spanish interest.[45] Italian aristocrats in most of Northern and Central Italy saw in the king of Spain a patron for their own ambitions, particularly in the military realm. He rewarded them with habits of the Spanish military orders,

---

[40] Signorotto, 'Milan et l'ennemi savoyard', 39–47.

[41] Giovanni Vittorio Signorotto, *Milano Spagnola: Guerra, istituzioni, uomini di governo (1635–1660)*, 2nd edn (Milan, 2001), 22–9; Stefano D'Amico, *Spanish Milan: A City within the Empire, 1535–1706* (Basingstoke and New York, 2012), 123–45.

[42] Giovanni Muto, 'Noble Presence and Stratification in the Territories of Spanish Italy', in T. J. Dandelet and J. A. Marino (eds), *Spain in Italy: Politics, Society and Religion 1500–1700* (Leiden, 2007), 251–97.

[43] Luis A. Ribot Garcìa, 'Las Provincias italianas y la defensa de la Monarquìa', in A. Musi (ed.), *Nel Sistema imperiale, l'Italia Spagnola* (Naples, 1994), 67–92.

[44] Giovanni Francesco Fossati, *Memorie historiche delle guerre d'Italia del secolo presente* (Milan, 1640), 127.

[45] Archivo General Simancas, Estado, 3833, letter of the Marques de Castel Rodrigo, 17 Nov. 1633.

which made them a 'friend' of the Catholic King, further enhancing the prestige that was the currency of nobility.[46] The contrast is striking between the king of Spain's largesse and confidence in Italian aristocrats, and Richelieu's suspicious control of French political elites and his projects to diminish or extinguish the satellite princes around the kingdom's borders.

With so many friends among the social and political elites of Northern Italy, Spanish ambassadors in Venice, Genoa, and Rome were able to keep Olivares and Philip IV very well informed of French initiatives. The new Governor of Milan, Cardinal Albornoz, who was not a soldier like most of his predecessors, relied on Don Carlos Coloma, fresh from the Low Countries, to assume military command. As a French invasion loomed in 1635, they began to hire soldiers from wherever they were available. Everyone considered the ethnic Spaniards to be the best soldiers, but initially there were barely 2,000 of them in all of Lombardy. Castile alone mobilized 21,000 men in the first year of the war against France, of whom 8,000 were destined for the Italian theatre.[47] The Neapolitans, less highly regarded, made up a good portion of the garrisons. The viceroy of the kingdom of Naples, Emanuel de Guzman, Count of Monterey, brother-in-law of the valido Olivares, made every effort to draw men and resources from Southern Italy from his arrival there in 1631. He established a gun foundry in the Arsenal of the great capital (by far the largest city in the entire Spanish Empire) and cast hundreds of guns there in the following years. He reformed the kingdom's cavalry, lightening their armour and weapons and supplying them with smaller, more economical mounts. Between 1632 and 1634, Naples dispatched over 10,000 foot to Spain and Germany, where they figured prominently in the fighting in Alsace and at Nördlingen. Now in 1635, as the volunteers proved scarce, Monterey imposed conscription on both fiefs and towns. He spent some of the kingdom's resources hiring 1,700 veteran soldiers in Hungary and Germany. In Naples, he was not above seizing men by force and holding them penned in the Arsenal until galleys and transports carried them north.[48] Contingents of horse made the long trek across the neutral Papal States to Milan. Many Lombards enlisted too, under local colonels.

The Habsburg troops numbered about 20,000 early in 1635, of whom Coloma posted about a third to fortress duty. The general could not concentrate the rest in a single field army, but strung them out in posts along the threatened borders of Mantua, Parma, and the Alpine Valtellina valley. The western threat required two field forces, one south of the Po in order to protect the vital communications with the Mediterranean, and another in the plain north of the Po to protect Milan. Lombard aristocrats helped prevent a French and Savoyard conquest by recruiting and equipping companies of soldiers with arms and clothing at their own expense, sometimes in exchange for the right to command them.[49] The nobles also helped

[46] Hanlon, *Twilight of a Military Tradition*, 182–5.

[47] Davide Maffi, *Il baluardo della corona* (Florence, 2007), 94–6.

[48] Giuseppe Carignani, *Le Truppe napoletane durante la guerra de' Trent'Anni* (Florence, 1888), 8–12.

[49] Davide Maffi, 'Guerra ed economia: Spese belliche e appaltatori militari nella Lombardia spagnola (1635–1660)', *Storia* Economica, 3 (2000), 489–527.

organize a new peasant militia under centralized control (this existed in all the neighbouring states in 1635), which mounted guard in village castles, patrolled the border, and escorted supply convoys. As a final measure, Olivares ordered the galley flotilla from Naples under the command of Don Alvaro de Bazan, Marques de Santa Cruz, to seize strategic ports along the French Riviera in the spring. Galleys were vulnerable to bad weather, however, and storms wrecked part of the squadron off Corsica, delaying it by several months.[50]

INITIAL FRENCH SETBACKS

While some historians have laid the blame at Olivares's feet for not making concessions, this was Cardinal Richelieu's war, a long time in the planning, and pushed forward in the face of fierce domestic opposition.[51] In the months after the combat at Nördlingen, he mobilized more troops than any king of France for centuries previous, perhaps as many as 80,000 men.[52] Some of them replaced the Swedes garrisoning Alsatian towns. French soldiers operating in the Palatinate late in 1634 occupied the Rhine fortress of Philippsburg and then seized Heidelberg in order to cut Spanish communications with Flanders.[53] After the French blocked the Rhine passage, Spanish troops from Luxembourg seized Trier on the Moselle river to open a new route towards the Alps.[54] In Italy, Marshal Créquy stocked supplies in Pinerolo and reinforced the garrison in Casale Monferrato (Fig. 1.9), which would become the rear and forward bases of operations respectively. French soldiers marched in small detachments through the neutral republic of Genoa to reinforce the Duke of Parma's garrisons in Piacenza and Parma, which was accepted practice as long as they did not plunder civilians along the way. Not nearly all the soldiers dispatched to Italy arrived there, but early in the campaign, if one were to tally the men in French pay in the armies of Créquy, the Duke of Parma, and the Duke of Rohan, in addition to the strong garrisons in Pinerolo and Casale Monferrato, the total might comprise about 25,000 men, not counting ethnic Frenchmen serving the Duke of Mantua (Fig.1.10) and the Duke of Savoy and in the pay of those states.

For the execution of his projects, Richelieu selected trusted kinsmen and clients without giving them much autonomy. The Dutch ambassador in Paris, Hugo Grotius, thought that Richelieu was duplicitous and cruel, capable of anything.[55] The cardinal sternly opposed awarding command to talented soldiers, like Marshal

---

[50] AGS Estado 3837, Consulta of 18 June 1635.

[51] Besides Stradling, 'Olivares and the Origins', see David Parrott, 'The Causes of the Franco-Spanish War of 1635–1659', in Jeremy Black (ed.), *The Origins of War in Early Modern Europe* (Edinburgh, 1987), 72–111.

[52] John A. Lynn, 'Recalculating French Army Growth during the Grand Siècle, 1610–1715', *French Historical Studies*, 18 (1994), 890.

[53] Sven Externbrink, 'L'Espagne, le duc de Savoie et les "portes": La politique italienne de Richelieu et Louis XIII', in Ferretti, *De Paris à Turin*, 15–34.

[54] Ibid.

[55] Lucien Bély, *Les relations internationales en Europe, XVIIe–XVIIIe siècles* (Paris, 1992), 76.

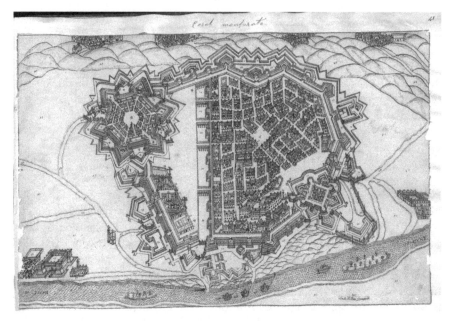

Fig. 1.9. Casale Monferrato, *c.*1640: Technically belonging to the Duke of Mantua, the strong city and its powerful citadel on the Po river housed a strong French garrison after 1628. It served as an almost-impregnable advance base and magazine for France until its capture in 1652.

Toiras, who might plot with his many enemies, preferring the less capable Créquy. Charles de Créquy de Blanchefort (Fig. 1.11) was no stranger to Northern Italy or to Victor-Amadeus. His father was a gentleman of Dauphiné who adhered to the Catholic League during the French wars of religion. His widowed mother abandoned the extremist wing after it called the Duke of Savoy Charles-Emanuel to intervene in their favour. After rallying to Henri IV and commencing service in Picardy, he married the daughter of a senior Huguenot warlord, the duc de Lesdiguières. The king commissioned him to raise a regiment in 1601 for service in Savoy, and after 1615 Lesdiguières, Créquy and the latter's son the Comte de Sault fought against Spain under Savoyard direction in Piedmont. Créquy and his father-in-law also led the Franco-Savoyard invasion of Genoa in 1625, in collaboration with Victor-Amadeus. Unlike his wily father-in-law, Créquy had no patience for cunning or dissimulation. 'Viveva alla grande', noted one potted biography of the general, who once deserted a siege to chase stags. He was very much an alpha male in matters of honour, and killed in a duel Don Filippino of Savoy, bastard son of Duke Emanuel Philibert, uncle of Victor-Amadeus.[56] He influenced men more by his charm, his winning demeanour, lithe body, and handsome face, enhanced

---

[56] Biblioteca Estense Modena, Ms Sorbelli 1410, *Vite e morti di personnaggi illustri*, *c.*1650; also Guadenzio Claretta, *Storia della Reggenza di Cristina di Francia, duchessa di Savoia* (Turin, 1868), i. 148–50; Ercole Ricotti, *Storia della monarchia piemontese* (Florence, 1865), v. 85–9.

CAROLVS GONZAGA DVX Mantuæ Montisfer. Cliu.
Niuer. Rhetel. Mayen. Princeps Supremus Archiensis
Vicarius S.R.Imperij. Comes Portian Altissiod S.Mench.
Vicecomes S.Florentini Baron D'erny etc.

Gonzague (Charles de) Duc de Mantoue et de Montferrat
+ 1637.

Fig. 1.10. Charles de Gonzague (Carlo Gonzaga), Duke of Mantua, a reluctant participant in the French alliance hoping to recover Casale Monferrato from French control. He deliberately made only minimal efforts to assist his allies.

by a cheek scar emphasized by a black velvet patch over it.[57] In battle he displayed as much rashness as courage, and collected a series of wounds over the years. Created Duke and Peer of France after his father-in-law died in 1626, Créquy got along well with Cardinal Richelieu, who plied him with military and diplomatic functions in the Italian theatre. Senior command was generally the preserve of these *Grands*, a group of about sixty or seventy families conspicuous at court.[58] The duke and his father-in-law possessed rich estates in Dauphiné, Languedoc, and

[57] Nicolas Chorier, *Histoire de la vie de Charles de Créquy de Blanchefort, duc de Lesdiguières* (Grenoble, 1684), 248 and 267. On his rashness and duels, 38–45 and 72.

[58] David Parrott, *Richelieu's Army: War, Government and Society in France, 1624–1642* (Cambridge and New York, 2001), 463.

CHARLES SIRE DE CREQVI DVC DE ...
...L'ESDIGVIERES, *Pair de France Prince de...*

† 1638

marêchal de France en 1621.

Fig. 1.11. Charles de Blanquefort duc de Crequy, *c.*1633, client of Cardinal Richelieu, a Grand Seigneur in Dauphiné near the border with Savoy in the Alps. A commander offensively minded and impatient with his slippery ally, the Duke of Savoy.

Provence, provinces closest to Italy, and could draw upon a vast network of clients both Catholic and Protestant. Créquy also possessed substantial domains in northern France and a Parisian pied-à-terre of forty-nine rooms in the fashionable Marais district.[59] No one considered Charles II de Blanchefort, duc de Créquy (1578–1638), to be the most gifted of Richelieu's generals, but he was not out of place at the head of a French army and most of all, he was unwilling to let Victor-Amadeus lead him by the nose.

It was Créquy's predicament to conquer Lombardy, notwithstanding the lukewarm support from his allies. Another smaller French army under the Duke of

---

[59] In addition to the Chorier biography, see Stéphane Gal, *Lesdiguières: Prince des Alpes et connétable de France* (Grenoble, 2007), 158.

HENRY DVC DE ROHAN PAIR DE FRANCE
PRINCE DE LEON COMTE DE PORHOVET.
Balthasar Moncornet ex   LP 20-42

pair de france, colonel général des Suisses a grisons, chef des Calvinistes.

+ 1638.

Fig. 1.12. Henri duc de Rohan, brilliant leader of the French Protestant rebellion in the 1620s, as a servant of Cardinal Richelieu he tried to keep the support of the Swiss German Grison League which wanted to recover the Italian-speaking Valtellina with French support. Richelieu promised much but could not deliver.

Rohan (Fig. 1.12), comprised of about 8,000 French and Swiss Protestant troops, crossed the Alps into the strategic corridor of the Valtellina, north-east of Milan in late March 1635, intending to cut off the direct line of communication between Spanish and German Habsburg territories. This strategy of Napoleonic scope and ambition proved bolder than seventeenth-century conditions allowed. Only Duke Odoardo of Parma was a willing ally, but his small state sat in an awkward position and his contribution would not be very large. Venice confined its support to allowing Rohan to draw supplies and recruits across its territory.[60]

---

[60] Giovanni Francesco Fossati, *Memorie historiche delle guerre d'Italia del secolo presente* (Milan, 1640), 140.

At the end of August the Marshal Créquy and his field army of 15,000 men filed out of Casale without waiting for Victor-Amadeus to give them an express order, and proceeded eastward along the Po with the intention of operating a junction with the 5,000 soldiers of the Duke of Parma, who were marching the 80 or 90 kilometres west from Piacenza. The two commanders quickly agreed to lay siege to Valenza overlooking the Po river on 11 September, expecting the weakly fortified place to capitulate quickly. For two weeks, however, Victor-Amadeus refused to isolate the town from the north bank, allowing Carlos Coloma to feed troops and provisions into the place and nourish a spirited defence of the fresh earthworks in front of the walls. Without the prospect of easy booty, French and Italian troops soon deserted en masse and continual reinforcements from France did not counterbalance their losses. Even after Victor-Amadeus finally arrived with his own contingent to cut the fortress off from relief, the confederate army was too small to prevent Spanish reinforcements from slipping through. In the stubborn trench fighting at close quarters, in the ability to maintain formation and fire discipline, and in the use of deadly countermines to collapse the French approaches, the siege of Valenza demonstrated the technical superiority of Habsburg troops. French gunners failed to concentrate enough fire on vulnerable sections of the ramparts. Meanwhile Coloma gathered a small field army of his own and erected a fortified camp in proximity to the siege on the north bank of the Po after 20 October. An attack by the coalition army on 24 October to dislodge them stalled and was then abandoned, and in the aftermath the three confederate commanders quarrelled with each other over their respective shortcomings. Finally on 26 October, Coloma stormed the siege lines on the north bank of the Po and conveyed troops and munitions in large quantities into the town after breaking its encirclement. Créquy, Duke Odoardo of Parma, and Victor-Amadeus withdrew to Casale and left an abundance of supplies behind them in the trenches. It was too late in the season to begin any fresh projects.[61]

The Italian theatre proved a great disappointment for Richelieu, while the French and Dutch operations in the Low Countries failed too, in part thanks to the energy and skill deployed by Prince Tommaso of Savoy. Olivares hoped that these disappointments would result in Richelieu's dismissal and the reversal of French policy. Spain's proposals for peace appealed to a broad spectrum of the French court aligned with the Prince Gaston d'Orléans, heir to the throne, and the exiled queen mother.[62] The widespread refusal of much of France to pay ever-higher taxes added to Richelieu's troubles. He ordered commanders to withdraw troops from the borders to enforce tax collection and to restore order in major cities like Bordeaux, and throughout rural Aquitaine, which was a region of endemic fiscal rebellion.

Even winter quarters brought their share of disillusionment. If many deserters rejoined the colours to pass the winter season in warm accommodation, feeding them proved a problem. Providing fodder for the horses and oxen necessary for

[61] For a detailed account of the siege, see Hanlon, *Hero of Italy*, 96–122.
[62] Charles Gregory, 'The End of Richelieu: Noble Conspiracy and Spanish Treason in Louis XIII's France, 1636–1642', unpublished D.Phil. dissertation, Oxford University, 2012, 13: I would like to thank the author for sending me the study and some of its supporting materials.

army transport and the cavalry proved an even bigger headache. Bulky fodder could not be carted from very far away due to the high cost of transport: armies typically acquired it locally. The Monferrato district had already been 'eaten' during the previous campaign, so the French would have to draw their own supplies at considerable expense from over the Alps.[63] Winter fodder for the draft animals was an absolute requirement, and it was likewise a strategic necessity to deny it to the enemy. Haylofts present in every farm were the equivalent of a modern petrol depot, so local commanders did their best to remove them and the large livestock to the shelter of village castles. The castles themselves, which were helpless against artillery, became the targets of small-scale expeditions seeking the capture of both the animals and the forage, and whatever other precious commodities the population squirrelled away there.[64]

In an attempt to consolidate the slender portion of Spanish territory they held in western Lombardy, Créquy and Victor-Amadeus built a fortress of packed earth around the village of Breme, which was close by the Po river in such a way that it helped protect the boat bridge across the Po at Casale Monferrato. Earthen walls rose quickly around the place, but money and supplies for the soldiers garrisoned there were cruelly inadequate. Lacking equipment to fell the trees in the fields, soldiers often tore down houses in order to find firewood to burn. Even this did not prevent widespread mortality among the troops and horses in winter for the lack of provisions and fodder.[65] Duke Odoardo's little army became a burden to him while his distant duchy remained unprotected.[66] Ambassador Hémery proposed to give him French troops to send him home, but headstrong Odoardo wished instead that Louis XIII would place him at the head of a strong French army certain to clinch victory in the coming campaign.[67]

Victor-Amadeus and Créquy were at each other's throats in the aftermath of the failed siege of Valenza, the first accusing the second of incompetence, the latter accusing the duke of treachery and double-dealing.[68] The three coalition commanders eventually decided to send the remnants of the Parman contingent home (perhaps 2,500 men, most of whom were by now ethnic Frenchmen), with the powerful escort of a thousand Savoyard cavalry commanded by the energetic count Guido Villa, a Ferrarese mercenary colonel. Unencumbered by artillery and many wagons, the column skirted Alessandria and Tortona south of the Po and stormed across a Scrivia river ford on 23 December before Leganés, the new Governor of Milan, could concentrate enough troops to stop it (Fig. 1.13).[69] They constituted a badly needed garrison for Odoardo's cities. Piacenza became the base from which French and Parman columns could raid the southern periphery of the duchy of

---

[63] Mun, *Richelieu et la maison de Savoie*, 112.

[64] Girolamo Ghilini, *Annali di Alessandria*, ed. A. Bossola (Alessandria, 1903), 112.

[65] Souvigny, *Memoires du comte de Souvigny, lieutenant-général des armées du roi*, ed. Ludovic De Contenson (Paris, 1906), i. 302.

[66] Giovanni Pietro Crescenzi Romani, *Corona della nobiltà d'Italia, ovvero compendio dell'istorie delle famiglie illustri* (Bologna, 1639–42), 298.

[67] Bibliothèque Nationale de France, Ms Fr 16929, 'Relation de M. d'Esmery de ses negociations en Piedmont en 1635 etc'., fos. 551–2.

[68] Claretta, *Storia della Reggenza*, 148–50.   [69] Hanlon, *Hero of Italy*, 123–4.

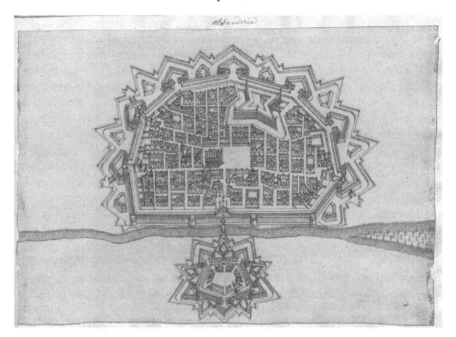

Fig. 1.13. Alessandria, with its citadel, south of the Po river, protected the vital communications between Milan and the Genoese Riviera by which supplies and reinforcements arrived from Spain and Naples.

Milan, but these could not be easily reinforced, nor could their actions be coordinated from Casale Monferrato. Odoardo left for Paris in February to lay his case for command of a French army before Louis XIII and Richelieu in person.

As Créquy's French forces dwindled, and deserters left to visit Rome or Venice like tourists, Spanish strength built steadily.[70] The sinews of war then, like now, were financial. The Governor of Milan oversaw tax collection in Lombardy, and managed funds sent from Madrid, Sicily, and Naples with a relatively free hand.[71] In 1635, Madrid disbursed enough money to cover about 80 per cent of the most urgent expenditures, and the kingdoms of Naples and Sicily provided most of the remainder. Madrid considered creating judicial offices that eligible candidates should purchase, as in France, but the Milanese Senate stood firm against the innovation and the crown backed off.[72] Another novelty perceived as an assault on urban privilege obliged citizen landholders living in the subject cities like Cremona, Lodi, Como, etc. to pay the rural taxation rates for their landed estates, which were higher than the urban rates they had paid until then. Other arbitrary measures included requisitioning carts, teams of oxen and their drivers, hundreds at a time, without any kind of compensation.[73] Whenever possible, Leganés obliged rural

---

[70] Galeazzo Gualdo Priorato, *Historia delle guerre del Conte Galeazzo Gualdo Priorato* (Venice, 1646), xi. 301–2.
[71] Maffi, *Il baluardo della corona*, 156.
[72] Ibid. 365.   [73] Ibid. 375.

communities to lodge troops on the move or in winter quarters, so that these costs did not appear as crown expenditures. Like rulers elsewhere, he aimed these measures primarily at communities or single individuals who owed back taxes.[74]

Leganés and his diplomatic assistant Don Francisco de Melo determined that the army required a minimum of 200,000 scudi every month, which did not include pay for most of the soldiers or money to purchase a thousand expensive cavalry remounts every year.[75] This sum far surpassed the total ordinary and extraordinary revenues of the state of Milan, which oscillated around 1.2 million scudi annually, levied on some 800,000 inhabitants. Revenues never recovered from the catastrophic plague of 1630, and in 1636 these were still about 20 per cent lower than fifteen years previous. Davide Maffi has calculated that Lombardy spent more than 2 million scudi annually for the prosecution of the war, and 2.6 million between August 1635 and September 1636, not including the costs of arms and ammunition.

War always occasioned massive borrowing and long-term state indebtedness. In Milan, Naples, Madrid (and Paris too), ministers earmarked much of their tax revenue to pay the interest on the huge accumulated debt. The Milanese public debt already devoured much of the duchy's revenue, which in the aftermath of the plague amounted to 21 million scudi. Ministers contracted new loans with willing financiers, chiefly Genoese, who anticipated 8 to 10 per cent interest annually, paid punctually unlike local lenders.[76] Wealthy individuals (including foreigners) and corporations (such as monasteries) consented to advance new loans only under duress. Before 1636 was out, and with interest payments on previous loans devouring three-quarters of the tax revenue, the Governor of Milan Leganés imposed forced loans on the principal state bondholders. These would no longer receive interest payments on previous loans unless they advanced more funds. To soften the political backlash, he exempted from this drastic measure the inhabitants of Milan proper, all the ecclesiastics, the churches and charitable institutions, and the modest bondholders.[77] Great feudal dynasties resident in Milan exempt from the forced loans contributed generously to recruiting and equipping new levies for the defence of the region. The most conspicuous example of loyal service was Cardinal Prince Teodoro Trivulzio, the principal feudatory in the lush lands near the Po, whose son had already received the collar of the Golden Fleece in 1634. The cardinal levied and deployed some 3,000 soldiers for the king's service, principally along the border with Parma.[78] Spain could not have retained Milan without the unflagging support of *potentados* like these. Fairly knowledgeable of international

---

[74] Ibid. 247–9; on troop lodgings generally, Alessandro Buono, *Esercito, Istituzioni, Territorio: Alloggiamenti militari e case herme nello stato di Milano, secoli XVI e XVII* (Florence, 2009).

[75] AGS Estado 3344, no. 45; letter of the Marques de Leganés, 26 May 1636.

[76] Maffi, *Il baluardo della corona*, 334.

[77] Marco Ostoni, *Il tesoro del Re: Uomini e istituzioni della finanza pubblica milanese fra Cinque e Seicento* (Naples, 2010), 137–41.

[78] Signorotto, *Milano Spagnola*, 127–8; Mario Rizzo, '"Ottima gente da guerra": Cremonesi al servizio della strategia imperiale', *Storia di Cremona: L'Età degli Asburgo di Spagna (1535–1707)*, ed. G. Politi (Cremona, 2006), 126–45.

events via broadsheets published in Milan and Venice, feudatories earned the king's favour and the gratitude of his powerful ministers.[79]

The clergy, on the other hand, pretended to be deaf, secure in their sense of entitlement. In previous emergencies, the king of Spain prevailed upon the archbishop of Milan to help impose contributions on both the secular clergy and on the religious orders, both major landowners. Pope Urban VIII proved helpful by authorizing such payments in 1624, but the Lombard clergy offered only a derisory sum and then obstructed any measures designed to assess their revenues. The crown threatened the clergy with arbitrary lodgings of soldiers on ecclesiastical estates, and turned to the papacy again in order to outflank its opponents.[80] This gentle patience of the king of Spain took time and obtained little. Duke Odoardo of Parma routinely imprisoned churchmen who protested the taxes he levied on them, and not surprisingly they constituted something of a fifth column in his duchy.[81]

Milan was the central hub of a constellation of self-governing towns and cities that benefited in various ways from Spain's military presence. Still one of Europe's great industrial cities, Milan was a great inland port, fed by several important navigable canals that floated not only food, but firewood and charcoal crucial for industry from the Alpine lake district. The same canals powered a multitude of flour mills and industrial equipment of all kinds.[82] The troops lodged in Lombard citadels were principally Spaniards.[83] Milan's castle garrison of perhaps 500 men was the largest of these, guaranteeing the loyalty of a city numbering *c.*80,000 inhabitants. In Pavìa, Cremona, Alessandria, and Novara garrisons normally barely surpassed one or at most two hundred men, who did not represent an intolerable burden on citizens. The crown poured tax revenues from near and far into the principal cities of the duchy. Merchants nimble enough to honour government contracts for bread, the rental of horses, mules and wagons, and other stores could enrich themselves, or at least make paper fortunes they could one day redeem for rewards and advantages of other kinds. The suppliers were not necessarily subjects of the king: army administrators welcomed bids from Brescian, Genoese, Florentine, Venetian, and Lucchese entrepreneurs too.[84] The armaments manufactures located in Lombard cities equipped not only local garrisons, but troops in

[79] Signorotto, *Milano Spagnola*, 22–36.

[80] Massimo Carlo Giannini, 'Risorse del principe e risorse dei sudditi: Fisco, clero e comunità di fronte al problema della difesa comune nello stato di Milano (1618–1660)', *Annali di Storia Moderna e Contemporanea*, 6 (2000), 173–225.

[81] Hanlon, *Hero of Italy*, 133–4.

[82] Yves-Marie Bercé, 'Les guerres dans l'Italie', in Y. M. Bercé, G. Delille, J. M. Sallmann, and J. C. Waquet (eds), *L'Italie au XVIIe siècle* (Paris, 1989), 311–31.

[83] Maffi, *Il baluardo della corona*, 138; the author provides a table indicating normal garrison sizes.

[84] Maffi, 'Guerra ed economia'; see also Ribot Garcia, 'Las Provincias Italianas', 67–92; by the same author, 'Milano, piazza d'armi della monarchia spagnola', in Federico Motta (ed.), *'Millain the great': Milano nelle brume del Seicento* (Milan, 1989), 349–63; the overall economic impact of the war is weighed by Mario Rizzo, '"Rivoluzioni dei Consumi", "State building" e "Rivoluzione militare": La domanda e l'offerta di servizi strategici nella Lombardia Spagnola, 1535–1659', in I. Lopane and E. Ritrovato (eds), *Tra Vecchi e Nuovi Equilibri: Domanda e offerta di servizi in Italia in età moderna e contemporanea* (Bari, 2007), 447–74.

Spain and Germany also. The foundries produced cannon and cannonballs but also thousands of picks, shovels, and sledgehammers, chains, iron bars for the artillery. Close to eighty musket-manufacturers existed in Milan alone, and more operated in each subject town. The Valsassina mountain valley north-east of the city close to Venetian Bergamo was home to scores of separate enterprises producing weapons and war materiel on a considerable scale. In 1636 Leganés ordered 10,000 muskets for the army, exclusive of the bullets, the powder (100 tonnes annually), wicks and the great variety of implements to furnish the artillery.[85] The cavalry required more than a thousand horses every year as remounts, each one costing double or triple the income of a peasant family. Horses were rare and expensive in Italy, relative to Northern Europe where population densities were lower and pastures and fodder were more easily available.

Just as vital to Spanish resilience as the loyalty of its subjects was the monarchy's ability to mobilize the resources of its friends and allies. We often envisage war and peace in all-or-nothing terms, but in all periods bystander states adopt varying stances of semi-belligerence or semi-neutrality in order to reap the advantages of both. The French invasion taught Philip IV and Olivares who Spain's true friends were. Duke Ferrante Gonzaga of the tiny principality of Guastalla (on the Po near Mantua) was an unconditional Habsburg ally: he supplied his uncle Don Vincenzo Gonzaga with enough cash to operate a company of horse, even though it was a considerable drain on his finances.[86] Florentine contributions were considerably more substantial, but the Grand Duke of Tuscany Ferdinando II maintained a façade of friendliness with Spain's enemies, hoping to remain everyone's friend. He owed homage to the king of Spain for his fief of Siena, and agreed to pay 30,000 ducats monthly for the war in Lombardy, in addition to supplying ships for an expedition to Brazil against the Dutch.[87] There was a written understanding that the grand duke should provide a powerful expeditionary force of 4,000 foot for the Lombard theatre, maintained at that level by continuous recruitment. Tuscan galleys ferried troops from Naples to Genoa and Finale Liguria, besides the 700 Florentine infantry who disembarked there just after Christmas 1635 (Fig. 1.14). Army administrators collected the men with great difficulty at Livorno and then shipped out batches of them to join the others posted to garrison duty in the duchy of Milan (Fig. 1.15). Early in March 1636 the eight companies amounted to only 640 men, of whom just over 500 were fit for duty.[88] Of the 700 soldiers disembarked near Genoa early in May, over 300 deserted immediately, provoking loud protests from Don Francisco de Melo. The Tuscans retorted that Leganés provided them with the worst lodging conditions, and they were always the last to receive their pay. Nonetheless, when the campaign began in May, the Tuscan contingent numbered twenty companies of foot totalling almost 2,000 men, and another four

---

[85] Davide Maffi, 'Guerra ed economia'.

[86] ASPr Archivio Gonzaga di Guastalla 63: Lettere, 16 June 1636; like other Italian princes, the Gonzaga of Guastalla were feudal lords of sizeable towns in the Kingdom of Naples.

[87] AGS Estado 3837, Consulta of 29 Aug. 1635.

[88] Archivio di Stato Firenze (hereafter ASF) Mediceo del Principato 3180, fo. 670, note of 7 Mar. 1636.

Fig. 1.14. Stefano della Bella, Loading a Tuscan galley in Livorno for departure. Tuscan galleys like the one depicted here served the Spanish empire between Naples and Liguria, transporting both Florentine and Habsburg troops in 1636. The commanders had orders not to engage the French without prior approval from Grand Duke Ferdinando II, however.

Fig. 1.15. Stefano della Bella, Tuscan troops embark on transports in Livorno. Tuscany's unenthusiastic support for the Spanish alliance produced enough troops in the spring and summer of 1636 to tip the balance in Lombardy.

companies of horse numbering 283 effective troopers.[89] The Medici dynasty also maintained an unspecified number of officers and men following Prince Matthias in Germany.

The Duke of Modena Francesco I d'Este pondered his response to the crisis more carefully. Like the kings of France and Spain, like his brothers-in-law Victor-Amadeus and Odoardo of Parma, he craved an occasion to accomplish great deeds on the battlefield and to expand his territories at the expense of his neighbours. This meant that he was liable to pass from one alliance to another at the right moment. In the meantime, he would try to extract the maximum from the Catholic King for the Este dynasty. His ambassador in Madrid presented a long list of requests to Olivares, beginning with the repayment of over half a million ducats in unpaid pensions and favours, superior to the annual income of his duchy. It was soon clear that Spain had no money to award, so the duke changed his objectives. High on the list was the international recognition of his title of Highness: Victor-Amadeus was a Highness, as was Ferdinando II, Duke Charles of Mantua, and Odoardo of Parma. Francesco was a mere Excellency. In addition he desired the award of a large and populous fief in Lombardy, preferably near his Po river border. (Spain offered a fief in the kingdom of Naples or Sicily.) Francesco also desired a senior military command in the Spanish army for his uncles Borso and Foresto, who were fighting in Germany, a pension for his infant son Prince Cesare, a collar of the Golden Fleece for himself.[90] After Ronchi's death in 1633, Francesco confided in Fulvio Testi, his ambassador in Rome, who warned him of the danger posed by a resurgent France in Italy.[91] Francesco was momentarily seduced by Richelieu's offer of protection and rewards early in 1635, but, noting Venice's refusal to join the French alliance, reluctantly decided not to sign the Treaty of Rivoli in July. He would serve the House of Austria as a prince of the Empire. His loyalty was nothing if not opportunistic, for in exchange Spain would transfer to his jurisdiction the rich fief of Correggio, held by a Spanish garrison.[92] Relations with Spain soon soured as Olivares had no intention of withdrawing Spanish troops from a fortress so close to Mantua and Parma. Francesco promised to the Spanish alliance 3,000 infantry, and pay for the thousand men holding Correggio, but Modenese contingents never amounted to more than a small fraction of that.[93]

Just as Spanish contributions to the Imperial war effort first helped stall and then crush the Swedes in 1633 and 1634, now it was the turn of the Emperor Ferdinand II to allow his cousin Philip IV to recruit men in Germany for the Italian theatre. Some Imperial contingents were purchased 'off the shelf' under officers commissioned by the emperor, and not subject to the military codes of Spain.[94] The emperor

[89] ASF Mediceo del Principato 3180, fos. 495, 542, 980, 1110; also 3258, fo. 233, letter to Don Francisco de Melo of 26 May 1636.

[90] Paolo Negri, *Relazioni Italo-Spagnuole nel secolo XVII* (Rome, 1913), 16–24.

[91] Signorotto, 'Modena e il mito della sovranità eroica', 11–50.

[92] AGS Estado 3343, no. 35; Daniela Frigo, 'Negozi, alleanze e conflitti. La dinastia estense e la diplomazia del Seicento', in Fumagalli and Signorotto, *La Corte estense nel primo Seicento*, 51–92.

[93] Odoardo Rombaldi, *Il duca Francesco I d'Este (1629–1658)* (Modena, 1992), 25.

[94] Fernando Gonzalez de Leon, *The Road to Rocroi: Class, Culture and Command in the Spanish Army of Flanders, 1567–1659* (Boston and Leiden, 2009), 232.

employed no fewer than 101 expensive cavalry regiments in 1636, substantially more than he could afford. Since everyone considered German cavalry to be of higher calibre than their Spanish counterparts, Olivares offered to hire some of these in the Low Countries and Italy and provide for their subsistence.[95] Most German auxiliary units were infantry, eager for better pickings than what ravaged Central Europe could offer. Some aristocratic Italian officers, like the Modenese Prince Borso d'Este or the Tuscan Ottavio Piccolomini, were prepared to pass from Spanish to Austrian service, and then back again.[96] Spanish money enabled one of Wallenstein's most promising colonels, Gil de Haes (originally a baker's helper from Ghent in the Spanish Netherlands) to levy troops in Tirol. The first of these contingents, described as fit and refined by one of our sources, arrived in Lombardy in January along with their 1,500 women (*garces*, in the more disparaging French account), children, and invalids. They clamoured for permission to plunder enemy territory immediately in order to subsist, and accounts from Milan assure us that they plundered friendly territory also.[97] A priest in Busto Arsizio where these men were posted complained that, to feed them, secular authorities imposed illegal levies on church revenues for the duration of the war.[98] Five more regiments of Germans crossed the Saint Gothard pass as soon as it was free of snow.[99]

Fresh contingents from Naples, from Spain, and Lombardy itself were soon at the disposal of Coloma's replacement, Diego Mejia de Guzmàn, the Marques de Leganés, Cardinal Albornoz's successor as Governor of Milan. The Spanish favourite, like Cardinal Richelieu, entrusted key posts to men belonging to a few families related to him.[100] As a cousin of the powerful chief minister Olivares, Leganés's career accelerated in his forties, when he received his title and married Polissena Spìnola, daughter of the celebrated Genoese general Ambrogio Spìnola, with a princely dowry of 200,000 ducats. Leganés was well known for his artistic flair and lived in a richly ornate palace, but the king annoyingly cherry-picked his most prized objects to furnish the Buen Retiro palace in 1633. Drawn naturally to mathematics and the sciences, he became a leading Spanish artillery specialist, and served as a senior technical adviser for the army in Madrid. Olivares then posted him to the Low Countries under Carlos Coloma, another partisan of more technical warfare, before awarding him his first command in Alsace in 1634. Not incidentally, he figured as one of the heroes of Nördlingen the same year.[101] Olivares

---

[95] Vladimir Brnardic, *Imperial Armies of the Thirty Years' War: Cavalry* (Oxford, 2010), 15.

[96] Bérenger, 'La collaboration militaire austro-espagnole aux XVIe–XVIIe siècles', *L'Espagne et ses guerres: De la fin de la Reconquête aux guerres d'Indépendance* (Paris: 2004), 11–33; on these careers, see my *Twilight of a Military Tradition*, 93–134.

[97] *Gazette de France*, 30 (1636), 9 Feb.; on their misbehaviour in Spanish Lombardy, see the diary of Alessandro Giulini, 'Un diario secentesco inedito d'un notaio milanese', *Archivio Storico Lombardo*, 57 (1930), 466–82: 22 Jan. 1636.

[98] Giovanni Battista Lupi, 'Storia della peste avvenuta nel borgo di Busto Arsizio, 1630 (1632–1642)', in Franco Bertolli and Umberto Colombo (eds), *La peste del 1630 a Busto Arsizio* (Busto Arsizio, 1990), 203.

[99] *Le Mercure François* (Paris, 1635–7), 147.   [100] Elliott, 'Staying in Power'.

[101] Gonzalez de Leon, *The Road to Rocroi*, 151; also Francisco Arroyo Martin, 'El marqués de Leganés. Apuntes biograficos', *Espacio, Tiempo y Forma, serie IV, Historia Moderna*, 15 (2002), 145–85.

paired Leganés at the outset with the diplomat Felipe de Rivera, duque de Alcalà, Spain's plenipotentiary designated to negotiate a quick end to the war, but the latter soon departed for fruitless peace talks in Germany.[102] Leganés's brother-in-law Filippo Spìnola, colonel of a Neapolitan tercio (an administrative unit of multiple infantry companies, ancestor of the modern regiment), spent part of his winter in the southern metropolis to levy recruits.[103] The naval flotilla in Liguria received additional units, until it totalled thirty-eight galleys and twelve sailing vessels, manned by thousands of soldiers and seamen.[104] Leganés received orders from Madrid to besiege and capture the city of Parma, but Governors of Milan treated their instructions with a great deal of liberty. Leganés felt that, although Parma's capture might be feasible, it would further antagonize Pope Urban VIII, whose policy had been far from Hispanophile. Rome ceased subsidizing the Habsburg war in 1635 now that it was no longer a confessional struggle against Protestants.[105] Better, Leganés thought, to press the French back into the Monferrato off Spanish territory, and try to pick apart the enemy alliance.[106] He employed the winter months to reform companies so as to keep a proper ratio between the number of officers and the soldiers, and sent home the officers who proved to be ineffectual.[107] He 'reformed' several of the seven Neapolitan tercios sent the previous year and allotted their remaining soldiers to fill out the Lombard tercios of Cardinal Trivulzio and Ludovico Guasco.[108]

Spain's situation in Italy at the end of 1635 was not nearly as dire as Richelieu had predicted. The Catholic King's ministers had galvanized Lombard social elites to rise to the challenge of invasion from several directions simultaneously.[109] Marshal Créquy's task was to mobilize an unwieldy alliance to effect a quick conquest of Spanish Lombardy in 1636. Generals knew better than to attempt large-scale operations over the winter months, due to the lack of fodder for the horses and the risk of illness from exposure for the men. Guido Villa's Savoyard cavalry in the duchy of Parma still needed to be fed, as the arrival of a thousand horse in the little state had not been anticipated. Skirmishing parties along the western border of that duchy drew Spanish forces there and prevented Villa from drawing supplies from that quarter. At the end of January, probably on the instructions of Duke Odoardo, Villa invaded the semi-neutral duchy of Modena in search of fodder. This rash action made a bad situation much worse. Odoardo seethed

---

[102] For an account of these talks, frustrated principally by Cardinal Richelieu, see the book by Daniel Séré, *La Paix des Pyrenees: Vingt-quatre ans de negociations entre la France et l'Espagne (1635–1659)* (Paris, 2007).

[103] *Gazette de France*, 3 (1636): news sent from Rome on 5 Dec. 1635. Another dispatch sent from Genoa on 28 Dec. announced the arrival of 700 reinforcements disembarking there en route to Milan.

[104] R. C. Anderson, 'The Thirty Years War in the Mediterranean', *The Mariner's Mirror*, 56 (1969), 435–51.

[105] Klaus Jaitner, 'The Popes and the Struggle for Power during the Sixteenth and Seventeenth Centuries', *1648: War and Peace in Europe* (Munster, 1998), i. 61–7.

[106] Maffi, *Il baluardo della corona*, 18.

[107] AGS, Estado 3343, no. 140, 27 Mar. 1636.

[108] *Gazette de France*, 10 (1636).

[109] Gianvittorio Signorotto, 'Milan et l'ennemi savoyard dans la première moitié du dix-septième siècle', in Ferretti, *De Paris à Turin*, 35–58.

with spite because his brother-in-law Duke Francesco would not join the coalition against Spain, after letting it be understood that he would. He considered plundering the duchy to be just punishment for Francesco's breach of faith. For good measure, Odoardo's subjects carted wagonloads of confiscated Modenese grain into Parma city magazines. Duke Francesco immediately mobilized a militia army of his own, but realized that it could not repel an invasion by professional soldiers. Leganés dispatched immediate assistance, to demonstrate that the king of Spain stood by his allies, even lukewarm ones. Spanish and Neapolitan troops arrived in the duchy from Cremona under the command of Juan Vasquez de Coronado only days after Francesco issued a cry for help. After mid-February, it was the turn of the rich district of Parma to suffer expeditions of Spanish and Modenese soldiers seeking plunder in the vulnerable countryside. In March, another Spanish contingent invaded the duchy from the mountainous south, under the command of the Genoese Prince Gian Andrea Doria, some of whose fiefs the Farnese Dukes of Parma usurped in the late sixteenth century. They plundered and set ablaze villages and farms as they advanced down the river valleys, with the local Farnese militia levies helpless to prevent it. In Paris, Odoardo suddenly took fright at the vulnerability of his duchy and demanded that the coalition do something to come to its aid.[110] The confederate commanders dreaded the invasion of the duchy of Parma from three sides in February and early March, because they knew that Odoardo Farnese's subjects had no stomach for the war and would have been happy to capitulate. Unhappy priests and nobles, and even a mercenary captain in Piacenza fed detailed information to the Spaniards on the number and deployment of Odoardo's soldiers.

In order to take some of the pressure off their beleaguered ally, Créquy and Victor-Amadeus collected a large force of 9,000 foot and 1,500 horse together with a small battery of four cannon to make a demonstration beyond the Sesia river border, with the nearest castles and their stores as immediate targets. Fighting over the control of castles and their precious supplies was a normal feature of this war, in part because the attacking soldiers shared the booty in lieu of pay. The winter months were ideal for these actions because enemy field armies retired to winter quarters, dispersed over the entire duchy.[111] The most important posts were held with small detachments of professional soldiers, assisted by militiamen, but smaller centres relied entirely on local forces. Normally the militia defenders opened the gates at the first appearance of enemy artillery, which could knock them down in a few minutes. Even regular troops defending such places were not always up to the task, like the newly arrived subjects of the Grand Duke of Tuscany guarding village castles along the Sesia border with Piedmont. Savoyard troops assaulted the sixty men in garrison at Confienza with such vigour that the Florentine commander arranged a pact with his attackers. Honour and reputation required the defenders to put up a decent fight: however he promised that his men would

[110] Hanlon, *Hero of Italy*, 152–4.

[111] George Satterfield, *Princes, Posts and Partisans: The Army of Louis XIV and Partisan Warfare in the Netherlands, 1673–1678* (Leiden and Boston, 2003), 134.

not load their muskets with bullets if the Savoyards would do the same. After a suitable expenditure of gunpowder, they surrendered the castle and constituted themselves prisoners. The following day another garrison surrendered at nearby Robbio on similar conditions. Micro-advances such as these enabled French and Savoyard raiding parties to penetrate the rich Lomellina district in search of fodder and booty. What they could not remove, they burned.[112]

Hoping to profit from the absence of strong opposition, the Franco-Savoyard army crossed the narrow Agogna river and seized the castle at Vespolate on 23 February, where the peasant militia fought for several hours to protect their stores of grain and wine.[113] Tributaries of the upper Po were not normally serious obstacles because of their wide, stony beds, which became raging torrents only after days of heavy rain. Forced to react, Leganés ordered his general of cavalry, the Neapolitan Gherardo Gambacorta, to withdraw from the western edge of the duchy of Parma, and to move on Abbiategrasso, where he joined him with troops drawn from Milan's citadel, some recently arrived German horse and foot, and a large body of militiamen. These crossed the Ticino river to rescue the weakly fortified city of Vigevano, whose two-kilometre circumference lacked stout walls, bastions, a moat, and everything else necessary for its defence.[114] Companies marched scores of kilometres from their winter quarters to augment this force, while artillery and its ponderous train arrived from Pavìa on 27 February.

The next day Leganés marched from Vigevano at the head of this modest host of 6,000 professional foot and 2,000 horse. The vanguard consisted of eleven companies of horse of the State of Milan under Gambacorta's direction, with some supporting Spanish musketeers, and a German regiment of dragoons under the Spanish colonel Juan Lope Giron. The main body of foot, mostly Spanish and German, followed behind with the cannon, while the less reliable Florentines and the Neapolitan tercio of Lucio Boccapianola brought up the rear. This force marched north towards Novara in classic battle order, keeping its baggage train to the east near the Ticino river. The Savoyard vanguard of 1,500 horse and 1,000 musketeers advanced slowly towards them across the wet rice paddies as far as the village of Sozzago, with a larger detachment behind it at Vespolate.[115] Leganés ordered Gambacorta to take some mounted arquebusiers with the heavy cavalry and force the Franco-Savoyard vanguard to withdraw. After his musketeers and dragoons softened up the enemy with sustained fire and destabilized their formations, the cavalry (which included a company of lancers) charged with such vigour that the Franco-Savoyards fell back precipitously. Gambacorta pursued them for a couple of kilometres but suspected an ambush in the densely planted flat countryside, where rows of trees and hedges severely restricted visibility. Créquy formed up

[112] Archivio di Stato Torino, Materie militare, mazza 1, no. 30; Giornaliere della Guerra fatta da S.A.R. e truppe confederate contro il duca di Mantova [sic] e dello Stato di Milano, reports on 21 and 22 Feb. 1636.

[113] Biblioteca Nacional Madrid, MS 2367, Italia 1636, p. 29.

[114] ASF Mediceo del Principato 3180, fo. 292, inspection of Vigevano's fortifications, 22 Mar. 1636.

[115] Alexandre de Saluces, *Histoire militaire du Piémont*, iv (Turin, 1818), 18.

his own troops outside Vespolate and posted his musketeers in the chokepoints, or *passos angostos*, thinking initially that the cavalry that routed his advance elements were only foragers. The main body of the Spanish force formed up in battle order outside Cerano six kilometres away and prepared to pass the night there. Isolated detachments of French horse withdrew to rejoin Créquy and Victor-Amadeus and the two armies readied themselves for a general battle. Before dawn, however, the Franco-Savoyards marched away in the direction from whence they came, and later the same day recrossed the Sesia river border with their baggage. Gambacorta's cavalry and some supporting infantry followed them closely to watch and collect intelligence, with swift couriers relaying the news and its confirmation (an important precaution) to Leganés in Novara. The Spanish commander formed up his army in battle once again at Granozzo, about six kilometres from the leading French outposts, until he received final confirmation from his scouts and from the local inhabitants on 2 March that all of the enemy forces had withdrawn. He then hastened to disperse the men into warm quarters before the cold weather depleted his outnumbered infantry still further. This action near Vespolate inflicted by Spanish estimates about 150 killed, to the Piedmontese and Savoyards primarily, and netted 72 prisoners, exclusive of the wounded of whom many would die. The French account proclaims that Victor-Amadeus retired from Vespolate 'after having pillaged and burned all the enemy villages and conveyed the grain and fodder to Breme'.[116] This was a typical 'action', of which there were many examples during the era, in winter as in summer, fighting over control of the countryside and its precious resources.[117] A formal battle would have been pointless for no defensible town could have been besieged during the winter months. The confederate commanders proved unable to force the Spanish to relinquish any fortified posts they held in the duchy of Parma, making this diversion doubly fruitless.

Generals and army administrators on both sides then went about preparing the coming campaign scheduled to start towards the end of May. Richelieu intended to give Créquy and the Italian theatre greater priority of men and resources, but perhaps half of the troops intended for the theatre deserted en route.[118] The situation of the duc de Rohan's army in the Alpine Valtellina was especially worrying for the lack of warm clothing, and the increasingly tense relations with the Grison Swiss allies.[119] The Habsburgs and their adversaries had been competing for the control of the valley for over a decade. The district had been in the jurisdiction of the Swiss Calvinist Grison League to the north for more than a century, conquered from the duchy of Milan. In 1620 the Italian Catholic population of the valley rose up and slaughtered several hundred Italian and German Protestants who ruled them. Spanish and Italian troops dispatched by the Governor of Milan seized the strategic corridor and defeated a Swiss Protestant army sent to reclaim the territory. Since Venice relied heavily on this valley for the easy passage of the German mercenaries it employed, the event triggered an international crisis,

[116] *Gazette de France*, 49 (9 Mar. 1636).   [117] BNM, Ms 2367, 32–6.
[118] Gualdo Priorato, *Historia delle guerre*, xi. 305.
[119] Pierre Deyon and Solange Deyon, *Henri de Rohan, huguenot de plume et d'épée, 1579–1638* (Paris, 2000), 175.

where France aligned itself with Venice. The Republic tried unsuccessfully to eject the Habsburg forces in the brief war of 1625–6.[120] Papal troops eventually served as a neutral peacekeeping force, but these allowed Spanish and Imperial troops to pass unobstructed in both directions for over a decade. It was by this route that Spanish troops bound for the Low Countries in 1633 and 1634 joined the Imperials and swung the fortunes of war in Germany back in the direction of the Catholics. Rohan occupied the valley in April 1635 with a Franco-Swiss army numbering at most 8,000 men (for no more could be fed) and in brilliant campaigns for the textbooks defeated Spanish and Imperial contingents in turn. Louis XIII and Richelieu gave Rohan strict orders however not to allow the German-speaking Grisons to re-establish Protestantism in the territory, for it would only alienate the population. The Swiss resented this aspect to Rohan's instructions, which placed the French Calvinist commander in a difficult position with his allies.[121] The Swiss also expected French money that was not forthcoming, since Richelieu's great mobilization against Spain and Austria dried up all the cash reserves.

The coalition commanders devised a strategic plan for the 1636 campaign to resolve these different problems. Rohan would strike out of his mountain valley and bypass the powerful Fort Fuentes blocking its mouth at Lake Como. Somehow he would penetrate the lush Italian plain south-west of Lecco and join the main Franco-Savoyard army marching east past Novara. Their rendezvous near Milan would spark the long-awaited uprising of the oppressed Lombards against the king of Spain. Surely, they thought, the cities would throw open the gates to their liberators. Meanwhile, Duke Odoardo of Parma, with a French army of his own, would march presumably unopposed south of the Po to return to his duchy. Casale Monferrato served as the central, almost impregnable pivot of the coalition army, with the new fortress of Breme fifteen kilometres downstream to protect it. A floating bridge across the Po there enabled easy passage of troops in either direction, for the river was otherwise a serious obstacle. Victor-Amadeus, when not in Turin with his cherished royal duchess, preferred to reside in the strong border fortress of Vercelli twenty-five kilometres north of Casale, out of Créquy's shadow but not far away. The fortress city of Asti, situated forty kilometres south-west of Casale, strongly garrisoned with Savoyards, blocked the other avenue of invasion of Piedmont along the Tanaro river valley. All four fortresses constituted powerful advance magazines, which could provide food and munitions to an advancing army.

Winter quarters did little to heal the rift between the French and the Savoyard high commands. Christine of France warned her husband in the aftermath of the siege of Valenza, 'Le maréchal de Créquy n'est pas votre ami, il a tenu ici des dis-

---

[120] Stefano Andretta, *La Repubblica inquieta: Venezia nel Seicento tra Italia e Europa* (Rome, 2000), 45–61.

[121] Yves-Marie Bercé, 'Rohan et la Valtelline', in Bély (ed.), *L'Europe des traités de Westphalie*, 321–35; Rohan was something of a cultural Catholic and an unabashed Italophile, which would have irked his German Swiss backers. See Jonathan Dewald, 'Rohan's World: A Political Culture in Seventeenth-Century France', accessible from the author's page on <www.Academia.edu>.

cours à des dames fort malicieux ... il a envie de vous perdre.' The ducal couple did not trust the French ambassador Hémery either, rightly seeing him as a tool of Cardinal Richelieu.[122] The Duke of Savoy's principal ally in Paris was the papal nuncio Giulio Mazzarini, who sought to assuage the mutual and well-founded mistrust between Paris and Turin.[123] Victor-Amadeus did his utmost to eject Créquy from his command and to substitute him with Toiras, a Frenchman he trusted, but Richelieu would not relent. Notwithstanding the mutual distrust, the coalition partners patiently gathered men for the upcoming campaign.

[122] Claretta, *Storia della Reggenza*, i. 148–50.
[123] Guido Quazza, 'Giulio Mazzarini mediatore fra Vittorio Amedeo I e il Richelieu (1635–1636)', *Bollettino Storico-Bibliografico Subalpino*, 48 (1950), 53–84.

2

Onward to Milan

THE OPPOSING ARMIES

By the middle of May the Franco-Savoyard field forces consisted of 16,000 French and 6,000 Piedmontese infantry and about 4,000 cavalry, two-thirds of these last on the Savoyard payroll. Victor-Amadeus distributed at least 4,000 other Piedmontese foot to his principal fortresses of Vercelli and Asti, and several smaller contingents screened his southern border in the Langhe hills. He was not about to allow French troops under Cardinal Richelieu's orders help him garrison his own towns.[1] Surprisingly, however, a large portion of the duke's officers and men—perhaps the majority of the field army—were French subjects. The correspondence between the duke and his brother Felice, Governor of Savoy, mentions eight regiments by name over the course of 1635. Three appear to be Savoyard (Monthoux, Sacconey, and Val d'Isère), while two others belonged to French Huguenot colonels (Boisdavid and d'Allot). The largest regiment, Senantes, belonged to a French opponent of Richelieu, while I could not find anything on the remaining two, that of Monsieur de la Tour, and La Ferté.[2] Several of these regiments passed into French pay the following year. Nicola Brancaccio, who has studied Savoyard regiments closely, identifies several Italian infantry regiments in the order of battle as well (Catalano Alfieri, Brunacci, Ressano, Mazzetto, Prince Carlo Emanuele, and the Serenissimo Principe), and a small Swiss German regiment too (Amryn), but none of these marched with the field army.[3] Apart from Augusto Manfredo Scaglia, Count of Verrua, a Piedmontese courtier-soldier, French officers dominated Victor-Amadeus's

[1] Archivio di Stato Torino, Materie militari, 1, no. 30; Memoria in forma d'Istruzione al Marchese de S. Morizio, ambassador to France, 1636 (n.d.); we have no evidence as to the ethnic makeup of his troops, unfortunately.

[2] Archivio di Stato Torino, Materie politiche interne; lettere del duca Vittorio Amedeo, vols. 55 and 56, 1635–6; the list of regiments in French service compiled by Louis Susane notes that the regiments of Boisdavid, Peyregourde, Senantes, and La Ferté had recently been raised in the winter of 1636. This is inexact; they were already in existence on the Savoyard roster, and simply passed into French pay from that date. See Louis Susane, *Histoire de l'Ancienne infanterie française*, iv (Paris, 1852), 138–42; Savoy's peacetime army in 1632, some eighteen infantry regiments, was largely composed of French soldiers. Claudio De Consoli, *Al soldo del duca: L'amministrazione delle armate sabaude (1560–1630)* (Turin, 1999), 196.

[3] Nicola Brancaccio, *L'Esercito del vecchio Piemonte: Gli ordinamenti, parte 1: Dal 1560 al 1814* (Rome, 1923), 130–4; Paola Bianchi, in her recent book on the use of foreign contingents in the Savoyard service, deplores the lack of good sources by which to pinpoint the precise origin of the rank and file. See *Sotto diverse bandiere: L'internazionale militare nello Stato sabaudo d'antico regime* (Milan, 2012), 124.

senior staff, made up of aides-de-camp of diverse status without fixed attributes or a clear hierarchy.[4] In Turin, Field Marshal Toiras, the duke's most trusted adviser, was safe from persecution by Cardinal Richelieu. Two others figure repeatedly in dispatches. Jacques de Borelli de Roqueservières, hailing like Toiras from lower Languedoc, and qualified as a simple captain in the Roure regiment in 1635, would later rise to colonel in the French army. Olivier de Castelan, from Airagues near Arles was simple 'sergent de bataille', promoted colonel in October 1636, and killed in action at Tarragona in Catalonia in 1644. The memorialist Count Souvigny also served the Marshal Toiras in the capacity of aide-de-camp, hoping it would give him access to the French court later.[5]

Victor-Amadeus rebuked his brother-in-law the king of France for not meeting his commitments to provide 20,000 foot and 2,000 horse, but this was not for want of trying: reinforcements intended to swell the French army just replaced the deserters. John Lynn claims that, if the paper strength of the French army in 1636 was an unprecedented 200,000 men, the true number might have been only about half of that figure.[6] This force was much more homogeneous than that of the Catholic King; Lynn calls it a 'state commission army' wherein all the officers owed their position to the king and the Cardinal Minister. France employed no foreign regiments in Italy purchased off the shelf similar to Leganés's German auxiliaries, or feudal militia levies, something the same author calls an 'aggregate contract army' typical of the medieval era.[7] The cardinal and the king kept royal regiments under close watch through the army intendants, who managed accounts and discipline. They would not concede wide autonomy to colonels and generals such as existed in Imperial Germany, even if inadequate pay and supervision from the centre entailed losses of efficiency. While all the armies and navies of the period required the profit-seeking investment of private finance, the French army adhered closest to state control.[8] David Parrott claims that private contractors providing mercenaries were better adapted to the circumstances of the period, since officers who held a financial stake in their command had more incentive to be diligent in matters of supply. Instead, the Cardinal Minister in Paris encouraged officers at all levels to make up for the shortage of government funds out of their own pockets. The unintended consequence of this policy was a revolving door of colonels and captains who could not afford to serve for many years, and who did not identify overmuch with the men under their command.[9]

[4] Brancaccio, *L'Esercito del vecchio Piemonte, parte 1*, 73; princes were often reluctant to clarify the chain of command, preferring that way to distribute honour more widely; see Hervé Drévillon, *L'Impôt du sang: Le métier des armes sous Louis XIV* (Paris, 2005), 23.

[5] *Memoires du Comte de Souvigny, lieutenant-générale des armées du roi*, ed. Ludovic de Contenson (Paris, 1906), i. 308; for Roqueservières, M. Pinard, *Chronologie Historique-Militaire*, vi (Paris, 1763), 317; for Castelan, Dominique Robert de Briançon, *L'Etat de la Provence* (Paris, 1693), i. 480.

[6] John A. Lynn, *Giant of the 'Grand Siècle': The French Army, 1610–1715* (Cambridge and New York, 1997), 33–50.

[7] Ibid. 6; France did employ a German mercenary army under Bernhard of Saxe-Weimar in the Rhineland.

[8] David Parrott, *The Business of War: Military Enterprise and Military Revolution in Early Modern Europe* (Cambridge and New York, 2012), 265–75.

[9] David Parrott, 'France's Wars Against the Habsburgs 1624–1659: The Politics of Military Failure', in Enrique Garcìa Hernan and Davide Maffi (eds), *Guerra y sociedad en la Monarquìa*

Judging from the French companies serving in Parma and Piacenza, most of Créquy's soldiers, like their officers, were Dauphinois, Lyonnais, or Burgundians, hailing in large part from the cities and small towns of eastern and southern France. Significant additional numbers came from Languedoc, Aquitaine, and Poitou, a continuous area known as the Huguenot Crescent. Gascon gentlemen, both nobles and commoners, so numerous on both sides during the Wars of Religion, figured prominently in this army too.[10] Few companies drew very heavily from a single region, however. Army recruiters set up a table in the market squares of towns and beat the drum to draw the attention of onlookers to the attractive signing bonus. In smaller locales the captain visited the houses of likely prospects and used his local influence to entice lads to follow him on campaign. This is why Victor-Amadeus enjoined his colonels to select their captains carefully.[11] One of the rare studies of the social origins of French soldiers has noted that they were dispropor-tionately urban. The data for Parma reflect that finding but we must remember that seventeenth-century cities did not teem with masses of marginal young men. A third of them claimed to come from cities of more than 10,000 people, and half that proportion again hailed from the dense network of smaller cities and towns where one could live with decorum.[12] If one had to confer on them an equivalent social ranking to civilians, the class of artisans first comes to mind. There is a myth that soldiering was a trade for ne'er-do-wells caught in a spiral of misery and looking forward to a lottery windfall on campaign. John Keegan laments that aca-demics often dismiss the hold that war exerts over the male imagination. Army life was rich in symbolic rewards and offered a sense of close companionship and escape from dreary routine.[13] These were armies formed of *volunteers*, and it was easy enough for them to desert when the life grated on them. Many deserters simply changed units or found more attractive army service elsewhere. At the outset, the new recruits might find the soldier's life appealing: 'food and profit; there was also adventure, travel, friendship, local loyalty and enthusiasm for the cause... There were tourist pleasures derived from seeing new sights and places. There was also the release from civilian prohibitions against destruction, violence and predation.'[14] Very few were beardless youths. The mean age of Frenchmen in Parman service tended towards 27, identical to the Parman and even Neapolitan infantry recruits.[15]

Hispanica: Politica, estrategia y cultura en la Europa Moderna (1500–1700) (Madrid, 2006), 31–48; also 'Cultures of Combat in the Ancien Régime: Linear Warfare, Noble Values and Entrepreneurship', *International History Review*, 27 (2005), 518–33.

[10] Véronique Larcade, *Orphelins d'une Amerique: Les capitaines gascons à l'époque des guerres de reli-gion* (Paris, 1999), 85–111.

[11] ASTo Materie politiche interne: lettere del duca Vittorio Amedeo, vol. 56. Letter of 20 July 1636, 'Ci vuol dare 4,000 ducatoni a dieci capitani per fare la levata, e conviene sapere chi sono questi dieci capitani, che siano persone a dare soddisfazione.' See also Keith Roberts, *Matchlock Musketeer 1588–1688* (Oxford and New York, 2002), 11–12.

[12] Robert Chaboche, 'Les soldats français de la Guerre de Trente Ans: Une tentative d'approche', *Revue d'Histoire Moderne et Contemporaine*, 20 (1973), 10–24; Lynn, *Giant*, 323–35.

[13] John Keegan, *A History of Warfare* (New York, 1993), 226.

[14] Barbara Donagan, *War in England, 1642–1649* (Oxford and New York, 2008), 220.

[15] Gregory Hanlon, *The Hero of Italy* (Oxford and New York, 2014), 58–68; Chaboche calculates an average age of recruits later admitted to the Invalides at 24. These men may have been keen to fight, for they had exceptionally long careers; Chaboche, 'Les soldats français'.

The soldiers' first training taught them to recognize the dozen different drumbeats, which served to reinforce orders in camp, on the march, and eventually, in battle.[16] Bonding in these French companies seems to have been enhanced by the general attribution of a nickname, rarely corresponding to their patronym, and referring only occasionally to their region of origin, *La Touraine, Champagne.* This *nom de guerre* might reflect a special skill or the trade they practised in civilian life, *Patissier, Milledroghe, La Boutonnière.* Often it reflected an individual penchant that set them apart from their comrades, *La Vedette, La Patience, La Folie, Gazette, La Culture, L'Honnetété, L'Espérance, La Brave, La Bonté, La Jeunesse* (for one 18-year-old), *Le Vieux* (aged 25), *La Croix,* and the distinctly unbellicose *Chaton* (kitten). Recruits might have showed a special fondness for food and drink, like *Ripailles* and *Salade.* But most army nicknames did not reveal much imagination or individuality. Single companies could contain more than one *La Croix, La Roche, La Grange, La Fontaine, La Vallée, La Forest, La Montagne, La Fleur, La Violette, La Vigne, La Verdure,* and so on.[17]

As these recruits crowded the billets and swelled the bivouacs, the coalition commanders deployed them into several large corps and returned to their plans for the upcoming campaign. The deep divisions among confederate commanders were partly the result of divergent political aims, and partly personal rivalries for influence. Duke Odoardo of Parma returned to Casale Monferrato in April triumphantly waving a letter from Louis XIII instructing Victor-Amadeus and Créquy to detach a strong contingent from their forces, 8,000 or 9,000 men, for his personal command. Apart from the disappointing siege of Valenza the previous year, Odoardo had no military experience to speak of, yet in his own mind he was a budding Gustavus Adolphus. The commanders in Italy feared that he would use this army as an instrument of vendetta against his brother-in-law Francesco d'Este, Duke of Modena, out of touch with his coalition allies and completely out of control.[18] It was important to mollify him, however, for Parma's location forced Leganés to draw troops away from the Piedmontese border. Victor-Amadeus and Créquy eventually consented to give Odoardo a force of about 4,000 foot and 500 cavalry, almost all French, assisted by a junior commander, the sieur Dauriac to serve as liaison officer, for French troops were reluctant to follow other officers than their own. This contingent would wait at Nizza Monferrato for a signal to move towards Piacenza. A great French fleet assembled in Toulon would bring Odoardo an equal number of reinforcements by sea, who would disembark and march over the Apennines. The French navy was a recent creation of Cardinal Richelieu, who as its 'grand maître' held a near monopoly on officers' commissions. By 1636 no fewer than thirty-eight warships owned by the crown assembled in Provence in

---

[16] Roberts, *Matchlock Musketeer,* 21; also Galeazzo Gualdo Priorato, *Il Maneggio dell'armi moderno* (Vicenza, 1642), 14–39.

[17] ASPr Collatereria Generale 362 and 363, companies of Baron Faino and Jean de la Haie, selected at random among many others. Army scribes recorded nicknames for the soldiers and employed them above all others. Italian soldiers in the same army almost never owned one, on the other hand.

[18] Gabriel de Mun, *Richelieu et la maison de Savoie* (Paris, 1907), 124–7.

order to join the galley flotilla and to collect troops on transports.[19] Infighting among the officers leading that expedition delayed their departure, however, and the amphibious forces of the Marquès de Santa Cruz encrusted like a barnacle along the Ligurian Riviera would have to be dislodged before the seaborne route would be secure.[20]

Duke Charles of Mantua remained a coalition partner, but ever since the epic siege and sack of 1630 his fortress capital was only a shadow of its former self. The Duchess Margherita of Mantua, sister of Victor-Amadeus and grand-daughter of King Philip II of Spain married Duke Francesco IV shortly before his death in 1612 but this dowager duchess spent much of her time in Turin. She returned to Mantua in 1631 expressly to create a pro-Spanish faction at court, but after she refused to take a pension from Cardinal Richelieu in 1633, French pressure forced her out. She became viceroy of Portugal for the Spanish crown in 1635. Her daughter Maria Gonzaga, married the Duc de Rethel, son and heir of Duke Charles who died in 1631 and she was mother to the future heir, Prince Charles. She also actively fed intelligence to the Governor of Milan and the Spanish ambassador in Venice.[21] Duke Charles and Leganés both considered it best to treat the duchy of Mantua proper as neutral territory, guaranteed against a hostile takeover by a garrison financed by the Venetian Republic.[22] Leganés feared that the duke might attack from the east as the French begged him to do, but the Spanish commander and the Gonzaga prince kept open discreet channels of communication ensuring the status quo.[23] Mantua maintained a resident in Milan during the war, which facilitated the courteous exchange of correspondence on a variety of subjects between the enemy governments.[24] Duke Charles limited Mantuan military participation to the Monferrato district, and contributed little to the coalition apart from providing fodder to the French and guarding his villages with militia.

While the confederate commanders made their plans, Leganés built up his forces to prevent their success. The Spanish army in 1636 opposite Créquy was the oldest large standing force in Western Europe and the proud heir of more than a century of victories against many adversaries. The term 'Spanish' army disguises the multi-ethnic reality that persisted for centuries. Alongside the ethnic Castilians marched tercios of Neapolitans, Lombards, and what we would today call Belgians (these last rare in Italy), all subjects of the Catholic King, as well as German mercenaries. Burgundian, Sicilian, Sardinian, Catalan, and Portuguese tercios served

---

[19] Alan James, *The Navy and Government in Early Modern France* (Woodbridge and Rochester, NY, 2004), 77–89.

[20] R. C. Anderson, 'The Thirty Years War in the Mediterranean', *Mariner's Mirror*, 15 (1969), 435–51, and 16 (1970), 41–57; E. Delahaye, 'Une campagne de l'armee navale sous Louis XIII: La reprise des îles de Lérins et le secours de Parme (1636–1637)', *Revue Maritime* (1929), 13–37; J. A. Durbec, 'Un episode de la Guerre de Trente Ans: L'occupation des Iles de Lérins par les Espagnols de 1635–1637', *Bulletin de la Commission Royale d'Histoire* (1951–2), 41–74.

[21] AGS, Estado 3338, Consulta of 25 June 1636, discussing a dispatch from the Count of Monterrey in Venice, dated 17 May 1636.

[22] Giancarlo Malacarne, *I Gonzaga di Mantova, una stirpe per una capitale europea*, iv. *Morte di una dinastia, 1628–1708* (Modena, 2008), 107–23.

[23] AGS, Estado 3344, no. 45, dispatch from Leganés, 26 May 1636.

[24] Archivio di Stato di Mantova, Archivio Gonzaga 1761, corrispondenza Milano 1636.

in other theatres. The primitive bonding criteria like blood and language greatly outweighed the ideological alignment of men fighting for king and religion.[25] Commanders considered these ethnically homogeneous infantry tercios and cavalry companies (for no larger formation yet existed in Spanish usage) to be more cohesive organizations than blended bodies of men drawn from far and wide.[26] Ethnic friction among these nationalities has not emerged from our sources, unlike in the Low Countries, where it festered for decades. The commanders themselves recognized a hierarchy of national military abilities, ranking the Spaniards at the top, the Germans and Lombards next, and the Neapolitans lower still. All of them derided the lack of combative spirit in the Tuscans and Modenese.[27]

This principle of emulation fit the dynastic traditions of noble houses too, where each succeeding generation sought to match the standards of its predecessors. Noblemen comprised the overwhelming majority of the officers in all the contingents. Conventional wisdom held that noble status constituted in itself a good criterion for military appointment and a prerequisite for high command.[28] Olivares sought to groom a new generation of Iberian commanders by attaching likely candidates to the various field armies. He identified Francisco de Melo, the Portuguese career diplomat, as someone with command potential, and appointed him to serve as an understudy to Leganés. He would be responsible for the great defeat at Rocroi in 1643.[29] In the winter of 1635–6, de Melo occupied himself primarily with non-military functions such as purchasing grain for Milan. He also planned with Prince Gian Andrea Doria the diversionary invasion of the duchy of Parma over the Apennines.[30] Olivares intended to keep a tight control over officer promotion, but Leganés confiscated this authority as much as he could, for the Governor of Milan was keen on rewarding faithful Lombard subjects, who might become French sympathizers if he left them in obscurity.[31] It is not easy to discern how talented various individual tercio commanders were, but they possessed undoubted experience, and Leganés periodically entrusted each of them with autonomous larger detachments to effect some specific purpose. Don Martin d'Aragon, who displayed much initiative, commanded the Spanish tercio of Lombardy after 1630. He enjoyed a mostly successful career, until he was killed repulsing a French attack in Piedmont in 1639. Don Antonio Arias Sotelo, whose particular specialty was artillery and fortification, was sergeant-major of the tercio of Savoy until the commanding officer Azevedo was killed in a fight against the Parmans in 1635. Thereafter he held unofficial command over the same unit. Francisco de Orozco, Marqués de Olias y de Mortara, served adequately in Lombardy, before passing to Catalonia with his own command in the early 1640s: there he defeated the French on two occasions. He rose to become viceroy of Catalonia in the late 1650s and

---

[25] Lionel Tiger, *Men in Groups* (New York, 1969), 180.

[26] Angelantonio Spagnoletti, 'Onore e spirito nazionale nei soldati italiani al servizio della monarchia spagnola', in C. Donati and B. Kroener (eds), *Militari e società civile nell'Europa dell'età moderna* (Bologna, 2007), 211–53.

[27] Davide Maffi, *Il baluardo della corona* (Florence, 2007), 117.

[28] Fernando Gonzalez de Leon, *The Road to Rocroi* (Boston and Leiden, 2009), 160–7.

[29] Laurent Henninger, *Rocroi, 1643* (Paris, 1993), 26.

[30] *Gazette de France*, 3 (1636).   [31] Maffi, *Il baluardo della corona*, 156 and 195.

Governor of Milan just before his death in 1668. Another future Governor of Milan, only 28 years old in 1636, was Luis de Benavides Carillo, Marqués de Caracena, a high-born Valencian whose crowning achievement would be the capture of Casale Monferrato in 1652. A cavalry officer when he was wounded in a fight against the Parmans early in 1636, he was designated an infantry colonel when he recovered, despite having no experience in that arm.[32] His career ended in disgrace decades later after an ill-fated campaign against Portugal in 1665. Don Filippo Spìnola, son of the great Genoese soldier-financier-statesman Ambrogio, was already Grandee of Spain and a Knight of the Golden Fleece since 1631. While not blessed with his father's gifts, he served as a general in Catalonia in 1640, and one of his sons, born in Milan in 1628, would be Spanish governor there in later years. Among the Neapolitans, Carlo della Gatta, the son of a colonel serving in Flanders under the great Duke Alessandro of Parma, served in Italy and Flanders as a captain and returned to duty in 1634 to command his own tercio. He managed the Parman sector largely on his own initiative in June 1636. Lucio Boccapianola, marchese of Brindisi, enlisted as a simple soldier to serve in Flanders early in the century. He held the rank of captain of Neapolitan infantry at the battle of White Mountain in 1620, was colonel at the siege of Verrua (1625) and Casale Monferrato (1630), before distinguishing himself again at Nördlingen. He would later die in a skirmish with the French near Breme in 1637. The parents of Gherardo Gambacorta initially destined their son for the priesthood but he followed his own inclinations to fight against Savoy in 1617. In the late 1620s he was commissary-general of cavalry in Lombardy, and after his critical role against the Protestants at Nördlingen, Olivares appointed him general of cavalry in Northern Italy and Knight of the Order of Santiago.[33] Aged 50 in 1636, Gambacorta enjoyed a reputation as one of the leading duellists of the army. Some officers at lower ranks were also considered rising stars. Gioan Tomaso Blanch, Marchese dell'Oliveto, who distinguished himself at Nördlingen, served as Gambacorta's understudy at the battle of Tornavento, where he was grievously wounded. The following year Olivares sent him to clear French invaders from Sardinia. Another famous duellist, the Baron Batteville from Franche-Comté, commanded a cavalry squadron. He would eventually rise to the dignity of Spanish ambassador to Great Britain in 1660. Talented commoners existed among the officers too. Francesco Picinino from Novara, after being declared an outlaw in Milan, served in the French army as a sergeant. He earned his pardon in 1629 by delivering a gate of Casale Monferrato to Spanish troops. In 1636, he published a book of tactics, *Il modo di formare squadroni*, and went by the moniker Capitano Spadino.[34] This talented commoner served at Valenza the year before, as an inspector of fortification and as captain of spirited skirmishers. He led the final infantry assault on the French fort

---

[32] Ibid. 213.

[33] Giuseppe Carignani, *Le Truppe napoletane durante la guerra de' Trent'Anni* (Florence, 1888), 11.

[34] Much of this information is available online under the name of each officer. Biographical material on the Neapolitans is contained in the work of P. Fra Raffaele Maria Filamondo, *Il Genio bellicoso di Napoli: Memorie istoriche d'alcuni capitani celebri Napolitani c'han militato per la fede, per lo re, per la patria nel secolo corrente* (Naples, 1694).

whose fall liberated the city. By early 1636, Picinino had risen socially to captain of horse, posted to Novara. A celebrity whose destiny attracted notice in both camps, as a commoner without wealth he was thereafter probably unpromotable in the Spanish system.[35] Another exceptional commoner was Flemish-born baker's assistant Colonel Gil de Haes who enjoyed an exceptional career born of luck. Leaving Ghent with the Spanish army at age 27 after being spurned by a maiden, he rose to the rank of lieutenant in five short years, in itself unremarkable. Under Marshal Aldringen, a Luxemburger in Imperial service in Italy, he advanced to lieutenant-colonel, and then reaped a colossal windfall in the 1630 sack of Mantua. This gave him the means to purchase his own regiment, with which he plundered Saxony in 1632. Accused by Wallenstein of lukewarm participation in the battle of Lützen, he showed his mettle at the siege of Ingoldstadt and the battle of Nördlingen. He raised new men for Spain in Tirol during the spring of 1635, and helped contain Rohan in the Valtellina.[36] He would serve both in Italy and Germany, before rising to the rank of general for the Venetian Republic fighting the Turks, with the title of *Eccellenza*.

We possess two company-level tallies of the Spanish army, both garrison troops and field forces, from before and after the battle of Tornavento. It does not include the troops of Cardinal Trivulzio facing Parma along the Po, the contingent under Prince Doria in the Apennines, or the amphibious force under the Marqués de Santa Cruz operating along the Ligurian Riviera, which totalled at least 3,000 or 4,000 additional soldiers. Included in the tally but not directly under Leganés's supervision was Giovanni Serbelloni's force blocking the duc de Rohan in the Valtellina. In May these were Spanish tercios under Juan de Garay, Juan Vasquez Coronado, and a Lombard one under Ludovico Guasco, totalling almost 3,500 professional infantry. The field army under Leganés's direct purview consisted of eleven tercios and regiments, six of which were comprised of ethnic Spaniards (Aragon, Sotelo, Mortara, and parts of Caracena, Garay, and Vasquez Coronado), three Neapolitan (Della Gatta, Boccapianola, and Spìnola), and two German (de Haes and Lener), all totalling 7,733 officers and foot. It would be too hasty to determine the number of soldiers per tercio by making a mean, for garrison troops were drawn from the same units. In theory, infantry tercios numbered 3,000 men, but such large bodies never existed.[37] The tercios and regiments in Lombardy were not uniform in size; six of them contained between fifteen and nineteen companies, and some others ten and fewer. The Spanish tercios contained the most companies, and the Germans the fewest. The mean strength of a company hovered around 109 men, but varied from 134 for German formations, to 105 for the Spaniards, 93 for the Lombards and only 89 for the Neapolitans. Within each

[35] Francesco Gasparolo (ed.), 'Narrazione dell'assedio di Valenza nel 1635, fatta da Bernardino Stanchi, sotto nome di Randiberno Caston', *Memorie Storiche Valenzane* (Casale, 1923; re-ed. Bologna, 1986), iii. 258–96. On Captain Spadino, 278 and 291; see also Archivio di Stato Novara, Comune Novara 1875, letter 19 Jan. 1636.

[36] Charles Rahlenbeck, *Gilles de Haes* (Ghent, 1854).

[37] Julio Albi de la Cuesta, *De Pavìa a Rocroi: Los tercios de infantería española en los siglos XVI y XVII* (Madrid, 1999), 46.

company, the men sorted themselves into little groups of about ten men who messed together and who integrated newcomers by teaching them the ropes.[38] Two-thirds of the foot carried muskets and the remainder held pikes, which was the standard proportion in European armies in 1636.[39]

The horse belonged to two separate organizations, with two different pay-masters; the cavalry of the State of Milan, and a smaller group of Neapolitan companies.[40] In 1638, Lombards comprised about half the cavalry in the army, as opposed to only 16 per cent of the infantry.[41] Cavalry companies were much smaller than the foot; forty-three Spanish and Italian companies averaged sixty troopers and officers each. Imperial armies combined companies into regiments of six to eight hundred men early in the seventeenth century.[42] The ten companies of Schlick's German regiment averaged ninety troopers each, and the German dragoons under Lopez Giron numbered on average eighty-two. The effectives of horse, without the dragoons, totalled 391 officers and 3,884 troopers, considerably more than those of Créquy and Victor-Amadeus combined. Coloma and Leganés candidly admitted that the Spanish and Italian cavalry was not very good and was certainly inferior to the French. This did not reflect backwards tactics (there was a single company of lancers among them), as much as the fact that the French cavalry rode larger horses and recruited the most bellicose subjects who prided themselves on their daring.[43]

It was not the practice in Lombardy to alternate whole tercios between field service and garrison duty.[44] Leganés assigned the weakest units entirely to fortresses, like the small tercios of Crivelli and Corata (both Lombards) and the Modenese allies, who consisted of a paltry 250 men in five companies.[45] In the summer of 1635, combat, sickness, and desertion reduced the Neapolitan tercio of Carlo Caracciolo (withdrawn from the fighting at Valenza) to fewer than 500 soldiers, so Coloma consigned it to serve in Pavìa before he disbanded it and reassigned the survivors elsewhere.[46] The garrisons included in the May tally were only those in strongholds considered threatened. Alessandria (with over 2,000 officers and soldiers) and Valenza (with almost 5,000, including some militia contingents) were almost impregnable. North of the Po, militia constituted almost half of the 1,500 officers and men in Novara's garrison. Likewise Mortara, where 600 of the 1,400

---

[38] Ibid. 69.

[39] Ibid. 228. This was made official in a directive published by the Cardinal-Infante on 20 Mar. 1636.

[40] Maffi, *Il baluardo della corona*, 89.   [41] Ibid. 118.

[42] Vladimir Brnardic, *Imperial Armies of the Thirty Years' War: Cavalry* (Oxford, 2010), 3.

[43] Albi de la Cuesta, *De Pavìa a Rocroi*, 117; on French cavalry panache, see Hervé Drévillon, *L'Impôt du sang* (Paris, 2005), 356–64; indispensable, the new book by Fréderic Chauviré, *Histoire de la Cavalerie* (Paris, 2013), 278–83.

[44] Gonzalez de Leon speaks of such a practice in Flanders, *Road to Rocroi*, 57.

[45] *Gazette de France*, 69 (1636). In April, his duchy free of the Parman threat, Duke Francesco d'Este withdrew from active hostilities, but the troops he sent to aid Leganés remained under Spanish direction and pay. The duke continued to subsidize them, and authorized Spain to recruit men in Modenese territory.

[46] AGS Estado 3337, Consulta of 10 Sept. 1635. Coloma also complained of the excessive number of Neapolitan officers not holding specific commissions, whose stipends overburdened his finances.

men garrison were armed peasants. The other forts, Sandoval (across the Sesia river from Piedmontese Vercelli) and Fontaneto, each contained only a few hundred men, in the latter case militiamen exclusively. Rottofreno's garrison in Parman territory numbered about 700 men, almost all German professionals.[47] Career soldiers no doubt garrisoned forts and cities not considered threatened, such as Pavìa, Cremona, Lodi, Como, and the citadel of Milan, but they do not figure in the document and there is no way to determine their number. In 1647, while the war still raged in Lombardy, the citadel of Milan contained 600 Spanish soldiers, while the port of Finale Liguria numbered only 200. Most of the cities hosted about 100 men, lodged in the citadels.[48]

The high number of officers listed in all the Spanish units is striking: around 12 per cent of the total for the infantry, and 10 per cent for the cavalry, who proved a great financial burden to the Spanish crown.[49] Each tercio contained between six and nine *officiales mayores* above the company level, such as the regimental sergeant-major, the provost entrusted with discipline, the quartermaster, and perhaps some assistants. At the company level the officers are so numerous in the roster that they must have included non-commissioned officers like sergeants and corporals, below the lieutenant and the ensign.[50] In an attempt to entice aristocrats into royal service, who might (like in France) employ their private fortunes to advance the royal cause, Olivares routinely passed over long-serving captains of modest means. Maffi notes that forty-four of the forty-nine Lombard colonels (maestro di campo) serving in the war were titled aristocrats. Of the thirty-four captains of Spanish infantry serving in the field, fully twenty-eight bore the title 'don'. Leganés and his predecessor Carlos Coloma both deplored this aristocratization, and merit might have characterized the officer class in Italy more than in Spain or the Low Countries.[51] Commanders feared that the feudatories who paid dearly to raise their own regiments might not employ capable officers at junior levels, employing relatives or clients instead. Gonzalez de Leon blames this policy for the decline of Spanish cavalry with respect to the French, and the slowness to adopt the most modern tactics. Of the thirty-nine Italian companies on the roster identified by their commanding officer in May 1636, twenty-seven were led by various counts, marquis, and those bearing the title of 'don'; some of those not so identified were authentic aristocrats, like the general himself, Gherardo Gambacorta, Filippo Spìnola, and Francesco Maria Lampugnani. The representatives of Lombard feudatories were numerous among these captains, with the Gonzaga, Beccaria,

---

[47] AGS Estado 3344, no. 117; no date, but it would probably have dated from mid-May 1636, after the reconquest of Castel San Giovanni by the Farnese forces.

[48] Luis Ribot Garcia, 'Milano, piazza d'armi della monarchia spagnola', in F. Motta (ed.), *'Millain the Great': Milano nelle brume del Seicento* (Milan, 1989), 349–63; A complete list of fortified places can be found in the article by Sara Pedretti, 'Ai confini occidentali dello Stato di Milano: L'impiego delle milizie rurali nelle guerre del Seicento', in C. Donati (ed.), *Alle frontiere della Lombardia: Politica, guerra e religione nell'età moderna* (Milan, 2006), 177–200; the additional forts were Domodossola and Arona in the Alps north of Milan, Vigevano in the plain, the Forte di Fuentes and Lecco in the upper Adda valley near the Valtellina, Trezzo, Pizzighettone, la Gera to the east, Tortona and Serravalle in the south. Some of these were bereft of modern fortification, however.

[49] Maffi, *Il baluardo della corona*, 228.   [50] Gonzalez de Leon, *Road to Rocroi*, 17–20.

[51] Ibid. 151 and 177; see also Maffi, *Il baluardo della corona*, 167–76.

Montecastelli, Soresina, Landolfi, and Mainardi figuring prominently on the roster. Since each of these men enjoyed connections with the court, and drew recruits from villages, it proved difficult to 'reform' or abolish companies and tercios when the rank and file's numbers withered.[52]

Unfortunately, we lack the individual company rosters for the Habsburg soldiery that we have for the French and Italian troops in the pay of the duke of Parma, which permit one to calculate rates of desertion or sickness. Davide Maffi concludes that tercios lost about a third of their complement every year, due mostly to those two things.[53] It is by no means certain that all the men in the Spanish tercios were effectively Iberians: they too recruited locally to compensate for their depletion. Their desertion was probably inferior to that of the Italians, for Spaniards would remain conspicuous wherever they went.[54] One would be too quick to label the rank and file as mercenary soldiers, especially when they were subjects of the Catholic King: soldiers in national armies today expect to be paid for their services.[55] The Germans, the Florentines, and the Italian soldiers from neutral or enemy territories joining the Lombard tercios resemble contemporary definitions of a mercenary, that is, *foreign* soldiers fighting for pay or plunder. Gualdo Priorato describes them as moths attracted to the glimmer of coin. Hiring mercenaries had the distinct advantage of leaving the peasants and artisans in their homes, where they continued to pay taxes. 'Whoever loses the foreigner, loses only the expenditure; whoever loses the native-born, loses the capital.'[56] The bonds of language and region of origin in the Catholic King's various tercios helped foster their extraordinary *esprit de corps*. The best soldiers maintained close ties to their officers, and might desert if the latter died or retired. Some colonels and captains rewarded deserving soldiers from their own pockets, or gave them symbolic rewards that tightened those personal bonds.[57] Over the course of the war, an astonishing number of men, 100,000 over a quarter-century, joined up in Lombardy, a state of some 800,000 inhabitants. Even if not all of them were subjects of the king of Spain, 4,000 recruits constituted 2 or 3 per cent of the entire male population, maybe one man in forty every year![58]

Spanish ministers, confident enough in the loyalty of the population to reconstitute a large peasant militia in 1635, initially intended it to number 8,000 fit men

[52] *Gazette de France*, 10 (1636). The *Gazette* reports that Neapolitan tercios were disbanded to the benefit of two Lombard units, Trivulzio and Guasco. There is no mention of the Caracciolo tercio in 1636.

[53] Maffi, *Il Baluardo della Corona*, 133–5.

[54] Luis Ribot Garcia, 'Las provincias Italianas y la defensa de la Monarquia', in A. Musi (ed.), *Nel sistema imperiale, l'Italia Spagnola* (Naples, 1994), 67–92.

[55] Parrott, *Business of War*, 6–21.

[56] Galeazzo Gualdo Priorato, *Il guerriero prudente e politico*, ed. A. Tamborra (Naples, 2000; 1st publ. 1640), 35.

[57] Maffi, *Il baluardo della corona*, 228; Spagnoletti, 'Onore e spirito nazionale', 222; Gonzalez de Leon, *Road to Rocroi*, 112.

[58] Mario Rizzo, '"Rivoluzione dei consumi", "State-building" e "Rivoluzione militare": La domanda e l'offerta di servizi strategici nella Lombardia Spagnola, 1535–1659', in I. Lopane and E. Ritrovato (eds), *Tra Vecchi e Nuovi equilibri: Domanda e offerta di servizi in Italia in età moderna e contemporanea* (Bari, 2007), 447–74.

between the ages of 18 and 50, or 1 per cent of the total population, but by 1636 they reportedly levied over twice that.[59] Commanders employed them to guard village castles or supplement fortress garrisons, but thousands of musketeer militiamen tagged along behind each detachment of professional soldiers in the field. Over the winter of 1636, these detachments hauled the crops from vulnerable villages and weak castles into the principal fortresses in order to prevent their seizure by the French in the coming campaign.[60] In the expectation that the coalition army would attempt to march to the relief of Piacenza south of the Po, Leganés conscripted a militia army to dig solid entrenchments for over twenty kilometres along the east bank of the Scrivia river, from Villalvernia south of the fortress of Tortona, to its confluence with the Po.[61] Thousands of peasants dug these works and hauled supplies with their draft animals, without any kind of compensation; small wonder that many inhabitants fled the district into neutral territory. Rich and influential landlords decried the sudden dearth of available labourers at the height of the harvest season.[62]

Both armies had to bide their time even after the return of warm weather in order to harvest the hay and tall grass. Long months of being restricted to dry fodder weakened horses and oxen. During the month of May grooms purged the fragile horses by 'grassing' them on vitamin-rich fresh grass or standing hay in pastures. Cavalrymen provided them with grass or unripe crops collected from further away, in addition to the oats, barley, and pulses they required if they were going to be fit to pull heavy loads.[63] By the end of May even the horses were ready for the campaign.

THE INVASION OF LOMBARDY

Rohan decamped as soon as the snows melted in the first week of April and marched along the top of Lake Como in search of a feasible route into the Po valley. He also needed to seize food stores for his famished soldiers and booty

---

[59] Galeazzo Gualdo Priorato, *Historia delle guerre del Conte Galeazzo Gualdo Priorato* (Venice, 1646), x. 269; see also Sara Pedretti, 'Ai confine occidentali dello Stato di Milano: L'impiego delle milizie rurali nelle guerre del Seicento', in Donati, *Alle frontiere della Lombardia*, 177–200; Davide Maffi, 'Le milizie dello Stato di Milano (1615–1700): Un tentativo di controllo sociale', *Las milicias del Rey de España (siglos XVI y XVII)* (Madrid, 2009), 245–67. My fulsome thanks to the author for allowing me to read work still unpublished.

[60] *Gazette de France*, 3 (1636), Dec. 1635; Giovanni Battista Lupi, 'Storia della peste avvenuta nel borgo di Busto Arsizio, 1630 (1629–1642)', in F. Bertolli and U. Colombo (eds), *La peste del 1630 a Busto Arsizio*, (Busto Arsizio, 1990), 203.

[61] Archivo General Simancas, Estado, Legajo 3344, dispatch by Leganes from Tortona, 26 May 1636.

[62] Archivio Storico Civico di Milano; Archivio Sola Busca: Serbelloni 53; 25 Sept. 1636, Memoriale of the Nuns of Sant'Eufemia of Tortona, claiming it was impossible to find labourers to work their fields, given that so many had fled the district or else were simply not available.

[63] G. Perjés, 'Army Provisioning, Logistics and Strategy in the Second Half of the Seventeenth Century', *Acta Historica Academiae Scientiarum Hungaricae*, 16 (1970), 1–51; see also Peter Edwards, 'Les chevaux et les guerres civiles anglaises au milieu du XVIIe siècle', in Daniel Roche and Daniel Reytier (eds), *Le cheval et la guerre du XVe au XXe siècle* (Paris, 2002), 243–9.

enough to compensate them for lack of pay.[64] His troops sacked and put to the torch all the lakeside villages they entered. This advance immediately drew off Habsburg forces harassing the duchy of Parma, which moved northwards to block him. Serbelloni outfitted a flotilla of galleys that gave him an amphibious interdiction capacity against Rohan's supply lines, if the Protestant warlord followed the narrow road along the lake shore, overlooked by high cliffs. On 29 May Rohan's army of 4,000 foot and 500 horse struck southwards, through a circuitous alpine route avoiding the lakeshore. Brushing aside Spanish soldiers and militia strung out in small posts, Rohan halted for two days to destroy the weapons workshops in the Valsassina valley. Resuming his march, he finally stopped just outside the town of Lecco on the Adda river near the Venetian frontier on 3 June.[65] A Milanese chronicler echoed the reports that his troops had plundered a convent and desecrated the Holy Sacrament on the altar, and shamed the nuns themselves. The term is cryptic: it may have designated rape, or (I believe) merely exposing the nuns to public view in violation of their vows. Rohan's men reportedly seized 6,000 head of livestock, from sheep and goats to oxen and mules, whose frightened owners fled the district. The invaders trampled crops and cut down fruit trees and vines for several days in early June. To prevent their progress, thousands of Lombard militiamen from the Como district converged on the heights across the Adda river, and dug themselves in alongside Serbelloni's tercios.[66] Rohan's men stood only fifty-five kilometres from the walls of Milan, without a single fortress in their way. Here, with both his French and his Swiss regiments on the verge of mutiny for the lack of pay and basic necessities, Rohan vainly waited a week for news of the Franco-Savoyard army's advance in his direction.

Leganés could not predict with certainty the direction of the coalition advance from the west, so he dispersed his field force across a hundred kilometres in several scattered contingents, from south of Tortona to north of Novara. These detachments without heavy artillery or long baggage trains, called flying columns, he placed under the command of the most experienced senior officers. They concentrated their forces at strategic crossroads, or dispersed them into multiple strongpoints as the situation evolved, in order to delay the enemy advance while reinforcements arrived. These mobile detachments would not be able to stop a full-scale invasion in their sector, but they could provide a powerful reinforcement to a nearby fortress. Alessandria, Valenza, Novara, and Pavìa were all substantial strongholds that could not be taken by storm. Gherardo Gambacorta manned the Scrivia river entrenchments south of the Po with a mixed force of cavalry and infantry. A detached force along the Bormida river guarded the access to the vital port of Finale Liguria. At Valenza the Spaniards stretched chains across the Po in order to impede the passage of boats travelling downriver with the intention of reaching Piacenza. Across

[64] Sandro Massera, 'La spedizione del Duca Henri de Rohan in Valtellina (1635–1637)', in Sandro Masseri (ed.), *La Spedizione del Duca di Rohan in Valtellina: Storia e memorie nell'età della Guerra dei Trent'Anni* (Milan, 1999), 73.

[65] Ibid. 74–5.

[66] Alessandro Giulini, 'Un diario secentesco inedito d'un notaio milanese', *Archivio Storico Lombardo*, 57 (1930), 466–82.

the Po a contingent of several thousand men waited near Mortara whose weak and makeshift fortifications probably comprised of earthen bastions. Still another force under Don Martin d'Aragon watched the right flank around Novara.[67] A strong reserve sat behind the centre at Pavìa ready to march in any direction.

Victor-Amadeus threw a bridge across the Tanaro river on 19 May and marched to Felizzano, upstream from Alessandria, to induce the Spanish into thinking that the army would advance towards Piacenza. The combined Franco-Savoyard field force, said to number 18,000 foot and 5,000 horse, would have overwhelmed the Habsburg army had it stood fast to give battle.[68] Leganés waited for it further east at Tortona, with about 11,000 foot and 3,000 horse.[69] At first, on 21

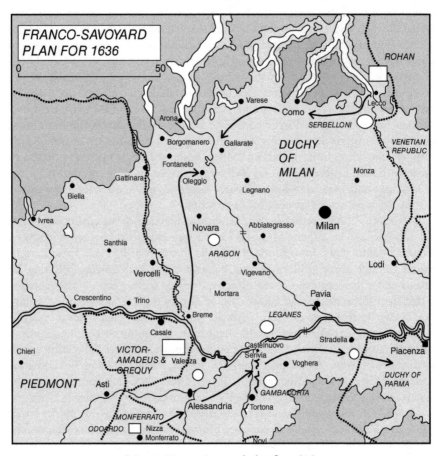

Map 3. Franco-Savoyard plan for 1636.

[67] Archivio Comunale Pavia, Ms II 59, Gabrio Busca, *Descrizione delle fortezze di frontiera dello Stato di Milano*, *c.*1600. On inspection, the engineer Gabrio Busca recommended earthen works for Mortara in order to husband resources for more important fortresses, like Novara and Alessandria.

[68] *Memoires du Comte de Souvigny*, i. 303, 1613–38.

[69] AGS Estado 3344, no. 45, letter from Tortona, 26 May 1636.

May Victor-Amadeus did precisely as the Spanish general expected, approaching the Scrivia lines until he determined they were too strong to storm. Only a few fords across the river were passable to wagons and artillery and these were especially well guarded with fortified bridgeheads.[70] Meanwhile, Leganés threw a boat bridge across the Po at Casa Gerola south of Pavìa and rushed reinforcements to the threatened lines. The principal commanders of the Spanish army converged on the sector hoping that the French would attack them there.[71] The Duke of Savoy's south-eastward movement was perhaps only a feint, made slower by heavy rains, for the confederate army soon withdrew towards Casale Monferrato while Créquy transferred his artillery and its impedimenta across the Po to Breme. Créquy on 1 June advanced along the north shore of the Po hoping to seize the Spanish bridge at Gerola, and float provisions and men in boats towards Piacenza from that point. Leganés's troops disassembled their bridge and placed batteries along the banks to make this movement impossible too.[72] Victor-Amadeus with his contingent camped just across the Po from Valenza, where a vigorous sally by the garrison on 6 June repulsed his cavalry and killed some leading officers. Exceptionally rainy weather in late May, which turned all the rivers into swollen torrents, hampered the coalition army's movements. Near the mouth of the Po the raging river burst the levees on 27 May and drowned people and animals. Créquy sat in this position for the better part of a week, hoping for a break in the weather, but with every passing day, Leganés assembled more troops across from him.[73]

Having failed to achieve any surprise, the coalition army recoiled once again and built ovens to bake their biscuits near Breme. This necessary operation immobilized all armies every five or six days, for firewood was a bulky commodity that could not easily be transported (Fig. 2.1). Nor could soldiers carry provisions for more than a few days, in addition to their armour, weapons, and personal effects. The confederate field army would have consumed at least 20,000 rations daily, and transporting loaves of bread would have required close to sixty wagons for a single day.[74] Instead, the army carted with it the bricks and other materials for assembling ovens. At this stage of the campaign, they milled their grain and drew their stocks of firewood from nearby Breme, a great magazine.[75] The clock was ticking, however: weather and fodder availability restricted campaigns to fifteen or twenty weeks, and Créquy and Victor-Amadeus lost the first three weeks without anything to show for it.

The coalition partners reverted to the plan suggested by Victor-Amadeus during the winter. From Breme they planned to march north past the enemy fortresses of Mortara and Novara, and then seize the walled town of Oleggio near the Ticino

---

[70] *Memoires du Comte de Souvigny*, i. 303.

[71] Biblioteca Nacional de España, Ms 2367, fo. 46.

[72] Girolamo Ghilini, *Annali di Alessandria*, ed. A. Bossola (Alessandria, 1903), 117; see also the *Gazette de France*, 93 (1636); a letter from Victor-Amadeus to the comte Tallard spells out these early problems as well, ASTo Materie Politiche dell'Interno: Registro di lettere alla Corte 38, 3 June 1636.

[73] Edouard Hardy de Perini, *Batailles françaises* (Paris, 1894–1906), iii. 213.

[74] Lynn, *Giant*, 115–20.   [75] Perjés, 'Army Provisioning'.

Fig. 2.1. Stefano della Bella, Commander supervising an army's march. Armies travelled in several separate corps along the same road, each section entrusted with specific functions.

river. The Duke of Rohan would emerge from the Adda river frontier near Lecco and march west to join up with them. The Duke of Parma sat in Nizza Monferrato with an army of about 5,000 men under his own command. With the Spaniards fully engaged north of Milan, he could march over the empty trenches behind the Scrivia and return home unopposed.

Victor-Amadeus and Créquy decided to keep their army split into two roughly equal contingents when they left Breme on 8 June. For the better part of a year, the Duke of Savoy tried to obtain Créquy's dismissal, and his substitution by his friend Marshal Toiras, who supervised the daily operations of the Savoyard contingent. Richelieu, on Mazarin's urging, finally consented to admit Toiras to Victor-Amadeus' staff, but on condition that the Duke of Savoy would camp separately from Créquy's contingent so as not to undermine his authority.[76] The two commanders suspected each other's good faith a great deal, and the French general thought that Victor-Amadeus harboured the intention of sabotaging the campaign.[77] Even civilians confided to their journals the conviction that the Duke of Savoy was secretly a Spanish ally.[78] Créquy wanted to advance on Milan at all costs in order

---

[76] Guido Quazza, 'Giulio Mazzarini mediatore fra Vittorio Amedeo I e il Richelieu (1635–1636)', *Bollettino Storico-Bibliografico Subalpino*, 48 (1950), 53–84.

[77] Mun, *Richelieu et la maison de Savoie*, 127.

[78] Giuseppe Giorcelli, 'Annali Casalesi (1632–1661) di Gian Domenico Bremio, speciaro di Casale Monferrato', *Rivista di Storia, Arte, Archaeologia della provincia di Alessandria*, 18 (1909), 381–436, 393 (1636).

to make up for his failures the previous year and to mollify the impatient cardinal. On the advance to Oleggio there was general agreement. The two contingents marched separately but not far from each other in a northerly direction. Pioneers who repaired roads and removed obstacles slowing the baggage wagons, led the way, behind the cavalry scouts. Armies did not move very quickly in enemy territory for it was important for its contingents to be ready to fight at all times. A *maréchal de camp général*, supervised troop movement day by day.[79] The *Gazette de France* reported the daily movement of Victor-Amadeus's army; it travelled fifteen, seventeen, nine, and twenty-three kilometres on the first four days, never straying more than ten kilometres from the Piedmontese border on the Sesia river.[80] Créquy's army advanced parallel to the east, but never far away from the other detachment. After five days of marching over bad roads not yet drained of the previous downpour, the generals halted to rest the horses pulling the cannon and the munitions wagons, set up the ovens and baked more bread. Geza Perjés, who has developed the most cogent model of field operations, notes that 'an army was not only a war machine, but an immense milling, baking, foraging and transportation device at the same time'. Meanwhile, advance parties of mounted scouts scoured the territory for signs of the enemy (Fig. 2.2).

The main body accompanying the baggage and the artillery fortified its camps from day to day, like the Romans. The first units to move needed to arrive at the designated encampment early enough in the day in order to fortify it, while successive regiments arrived behind them (Fig. 2.3). The basic rule governing the layout of temporary encampments was that the *maréchal de camp* should entrust the officers and men with specific tasks. He first made a quick sketch of the ground after choosing it on the basis of the availability of wood and water, and then allotted each unit a portion of the space. Assistants staked out their quarters on right angles, with 'streets' and 'squares' to facilitate movement and assembly. Alongside emplacements for soldiers' tents and huts, and shelters for horses and their grooms, he designated space for the general officers and their assistants, the sutlers, the artillery, and its many wagons.[81] Each cannon required teams of oxen or horses to haul it over the muddy roads; a heavy siege gun would have required thirty animals, not including those hauling the wagons carrying the necessary hardware.[82] The *maréchal de camp* assigned other detachments to collect forage, for the 10,000 horses and oxen with the army (a minimum figure) would have required something like 300 tonnes of it daily (Fig. 2.4). Cavalry troopers dismounted in order to scythe the grass and the standing crops in the fields, which

---

[79] Paul Azan, *Un tacticien du XVIIe siècle* (Paris, 1904), 40; Perjés, 'Army Provisioning'; on the perennial nature of these constraints over the centuries, see Keegan, *History of Warfare*, 301–4.

[80] *Gazette de France*, 93 (1636).

[81] The most detailed description is that of John Cruso, *Castramentation, or the measuring out of the quarters for the encamping of an army* (London, 1642). Cruso was a diligent purveyor of specialized information for a public avid for it, but he does not seem to have had any direct experience of the thing. Much of that booklet he derived from the well-known work by the Sieur du Praissac, which he translated into English. I have used the last edn of that book, Sieur du Praissac, *Discours et questions militaires* (Paris, 1638), 28–39.

[82] Marcello Manacci, *Compendio d'Instruttioni per gli bombardieri* (Parma, 1640), 32–3.

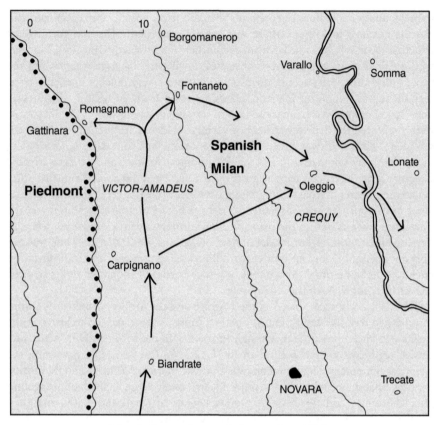

Map 4. Franco-Savoyard advance, June 1636.

Fig. 2.2. Stefano della Bella, Officer acquiring information from a peasant boy. Cavalry patrols were the eyes of every army, collecting information on the whereabouts of enemy forces.

Fig. 2.3. Stefano della Bella, The artillery train, *c.*1630. Siege artillery required abundant hardware to operate and transport the heavy tubes, pulled by numerous horses and oxen requiring large quantities of fodder.

Fig. 2.4. Jacques Callot, Farm in Italy. Each farm stocked hay, straw, and precious fodder to feed the indispensable oxen. For an army on the march, a farm was a filling station cleaned out by cavalry foragers.

Fig. 2.5. Anonymous, Castle of Cortemaggiore (Piacenza province). Every large village and small town had a medieval castle incapable of withstanding a siege, but peasants stocked them with food, fodder, and animals nevertheless. Well-armed militiamen defended them against enemy foraging patrols.

they bundled into (stolen) sheets to carry back to camp.[83] Officers detailed still other troops to fetch water for cooking and refreshing the horses and oxen. Men, women, and boys scoured the vicinity for firewood and branches to construct huts. Most soldiers preferred two-man huts to tents, for these kept them warmer and drier than the canvas sheets, which spoiled quickly. These shelters could be made more livable by cutting a small furrow in the narrow space between them for water runoff, and piling their sleeping quarters with straw, a commodity the army consumed in great quantities.[84]

Fodder requirements made it necessary for the army to seize all the castles and fortified places that lay on their march path, for the inhabitants stocked them with whatever grass and grain they possessed, along with their carts and livestock (Fig. 2.5). Few strongpoints could withstand a prolonged artillery bombardment, for medieval castles with thin walls and high towers could not support the weight of cannon that could return the fire. Peasant militiamen defending these castles understood that prolonged resistance was futile and would only serve to frustrate and antagonize the assailants. Everyone judged it opportune to negotiate a satisfactory capitulation through designated non-combatant intermediaries (priests and friars as a rule), and hope for the best. This might protect villagers' personal belongings from indiscriminate looting, and place the women off limits to the

---

[83] Lynn, *Giant*, 127.   [84] Du Praissac, *Discours et questions militaires*, 30.

soldiers. The comte de Souvigny recollected his role in negotiating the surrender of one such stronghold, Castel Sant' Angelo, seven kilometres west of Mortara, the day before the main body of the army was to pass by. The militia defenders feared for their lives and their goods and so put up stout resistance against the French attackers. Souvigny presented himself below the battlements and requested an interview with the parish priest. After fifteen minutes of parley the inhabitants opened the castle gates on the understanding with Souvigny personally that his men would not plunder them.[85] We have only his word for it that his soldiers respected these promises.

The peasants were right to be fearful. It was a theoretical maxim of war that the invaders should strike terror in the hearts of the civilian population. War's grim reality for civilians has not found much space in military history books, but thanks to historians like George Satterfield, Bernard Peschot, and Simon Pepper we are beginning to understand its importance today.

> In the lengthy intervals of campaigning between battles... low-intensity warfare took place on a daily basis. Patrols skirmished; foragers seized provisions and animals; raiding parties burnt villages and crops to deny them to the enemy, whilst others destroyed them in reprisal for the failure to pay contributions. What was known universally as 'small war' was waged on a scale that was anything but small. Indeed, for many soldiers, for much of the time, small war almost certainly provided their primary experience of active service and combat.[86]

Commanders should ensure that their troops destroy the infrastructure of mills and farms along their march path, noted Raimondo Montecuccoli, in his influential textbook on the art of war.[87] Another treatise, by the chevalier Antoine de Ville (1639) recommended systematically ravaging enemy territory, plundering everything possible and burning whatever could not be carried off (Fig. 2.6). Crops in the fields should be burned or trampled, and the local inhabitants (probably only the notables) taken hostage. He recommended sparing three categories of people, however; women in general, the clergy in their churches, and any man who laid down his arms, for harming these people were actions that cried out for vengeance.[88] In the absence of detailed information from the villages west and north of Mortara and Novara it is impossible to know if Franco-Savoyard invaders respected these limits. It is certain, however, that the coalition soldiers received express orders

---

[85] *Memoires du Comte de Souvigny*, i. 306.

[86] Simon Pepper, 'Aspects of Operational Art: Communications, Cannon and Small War', in Frank Tallett and D. J. B. Trim (eds), *European Warfare 1350–1750* (Cambridge and New York, 2010), 182; see also George Satterfield, *Princes, Posts and Partisans: The Army of Louis XIV and Partisan Warfare in the Netherlands, 1673–1678* (Leiden and Boston, 2003).

[87] Marco Costa, *Psicologia militare: Elementi di psicologia per gli appartenenti alle forze armate* (Milan, 2003); Costa's second chapter synthesizes Raimondo Montecuccoli's 'Aforismi dell'arte bellica' (1670), which he composed during his capitivity in Germany in the late 1630s. The Modenese aristocrat's handbook, written c.1640, was the most influential of all the 17th-century treatises on the art of war.

[88] Bernard Peschot, 'Les "lettres de feu": La petite guerre et les contributions paysannes au XVIIe siècle', in C. Desplat (ed.), *Les Villageois face à la guerre, XIVe–XVIIIe siècle* (Toulouse, 2002), 129–42; Antoine de Ville, *De la charge des gouverneurs des places*, last edn (Paris, 1674), 397–9.

Fig. 2.6. Jacques Callot, Camp scene *c.*1630. The camp was security, plenty, relaxation, but it depended upon the busy accomplishment of specialized tasks. A woman and child figure just left of the tree trunk. Armies in Italy probably included only modest numbers of these.

to devastate the region. Hémery boasted in a letter to the king that the army wrecked the canals leading to Novara and Mortara.[89] The mills in particular constituted strategic objectives; in the invaders' hands they enabled the army to convert its grain into flour. A large invasion force required the services of many mills in order to provide enough flour every day. Moreover the mill streams directed runoff water onto precious meadows, irrigated fields and rice paddies.[90] The destruction of mills alone inflicted several million crowns worth of damage on this densely populated district, in Hémery's estimation. Other detachments halted in order to scythe the fields of ripening grain that they carted back to Breme's magazines.[91] The army was moving too quickly to strip the countryside of all its resources, however. Créquy recommended using the cavalry to burn all the crops that could not be harvested by the troops, for the same task would tie down too many infantry.[92] Foraging parties stripped whatever they could from the land, often in the face of enemy parties (the members of whom were 'partisans'). 'La petite guerre nourrit la grande', writes Bernard Peschot à propos of these activities.[93] Du Praissac thought that a good half of soldiers joined the colours seeking just such opportunities and quickly deserted when the pickings declined.[94]

---

[89] Archives des Affaires Etrangères, Correspondance Politique Sardaigne 24, 16 June 1636.

[90] ASPr Magistrato Camerale di Parma, Memoriali 23; Giovan Stefano Bolzoni pleaded for compensation after war reduced his investment in mill water rights to nothing. Mills were a central part of rural infrastructure.

[91] Lupi, 'Storia della peste', 203.

[92] Archives des Affaires Etrangères, (La Courneuve), Correspondance Politique, Sardaigne, vol. 24, letter of 16 June.

[93] Peschot, 'Lettres de feu'.   [94] Du Praissac, *Discours et questions militaires*, 8.

After 13 June, the two contingents separated further, with Créquy arguing for a rapid march on Milan, and Victor-Amadeus preferring to make haste slowly (Fig. 2.7). 'The interests of Monsieur de Savoye are more important to him than any others, and he does what he wants', complained Hémery in a letter to Cardinal Richelieu on 11 June. The ambassador was unsure whether or not the duke maintained secret intelligence with the Spaniards, as many French officers thought.[95] Just as Créquy was about to pounce on Oleggio and cross the Ticino river towards Milan, Victor-Amadeus announced his intention to capture the castles to his rear and to the north at Arona on Lake Maggiore. His dilatory strategy of methodical conquest was not absurd, for the procedure rendered more secure the supply convoys travelling east from Piedmont. But it slowed down the advance. Victor-Amadeus sent Marshal Toiras with a few cannon to capture the walled village of Fontaneto, defended only by militiamen.[96] Resistance was stiffer than he anticipated, so the famous general called for more artillery and opened a sap: that is, his men dug zigzag trenches towards the walls so that a battery set up there could demolish

Fig. 2.7. Jacob Duck, Soldiers leaving quarters to march *c.*1630. These soldiers have spent the night, relatively comfortably, in a house. A company has formed up outside their door, ready to march.

[95] AAE, Correspondance Politique, Sardaigne, vol. 24, 11 June.
[96] AGS Estado 3344, no. 118, State of garrisons in the state of Milan. In May, Fontaneto's garrison was given as 146 officers and men of the Novara peasant militia.

them at closer range.[97] A number of senior French officers were killed and wounded (including Souvigny) through their lack of caution in the approaches. A militia marksman felled Toiras himself after he stepped in front of a cannon emplacement in order to see the effects of the shot. The plucky garrison surrendered on conditions and marched off to Novara several days later (17 June) only after the Savoyard battery of six large cannon made a viable breach in the walls (Fig. 2.8). In order to hold the wider district more securely, Victor-Amadeus posted no fewer than 900 men in garrison there, almost two regiments! It provides a good illustration of the difficulties of an offensive: the further an invading army advanced, the more contingents large and small had to be left in the castles and towns along its supply route.[98] The death of the gifted Marshal Toiras deprived Victor-Amadeus of someone he could trust among the French senior command and the chasm of mistrust between the commanders deepened as a result.[99] Meanwhile, French soldiers trickled rearwards on various pretexts to go home, congregating around Pinerolo where the governor formed a special detachment to round them up.[100]

Créquy seized Oleggio, a small town without modern defences or a proper garrison, on 14 June. It surrendered meekly after the general promised not to plunder

Fig. 2.8. Stefano della Bella, Bombardment of a town, *c.*1630. Cannon inflicted much greater damage if placed close to the ramparts, but this entailed greater danger for their crews.

---

[97] Marcello Manacci recommended getting as close as possible to speed the breaching process, no further than 500 metres to begin with. Manacci, *Compendio d'Instruttioni*, 58.

[98] AAE, CP Sardaigne, vol. 24, Hémery to King Louis XIII, 16 June 1636.

[99] BNF, Ms Fr 16929, Relation de M. d'Esmery de ses negociations en Piedmont en 1635, fo. 565.

[100] Archives du Service Historique de la Défense, A1 27, no. 15, letter from Louis XIII to Monsieur de Malissy, 13 June 1636.

it or violate the women there. The feeble remnants of its medieval defences precluded fortifying the town as a forward base. Strong French cavalry patrols pushed the Spanish scouts and skirmishers back into Novara, leaving the coalition army in complete control of the countryside. Everywhere around their advance, French parties cut the ripening crops and carted them back to Breme or Gattinara for their magazines, while the rural population fled eastward.[101] After a French column raided the female monastery of Santa Marta, soldiers allowed the nuns to march two-by-two in procession behind their cross to the protection of Novara. The well-fortified city of about 4,000 or 5,000 inhabitants was crammed to the ramparts with garrison forces, who occupied houses and took shelter wherever there was space. Instead of demolishing the suburbs outside the gates, which facilitated defence in time of siege, the governor billeted men and horses there too. City authorities feared there would not be enough food and money to go around, but it was the fodder that was always in short supply.[102] There was a distinct danger, perfectly understood by Victor-Amadeus, that if the coalition army crossed the Ticino towards Milan, strong sallies north or west from Novara would cut off their supplies.[103]

The disunited command now expressed two starkly opposing views of the campaign's objective. On to Milan!, urged Créquy. Fearing that Leganés's German reinforcements would descend from the north, and hoping to force them to take a more lengthy route, the Duke of Savoy decided instead to seize the Lake Maggiore port of Arona, whose capture would interdict river-borne supplies to much of Spanish Lombardy. It was guarded by a medieval castle built on an outcropping, connected to the town below by a simple trench.[104] Victor-Amadeus thought Arona, and Angera on the opposite shore, were easy targets.

And then, a stroke of luck. Don Martin d'Aragon ordered all the boats along the Ticino to be rowed to the eastern shore, as a sensible precaution. But Pietro Francesco della Croce, commander of Lonate's militia, entrusted to cut the ferry cable across the river on 13 June, delayed carrying it out until the following dawn in order to allow escape to frightened refugees.[105] At dawn of 14 June, six Monferrato cavalrymen (thus ethnically Italian) in a French cavalry detachment outside Oleggio wrapped red sashes diagonally around their torsos, (the customary identification for Habsburg troops) and approached the edge of the river where the

[101] Lupi, 'Storia della peste', 203.

[102] ASNo Comune di Novara. Parte Antica 1823: Corrispondenza, Letter of the delegates of the city to Cardinal Albornoz, 30 Aug. 1635; Parte Antica 1875: Memoriali, 19 Jan. 1636, complaining of the excessive demands of the cavalry companies on fodder supplies.

[103] ASTo Materie politiche interne: lettere ministri, Francia mazzo 34, 19 June 1636, Letter from Victor-Amadeus to his ambassador in France the Marquis de St. Maurice. 'Le danger est que si les ennemis mettaient seulement quelque peu de cavallerie dans Novare, n'y ayant delà que 5 ou 6 petites milles jusqu'aux lieux où il faut que nos provisions passent.' This is an exaggeration, unless a Piedmontese mile was 3 km, for convoys moving northward from Vercelli would have been over 20 km distant, and at least 15 km away from those moving east towards Oleggio.

[104] Archivio Comunale Pavia, MS II 59, Gabrio Busca, *Descrizione delle fortezze di frontiera dello Stato di Milano* (1600?), fo. 35.

[105] 'Relazione del curato Francesco Comerio di Lonate', in Bertolli and Colombo, *La peste del 1630 a Busto Arsizio*, 438–41.

ferry cable ran to the other side. Pretending to be Habsburg cavalry cut off and fleeing from the French, they convinced the boatman on the other shore to come over and rescue them. The soft-hearted or greedy boatman crossed the channel where the troopers promptly killed him for his pains. Soldiers hiding nearby filled the capacious boat, designed to float carts and livestock, and crossed to the eastern bank, where they secured the other end of the cable and collected five or six boats more in order to fetch reinforcements. Before long, some 500 soldiers were busy throwing up earthworks on the eastern bank in order to hold the position, while the remainder of Créquy's corps converged towards it.[106] Della Croce mobilized the militia to the sound of the village bells, and ordered men down to the river's edge to contest the passage with their musketry and to cut the cable if they could. The local priest claims that the militiamen fired continuously all day, until they had exhausted their munitions, inflicting (by his own unsubstantiated claim) scores of dead and injured on the swelling number of French troops for only two casualties of their own. But while militiamen carried modern muskets, they had no experience of fighting professional soldiers at close quarters with pikes and blade weapons, and were unable to stanch the flow.

This was bold Créquy's hour. He reinforced the first detachment with more cavalry, and then aligned the coalition army's fifteen wagon-borne boats across the Ticino to form a floating bridge, which was ready the next day.[107] The crossing point marked the point of entry to a navigable canal, or *naviglio*, flowing to Milan. It irrigated en route the lush meadows and rich grain fields of Lombardy, making it doubly important strategically. There sat a customs house along the shore, the Casa della Camera, where Créquy established his first headquarters. He instructed his troops to block the water intake next to it and render the canal unusable. Cavalry patrols trotted south along the *naviglio* towpath, past Turbigo to Boffalora, wrecking everything they could. The infantry dug entrenchments in the gravel at the canal entrance, but the unstable valley bottom, all sand and stones, made it futile. Detachments then threw up more entrenchments at the crest of the plateau some 600 metres distant and 60 metres above the river level, and eventually ventured further out onto the plain as their numbers increased. The coalition commanders debated how to use the canal as leverage over the Milanese. Hémery suggested leaving it operable if the city was willing to pay the army's subsistence costs. Victor-Amadeus preferred to destroy the works first, certain that the Milanese would pay dearly for its restoration once they began to suffer from the inconvenience.[108]

The successful crossing galvanized the entire invasion army. The *maréchal de camp* Du Plessis-Praslin announced to Richelieu the important shift in its mood. 'I can tell you that the king's whole army, from the general down to the last soldier,

---

[106] *Memoires du Comte de Souvigny*, 308; he identifies the first troops across as the Pierregourde regiment, selected because it had made a similar crossing of the Rhone river.

[107] Girolamo Brusoni, *Delle Historie memorabilia, contiene le Guerre d'Italia de' nostri tempi* (Venice, 1656), 30.

[108] AAE C.P. Sardaigne, vol. 24, Hémery to Cardinal Richelieu, 17 June 1636.

Fig. 2.9. Stefano della Bella, Cavalry skirmish. Advancing French troops needed to chase Habsburg cavalry patrols back into their fortress bases, in order to forage in relative security.

desire only to serve you.'[109] On the evening of 16 June, a multitude of French infantry and cavalry descended upon Lonate three kilometres from the river's edge, 'con barbarico furore e arte diabolica', intent on looting the churches and private houses (Fig. 2.9). They reportedly brutalized an inhabitant in the parish church before making off with the sacred vessels. Parties returned the following day to plunder the convents, and then moved on to villages nearby. The eyewitness parish priest Francesco Comerio made veiled comments about the 'carnal sins' visited upon some women by the soldiery, but laid his emphasis rather on the spoliation and desecration of the churches. Over four days, troops scythed the grain and set some fires in the neighbouring villages of Magnago, Ferno, Cardano, Samarate, and Compagna. They pastured their horses in the fields in a radius of five or six kilometres from their crossing point, and helped themselves to the food stores. Whatever wine they did not drink they spilled out onto the cellar floors.[110] French parties arrived at Busto Arsizio, a small town, where the panicked inhabitants crowded into churches for protection with their household furnishings and their livestock. Soldiers exacted booty and contributions on the threat of setting fire to the houses of those who fled or refused to pay. Thereafter they made examples of particular persons instead of plundering the whole town. Twice they returned, but accepted 50 scudi each time in exchange for not committing outrages on the persons living there. After the second visit the inhabitants raised entrenchments around the town to prevent enemy parties from penetrating its perimeter, and committed thirty men every day to sentry duty, while thirty militiamen served on work details. An additional party of thirty horse served as scouts. It would have

---

[109] AAE C.P. Sardaigne, vol. 24, Du Plessis-Praslin to Cardinal Richelieu, 15 June 1636.
[110] Lupi, 'Storia della peste', 204–5.

been too onerous to maintain hundreds of militiamen under arms continuously, so each had to serve one day in four in one of these capacities.[111]

'We have spread such terror that from Milan to Como there is not a single peasant' (harvesting the crops), crowed Hémery on 18 June.[112] The urban Milanese were frightened too, for Leganés was nowhere to be seen. 'The populace (*popolo minuto*) of Milan began to take fright, complaining that the country was going to ruin, first from eighteen years of intolerable troop lodgings, and now they were suffering the plunder of the countryside, and not only were the Spaniards not giving any help, but they were not permitting the country to defend itself like people offered.'[113] Leganés suspected at first that the enemy's march northwards and then around Novara was a simple feint, for Duke Odoardo's detachment still sat south of the Po ready to march.[114] Many people around him speculated early on that Rohan would rendezvous with Créquy near Oleggio. Leganés nevertheless sat where he was near Tortona and waited for developments. He diverted some of the German reinforcements eastwards towards Lecco to keep Rohan from attempting to break into the plain by some unlikely road. Don Martin d'Aragon with 6,000 or 7,000 men (including militiamen) converged on Boffalora south of Tornavento to slow Créquy's advance. The 2,500 German soldiers under Prince Borso d'Este freshly arrived and placed under his command refused to march with him. They grated on the local inhabitants, for their *infinite estorsioni*, and their refusal to submit to Spanish military discipline. Leganés reacted to the news of the Ticino river crossing with growing alarm, and finally left Tortona for Pavìa on 15 June with what we would call his general staff. He called for scattered contingents and detachments from various garrisons to assemble at Abbiategrasso, twenty-five kilometres west of Milan. Francisco de Melo hastened to the capital to provide for the citadel, and to rally the citizenry. The principal senators and feudatories of Milan assembled before the Grand Chancellor of the state, Don Antonio Ronquillo, and begged him to do something. He and Leganés called all fit citizens to form companies to patrol the city walls and gates. Six thousand citizens enlisted under six militia colonels while other officials proceeded to requisition horses and carts for army transport.[115] The Lombard count Francesco d'Adda, an old soldier no longer fit for active service, drilled the recruits in the use of their weapons. Thousands more militia under the Milanese Paolo Sormani assembled to support the 4,000 professional soldiers under Giovanni Serbelloni, dug in on the heights overlooking Lecco, in case Rohan should emerge from the Valtellina once again.[116]

[111] The rotation of militiamen in their duties was established practice; see Mario Rizzo, 'Istituzioni militari e strutture socio-economiche in una città di antico regime: La milizia urbana a Pavia nell'età spagnola', in C. Donati (ed.), *Eserciti e carriere militari nell'Italia moderna* (Milan, 1998), 63–89.

[112] AAE, C.P. Sardaigne, vol. 24, Hémery's dispatches to Cardinal Richelieu, 17–18 June 1636.

[113] Giulini, 'Un diario secentesco', 477.

[114] Archivio di Stato Modena, Ambasciatori Milano 107, fasc. 21, letter of 11 June from the Lombard aristocrat Fra Ferrante Attendolo Bolognini to Duke Francesco. Bolognini was an officer in the Spanish army, expert in fortification and siegecraft, in addition to his function of liaison with the Modenese court.

[115] Giulini, 'Un diario secentesco', 478; the chronicler confirms Girolamo Brusoni's account years later, *Delle Historie memorabili* (1656), 31–2.

[116] Abbate Giovanni Fossati, *Memorie historiche delle guerre d'Italia del secolo presente* (Milan, 1640), 163.

The feudatories and wealthy Milanese consented on 20 June to raise almost 300,000 lire in emergency financing, with Captain Carlo Arconati promising 11,500 lire from his private funds.[117] The prominent place of Protestant troops and the widespread desecration of churches by the invaders served to focus everyone's energies.[118]

Both Victor-Amadeus and Créquy sent frantic letters to Rohan begging him to march in their direction, but he replied that it was impossible, since his troops were hungry and on the verge of mutiny.[119] A worrying plague had also just broken out in the Valtellina, Rohan reported, and it was beginning to infect his men. He proposed that the coalition army should advance due east towards Como so that it would reduce the distance he had to march. Créquy and Victor-Amadeus were not aware of Rohan's inability to move before some time had elapsed, and sensed that a 'combat général' might be in the offing, as Hémery reported to Cardinal Richelieu in a dispatch on 17 June. They knew that the marquis de Leganés had reached Boffalora and had called for troops to join him there. Half the Franco-Savoyard army crossed the bridge of boats over the Ticino, and erected earthworks.

Strategic though it was, the Tornavento position had one important weakness: the bridgehead could not be properly fortified, given that the river plain was all sand and gravel. The earthworks erected on the heights were too far away to offer adequate protection, and their defence on both banks would tie down too many men. Similarly the soil on the western shore would not permit the erection of strong earthworks guarding the bridge's approach. Oleggio was three kilometres distant from the river, and could only serve as an enclosure to the baggage. In the absence of a viable bridgehead, the army could not advance from its position towards Milan or Como, for a Spanish column could storm the bridge approaches on either side of the river and cut the coalition army off from its supplies. Another looming problem was that, after five or six days, the army had stripped the district of its available fodder. Cavalry patrols ranged eight or ten kilometres in search of hay to bring back to camp.[120] The Sergeant-Major-General of the army, the sieur Castelan, and his aides Le Camus and Roqueservières recommended a better crossing at Casteletto, about fifteen kilometres further north. Troops disassembled the bridge early on 20 June and placed the boats on wagons or towed them upriver from the western bank. The next day the two contingents marched north, one on each side of the wide Ticino river. Créquy's smaller force of about 6,000 infantry and 1,200 cavalry advanced across the heath towards Sesto. Victor-Amadeus led perhaps 8,000 foot and 1,500 horse towards Varallo Piombo on the western shore, together with almost all of the artillery and most of the baggage. The perfect crossing point remained elusive, however, for the river was either too wide, or the current too

[117] Archivio Storico Civico di Milano, Archivio Sola Busca: Serbelloni b. 53, Imposizioni, 20 June 1636 (printed broadsheet).

[118] This accusation figures prominently in the declaration of loyalty of the city of Novara to the Governor of Milan in Aug. 1635, denouncing the 'nemici crudeli sterminatori del culto divino e della Santa Fede Cattolica'; ASNo, Comune di Novara Parte Antica 1823: corrispondenza, 30 Aug. 1635.

[119] BNF Ms Fr 16929, Relation de M. d'Esmery de ses negociations en Piedmont en 1635 etc., fo. 568.

[120] ASTo Materie politiche interne: Lettere ministri Francia 34, letter from Victor-Amadeus to his ambassador in France, the Marquis de St Maurice, 19 June 1636.

strong, which made hauling the boats upstream slower than anticipated.[121] Victor-Amadeus sent a column further north in the hopes of seizing Arona, which controlled the exit from the Lake Maggiore, but the militia garrison under its alert commander Count Giulio Cesare Borromeo, feudal lord of the place, repelled a surprise assault. Lombard militia parties in front of Victor-Amadeus felled trees across the road and did their utmost to hamper his advance.[122]

Spanish generals usually let pass the chance to fight the French in the open field, for battles were risky events with unpredictable outcomes. Leganés feared in particular that his cavalry would be outclassed by the enemy horse. Should he fight and lose, the nearest reinforcements were available from distant Germany or the kingdom of Naples. The duchies of Modena and Tuscany, Spain's two principal allies nearby, provided few soldiers, with no stomach for fighting. Thus it would rarely be worth gambling the fate of the rich and strategic duchy of Milan in a single day's battle.[123] Leganés could legitimately have done nothing more than dig in across from the coalition bridgehead and force a stalemate. With German and Neapolitan reinforcements on their way, political observers understood that the balance of forces would soon be reversed.[124] But it was impolitic for him to ignore the pleas for action from influential Milanese citizens. Many of these were carting their belongings off to neutral Venetian territory. 'All that could be heard were laments and curses against Leganés in the squares, the streets and the houses.'[125]

The timely arrival of thousands of professional soldiers from Germany and Naples emboldened the commander-in-chief to risk a 'generous action' (the term is Gualdo Priorato's) in order to give courage to the Milanese. Prince Borso d'Este's 4,000 veterans marched towards the Alps around 10 May, with his own regiment of 2,000 men in the lead.[126] Another contingent of long-awaited German horse, mostly dragoons, reached Milan just behind Borso d'Este's foot. Simultaneously, Neapolitan cavalry trekked up the peninsula, crossing neutral and friendly territory on their way. Duke Ferrante Gonzaga in Guastalla, fearing that these men might plunder this friendly district's valuable dairy assets, dispatched a letter to his neighbour the Duke of Modena. 'Guard my cows!' he pleaded, hoping Francesco would post soldiers around the farms near the march route. The Duchess of Mantua also helped round up the precious livestock in exposed pastures, to place them out of the soldiers' reach.[127]

Leganés finally called Gherardo Gambacorta away from the Scrivia lines with his remaining infantry and cavalry (6,000 foot and 2,000 horse by one account),

[121] *Memoires du Cardinal de Richelieu*, in Michaud and Poujoulat (eds), *Nouvelle collection des Memoires pour servir à l'histoire de France* (Paris, 1838), ix. 48.

[122] Biblioteca Universitaria Bologna, vol. 473, Misc. H, 15; Anonymous Italian, 'Relatione del fatto d'Arme seguito fra l'Esercito spagnolo e francese nelle selva di Soma di là del Ticino e Tornavento e Ca' della Camera, il 22 giugno 1636'.

[123] Galeazzo Gualdo Priorato, *Il guerriero prudente e politico*, ed. Angelo Tamborra (Naples, 2002; 1st publ. 1640).

[124] ASPr Archivio Gonzaga di Guastalla 63, Lettere, 17 June 1636.

[125] Brusoni, *Delle Historie memorabili*, 31.

[126] ASMo: Casa e Stato. Carteggi fra Principi Estensi 209, letters of 25 Feb. and 2 May 1636.

[127] ASPr Archivio Gonzaga di Guastalla 63, Lettere, 28 May 1636.

leaving only 1,000 professional soldiers under Carlo Della Gatta to guard the lines south of the Po river and box in the French and Parman troops in Piacenza.[128] With these final reinforcements on the way, the Spanish commander decided on 20 June to venture from his entrenched camp at Abbiategrasso, where he had collected his provisions, to Boffalora only eighteen kilometres distant from Tornavento. This force is thought to have totalled 15,000 foot and 4,500 cavalry, but it includes troops still on the march like Gambacorta's, who had orders to join him as quickly as possible, as well as a militia contingent of several thousand infantry who could not be expected to fight.[129] The next day, he ordered all his available units to rendezvous just outside Castano Primo, six kilometres from the Tornavento crossing.

Créquy had only reached the village of Somma on Saturday 21 June, a scant dozen kilometres north of Tornavento when a dispatch from Victor-Amadeus warned him of Leganés's advance. A spy or deserter from the Spanish camp hastened to warn the Duke of Savoy of the impending fight.[130] Victor-Amadeus wanted to throw a bridge across the Ticino right where he was, but the river's great width and rapid current made it impossible. In a short meeting on the western shore, the two generals agreed to hasten to Tornavento to occupy the abandoned entrenchments before the Spanish seized them. Victor-Amadeus dispatched word to the Duke of Parma a hundred kilometres away to join them with his contingent, or else to march immediately towards the Scrivia lines. Créquy ordered a strong French cavalry detachment under Du Plessis-Praslin to chase away the first Spanish advanced parties at Tornavento, while the infantry and their two small cannon (called sakers) followed close behind in battle order. After some spirited skirmishing by the cavalry, the Spanish scouts withdrew. Meanwhile, Victor-Amadeus and his engineers rushed back to the previous crossing point and set to work assembling the bridge in the evening. The two armies reached the zone at approximately the same time, with Leganés's lead infantry column halting at the small village of Vanzaghello just three kilometres east of Tornavento.[131]

The exact site of the battle and the deployment of each army are not difficult to determine in general terms, but many crucial particulars are obscure today due to centuries of almost continuous development. Tornavento was then a mere hamlet dominated by a large *cascina*, or multi-household farm, flanked by a small church and a few modest houses, perched at the crest of the wooded heights 60 metres above the valley floor. Passing just under the crest was a large irrigation ditch called Panperduto, but a few hundred metres from Tornavento it veered

---

[128] Bologna Biblioteca Universitaria, vol. 473, Misc. H, no. 15, Relazione del fatto d'Arme seguito fra l'Esercito spagnolo e francese; ASF Mediceo del Principato 3180, fos. 1118–21, letter to Pandolfini in Milan, 24 June 1636.

[129] Gualdo Priorato, *Historia delle guerre*, xii. 335.

[130] ASFi Mediceo del Principato 3258, letter from Florence to Francisco de Melo, 1 July 1636. The court in Florence learnt of this in the aftermath due to its own high-ranking spy (not named in the letter) in the entourage of Victor-Amadeus. Hémery confirms that Créquy learnt of the Spanish advance from the duke. BNF Ms Fr 16929, Relation de M. d'Esmery, fo. 569.

[131] *Gazette de France*, 99 (1636), 'La Sanglante deffaite des Espagnols dans le Milannez: Par l'armée de France et de Savoye', 405–12. This account was published in early July, barely more than two weeks after the event and appears to be based on the information brought from the field by the comte Palluau.

south-east onto the gently sloping plateau towards Castano. This medieval irrigation course drew water from the Ticino upstream, and passing just north of Castano it continued towards Milan. Today its trace south-east of Tornavento is still perceptible from satellite photography, and its emplacement around the village probably follows the Canale Villoresi, dug in the late nineteenth century. Levees broad enough to plant cannon on top of them contained this irrigation water on the plateau. The plain at the top of the crest, not entirely lacking planted fields, was mostly devoid of the dense promiscuous cultivation characteristic of Northern Italy between the late sixteenth and the mid-twentieth century. That is, the land on the heights above the river was of poor quality for agriculture and was covered by scrub vegetation only a few centimetres high. One French source speaks of some hedges, vines, and mulberry trees behind the earthworks where cavalrymen rested (Fig. 2.10).

The French position was defined by the ring of entrenchments erected the preceding week, and soldiers strengthened it throughout the night before the battle. There are no crop markings showing traces of these today, although one might discern a ravelin just east of the road leading to Malpensa airport in an old aerial photograph. North–south across the eastern edge of the French position ran another, smaller irrigation ditch, the Fosso Cerca, which joined the Panperduto work just south of Tornavento, but this too has since disappeared.[132] The local historian Gian Domenico Oltrona Visconti represented these entrenchments in his summary of the battle as a simple semi-circle with the *cascina* in the centre. These were certainly more complex than his sketch implies. Brusoni, who probably never visited the site, claims that the eastern levee of the Panperduto ditch was incorporated into

Fig. 2.10. Ravenet, Landscape near Sissa (Parma province). This densely planted promiscuous culture covering most of Northern and Central Italy constituted a garden landscape that made reconnaissance difficult, and limited cavalry manoeuvrability.

---

[132] One may derive a general impression of the site via Google Earth, but what strikes the observer most is the extent of modern development. South of Tornavento today lie three sandpits, while running north–south is an expressway giving access to Malpensa airport.

the defences, along with the houses in the village. However Oltrona Visconti suggests that the 'fulcrum' of the battle more likely raged along the Cerca ditch further east, given that the Panperduto lay *underneath* the crest of the plateau behind the village.[133] There are few details concerning the trenches themselves but from the Spanish emphasis on the existence of strong French 'posts' it appears they conformed to the well-developed art of field fortifications. Rather than consisting of a single earthen parapet, raised by digging a ditch and piling the earth up behind it, officers studded the line with little forts at intervals. The forts constituted an enclosed space that the men posted there defended more strenuously—'cent soldats font plus de resistance dans un fort, que mille étendus derrière une ligne', wrote a contemporary tactician, François Dorignac, from long experience.[134] A redoubt 25 metres square and almost 2 metres high could contain a sizeable company of sixty-eight men.[135] While the parapet almost 2 metres thick gave protection from bullets to those standing behind it, it was not a major impediment to men assaulting it with cold steel. The ditch embankment atop the plateau was probably the firmest part of the perimeter. The weak section consisted in the little parapet constructed on the slope down to the edge of the canal, and across the narrow floodplain at the bottom where the soil was unsuitable for earthworks. Most accounts mention a small wood where musketeers sat ready (probably the wooded slope itself) and a small open plain adjacent to it on the extreme right of the French position joining the canal. The map representing the entrenchments is still somewhat conjectural, but it incorporates details emerging from the several narratives of both French and Spanish origin.

Créquy had now largely resolved his predicament, sitting in his earthworks astride the vital *naviglio* threatening Milan. Victor-Amadeus busied himself to his rear reassembling the bridge to come to his aid. The next day their combined armies would probably overwhelm the outnumbered Spaniards on the open ground, perfect for cavalry, and no further obstacles blocked their advance towards the prize.

---

[133] Oltrona Visconti, 19; the local historian's map has been reproduced in more dynamic form by Pierre Picouet, whose five-part summary of the day's fighting seems to correspond well with several accounts.

[134] Azan, *Un tacticien*, 36–8.

[135] Vaclav Matoušek, 'Building a Model of a Field Fortification of the Thirty Years' War near Olbramov (Czech Republic)', *Journal of Conflict Archaeology* (2005), 114–32.

3

The Ordeal of Tornavento, 22 June 1636

THE WILL TO FIGHT

One of the finest qualities of John Keegan's *Face of Battle* is the forthright manner in which he describes the soldiers' fundamental dilemma of carrying out their tasks against their instinct of preservation.

> The study of battle is therefore always a study of fear and usually of courage; always of leadership, usually of obedience; always of compulsion, sometimes of insubordination; always of anxiety, sometimes of elation or catharsis; always of uncertainty and doubt, misinformation and misapprehension, usually also of faith and sometimes of vision; always of violence, sometimes also of cruelty, self-sacrifice, compassion; above all, it is always a study of solidarity and also of disintegration – for it is towards the disintegration of human groups that battle is directed.[1]

This willingness of soldiers to fight and to risk death and injury constitutes an interesting problem, only recently approached by psychologists. It has often been written that the rank and file of armies were society's eternal victims, pushed by misfortune into destitution and with nothing to lose but their lives.[2] However, the participants in *this* battle volunteered twice to be placed in harm's way, once when they followed their captain into the theatre of war, and again by neglecting to desert as the possibility of a close engagement with the enemy loomed. In short, they *chose* to fight and took their chances. This willingness to fight and risk being killed or maimed appears to be a human universal.[3]

Both intraspecies aggressive, lethal violence and its mitigation through submissive postures are innate to humans and indeed predate the evolution of our particular species. In Darwinian language, lethal violence is a trait that has been selected for over many generations. Humans understand universally the 'Darwinian algorithms' of coalition formation, the cost and benefits of participation, and the risks involved. Chimpanzees engage in both hunting and warfare, the latter resembling raiding among humans. Their tight little groups rely on coordination and

---

[1] John Keegan, *The Face of Battle* (Harmondsworth and New York, 1976), 303.

[2] Bernhard Kroener, 'Conditions de vie et origine sociale du personnel militaire subalterne au cours de la Guerre de Trente Ans', *Francia*, 15 (1987), 321–50; Erik Swart, 'From "Landsknecht" to "soldier": The Low German Foot Soldiers of the Low Countries in the Second Half of the Sixteenth Century', *International Review of Social History*, 51 (2006), 75–92.

[3] For a survey of these human attributes, see Donald Brown, *Human Universals* (New York, 1991). The list of these continues to grow. A revised, expanded list figures as an appendix in Steven Pinker's book, *The Blank Slate* (New York, 2002).

stealth to take their chimpanzee enemies at a disadvantage. Failing surprise, the two groups exchange hostile vocalizations and aggressive posturing before they separate.[4] There are several good reasons for the capacity for violence against other members of our species to have evolved; to defend territory and resources, to maintain one's rank and the place of kin, and to show other members of the community that one could be trusted to help in dangerous situations. Prehistoric societies with no use for land or material goods are often the most warlike, for rival groups exploit their weakness by stealing their women.[5] Those who excel at war, on the other hand, attract other males to their kinship groups and enable them to leave much larger numbers of descendants.[6] These predicaments all influence our survival and reproduction, individually and at the group level. Evolutionary psychologists posit that the basic architecture of our psyche still governs our species today. 'Although humans now nearly universally live in state systems, our minds were formed during tens or hundreds of thousands of generations in small, horizontally-organized hunter-gatherer bands. The special psychological mechanisms to deal with coalitional aggression that evolved then are with us now, and influence modern human behavior in a wide variety of contexts.'[7]

The soldiers at Tornavento found themselves in a specific, historical predicament that mobilized their innate capacities. The first of these is a tendency of men, and especially men, to fight and to dominate. These same men lived and bonded in groups providing reciprocal aid to their members, and reacted aggressively when they were threatened. Solidarity towards the group has as its corollary of suspicion and hostility towards outsiders, particularly if the latter might have designs on the group's territory. And finally, members are quite willing to punish anyone deviating from a group's norms, especially those who enjoy the benefits of living in society without contributing to the costs.[8] One of the most important clauses in the 'risk contract' members of the military coalition signed on for was that there must be ways to enforce cooperation and punish defectors. All of the members were adept at 'keeping score'. This social cooperation is common in species where individual recognition plays a fundamental role in grooming and food access.[9] Lionel Tiger claims that male bonding is a biological propensity that *causes* them to form different types of groups.[10] The young male has a biologically driven need to prove himself to his peers; this display of prowess enhances a cumulative group feeling, but establishes a ranking order simultaneously. Boys and men issue each

[4] Lee Alan Dugatkin, *Cooperation among Animals: An Evolutionary Perspective* (Oxford and New York, 1997), 132.

[5] Napoleon A. Chagnon, *Noble Savages* (New York and London, 2013), 73–9.

[6] Ibid. 314–22.

[7] John Tooby and Leda Cosmides, *The Evolution of War and its Cognitive Foundations*, Institute for Evolutionary Studies Technical Report, 88–1 (1988), 10.

[8] Marco Costa, *Psicologia militare: Elementi di psicologia per gli appartenenti alle forze armate* (Milan, 2003), 81–2; see also Steven Pinker, *The Better Angels of our Nature: The Decline of Violence and its Causes* (London and New York, 2011), 31–3. Despite a tendency to hyperbole and his reliance on databases built from sketchy material that exaggerate the number of victims in the past, Pinker's description of the psychological roots of violence remains important for historians.

[9] Dugatkin, *Cooperation among Animals*, 39 and 118.

[10] Lionel Tiger, *Men in Groups* (New York, 1969), p. xvii.

other challenges, and assess the relative standing of members for bravery and toughness.[11] Small groups of men once made war spontaneously, but with the advent of states, hierarchies co-opted the means of war and mobilized men and resources on a vast scale. By the seventeenth century, states enjoyed something like a monopoly on legal violence and they were remarkably successful in compressing illegal violence while raising larger armies than ever before.

The officers usually chose this dangerous profession for reasons of personal advantage. For aristocratic societies that held excellence in war in high esteem, exemplary service enabled the army officer to reap non-material benefits in prestige and social ranking.[12] They earned the gratitude of higher powers and the esteem of their peers, friend and foe alike, for men appreciated this aesthetic panache of bravery and competitive assertiveness. Among the rank and file, the self-interest of the men who chose to fight is not as apparent. Mercenaries fought for money, before other considerations, but we know that the governments lacked the means to pay them. Most analyses that portray soldiers as victims, forced by circumstances to risk their lives just to survive, suffer from the myth of the average man. Many of these men were what today we would call 'adrenaline junkies', living in the present and *seeking out danger* and adventure. Research on sensation-seeking, a burgeoning area of psychological research, attempts to understand how people process risk and persist in seeking it out even when they understand its hazards. Across cultures, men score much higher for this kind of factor than women on most measurable scales.[13] There is every likelihood that risk-taking and dominance-seeking have deep genetic and biological roots, for castration curtails the aggressiveness of male animals. Sensation-seekers score high in testosterone levels, but display low levels of cortisol (released to alleviate stress) and serotonin (which influences the perception of social rank). Without thinking ahead to complications, these men not only seek risk for its own sake, but crave intensity of experience and novelty. Young men have shorter time horizons and place greater emphasis on living for the moment.[14] There is still a great disparity in individual assessments of risk, for people have different base levels of testosterone, and tend to gravitate towards groups sharing their values. Some people, principally males, will continue to seek out hedonistic enjoyment in thrill-seeking even after they have been burned.[15] They have a predisposition to engage in dominant behaviour, and engage in self-reinforcing cycles of social competition beyond the value of external rewards they might enjoy. 'In plain terms', writes Stephen Rosen, 'some people are more likely to fight when challenged, and they get great satisfaction from subduing challengers, and will go on to seize another occasion.'[16] Peer pressure appears to be the most powerful influence for several

[11] Ibid. 180–2.   [12] Gwynne Dyer, *War*, 2nd edn (Toronto, 2004), 18–20.
[13] Marvin Zuckerman, *Sensation Seeking and Risky Behavior* (Washington, DC, 2007), pp. xiii–xiv, 14.
[14] Stephen P. Rosen, *War and Human Nature* (Princeton and Oxford, 2005), 153.
[15] Jeffrey Arnett, 'Still Crazy After All These Years: Reckless Behavior among Young Adults Aged 23–27', *Personality and Individual Differences*, 12 (1991), 1305–13; anyone familiar with the film series *Jackass* will recognize this personality type.
[16] Rosen, *War and Human Nature*, 73–4.

kinds of risky behaviour. Thrill-seeking holds enormous importance in the military sphere, where some individuals volunteer for dangerous jobs just to repeat this rush of exhilaration. Exposure to the danger lowers the perceived risk of engaging in the activity another time, which explains why veterans are more trustworthy in battle.[17] It seems that there is such a thing as a 'natural' soldier. Military life still today attracts men who share some personality characteristics, such as the desire for adventure, the easy acceptance of authority, the need for praise from their peers. They are also easily bored, and enjoy risks and challenges.[18]

The volunteer armies of the seventeenth century—which typically comprised of 0.5 to 1 per cent of the total population, attracted many such adventurers to the colours, even though there was little chance they would advance beyond the rank of sergeant.[19] The roughly 90,000 Frenchmen fighting on all theatres of the war in 1636 would only have constituted 0.5 per cent of the kingdom's population (at most, for many of the soldiers were foreigners), and barely 3 or 4 per cent of adult males of their age bracket. We should not assume that soldiers adhered to the cause of the king, and still less to religious values, save in a residual way. Rather, the motivation for organized fighting derives much from the rules governing male sociability, status, and bonding, wherein each participant must demonstrate to the others that he is up to the task and can be depended upon to do his part.[20] 'The desire of glory and greatnesse', wrote Gualdo Priorato in 1640, 'reignes not onely amongst the better, but amongst the inferiour, yea the basest sort of men... the souldier fights, and looseth his life, to increase his fame amonst men; human desires not unlike to torrents, by how much they are more swolne with the waters of glory the more headlong doe they run, and oft times breake the banks or bounds of faith and promises.'[21]

How many soldiers in the opposing armies, as they gathered on the plateau east of the Ticino river on the evening of 21 June, had ever experienced a battle? A field encounter between armies was something rare in Italy; Davide Maffi counts only ten of them in the quarter-century of hostilities, and practically all of them were small-scale 'actions' that did not engage the greater part of the troops in the theatre.[22] Generals agreed only rarely to fight them. The priest Lupi in nearby Lonate wrote that 'On Sunday, the Marqués Leganés invited Monsieur Créquy to have a battle.'[23] The invasion unfolded on Créquy's initiative: he was a *fonceur*, bold to the point of recklessness. Leganés's own predicament was offering battle to

[17] Zuckerman, *Sensation Seeking*, 18–58 and 103–5.

[18] Costa, *Psicologia militare*, 127, 292–5.

[19] Rune Henriksen, 'Warriors in Combat—What Makes People Actively Fight in Combat?', *Journal of Strategic Studies*, 30 (2007), 187–223.

[20] Richard Holmes, *Acts of War*, 2nd edn (London, 2003), 285; see also Costa, *Psicologia militare*, 58–65.

[21] Galeazzo Gualdo Priorato, *The Warres, and other State-Affaires of the best part of Christendome, from 1629 to 1640* (London, 1648), unnumbered page in 'The author to the reader' (page 3).

[22] Davide Maffi, *Il baluardo della corona* (Florence, 2007), 75.

[23] Lupi, 'Storia della peste avvenuta nel borgo di Busto Arsizio, 1630 (1632–1642)', in Franco Bertolli and Umberto Colombo (eds), *La peste del 1630 a Busto Arsizio* (Busto Arsizio, 1990), 205; Lupi's actual words were even more picturesque, 'La domenica, il Marchese di Leganés, invitò Monsù Chirichi a fare giornata ...'

Fig. 3.1. Van Dyck and Paulus Pontius, Diego Felipe de Guzman, Marqués de Leganés: The Spanish commander was about 50 years old at Tornavento, the same age as his cavalry general Gherardo Gambacorta, Créquy, and Victor-Amadeus. He held his first command just two short years before. As governor of Milan, he enjoyed considerable military and diplomatic initiative.

the invaders. The senior Spanish commanders certainly understood what lay in store, for Leganés (Fig. 3.1), Spìnola, Francisco de Melo, Gambacorta, and others besides had been in the thick of the fighting at Nördlingen. Most of the German auxiliary officers and a good portion of the soldiers had too fought in at least one great battle, for they occurred more frequently north of the Alps. Leganés's veterans of the previous campaign skirmished against the French and their allies during the siege of Valenza, but those brief encounters usually entailed short rushes against small detachments. The experiences of the French religious wars of the 1620s mostly entailed skirmishing and siege work, for the Protestants were never numerous enough in one place to challenge professional troops in the open field. It would be difficult to claim that most French, Spanish, and Italian rank and file knew what they were in for.

A battle was an event too momentous to hazard without compelling reasons both political and military, and still less something to be improvised on the spur of the moment by an ambitious general. Battles give or take away whole kingdoms, wrote Raimondo Montecuccoli, author of the century's most influential handbook on the art of war; they pronounce final sentences upon great powers, they terminate wars, and they immortalize the generals. However, he warned, a commander must not hazard a battle without necessity, and only when he and his staff are persuaded that victory is likely.[24] The compelling political reason to fight, to reassure the city of Milan that he could prevent a French conquest and restore their confidence in the Catholic King, met Leganés's first condition. He also did not wish to appear to be a coward, writes Brusoni with some plausibility, for the mere suspicion of it would undermine the confidence in his abilities among his subordinates and the soldiers too, and undermine his political authority.[25] In that event, many Lombard notables would initiate on their own a political dialogue with Créquy and ambassador Hémery. Military reasons in favour of battle were more than satisfactory. The Ticino river bisected the enemy contingents and if he acted quickly, Leganés could overwhelm Créquy and annihilate half the invading force in a few hours. While he expected that the French would put up fierce resistance behind their parapet, he trusted that the courage and skill of his infantry would prevail.[26] He would have to act without delay, for his army could not remain on the parched heath very long for the lack of water and pasture for the horses. On the evening of 21 June Leganés gathered his tercio commanders for a council of war at Castano together with Francisco de Melo to discuss the situation again. Above all he wished to know if their troops had the stomach for fighting.[27] They reassured him that the men were as eager for a battle as he was.[28] This mutual confidence between the soldiers and their officers was essential to victory.[29] Before the break of dawn the officers discussed yet again their plan of attacking the French positions head-on. Upon learning of the enemy's frantic activity to rebuild the bridge across the Ticino, the senior command collectively decided that everyone was eager for a decision and that such a good opportunity was unlikely to arise again.

[24] Costa, *Psicologia militare*, 118.

[25] Girolamo Brusoni, *Delle Historie memorabili, contiene le Guerre d'Italia de' nostri tempi* (Venice, 1656), 35.

[26] Biblioteca Nacional Madrid, Ms 2367, Italia 1636, 49.

[27] Thomas M. Barker, *The Military Intellectual and Battle: Raimondo Montecuccoli and the Thirty Years War* (Albany, NY, 1975), 73. Barker translates and annotates Montecuccoli's important early text, 'Concerning Battle', 73–173.

[28] Contemporary writers like Brusoni and Gualdo Priorato claim that Leganés's troops were spoiling for a fight. The dispatch sent to Madrid after the battle also makes it clear the general had placed great confidence in the morale of his soldiers; AGS Estado 3344, letter in cipher from Abbiategrasso, 25 June 1636; in the *Relacion*, he writes that his men were ready for battle, 'con determinacion de pelear'.

[29] Rory Muir, *Tactics and the Experience of Battle in the Age of Napoleon* (New Haven and London, 1998), 6.

Most of the men passed the night sleeping on the treeless heath in battle formation, in the order in which they arrived on the field, as the textbooks recommended.[30] Only the low scrub vegetation separated the Spanish campfires from the French entrenchments, about two kilometres distant. Leganés put off his attack on the French positions on the eve of 21 June in the expectation that infantry reinforcements would reach the field by night march from Abbiategrasso before the French and Piedmontese completed their bridge. Gherardo Gambacorta appeared with his horse during the night, but the first foot detachments in his command made their entrance two hours after sunrise, at about 7 a.m. Gambacorta's reinforcements comprised only 4,000 men rather than the expected 6,000, sorely tired when it came time to form them up into battle array. These men had been drawn away from the Parman frontier a hundred kilometres distant and from the large garrisons in Alessandria and Valenza (over seventy kilometres as the crow flies, but surely further, given the river obstacles across their march path). Officers rested the men periodically en route due to the extreme heat of the day. Many more infantry were still on the road when the fighting commenced.[31]

Most of the Habsburg troops were fresh, having slept and eaten as according to the optimal conditions for battle. No source mentions the psychological preparation by the soldiers of the Catholic King, but it certainly included individual confession, then mass and communion. 'From that point on, the men need only think of facing the foe, their consciences clean.'[32] Friars attached to the companies, who prayed for the success of the Habsburg monarchy, sometimes blessed the standards.[33] Leganés and Francisco de Melo circulated through the different contingents and exhorted the men to live up to the best traditions of their nation, then posted themselves on the right flank where the battle would begin.[34] This appeal to tribalism revealed a good understanding of the Spanish imperial system, articulated through ethnic diversity.[35] The men's spirits were already buoyed by a clear understanding of what their commander was asking them: to throw themselves against an outnumbered enemy cowering behind entrenchments and to overwhelm them before help could be brought from across the river. If they succeeded, the enemy's baggage and their property were theirs! This clarity and simplicity of their objective was likely to have constituted a moral advantage.[36] Leganés encouraged them to believe that their future lay in their hands, that their past successes would be repeated on this day.

Leganés deployed his army in two sections, with the vanguard on the heath just west of Vanzaghello. This comprised of the German infantry of Gil de Haes, the

---

[30] Barker, *Military Intellectual and Battle*, 175.

[31] *Relacion del combate del exercito de su magestad con los de Francia y Saboya, en 22 de Iunio 1636* (Madrid, 1636).

[32] Barker, *Military Intellectual and Battle*, 128.

[33] Lorraine White, 'The Experience of Spain's Early Modern Soldiers: Combat, Welfare and Violence', *War in History*, 9 (2002), 1–38.

[34] Giovanni Francesco Fossati, *Memorie historiche delle guerre d'Italia del secolo presente* (Milan, 1640), 168.

[35] John Keegan, *A History of Warfare* (New York, 1993), p. xv.

[36] Dorothée Malfoy-Noël, *L'épreuve de la bataille (1700–1714)* (Montpellier, 2007), 44.

Neapolitan horse newly arrived in the duchy, the tercio of Lombardy under Don Martin d'Aragon (a Spanish formation), and the large German infantry regiment of Prince Borso d'Este, the uncle of the Duke of Modena and a veteran of the fighting north of the Alps. Leganés placed them all under the direction of sergeant-major Don Antonio Arias Sotelo, acting commander of the Spanish tercio of Naples. The larger component formed up north-west of Castano Primo, where Leganés pitched his headquarters tent, although the exact identity of all its components is unclear. Here figured two Spanish tercios of perhaps smaller dimensions, belonging to the Marqués de Mortara and the Marqués de Caracena, two Neapolitan tercios under Filippo Spìnola and Lucio Boccapianola, a smallish tercio of Tuscan allies under Camillo del Monte, another German infantry regiment under Erasmus Lener, and seven large German 'free companies' not formally incorporated into a regiment. A twelfth regimental formation of dragoons under Juan Lope Giron, which customarily fought on foot as highly mobile musketeers, counted nine captains and 600 troopers reflecting no single national origin.

Lacking room for a cavalry action, he arrayed most of the horse behind the foot, in order to remove any possibility of flight from the latter.[37] He understood that, despite the high morale of his troops, they must be forced to fight and deprived of the hope and means of drifting away from the firing line.[38] Following military usage on both sides, Leganés posted the army surgeons and barbers to attend to the wounded several hundred metres to the rear by the church of San Giovanni in Campagna.[39] Commanders almost always reserved churches for non-combatants, like modern Red Cross tents, and junior officers designated bearers in each company to assist the wounded off the field.[40] The Spanish general also placed one battery of cannon, given variously as four or five pieces, atop the embankment of the Panperduto canal as it veered eastward to the left of his position. These were not all the cannon at Leganés's disposal, and one source affirms that he readied a great battery of eighteen limbered guns, prepared to move forward when the opportunity presented itself. If Gualdo Priorato's numbers for the Spanish army are roughly accurate, 4,000 or 5,000 militia auxiliaries drawn from the district reluctantly formed up nearby to assist the attack. They would be prone to bolting if professional soldiers attacked them, and their panic was liable to shake even veteran soldiers.[41] Filippo Spìnola formed the infantry into nine large formations, called squadrons, five in the front line and four others in reserve.[42] A crude calculation of the size of Leganés's formations would simply divide the 10,000 infantry

---

[37] Costa, *Psicologia militare*, 122, from Montecuccoli.

[38] Barker, *Military Intellectual and Battle*, 82.

[39] GianDomenico Oltrona Visconti, *La battaglia di Tornavento* (Gallarate, 1970), 121; likewise at Fontaneto, where Souvigny and other casualties were carried into a church serving as a makeshift hospital close by the besieged village, *Memoires du Comte de Souvigny, lieutenant-général des armées du roi*, ed. Ludovic de Contenson (Paris, 1906), i. 306–7.

[40] Cristina Borreguero Beltràn, 'El coste humano de la guerra: mortandad, enfermedad y deserciòn en los ejercitos de la Epoca Moderna', in Fidel Gomez Ochoa and Daniel Macias Fernandez (eds), *El combatiente a lo largo de la historia: Imaginario, percepciòn, representaciòn* (Santander, 2012), 57–82.

[41] Galeazzo Gualdo Priorato, *Il guerriero prudente e politico*, ed. A. Tamborra (Naples, 2002; 1st publ. 1640), 81.

[42] Fossati, *Memorie historiche*, 168.

by nine, at just over a thousand men apiece. No source designates the nomenclature of each of these, but the muster of the field army in late May 1636 identified eleven tercios or regiments of unequal size.[43] The dimension of each of these large formations at Tornavento was never established. Companies in garrison in May appear to have joined their tercio for the battle in June.[44]

Infantry tactics evolved rapidly over the first twenty years of the Thirty Years' War. At the battle of White Mountain in 1620, the Catholic commanders organized contingents numbering over 20,000 foot into merely five lumbering formations of musket and pike.[45] These thick formations were particular to the Spaniards after 1630, and a traditional Anglo-Saxon historiography equating the Dutch and Swedish linear order with modernity long considered the former to be outmoded. By the time of Nördlingen, the Spanish squadrons numbering approximately 1,000 men apiece stood sixteen deep against the 'Swedes', who deployed only six or eight men deep.[46] More careful scholarship notes that Spanish armies usually prevailed against their enemies, resisting the Protestant onslaught at Nördlingen by their tight cohesion. Montecuccoli considered the large Spanish formations to be one of the few viable battlefield deployments, for large bodies of soldiers gave greater psychological assurance to the green troops standing in them. Moreover, they were difficult to outflank and almost impossible to break open.[47] Nobody mentions the depth of the Spanish formations at Tornavento, but if the pikemen deployed around sixteen men deep, only the first five ranks had immediate contact with the enemy.[48] Sergeant-majors placed the musketeers along the outer edges of the pike and then deployed them flexibly when they closed with the enemy. This separation of pike and shot entailed splitting up the individual companies. Slotting men into position was anything but a haphazard process. From the sergeant-major of battle at army level, down to the sergeants in each company, officers and non-coms drew up the foot. Sergeants initially gave a musket or a pike to a recruit according to their size and ability. In battle they assigned each man a place in the formation, towards the front or the rear according to their strength and completeness of their body armour. They took care to insert the best soldiers into corner positions. Corporals stood at the rear of each file in order to prevent the men from hanging back, and to dress the files and control the men in front. Sergeants also needed to leaven the inexperienced or untrustworthy men with more dependable soldiers standing next to them. Other positions, especially the dangerous ones,

[43] Estado 3344/117.

[44] Brusoni, *Delle Historie memorabili*, 34; Ottaviano Sauli's company in Valenza (May) fought at Tornavento.

[45] Olivier Chaline, *La bataille de la Montagne Blanche (8 novembre 1620): Un mystique chez les guerriers* (Paris, 1999), 114.

[46] Peter Engerisser and Pavel Hrnčirik, *Nördlingen 1634: Die Schlacht bei Nördlingen. Wendepunkt des Dreissigjahringen Kriegs* (Weissenstadt, 2009), 186–95; see also Giovanni Cerino Badone's thesis, 'Le seconde guerre d'Italia (1589–1659)', Università degli Studi del Piemonte Orientale, 2011, 204.

[47] Barker, *Military Intellectual and Battle*, 88–90; see also Clifford J. Rogers, 'Tactics and the Face of Battle', in F. Tallett and D. J. B. Trim (eds), *European Warfare, 1350–1750* (Cambridge, 2010), 203–35.

[48] Vladimir Brnardic, *Imperial Armies of the Thirty Years' War: Infantry and Artillery* (Oxford, 2009), 22.

were determined by drawing lots.[49] Soldiers tempted fate with cards and dice on a daily basis: their willingness to accept the outcome of chance or destiny was proof of their good character. Sergeants walked about to fix the formation and maintained this managerial function even in dire situations.

The principal tactical problem of the sixteenth and seventeenth centuries was to combine the pike with the shot (the musketeers) to the greatest advantage. All armies practised drill that multiplied the possible formations of musket and pike, following the lead of the Dutch Prince of Orange-Nassau in the late sixteenth century. Muskets were really effective at only 50 or 60 metres from their target, and required a complex procedure of reloading in dozens of steps that limited their rate of fire to one shot every two minutes. Gualdo Priorato claims that well-trained soldiers could reduce this complex procedure to six sequences and accelerate the rate of fire in the heat of battle. The matchlock musket was a cumbersome weapon weighing between 7 and 10 kg, too heavy to aim without resting it on a forked stick. Soldiers, while reloading, had to hold the musket, its support, and a lit wick used to detonate the powder charge. Each musketeer was festooned with a dozen measured charges of powder and shot hanging from his bandolier: he risked setting himself alight if he made a false movement with his wick lit at both ends (to enable him to relight it if one end extinguished). In order to fight effectively, soldiers needed to maintain their spacing, calculated in feet and paces (five feet, in one Neapolitan text, but the precise measurement, like the foot itself, varied from one place to another).[50] Normally, musketeers in an infantry battalion stood 1 metre from shoulder to shoulder, and about 2 metres from front to back.[51] Drill sergeants and corporals spaced the musketeers to enable them to function effectively.[52] Deep formations did not allow the rearward men much view of the enemy. The solution to this problem was the counter-march, wherein a line of musketeers would step forward just ahead of the protective pikes to release a volley, and then retire behind the formation to reload while the line behind them stepped forward with a loaded weapon to do the same. A formation ten soldiers deep could therefore deliver its fire at a rate of one salvo every ten seconds. Only 10 per cent of the musketeers fired at a time, however. Pikemen standing a metre apart allowed the musketeers to scurry through their files into a hollow space in the centre or rear of the battalion to reload. While textbooks emphasized the necessity of musketeers operating closely in conjunction with the pike, other detachments, or 'sleeves' of marksmen, deployed separately from them wherever they did not fear enemy cavalry. This would emerge time and again in the accounts of the fighting at Tornavento.

The pikemen, whose weapon was about 5 metres long, fulfilled two functions in a pitched battle. They protected the shot from enemy cavalry, for musketeers

---

[49] Francisco de Valdés, *The Sergeant Maior: A Dialogue of the Office of a Sergeant Maior* (London, 1590), 10–11.

[50] Domenico Marincola, *Trattato dell'Ordinanze di squadroni, et altre cose appartenenti al soldato in questa materia* (Naples, 1637), 58.

[51] Sieur du Praissac, *Discours et questions militaires,* last edn (Paris, 1638), 225.

[52] Julio Albi de la Cuesta, *De Pavia a Rocroi: Los tercios de infanteria española en los siglos XVI y XVII* (Madrid, 1999), 228; on tactical instruction, Marincola, *Trattato dell'Ordinanze,* 89.

would be unable to release more than a single inaccurate volley before the riders put them into headlong flight. When threatened by cavalry, the musketeers withdrew into the midst of a pike formation, which would close up ranks to present a dense and impenetrable array of steel points. Horses could not be trained to impale themselves on these polearms, which the soldiers held diagonally, planting the butt end of the weapon in the earth and holding it fast with their foot. Against infantry, the pikemen would stand further apart, lift their weapons horizontally and march towards the enemy to come 'point to point' in a grand melee. Musketeers drew their swords and joined them in a hand-to-hand struggle at close quarters until one of the two formations gave way.[53] The pikeman still wore a heavy breastplate, a backplate, a gorget (to protect the throat), and a steel helmet. Below the waist, overlapping plates called tassets covered their crotch and thighs.[54] Up near the front and centre of the pike in each formation stood the ensign, typically a young, well-armoured nobleman in visible attire, with a helmet decorated with bright plumes. His function was to hold the banner that served as the unit's rallying point amidst the smoke and confusion of battle.[55] He wielded only a sword as defence against the enemy at close quarters. The ensign could count on the presence nearby of friends and followers who would seize the banner should he ever become a casualty himself. Not far away were the drummers, sometimes mere lads, entrusted with beating the orders to the men, most of whom would not be within earshot of the colonel.

Rather than form a continuous line of soldiers opposite to the enemy, these squadrons constituted rectangular masses in a chequerboard array, close enough to offer fire support to others on their flanks. The combination of easy access to published drillbooks and the usual lack of detail on tactical formations in battlefield accounts has led historians to exaggerate the cohesion of these battalions and the discipline of their fire.[56] We have often relied on battle paintings to understand the deployment of formations, sometimes forgetting that these visual or iconographical documents obeyed several distorting conventions. King Philip IV com-

---

[53] William P. Guthrie, *The Later Thirty Years War: From the Battle of Wittstock to the Treaty of Westphalia* (Westport, CT, and London, 2003), 8–9.

[54] On the persistence of armour among the pikemen, who were destined to close with the enemy, see Brnardic, *Imperial Armies: Infantry*, 33; see also David Blackmore, *Arms and Armour of the English Civil Wars* (London, 1990), 61–3.

[55] Biblioteca Estense Modena, Ms Misc. Estense Ital. 635, Avvertimenti militari…composto per il Colonello Bartolomeo Pelliciari di Modena, fo. 57ʳ; for the emplacement of the ensign and his drummers, Marincola, *Trattato dell'Ordinanze*, 37.

[56] Brent Nosworthy discusses this problem in an earlier publication, but concludes that most of the tactical systems had their basis in the limitations of the weapons available. He concludes that they represented optimal solutions. Brent Nosworthy, *The Anatomy of Victory: Battle Tactics 1689–1763* (New York, 1990), pp. xii–xv; see also David Parrott, *Richelieu's Army: War, Government and Society in France, 1624–1642* (Cambridge and New York, 2001), 32–6. Parrott's great virtue is to show that reputedly 'outmoded' systems like the Spanish one that relied more on élan than on firepower were still routinely successful in the 1630s. Mass-market publications too reliant on drillbooks (which are now widely available online) include Keith Roberts, *Pike and Shot Tactics 1590–1660* (Oxford, 2010); and Christer Jörgensen, Michael F. Pavkovic, Rob S. Price, Frederick C. Schneid, and Chris L. Scott, *Fighting Techniques of the Early Modern World, AD 1500–AD 1763: Equipment, Combat Skills and Tactics* (New York, 2005).

missioned Pieter Snayers to commemorate a number of triumphal sieges and battles. He and other Flemish painters in the wake of Breughel patiently painted thousands of little figures in ways we have mistaken for photographic realism. These battle painters, who included Thomas Meulener and Sebastian Vrancx, rarely left their workshops and were not themselves witnesses to the events they depicted. If we were to take as an example Snayers's depiction of the battle of Honnecourt, we can make an accurate count of the men arrayed in each battalion in the middle ground, ten deep and seventeen wide, totalling about one-sixth the size of a typical tercio in full array. In a more exact reconstruction of a Spanish squadron, (remembering that formation depths were not set in stone and were sometimes thinner), sixteen deep would require about seventy men across, accentuating its rectangular shape. The deep Spanish tercio deployment would be close to 150 metres in breadth, six times its depth. Why would such meticulous artists commit such distortions? We should remember that such paintings immortalized the generals and their principal subordinates, who would be certain to scrutinize the image in search of their own emplacement. Above all, the patron required the artist to fit *everybody who counted* into the canvas, which required bunching the men up to conserve space. This convention exaggerates the compactness of the tercio formation. The paintings are rather better at depicting some of the tactics, particularly the 'sleeves' of musketeers advancing ahead of the pike to soften up the enemy. To this we will return.[57]

Consternation broke out in the French camp when they discovered the Catholic King's army in battle array first thing in the morning, for they were not ready! Victor-Amadeus and Créquy were hoping that a general battle would eventually take place, but they did not think that Leganés would oblige them, even though the Duke of Savoy reportedly received information to that effect the night before from a spy in the Spanish camp.[58] Créquy instructed the sergeant-majors to form up the men into battalions as quickly as possible. A contemporary stressed just how important it was for a general to intuit the likelihood that his adversary was likely to attack, given his understanding of the enemy's numerical strength and troop quality. Not being ready on the morning of 22 June demonstrated that Créquy had misjudged the situation.[59] This hasty defensive deployment was an added stress for the French, for they felt that attack was the natural posture more befitting their ardour.[60] Créquy sent word of his peril to Victor-Amadeus, who crossed the river to inspect the camp after giving orders for troops to assemble the men on his side of the river (Fig. 3.2). Deployment often took hours to effect, unfortunately, for the foraging parties would have to be recalled. The infantry retrieved its armour packed away in the baggage train, then the men fastened it to themselves and to each other by means of buckles, clasps, hooks, and straps. Following that, the companies lined up in order to cross the bridge and reform on

---

[57] For the discerning interpretation of Snayers's iconography by military historians, see Engerisser and Hrnčirik, *Nördlingen 1634*, 186–95.

[58] ASFi Mediceo Principato 3258, fo. 251.

[59] Paul Azan, *Un tacticien du XVIIe siècle* (Paris, 1904), 62.

[60] Ibid. 68; D'Aurignac repeats the commonplace that 'les Français sont faits pour l'attaque'.

Fig. 3.2. Ticino river and canal entrance. The river was about 200 metres wide at the entrance to the *naviglio*, too deep for soldiers to wade across with their weapons and armour. The low ground could not be fortified, due to the stones and loose soil.

the other side without losing any time. Several accounts claim that the engineers completed the bridge at daybreak. If correct, Créquy and Victor-Amadeus might have assumed that Leganés would surely not attack.[61] If so, they had both underestimated their opponent.[62]

As a commander, Victor-Amadeus was an unknown quantity; he displayed some ability in a war of mobility and harassment in the conflicts his father waged against Spain in Piedmont and the Monferrato. The House of Savoy usually waged war not with the aim of seeking a decisive battle, and still less achieving victory through long attrition, but rather through short siege and skirmish sought to achieve a better peace as quickly as possible.[63] Créquy served at Tornavento with his son François, comte de Sault, who carried the mantle of dynastic expectations

---

[61] Victor-Amadeus penned a number of letters describing in detail the events of that day, but they were private missives appended to official dispatches and so copies were not bound into the official records for the archives. However, Victor-Amadeus appears to have been the principal author of the official (self-censored) version of the battle carried to Paris and published in the *Gazette*. See ASTo Materie politiche interne: Lettere del duca Vittorio Amedeo, vol. 56, 10 July 1636, letter to his brother the cardinal Maurizio.

[62] BNF Ms Fr 16929, *Relation de M. d'Esmery de ses negociations en Piedmont en 1635 etc.*, fo. 569.

[63] Salvatore Foa, *Vittorio Amedeo I (1587–1637)* (Turin, 1930), 44 and 72; Claudio De Consoli, *Al soldo del duca: L'amministrazione delle armate sabaude (1560–1630)* (Turin, 1999), 200.

after another son, Charles, had died at the siege of Chambéry in 1630. Créquy's son-in-law Scipion de Grimoard de Beauvoir, comte de Roure, commanded another of the battalions. This member of the Languedoc warrior nobility belonged to the entourage of Prince Gaston, brother of Louis XIII and heir to the throne.[64] At the head of still another of Créquy's regiments was his young nephew Maximilien François de Béthune, Prince d'Henrichemont, sovereign prince of the little fief of Boisbelle in Berry. Henrichemont was the Calvinist grandson of Henri IV's great minister and comrade-in-arms the duc de Sully.[65] Créquy was ably seconded by another scion of the great court nobility twenty years his junior, César de Choiseul Du Plessis-Praslin, astute diplomat in Italy and future field marshal.[66] Both Créquy and Du Plessis-Praslin were trusted clients, or *créatures*, of the cardinal minister Richelieu. Alongside them rode another future field marshal from Poitou, Philippe de Clérambault, comte de Palluau (1606–65). Warfare for all these men was a way of life since their early years, but it was also the instrument of honour and wealth in the rarefied and competitive atmosphere of the French court in Paris. Battle was an opportunity to seize in order to enhance their reputation, so the occasion would not find them wanting.[67]

Créquy too was confident that his troops would perform well in a confrontation with the enemy, for many of his contingents and a fair portion of the soldiers had fought the Spaniards the year before, not in open battle, but in the gruelling close-quarters skirmishing at the siege of Valenza.[68] There the French infantry proved to be technically outclassed by their Spanish opposite numbers, but they were not afraid to fight. However, since desertion corroded such a large proportion of the complement it is difficult to determine just how many soldiers in 1636 had combat experience of any kind. Créquy's own regiment de Sault had belonged to his father-in-law the maréchal de Lesdiguières, and served throughout the later Wars of Religion. The Lyonnais regiment formed by the marquis de Villeroy back in 1616, and whose command was reserved for members of that lineage, had been 'reformed' or scaled back on several occasions. Several of Créquy's regiments had been bloodied in sieges and actions in Lorraine and Germany or at Valenza (Le Ferron, Florainville, La Tour, Bonne, Maugeron). About half of the regiments were new, however, having been raised in the previous six months (Henrichemont, Montclar, Roure, Roquefeuil, Forez, Marolles, Maillane).[69] David Parrott argues that French regiments were notoriously unstable due to excessive state control over

[64] Louis Moreri, *Le Grand dictionnaire historique* (Amsterdam, 1740), iv. 373.

[65] <http://heraldique-europeenne.org>; <http://gw1.geneanet.org>.

[66] *Memoires du Maréchal Du Plessis*, in Michaud and Poujoulat (eds), *Memoires pour servir à l'histoire de France depuis le XIIIe siècle jusqu'à la fin du XVIIIe siècle* (Paris, 1838), vii. 360.

[67] Brian Sandberg, *Warrior Pursuits: Noble Culture and Civil Conflict in Early Modern France* (Baltimore, 2010), 168–81.

[68] Brusoni refers to the French army as 'una forza disciplinata, e non un collettizio di gente nuova e inesperta'. This is probably true for a portion of the army at least, but desertion the previous year and over the winter had been considerable. Brusoni, *Delle Historie memorabili*, 34.

[69] Louis Susane, *Histoire de l'Ancienne infanterie française* (Paris, 1852), iv; and, by the same author, *Histoire de l'Infanterie française* (Paris, 1876), iii.

the officers, combined with inadequate financing.[70] This was not specific to France, however: Neapolitan and Lombard regiments were quickly raised and almost as quickly reformed, unlike the elite Spanish tercios that formed the backbone of Habsburg power.

Not having a recently acquired store of battlefield experience to draw upon, French and Savoyard regiments followed Dutch and Swedish methods, with their smaller, more linear formations of 600 men, called battalions. French regiments were smaller than the Spanish tercios, and the companies that comprised them often consisted of only fifty or sixty men, and even fewer as the campaign wore on.[71] The *Gazette* account implies that French battalions were smaller than the Spanish ones; Créquy's regiments of Peyregourde, Florinville, Sault, Aiguebonne, Henrichemont, Lyonnais, de Bonne, Roure, and Roquefeuil totalled *c.*6,000 foot, averaging about 650 men each.[72] This is a fictional mean, of course, for commanders routinely amalgamated understrength regiments until they totalled 500 or 600 men.

Créquy spread his units out behind the parapet, although no source tells us about the depth of his formations. We do not know if he arranged them ten deep (common in 1630) or six deep (the formation of the innovative French guard regiment in 1638) or some other figure in between.[73] A common depth for the German armies of the period was eight men, so that a battalion of 650 men would present a front of 80 soldiers, spaced at least 1 metre apart from shoulder to shoulder, which, added to the width of each man, would have extended about 133 metres total.[74] Commanders often adapted the depth to the task at hand: here it was necessary to deploy the foot behind the full extent of the entrenchments, while holding others back as a reserve.[75] Créquy could have consulted the *maréchal de bataille* on the best formation for the occasion. Placing individual soldiers into a battlefield formation was a technical skill overseen by the *sergent-major général*, the sieur de Castelan. The ensigns planted their standards in the unit's allotted location, and soldiers lined up around them. While each company and battalion put itself in order, the regimental sergeants-major and other senior officers trotted about on horseback armed with a baton, their own special weapon, with which to point and give instructions or else to bludgeon wayward soldiers reluctant to take their allotted places.[76]

The protective breastwork obscured the infantry's view of the enemy, especially given that men were typically 15 centimetres shorter than today. The textbook instructed the musketeers to march up to the firing step row by row, fire on com-

---

[70] David Parrott, *The Business of War* (Cambridge and New York, 2012), 265–9.

[71] Parrott, *Richelieu's Army*, 32–52.

[72] *Gazette de France*, 99 (1636): *La sanglante deffaite des Espagnols dans le Milannez*, 405–12.

[73] Parrott, *Richelieu's Army*, 49–52; see also John A. Lynn, *Giant of the 'Grand Siècle': The French Army 1610–1715* (Cambridge and New York, 1997), 477; the manual of the very experienced Count Galeazzo Gualdo Priorato specifies a depth of eight soldiers for the musketeers, *Il Maneggio dell'armi moderno* (Vicenza, 1642), 84.

[74] Gualdo Priorato, *Il Maneggio dell'armi moderno*, 8.

[75] Azan, *Un tacticien*, 63.

[76] D Valdés, *The sergeant maior*, fos. 10–23; Sieur de Lostelneau, *Le mareschal de bataille* (Paris, 1647), 252.

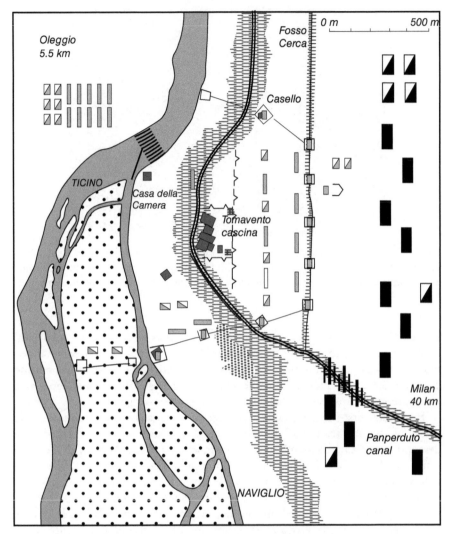

Map 5. Positions at Tornavento, morning 22 June.

mand, and then return to the rear to reload. About 2 metres behind the firing step, officers assembled the pikemen, ready to repel anyone who tried to clamber over the earthwork. Other parties of pikemen stood interspersed with cavalry just to the rear in order to rush to wherever the enemy succeeded in obtaining a toehold.[77] Not all the infantry deployed behind the parapet, since it was important to have reserves in case the forward line collapsed under the weight of the attack. Behind the foot Créquy posted his cavalry. Some troopers sheltered under the cover of the

---

[77] Gualdo Priorato, *Il maneggio delle armi*, 121; a similar disposition figures in the manual of Montecuccoli, *Memoires de Montecuculi, généralissime des troupes de l'Empereur* (Amsterdam, 1752), 186.

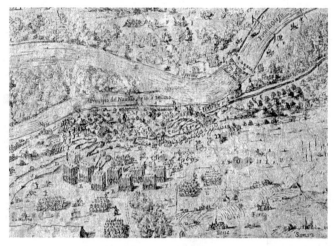

Fig. 3.3. Anonymous, Battle of Tornavento 1636. This conventional imagery depicts nine Habsburg formations in the lower left field, with Habsburg cavalry to their right. The French entrenchments and the troops manning them immediately above are almost invisible.

hedges, vines, and mulberry trees close by the *cascina* of Tornavento, while still others sat in their saddles waiting for orders.[78] A large group of 600 'commanded musketeers' detached from their regiments lurked patiently in a wood just outside Tornavento hamlet, probably on the slope facing west. They would serve as a hidden reserve corps ready to launch a surprise counter-attack.[79]

The several first-hand accounts and those of historians writing soon after the events of the day are remarkably concordant, although not very detailed. The description of the battle itself is much more fragmentary. Let's begin with the landscape on which it was fought. The engraving published subsequent to the battle reduces the space depicting the battle's fulcrum to a few square centimetres, and the topography that it depicts is not exempt from distortions (Fig. 3.3).[80] No archaeologist has ever worked on the site, to locate musket balls and horseshoe fragments, which might give a rough estimation of the spread and density of the fire and the deployment of horse.[81] The discovery of the emplacement of the Fossa della Cerca makes it easier to situate the perimeter of the French entrenchments, and therefore to calculate their circumference. All our accounts agree on a general chronology of the battle, but these are clearer for the beginning of the combat than for what came after. This falls within the norm for battle accounts, according to

[78] *Gazette de France*, 99 (1636), 407.

[79] Montecuccoli describes the usefulness of these impromptu detachments, Barker, *Military Intellectual and Battle*, 154.

[80] These warnings come from Malcolm Wanklyn, *Decisive Battles of the English Civil Wars: Myth and Reality* (Barnsley, 2006), 18–30.

[81] For an example of what could be done on this site with metal detectors, see James Bonsall, 'The Study of Small Finds at the 1644 Bbattle of Cheriton', *Journal of Conflict Archaeology* (2007), 29–52.

Malcolm Wanklyn, writing about the English Civil War where these are generally plentiful. As he reminds us, 'we do not have all the pieces and those we have are not necessarily true representations'. The historian of battle usually possesses only a number of partial and conflicting narratives.[82]

The three phases of the battle emerge not so much from the Spanish sources, as from the French ones. Much must be left to conjecture due to the spotty nature of the sources. In some instances (the losses of dead and wounded men, for example) conflicting partisan accounts cannot be reconciled. But our sources fortunately consist of several independent accounts, while the narratives published not long after the battle are remarkably even-handed. That of Count Galeazzo Gualdo Priorato meets criteria of impartiality that are admirable in any era. Girolamo Brusoni's description of the battle contains details present neither in the French nor in Spanish official records, but local manuscript records verify them. Both historians spoke with eyewitnesses or participants of the event. Where the sources let us down, I will try to signal the inconsistencies or leave the problem unresolved. Existing technologies, that is, the armament and tactics as they existed in 1636, channelled the manner of waging war. Raimondo Montecuccoli's influential manual on combat, written just two or three short years after the event at Tornavento, suggests that both Leganés and the resourceful Créquy were fighting 'by the book'. From his writings we might patch up some of the documentary lapses with working hypotheses that Wanklyn calls 'inherent military probability'.

THE SPANISH ONSLAUGHT

At 8.00 a.m. French time, 11.00 Italian time, anxious not to lose more time waiting for the rest of Gambacorta's infantry to arrive, Leganés gave the order to advance the portion of his army on the right (north) flank. Leganés, Filippo Spìnola, and the ambassador de Melo posted themselves up front on horseback and led the men into battle until they came within musket range (Fig. 3.4). The Madrid account emphasizes that Spanish troops on the right wing (the tercio of Naples) held the place of honour, while the German veterans of Borso d'Este marched just behind them on the right, and Neapolitan cavalry advanced nearby on their flank.[83] (The colonel of the Florentine tercio, Camillo del Monte, recorded the position of each of the attacking corps as well as the French deployment in a sketch for the Grand Duke of Tuscany, but it was separated from his written description of the battle and appears impossible to locate.[84]) Leganés intended to advance with an *esquadron* of two or three regiments combined at the part of the

---

[82] Wanklyn, *Decisive Battles*, 18–30.

[83] BNM Ms 2367 Italia 1636, Campaña de Italia del año de 1636, 49; for the tradition of posting the best troops on the right flank, which was practised by other armies too, Fernando Gonzalez de Leon, *The Road to Rocroi* (Boston and Leiden, 2009), 103. The Bologna manuscript indicates the position of each unit in this vanguard.

[84] ASFi Mediceo Principato 3181, fo. 415, letter from Camillo del Monte, 24 June 1636. I wish to thank the director of the Florentine Archivio di Stato, dott.ssa Carla Zarrilli for undertaking a search for this sketch.

Fig. 3.4. Stefano della Bella, The melee *c*.1630. The image renders effectively the confusion of a large-scale cavalry engagement, where troopers are protected by their heavy armour, often bulletproof to pistols except at very close range. Musketeers and pikemen stand close by.

line he wished to overwhelm, using them like the 'brigades' of three battalions employed by the late king of Sweden.[85] Battlefield convention conferred on units posted on the right flank the 'place of honour' and the privilege of initiating battle, and officers and soldiers in elite regiments set much store by its observance. But one can posit alongside an ideological motivation a sound practical one. By attacking only one sector Leganés hoped to pierce the French entrenchments and to roll back their army without engaging too many units of his own in an exchange of fire which would incur needless casualties. 'The first soldiers must be the oldest and the best, and not thrust back on the second line. No better tactic has been invented than to place the bravest troops wherever it is the habit to commence the battle,' wrote Montecuccoli, apparently echoing standard procedure.[86] This ponderous infantry advance committed 2,000 or 3,000 infantry and some cavalry, but I am not certain that they were engaged simultaneously. Accounts generally mention two tercios engaged at a time, implying that one withdrew to clean its muskets while the other advanced to keep the pressure up on the targeted segment of the enemy line. That way they competed with each other for the glory of their nation and bragging rights for their officers.[87]

The great Garganasta heath that separated the opposing armies, covered in grass only a few inches high, was perfect country for a cavalry fight, unlike most of Northern Italy, where hedges and vines sectioned the landscape into an infinite number of small parcels resembling garden plots. Créquy therefore deployed a

[85] Roberts, *Pike and Shot Tactics*, 51–5; at Rocroi in 1643, the Spanish infantry tercios consisted of about 1,000 men apiece. Laurent Henninger, *Rocroi 1643* (Paris, 1993), 45; on the 'esquadron', see Cerino Badone, *Le seconde guerre*, 202–3. Badone's discussion of these more evolved Spanish tactics is drawn from the work of Engerisser and Hrnčiřik, *Nördlingen 1634*, 185–94.

[86] Barker, *Military Intellectual and Battle*, 120; to keep most troops out of range, 143.

[87] Ibid. 85.

detachment of 300 French horse *outside* the defensive works under the sieur de Boissac. It advanced against this great body at a trot, led personally at the outset by Du Plessis-Praslin and the comte de Palluau.[88] A cavalry charge was a deliberate movement too, performed at speeds not greater than ten kilometres an hour, and stopping close enough to the great host in order to deliver pistol and carbine fire.[89] No text mentions whether or not they opposed the foot with the caracole tactic, in which the front row of cavaliers wheeled about after firing, galloped to the rear of their formation (about six troopers deep) to reload, while the rows behind them trotted forward similarly each in turn. Military writers commonly described this cavalry version of the counter-march as ineffectual if the aim was to break and pursue an opposing formation.[90] Here this tactic sought not to destroy the battalions by putting them to flight (which would have been impossible to do to such resolute infantry) but to delay them. Every minute counted!

Créquy supported this cavalry with an unspecified number of musketeers sheltering behind some earthworks or sconces placed just ahead of the defensive perimeter. By this common delaying tactic he intended to disrupt the momentum of the infantry assault.[91] He then ordered the entire Lyonnais regiment of 600 men out of its earthworks to reinforce this forward detachment, hoping no doubt that they would be able to take the advancing enemy in enfilading fire and still support the cavalry.[92] This brought them into range of the Spanish musketry, but even worse, of the enfilading artillery fire from the Spanish battery south of them, 'avantageusement planté'. Cannon fire followed the principle of bowling, in which the gunners sought the angle by which they could knock down the greatest number of 'pins'. The long rows of men directly in front of them constituted an irresistible target. Artillery pieces could fire only six or seven times an hour so as not to overheat the barrels and therefore this cannonade could only have thrown projectiles into the force at a rate of one every two minutes, and not all of them would have struck someone. Unlike a musket ball, which at longer range armour plate deflects, a cannonball's great momentum sweeps away all in its path, with gruesome effects on the unfortunate horses and men it encounters. People struck by the cannonballs themselves were probably not very numerous, but the impact on morale was multiplied by everyone who witnessed it. The principal effect of the bombardment was to psychologically 'soften up' the men, helplessly exposed to the projectiles arriving on their flank.[93] Everything about the cannon struck fear in the men it targeted; the burst of flame, the thunder of the detonation, and the fearsome power of the balls, wrote a technical expert for the Duke of Parma.[94]

[88] *Relation de la victoire obtenue en Italie par l'armée du Roy* (Lyon, 1636), accessed from <http://rohanturenne.blogspot.com/2009/09/french-account-of-battle-of-Tornavento.html>.

[89] Brusoni, *Delle Historie memorabili*, 36; for the best available depiction of cavalry tactics, see Frederic Chauviré, *Histoire de la cavalerie* (Paris, 2013), 81–5.

[90] Barker, *Military Intellectual and Battle*, 110; Montecuccoli criticizes Gambacorta in particular for useless caracole charges.

[91] *Memoires de Montecuculi*, 183.

[92] *Relation de la victoire obtenue en Italie par l'armée du Roy* (Lyon, 1636).   [93] Ibid.

[94] Marcello Manacci, *Compendio d'Instruttioni per gli bombardieri* (Parma, 1640). My heartfelt gratitude to Mario Zannoni, who brought my attention to this source.

The French foot exposed on the open plain, required to maintain their formation, could do nothing to protect themselves. Then they were set upon by the 'sleeves' of Spanish musketeers advancing ahead of their pike support, which constituted the 'body' of the formation.

The French horse, similarly 'extrêmement incommodée' by the cannon fire, waited for Gambacorta's cavalry to close in on them. This latter force advanced at a trot in a great body without keeping ranks, each trooper brandishing his pistol. Early in the Thirty Years' War, it was common for two bodies of cavalry to stop and exchange fire at about 30 metres' distance, before one side approached to mix with their adversary.[95] Cavalry engagements were brief, frantic actions where horsemen advanced without breaking into a gallop into each other's ranks from opposing directions. There was no 'shock' of horses and riders, if indeed the two bodies came within reach at all: rather, cavaliers tried to push their way into gaps in the enemy array and to break open their formation. The more 'porous' formation would quickly be dominated and seek to disperse and reform. In the tight spaces men fired pistols against their adversaries at close range, drew their sabres, and then slashed any opponent within reach, if they were able to retain their sang-froid to control their excited mount and to use their weapons effectively. Only a few minutes would elapse before buglers sounded the order to disengage and reform. Then a second line repeated the process until one of the formations decided to withdraw.[96] It was common enough for one of the formations, usually the Spanish, to refuse a melee and to withdraw before contact. No source describes the choreography of the engagement outside the trenches in detail, but under the weight of the cannon fire, the musketry, and the cavalry charges, the Lyonnais regiment began to disintegrate (probably from the rear).[97] The shaken foot hurried back into the shelter of the line of entrenchments behind them, and the horse followed soon after.

Sotelo's Spanish infantry advanced next on the principal earthwork, with the musketeers and the pikemen operating as separate bodies taking turns to accomplish their complementary tasks. Attacking foot could advance to the beat of the drums at the rate of close to 1 metre per second. Nevertheless it was imperative that they should not arrive in dispersed order across the heath. Tacticians recommended halting the battalions every 50 metres in order to dress the lines and files anew.[98] Once they were at the edge of the 'killing zone' less than 100 metres from the breastworks, the officers ordered the drummers to beat the attack and sounded the

---

[95] Barker, *Military Intellectual and Battle*, 147.

[96] Gavin Robinson, 'Equine Battering Rams? A Reassessment of Cavalry Charges in the English Civil War', *Journal of Military History*, 75 (2011), 719–31; see also Frédéric Chauviré, 'Le problème de l'allure dans les charges de cavalerie du XVIe au XVIIIe siècle', *Revue Historique des Armées*, 249 (2007), 16–27; the same author's recent book, *Histoire de la cavalerie*, constitutes the best introduction to date, 278–93; see also Jean-Michel Sallmann, 'Le cheval, la pique et le canon: Le rôle tactique de la cavalerie du XIVe au XVIIe siècle', in Daniel Roche and Daniel Reytier (eds), *Le cheval et la guerre du XVe au XXe siècle* (Paris, 2002), 253–67.

[97] Keegan, *Face of Battle*, 172.

[98] Azan, *Un tacticien*, 65; for the rate of advance on foot, Paddy Griffith, *Forward into Battle: Fighting Tactics from Waterloo to the Near Future* (Novato, CA, 1991), 41.

charge with the general's trumpet, which other trumpets and drums then relayed along the line in a way which must surely have impressed everyone who saw and heard it.[99] There is something primordial in this moment, akin to mobbing in fish and birds; the imposing size of the group reassures the participants and bolsters their confidence.[100] The pikemen stood briefly motionless beneath the gorgeous multicoloured banners of the tercios displaying images of the Virgin Mary, and the great flags bearing the jagged diagonal red cross of Burgundy that identified the units as Habsburg.[101] 'As the battle is close to being joined, the men will surely display a certain natural levity and eagerness for combat.' Soldiers were encouraged then to raise their battle cry, 'to heat up the blood and dissipate the melancholy fantasies of the mind, encouraging one's own men and terrifying the enemy. Whoever attacks has twice as much fortitude whereas waiting for the onslaught induces intimidation...There are two senses in man—visual and aural—by which fear penetrates the mind: the battle cries help establish this; the Spaniards bellow "Spania!"'[102] But this fleeting moment ends with the first contact.

As the Spanish troops neared the enemy parapet, the men of both sides held their fire, carrying their firearms obliquely across their torso until the last moment. The musketeers of this tercio of Naples then deployed ahead of the pikes and closed in to open fire at short range, perhaps the forty paces (*c.*60 metres) recommended by Giorgio Basta, perhaps closer still to offset the cover of the earthwork.[103] It was crucial to withhold fire until the last possible moment, preferably until the enemy fired first. If the defending troops fired too soon, they immediately lost heart, for the assailants had time to approach and fire at point-blank range with each marksman choosing his man. Attackers who survived an enemy volley had to seize the opportunity and rush forward without fear of a second salvo.[104]

One rarely finds specific information on the tactics employed in the thick of the fighting, and no source states unambiguously whether troops fired in controlled salvoes or individually. Volley fire emerged only recently in infantry warfare and officers did not think they could maintain it long after the first salvoes. The Swedish army delivered its bullets in deadly volleys at close range, but at Nördlingen the Spaniards had apparently evolved a parry for it, by having the men crouch when they heard the enemy order to fire.[105] Spanish tactics rotated parties of thirty to fifty musketeers at a time, closing to deliver their fire at close range and then retiring out of range to reload.[106] Formations about fifteen men deep could deliver their salvo every five or six seconds. They stood on each side of the pike, firing either directly to the front, or diagonally against a designated target. Officers

[99] Malfoy-Noël, *L'épreuve de la bataille*, 19.

[100] Dugatkin, *Cooperation among Animals*, 87; also for humans, Tooby and Cosmides, *Evolution of War*, 7.

[101] Brnardic, *Imperial Armies: Infantry*, 38.

[102] Barker, *Military Intellectual and Battle*, 135–8.

[103] Giorgio Basta, *Le gouvernement de la cavalerie legere* (Rouen, 1616), 16.

[104] Azan, *Un tacticien*, 62.

[105] William P. Guthrie, *Battles of the Thirty Years War: From White Mountain to Nördlingen* (Westport, CT, and London, 2002), 271–8.

[106] Keith Roberts, *Matchlock Musketeer 1588–1688* (Oxford and New York, 2002), 48.

instructed some of them to stand several files deep in front of the pike and deliver their fire from there, as close to the French as they dared.[107] There was no 'collision' of infantry in a great shock, but rather a prolonged musketry exchange row by row at ever closer ranges. For each shot, the musketeer was required to blow a couple of times on his wick to make it glow, taking care not to have it touch the priming pan or bassinette before he picked a man and aimed at his middle.[108] Having released the shot, he scurried to the rear, lifted the cover of the firing pan and blew on it in order to remove any smouldering powder, which would explode when he reloaded. Reloading was a cumbersome process:,

> the soldier held the musket obliquely, took a ball from his pouch and put it in his mouth. Then he stuck the patch or wad on his hat. Next he emptied the measure of powder from its capsule into the barrel and, using his ramrod, sealed it with the patch. Then dropping the ball down the barrel and sealing it with another patch, he stuck his fork into the ground, rested the musket on it, placed the priming powder in the pan, and closed the cover. Next, he clamped the match in the cock, blew on it lightly and opened the pan. Finally he pulled the trigger. The whole operation took about two minutes.[109]

A devastating volley from the French entrenchment might have halted the attackers and dissuaded them from approaching, but not here: braving heavy casualties as they advanced through a hail of bullets, the musketeers then gave way to the pikemen (Fig. 3.5).[110]

The lead assailants carried fascines (bundles of sticks or branches) or planks they set at the foot of the ditch to enable them to clamber over the breastworks. To the drumbeat of the attack, the first pikemen over the obstacle lowered their weapons towards the faces of their adversaries, projecting the pole as far in front of them as they could, right foot placed in the direction of the point. They pulled the weapon back, took a step forward, and pushed the pike forward again. If the front man went down, the man behind him immediately stepped into his place, followed by the men to his rear.[111] Maurizio Arfaioli's description of Swiss pike tactics a century earlier is pertinent here: pikemen 'viciously prodded and thrust with their long weapons to open gaps in the opposing formation with the vibrating pike staves jutting back and forth, while the iron tips searched for a path through the guard and the armour of their targets'. Wherever a gap opened up, men used swords or musket butts to strike the men resisting them.[112] The pikemen closed ranks and squeezed tightly together in order to facilitate their job of breaking up their opposite numbers, while the men behind them pushed forward to create an

---

[107] Barker, *Military Intellectual and Battle*, 100–1 and 146.

[108] Sieur de Lostelneau, *Le mareschal de bataille*, 5; also ASPr Governo Farnesiano, Milizie 33, Esercizio della militia a piedi (*c*.1630).

[109] Jaroslav Lugs, *Firearms Past and Present: A Complete Review of Firearms Systems and their Histories*, i (London, 1973; 1st publ. 1956), 17. For a demonstration of the reloading process in real time, visit <www.englishcivilwar.org/p/previous-events.html> for a video clip lasting just over a minute. The re-enactor uses a lighter matchlock, without the forked rest.

[110] Brusoni, *Delle Historie memorabili*, 36.

[111] Gualdo Priorato, *Il maneggio delle armi*, 62–5; see also the *Memoires de Montecuculi*, 183.

[112] Maurizio Arfaioli, *The Black Bands of Giovanni: Infantry and Diplomacy during the Italian Wars (1526–1528)* (Pisa, 2005), 7.

Fig. 3.5. Pieter Snayers, Battle of Bois-le-Duc 1629 (detail). The square battalions are not accurate depictions of infantry units formed up for battle. These have been compacted by about five-sixths in order to conserve space, and transform rectangular formations into squares. Sleeves of musketeers advance on each side of the pikemen to close with the enemy in the woods, but artistic licence reduces the distance there too.

irresistible momentum.[113] Meanwhile, musketeers in a rather loose order on each side of the pikemen reloaded and fired at their adversaries over the top of the parapet, and upon gaining a foothold themselves, fired on the exposed French infantry standing behind it. Once they carried them, the attackers found the little forts along the line especially valuable, since musketeers posted there could not easily be dislodged and could fire at close range at an advantageous angle into the defending formations. Parties of foot hurried forward with spades and picks to pull down the parapet between the forts to enable men and horses behind them to pass through the line. A few metres behind the trench, small parties of French pikemen standing five or six deep rushed the place where the adversary succeeded in clambering the barrier, killing the lead soldiers and pushing the others back.[114] The Spaniards did not carry the forward line right away, being subject to a withering hail of musketry.

The French initially defended their entrenchments vigorously. But eventually they tired or became hesitant and the outnumbered foot drifted backwards. Following their example, other soldiers made some opportune mental calculations and fled toward the river.[115] The continued retrograde movement by the Lyonnais regiment was largely uncontrolled by the officers, a large portion of whom were killed and wounded in the close fighting. Count Montecuccoli stressed in 1642 the importance of detailing men to aim their fire at these officers in the hopes of

[113] Barker, *Military Intellectual and Battle*, 111.
[114] Gualdo Priorato, *Il maneggio delle armi*, 120.
[115] Galeazzo Gualdo Priorato, *An History of the late Warres and other state affaires of the best part of Christendom* (London, 1648; 1st publ. 1641), 357.

demoralizing the men under their command. Many leaders were conspicuously mounted in order to have a better view of the combat swirling around them, and rode close to the front of their formations in order to be heard above the crackle of musketry. This backwards motion of the French foot encouraged the Spaniards to press forward into the smoke and over the parapets, followed by the pikemen, although they lost their formation in doing so. Spanish accounts stress the 'grandissima resistencia' the assailants encountered but they were determined to press forward, despite the fact that Antonio Sotelo was grievously wounded.[116] 'There are never, never, never two equal resolutions face to face', wrote the first scientific observer of soldiers in action, Ardant du Picq.[117] As the French lost most of their redoubts, they drifted to the rear under the weight of numbers, followed at a distance by the Spaniards. Some of the attackers would have broken ranks in order to plunder the dead and wounded, for in gathering the spoils on the battlefield, it was every man for himself. Leganés and his staff officers, probably identified by a pennant visible to messengers relaying orders and information, followed close behind, trying to get a sense of what was happening. The misadventure of Gustavus Adolphus at Lützen in 1632, killed when he ventured too close to the fighting, was fresh in everyone's minds.[118] But Leganés was never far away, since the French colonel De La Tour commanding the Lyonnais regiment, captured in the fighting, was presented to the Spanish commander not far from where he was seized.[119]

Men on both sides would have found the noise overpowering, with musket detonations, drumbeats, officers' shouts, the clang of blade weapons on others, the ricochet of balls off armour, and the howling of wounded men echoing continually in their ears.[120] Those closest to the enemy experienced a 'saturation of perceptions', an inebria of action proper to combat throughout history that distorted their sense of time and space. A mixture of burnt powder and dust stifled the soldiers, who could not escape the stench of blood and death nearby. Individuals flinched from bullets zipping by their heads, many times more numerous than direct hits. Above all, men were choked and blinded by the thickening smoke. The powder in the barrel and the priming pan created a cubic metre of thick smoke combustion, multiplied by many thousands in the constricted space.[121] In the windless sticky heat of a Lombard summer, this smoke hung thick and close to the ground, quickly caking each man with grime and powder residue on their faces, hands, clothing, and leather. In the single-minded focus of the fight, many would have soiled themselves without noticing it at the time. Combat distorted both the auditory and visual per-

---

[116] Biblioteca Nacional Madrid, Ms 2367, Italia 1636, 38; on casualties among the officers, ASFi Mediceo del Principato 3176, letter to Florence from the Tuscan resident Pandolfini in Milan, 24 June 1636.

[117] Charles Ardant du Picq, *Etudes sur le combat: Combat antique et combat moderne* (Paris, 2004; reproduction of the 4th edn of 1904).

[118] Azan, *Un tacticien*, 66.

[119] *Relacion del combate del exercito de su magestad*; on the placement of the general and his identifying pennant, Barker, *Military Intellectual and Battle*, 113.

[120] Malfoy-Noël, *L'épreuve de la bataille*, 53.

[121] Chaline, *La bataille de la Montagne Blanche*, 167; on the reaction to powder, Malfoy-Noël, *L'épreuve de la bataille*, 59.

ceptions of the men caught up in it, 'for the brain is screening out awareness of what it deems insignificant to the goal... This frightening situation literally shuts down forebrain processing.'[122] What some call 'combat narcosis' was an adrenaline-filled frenzy that gave men more agility in clambering over earthworks.[123]

One account held that the French foot drifted or fled back in direction of the Ticino river, followed closely by some Spanish or German musketeers eager for booty from the enemy camp.[124] Outpacing the more heavily armoured pikemen who advanced tentatively behind them, they found a second set of earthworks closer to the crest.[125] At this stage in the fighting, someone left the battlefield to carry a victory message to Milan, whose receipt prompted the cannon of the citadel to fire in sign of rejoicing.[126] The attackers were elated at this auspicious beginning, after the stress of closing with the enemy behind their entrench-ments, the musketry exchange at close range, and the melee of the pikemen with the defenders. However, the greatest moment of vulnerability is that of victory, for a *parasympathetic backlash* sets in, inducing a sense of safety that causes a physiological and psychological collapse among the relieved survivors.[127] 'Once the attacker's fury has been spent and he encounters trouble', echoed Montecuccoli, 'he becomes impatient and cowardly and may be repulsed easily. As soon as an attacker's ferocity is restrained, it becomes weakened.'[128] Reserve troops, not having experienced the adrenaline rush of the assault, were better suited to pursue the fleeing enemy and to parry any counter-attack, but these were not close by.[129] The space was too confined to support the forward infantry with squadrons of horse.[130]

Suddenly the battle changed complexion as several hundred French cavalry emerged from behind breaks in the parapet and galloped through the smoke behind Du Plessis-Praslin (Fig. 3.6). Musketeers and pikemen advanced behind them from the edge of the plateau.[131] They constituted the second, supporting line of troops drawn up in formations alternating infantry units with cavalry squad-rons, and possibly they included the hidden reserve of detached musketeers. It is unlikely that the Spanish and Germans saw them coming due to the smoke, and in any case the Catholic King's musketeers and pikemen in loose order were taken

[122] Dave Grossman, *On Combat: The Psychology and Physiology of Deadly Conflict in War and in Peace* (Mascoutah, IL, 2004), 57.

[123] James M. McPherson, *For Cause and Comrades: Why Men Fought in the Civil War* (New York and Oxford, 1997), 40.

[124] No document mentions the French camp. Montecuccoli recommended placing them 300 or 400 metres back from the earthworks, which would have situated them in the valley below the plateau; *Memoires de Montecuculi*, 112.

[125] Oltrona Visconti, *La battaglia di Tornavento*, 125.

[126] Biblioteca Universitaria Bologna, vol. 473, Misc. H, no. 15, *Relatione del fatto d'Arme*.

[127] Grossman, *On Combat*, 16.   [128] Barker, *Military Intellectual and Battle*, 142.

[129] Dave Grossman, *On Killing: The Psychological Cost of Learning to Kill in War and Society* (Boston and London, 1995), 70–1.

[130] *Relacion*. Filling in captured entrenchments to allow the passage of cavalry was standard oper-ating procedure for assaulting troops, *Memoires de Montecuculi*, 184.

[131] Biblioteca Universitaria Bologna, vol. 473, Misc. H, no. 15, *Relatione del fatto d'Arme seguito fra l'Esercito spagnolo e francese nella selva di Soma di la del Ticino e Tornavento e Ca' della Camera, il 22 giugno 1636.*

CESAR DE CHOISEVL COMTE DV PLESSY, PRASLIN, GOVVER
neur de Monsieur Frere unique du Roy, Marschal de France. Fils de Ferry de Choiseul
Côte du dit lieu, et de Magdelaine Barthelemy. cy deuant General des Armées de sa Majesté en Italie catalogne, Plandre, Luxembourg, Champaigne, et Picardie. Ou il a montré par tout de
marques de son courage et desa prudence. il gagna la bataille du Trancheron en Italie en
16   prit Fiombino et Portolongone, comandant conjointement auec le Marofchal de la Mof-
leraye et en 1645 Roses en catalogne. Sa Majesté reconnoissant alors ses seruices, l'honora du
baston de Marschal de France en l'année 1650. il secourut Guise ou il reduisit les Espagnols
à la derniere necessité, et pour couronner sa campagne gagna la memorable bataille de Rethel:
ou il desfit entierement l'Armée d'Espagne: qui y perdit ses canons, son bagage, et y eut
ses principaux Officiers morts ou prisonniers. il a espousé Dame Colombe Charron, du-
quel Mariage sont issus entr'autres Cæsar de Choiseul. leur fils aisné tué au siege de Cremo-
ne, et Auguste de Choiseul à la bataille de Rethel.

LP 31-19²

F 1675.

Fig. 3.6. Cesar de Choiseul, comte Du Plessis-Praslin: a young senior officer at Tornavento, he personally led a series of spirited counter-attacks by both horse and foot. The memoirs of this future field marshal published decades later contain only a little information on the battle, completely unreliable.

completely by surprise. Normally a cavalry charge would make no impression against a body of experienced pikemen, but if these were not in tight formation, they had no stopping power at all, and uncoordinated musketry had little effect.[132] The dry ground underneath the horses' hooves amplified the noise of the charge and unnerved the foot, who could hear more than they could see.[133] Each squadron, about six ranks deep and twenty files wide, advanced first at a trot and then progressively faster as the well-armoured horsemen approached the enemy.

[132] Gualdo Priorato, *Il maneggio delle armi*, 68.
[133] Malfoy-Noël, *L'épreuve de la bataille*, 25.

The second and subsequent rows of horse followed close enough behind to risk trampling the hooves of the horses in front. It was important to keep a measured pace of about twelve kilometres an hour in order not to disrupt the solid wall of oncoming horse, whose very mass constituted a psychological weapon.[134] One specialist describes the cavalry charge as a moving wall of centaurs, well over 2 metres high, whose voluminous physicality sweeps away the startled foot before them.[135] Men have a natural fear of being trampled by the horses, which in fact the horse avoids, even when soldiers lie prone on the ground.[136] The emotions of Leganés's infantry passed immediately from euphoria to panic. Startled soldiers seek only to get out of the way, and the exhortations of their officers have little effect. They were more likely to imitate the behaviour of other men fleeing around them.[137] Chasing the far more numerous foot was the moment of glory for cavalry troopers, whose own armour, reasonably effective at deflecting musketry and pistol balls except at close range, made them bold.[138] They chased all before them to the limit of the easternmost entrenchments they had lost soon before.[139]

SECOND WIND

Du Plessis-Praslin's stirring charge completely upset Leganés's plan, and confirmed once more the redoubtable effectiveness of the French horse in a set-piece battle. The initial assault infantry retired disorganized and demoralized, and was in no condition to reform and advance for a while. Behind the infantry squadrons, however, sat a good portion of the Habsburg cavalry formed up under Gherardo Gambacorta and awaiting orders. Reserve cavalry customarily waited behind the fighting in order to prevent collapses. Habsburg commanders formed great double-squadrons of 400 horse, in eighty ranks five deep. Cavalrymen arrayed more thinly tended to hesitate in a charge, the rearward ranks not always following the bravest men posted up front.[140] Gambacorta's predominantly Italian squadrons, more numerous than the French, first chased the enemy cavalry back behind the entrenchments and perhaps off the plateau completely. Leganés then ordered him to seize the earthworks too. Gambacorta understood, however, that it would be difficult for his horse (without supporting pike) to recover the trench, even though it was common for cavalrymen to fight dismounted. At first he contested the order,

---

[134] Chauviré, 'Le problème de l'allure', 16–27.

[135] Nicole de Blomac, 'Le cheval de guerre entre le dire et le faire: Quelques variations sur le discours équestre adapté à la réalité militaire', in Roche and Reytier, *Le cheval et la guerre*, 55–65.

[136] Ardant du Picq, *Etudes sur le combat*, 76–8; for the effect of panic, Holmes, *Acts of War*, 226–9; Malfoy-Noël, *L'épreuve de la bataille*, 77–80.

[137] On this moment of crisis, Malfoy-Noël, *L'épreuve de la bataille*, 72.

[138] On cavalry armour, see Blackmore, *Arms and Armour*, 7–9. Cuirassiers were sometimes known as 'lobsters', such was the hardness of their shells. Breastplates sported the proof-mark, where a pistol-shot had been deflected off it in a test; Vladimir Brnardic, *Imperial Armies of the Thirty Years' War: Cavalry* (Oxford, 2010), 15.

[139] On this 'esprit cavalier', see Hervé Drévillon, *L'Impôt du sang* (Paris, 2005), 354–66; on their impact on disorganized foot, Muir, *Tactics*, 131.

[140] Barker, *Military Intellectual and Battle*, 91–3 and 108–10.

but Leganés insisted, in words that were purportedly injurious to his honour: the general *dared* him to attack. Therefore, at the head of some 500 carabiniers (i.e. horsemen using a short musket as their principal weapon), Gambacorta trotted up to the breaches in the entrenchments through which the French horse might pass, with an equal number of cuirassiers (armoured heavy cavalry) under Agostino del Fiesco just to his rear. Leading from the front and displaying the firmness that his troopers expected of him, the general prepared to lead his men over the entrenchments before the enemy could man them in strength, when French musketry hit him in the helmet and knocked him off his horse. When he staggered to his feet and called for his men to follow him dismounted, several shots punched through his breastplate and killed him outright in front of his officers.[141] Gambacorta's glorious demise risked having serious consequences, because he died where cavalry commanders were expected to be, in full view of their troops. The heavy losses incurred here and the death of a prestigious leader risked demoralizing the officers and men, but the cuirassiers under Fiesco advanced immediately to drive back the French horse and foot.[142] Gambacorta's exemplary death at a key juncture of the battle figures in every account of the day's action. Luigi Caetani, another prominent Neapolitan nobleman, dismounted to recover the cadaver, but was himself wounded and captured.

French cavalry left the plateau and moved down the wooded slope towards the Panperduto ditch. Some of them shifted from north of Tornavento hamlet to reinforce the infantry on the plateau south of it, but that made them targets of the Spanish cannon on the Panperduto levee. After the northernmost infantry *esquadron* reformed, it renewed its pressure on the trench lines and redoubts carried by following Gambacorta's advance. Then Leganés ordered the centre of his line to advance against Créquy's positions around the Tornavento hamlet, which was surrounded by barricades.[143] The Spanish infantry tercio of the Marqués de Mortara clambered over the entrenchments south of the hamlet and proceeded to roll up the line of posts defended by Créquy's own regiment de Sault, but the attackers did not make much progress since a fresh wave of French cavalry several squadrons strong, with parties of musketeers in close support, charged them repeatedly.[144] Intense fire from the Habsburg musketeers drove the horse back towards the barricades around the Tornavento hamlet, but Du Plessis-Praslin led them back repeatedly. One of these sallies, led by the Count Palluau, numbered a mere twenty troopers, but these would have swept away a much greater number of foot if the lack of cohesion of musket and pike permitted it.[145] Cavalrymen wore, in addition to the helmet, iron or steel plate covering the torso, and more armour protecting the lower leg, in all, between 25 and 50 kg.[146] More timid than the troopers were the horses, made skittish by the noise to

---

[141] Filamondo, *Il Genio bellicoso di Napoli* (Naples, 1694), i. 316–21; Brusoni, *Delle Historie memorabili*, 36; on the innate qualities of leaders of his ilk, Malfoy-Noël, L'épreuve de la bataille, 161–2.

[142] *Relatione del fatto d'Arme*; on the impact of the death of trusted leaders, Costa, *Psicologia militare*, 251.

[143] Gualdo Priorato, *Historia delle guerre del Conte Galeazzo Gualdo Priorato* (Venice, 1646), 336.

[144] This tactic was a Swedish innovation, quickly adopted by the French. It proved decisive at Rocroi in 1643. See Henninger, *Rocroi 1643*, 42.

[145] Drévillon, *L'Impôt du sang*, 361–5.   [146] Bonsall, 'The Study of Small Finds'.

a point where their riders had difficulty mastering their fear.[147] 'It can be taken as axiomatic that no battalion of pikemen can be ruptured in a head-on attack, particularly by horse. Even the smallest things bring horses to a standstill. The noise and smoke of musketry frighten them. Feigned blows cause them to halt; fear of human beings automatically bridles them.'[148] It was all many cavaliers could do to keep their mounts in line and calm while awaiting orders, and musketry probably killed many more horses that day than the steel-plated troopers.[149]

German foot under Gil de Haes then relayed Mortara's Spaniards (the Tuscan account identifies them rather as Prince Borso's regiment) storming the adjacent French redoubts, fighting hand to hand with pikes and swords and reputedly butchering the stubborn defenders inside them (Fig. 3.7).[150] The more slender deployment of the French made them more vulnerable to be taken in flank. Habsburg musketry and artillery fire gradually drove Créquy's men back towards the hamlet of Tornavento and the edge of the plateau.[151] Desperate rushes of French horse through the smoke slowed Spanish and German progress for a time, but they contained the advance with diminishing success. Most of Leganés's horse sat out the battle behind the infantry, but a few seem to have charged their French counterparts in the tight space between the entrenchments and the village. Parties of musketeers tormented the advancing French cavalry with shot and after dropping some of the lead horses, the Habsburg cavalry would gallop in to break up and chase away the remainder. Coordinating parties of horse with musketeers in narrow spaces must have been difficult for both sides, for there would not have been much room at the top of the plateau left to the French (Fig. 3.8).[152] Créquy, well-armoured and astride his horse, moved forward and back near the fighting in order to have a better view of the situation. The published account of the battle considered him to be lucky to emerge from the combat unscathed. Battle, his biographer swore, was an occasion he relished. One of his colonels at Tornavento contrasted the effect of his intrepidity on the skittish French rank and file with Leganés's caution, which nullified the boldness of his soldiers.[153] The veteran Sault regiment was close to collapsing when the first unit to cross the bridge, that of Chamblay, climbed up the escarpment to its aid.[154] The firefight in this central portion of the field reportedly lasted three hours. Battle narratives tend to lose their clarity once the combat was well under way, and Tornavento is no exception. It

---

[147] Malfoy-Noël, *L'épreuve de la bataille*, 54; for similar cavalry tactics of a later era, see Muir, *Tactics*, 111–22.

[148] Barker, *Military Intellectual and Battle*, 101.

[149] Brnardic, *Imperial Armies: Cavalry*, 8–15.

[150] Biblioteca Universitaria Bologna, vol. 473, Misc. H, no. 15, *Relatione del fatto d'Arme*.

[151] Edouard Hardy de Perini, *Batailles françaises* (Paris, 1894–1906), iii. 27.

[152] Basta recommended keeping parties of musketeers close to squadrons of horse, no further than 30 or 40 paces distant. Basta, *Le gouvernement de la cavallerie legere*, 15; Montecuccoli emphasized how parties of friendly musketeers close by made cavalrymen braver, Barker, *Military Intellectual and Battle*, 106.

[153] Nicolas Chorier, *Histoire de la vie de Charles de Créquy de Blanchefort, duc de Lesdiguières* (Grenoble, 1684), 248–53.

[154] *Gazette de France*, 99 (1636).

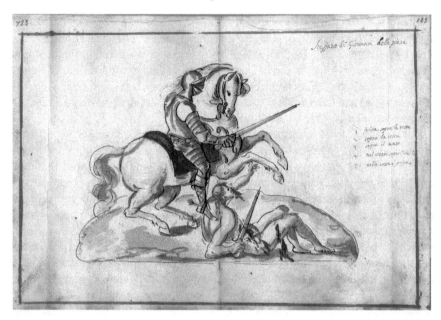

Fig. 3.7. Giovanni Polino, surgeon of Casale Monferrato, illustrates wounds inflicted by sword. Note the full armour worn by the Spanish or Italian cavalier, *c.*1630.

Fig. 3.8. Thomas Meulener, Cavalry melee with Habsburg musketeers in close support, Prado, Madrid. Montecuccoli, an expert on this subject, claimed that friendly musketeers nearby made the horsemen bolder.

becomes increasingly difficult to identify the Catholic King's formations committed to the attack, which lasted many hours still.

Failing to drive back the French from the plateau on his right flank, Leganés ordered his left flank to advance along the Panperduto canal, and then descend from the plateau to press the French along the *naviglio* and the edge of the Ticino river. The French held this sector weakly due to insufficient troops relative to the circumference of the entrenchments. Their account admits that the enemy descended from the plateau without much resistance, enjoying the greater momentum from the force of gravity.[155] Two regiments, perhaps understrength, of Peyregourde and Florainville waited at the bottom, with some cavalry in support on the flank next to the river. This fresh Habsburg *esquadron* of 2,000 or 3,000 foot (perhaps Don Martin d'Aragon's Spanish tercio of Lombardy, and likely the Spìnola regiment) overwhelmed the outposts in the mill before the entrenchments, while others descended the slopes and clambered over the breastworks where French defenders were fewest.[156] Above them on their right, the Spanish tercio of the Marqués de Mortara, and the German foot under Gil de Haes then pressed forward south of the Tornavento hamlet, pushing the French off the plateau.[157]

Créquy's right wing might have disintegrated and left the way free for the Spanish troops to reach the bridge and cut its cables, when cavalry, including the heavy *gendarmes*, rushed the assailants on the valley floor and drove them back to the edge of the breastworks. This respite permitted Colonel Peyregourd to rally his men and to reoccupy his trenches just as the first reinforcements began arriving from the other shore.[158] French soldiers in reserve busied themselves throwing up trench works around the bridgehead as a line of last-ditch defence. Du Plessis-Praslin led the first regiment from the other shore, that of Chamblay, back up the slope. Its twelve companies almost recaptured the trenches atop the plateau, but a long firefight cut them to ribbons and the survivors withdrew towards the protection of the Panperduto canal.[159]

According to the Italian 'Relatione', the action along the edge of the *naviglio* developed into a fierce contest of blade weapons, since the Habsburg attackers refused to give way to the fresh units who deployed on the French right wing in the river plain. In these tight spaces, infantry fighting took on a savagery uncharacteristic of the battlefield as a whole.[160] In a close melee, pikes become useless and even swords could not be wielded with full effectiveness. Soldiers up front wielded daggers, while the musketeers bludgeoned their adversaries with the butts of their firearm.[161] Giuseppe Poderico, an ensign in Lucio Boccapianola's Neapolitan regiment who perished while storming one of these entrenchments, received no fewer

[155] Barker, *Military Intellectual and Battle*, 79. 'Whoever holds the hill and lunges downward augments the rate of impulse with the weight of his body.'

[156] Biblioteca Universitaria Bologna, vol. 473, Misc. H, no. 15, 'Relatione del fatto d'Arme seguito fra l'Esercito spagnolo e francese nella selva di Soma di là del Ticino e Tornavento e Ca' della Camera il 22 giugno 1636'.

[157] *Gazette de France*, 99 (1636).   [158] Hardy de Perini, *Batailles françaises*, iii. 216.

[159] Biblioteca Universitaria Bologna, vol. 473, Misc. H, no. 15, *Relatione del fatto d'Arme*.

[160] Keegan, *Face of Battle*, 165–7.

[161] Gualdo Priorato, *Il maneggio dell'armi*, 66; Barker, *Military Intellectual and Battle*, 146.

than twenty-seven wounds from pikes, swords, and halberds in the affray.[162] The repeated cavalry rushes at the Habsburg foot soon gave way to the advance of the Senantes and Cevennes infantry regiments in battle array.[163] Even these forma-tions, among the first to cross the bridge behind Victor-Amadeus, were insufficient to stem the tide, after Leganés committed seven German infantry companies to push them back, supported with some cavalry squadrons to hold off their French counterparts.[164] The Bologna account claims that, after the assailants unleashed their initial musketry volleys, they surged forward with pikes and swords to engage a general melee. But these kinds of pitched hand-to-hand battles could not last for very long. Some of the assaulting Spanish and German companies descending the slope towards the Panperduto channel climbed back onto the plateau to regroup while the newly arrived Tuscans took their place. The remainder continued to exchange musketry with the Franco-Savoyards in order to beat back Victor-Amadeus's advancing reinforcements. In the lengthy action at the foot of the slope around the French entrenchments, companies started to come apart in the smoke. In the thick of battle soldiers failed to hear the orders through the din, or refused to follow the officers calling for them to advance.

All the troops, but particularly those of the Catholic King, suffered terribly from the heat and thirst. Leganés attributed his final failure to the lack of water for men and horses.[165] Standing in a packed battalion on a stiflingly hot summer's day, bur-dened with heavy steel breastplates and helmets gleaming in the sun, men were desperate for any source of water. Every attack loses men from the rear, who fall to the ground feigning wounds, or who find excuses to drop out from the company moving forward. Brusoni cites an unnamed writer who related that the Genoese foot in Ottaviano Saulì's company (part of Spìnola's regiment), suffering from the intense heat, discovered a pool of water behind a mill the French had fortified, and chased the enemy from it with a bold party of musketeers.[166] Soon men broke ranks to drink and dowse themselves in the pool, unknown to the French who might have profited from it had they but known. 'But this is not certain', warns the historian.[167] The disruption of the attack by men dropping out to seek water also figures in the anonymous Italian account in which men and horses posted next to the *naviglio* and the river were drawn irresistibly to refresh themselves there.[168] The manuscript account of the battle in the Biblioteca Nacional in Madrid, which bears the traces of official dispatches, claims that an entire regiment (not identi-

---

[162] Filamondo, *Il Genio bellicoso di Napoli*, 427.

[163] The Senantes regiment, commanded by François de Havart, seigneur de Senantes, was technic-ally a Savoyard unit. Its colonel was a French client of Prince Gaston d'Orléans, and a plotter against Richelieu who like Toiras had to flee to Piedmont to escape the cardinal's wrath. Aubert de laChesnaye des Bois, *Dictionnaire de la noblesse*, vii (Paris, 1774), 725.

[164] *Gazette de France*, 99 (1636).   [165] BNM MS 2367, Italia 1636, 39.

[166] Saulì, captain of a free company of 150 Genoese infantry at Valenza the previous year, is de-scribed as 'prode cavaliere e bravo soldato'. Stanchi, 'Narrazione dell'assedio di Valenza nel 1635, fatta da Bernardino Stanchi', *Memorie Storiche Valenzane*, doc. 131 (Casale, 1923), 286.

[167] Brusoni, *Delle Historie memorabili*, 37.

[168] Biblioteca Universitaria Bologna, vol. 473, Misc. H, no. 15, *Relatione del fatto d'Arme*.

fied) turned its back on the enemy in order to drink from the Ticino.[169] They dipped their flasks in the clear water of the river, filled their hats and helmets, and incautiously drank it back in long draughts.[170]

It has been written by a famous philosopher, on the basis of literary documents alone, that agents of Power transformed the soldiers of this era into 'docile bodies' that moved in battle according to elaborate choreographies of time and motion management. The individual soldiers carefully formed up into battalions that morning were just cogs in a vast machine, calibrated to obtain the optimum effect. The bravery or the strength of the single body ceased to constitute an important variable.[171] Rigorous training, and the punitive systems of discipline behind it, he considered enough to obtain this result. While it is undoubtedly true that young men are fairly malleable, and that officers can cultivate and develop men's warrior instincts by training, the soldier's stamina is as much due to peer pressure as to fashioning by the firm hand of authority.[172] Reading these pages, one is struck by the absence of evidence behind the argument. This vision of 1970, still widespread today, ignores the fundamentals of human nature. Soldiers were sentient beings too, just like philosophers. Pity that Michel Foucault had never encountered the writings of Charles Ardant du Picq, who based his *Etudes sur le combat* (written between 1865 and 1869) on first-hand observation of the *instincts* of men under the stress of great danger. The French colonel would have considered Foucault's elegant theory as the abstract vision of an *homme de cabinet*.[173] In a compelling combination of historical study of combat in ancient times, and a rigorous first-hand observation of modern infantry fighting in the Crimea and Algeria, supported by detailed questionnaires he collected from fellow officers, this contemporary of Charles Darwin concluded that men in peril have always remained fundamentally the same. In fighting, even between disciplined troops, the soldier's training fades before his *instinct de conservation*. Soldiers could not be trained to become robots. At best discipline kept them under the control of their officers for a longer period, but eventually their fear would get the better of them. Soldiers in battle might also be animated by passions such as religious fanaticism, national pride, lust for glory, and thirst for booty, but they reasoned too. They knew that the more numerous they were to advance towards the enemy, the more likely the latter was to retreat, thus diminishing their peril.[174]

---

[169] BNM MS 2367, Italia 1636, 50.

[170] Luca Antonio Porzio, *The soldier's Vade Mecum: Or, the method of curing the diseases and preserving the health of soldiers, I: in camps II: in garrisons III: during marches* (London, 1747; 1st publ. 1685), 9.

[171] Michel Foucault, *Discipline and Punish: The Birth of the Prison* (New York, 1977; 1st publ. 1975); see the chapter on Docile Bodies, 135–69.

[172] Dyer, *War*, 32.

[173] Ardant du Picq, *Etudes sur le combat*, 35; Stéphane Audoin-Rouzeau, 'Vers une anthropologie historique de la violence de combat au XIXe siècle: Relire Ardant du Picq?', *Revue d'Histoire du XIXe siècle*, 30 (2005), 85–97.

[174] Ardant du Picq, *Etudes sur le combat*, 83.

Officers might exhort the men to keep advancing, but the former would have to keep a sense of what was possible to ask of the latter. The emotions in the limbic system stirred by combat competed with the computations in the higher brain, where self-interest resided. The officers encouraged their men to dominate the enemy, and the soldiers could also see some feats accomplished by more ardent warriors around them, whose energy was contagious.[175] Inversely, the demonstration of resolve among the defenders had the result of disheartening and retarding the attackers' forward momentum. An officer's ability to simply maintain his troops arrayed beneath their standards went a long way to discourage the enemy from coming closer. On the attack or in defence, whether on foot or on horseback, the officers posted themselves where their subordinates could see them. Captains enforced the 'risk contract' and deterred defectors by posting lieutenants and non-commissioned officers around the unit with instructions to strike down any man who attempted to flee. Often the simple threat of enforcement was strong enough to dissuade men from leaving the ranks.[176] Officers directed the men to execute orders they would not be inclined to carry out on their own out of instinct for their own survival. 'The purpose of discipline is to make the men fight against their wishes.'[177] Montecuccoli recommended posting supernumerary officers throughout the line whose sole function would be to observe the behaviour of the officers and men so that rewards and punishments could be fairly distributed in the aftermath.[178]

Just as the pressure on the French lines from the more numerous attackers was becoming unbearable late in the morning, the first reinforcements began to arrive. The exact moment the engineers completed the bridge was the object of debate. Souvigny (who was not present) claims that it was ready only around noon, four hours after the fighting started.[179] In his letter to Cardinal Richelieu, Créquy simply stated that the bridge was ready the day after his arrival, without specifying a time. The Grand Duke of Tuscany relates in a dispatch to Don Francisco de Melo a week after the fight that a Tuscan spy well placed in the Savoyard camp was present throughout the battle. By his account the bridge was complete at 7.00 (an hour before the onset of the battle) and Victor-Amadeus crossed it to inspect Créquy's position before Leganes attacked.[180] Hémery also establishes that the bridge was ready at sunrise, but that the battalions had not been formed up to cross it.[181] The Tuscan resident writing to Florence just after the battle claims that they

[175] John Keegan, 'Towards a Theory of Combat Motivation', in Paul Addison and Angus Calder (eds), *A Time to Kill: The Soldier's Experience of War in the West* (London, 1997), 3–11.

[176] Tooby and Cosmides, *Evolution of War*, 8–9.

[177] Ardant du Picq, *Etudes sur le combat*, 128.

[178] Barker, *Military Intellectual and Battle*, 113.

[179] Souvigny, *Memoires*, i. 313; while the exact expression, 'sur le midi', designates midday, it was closer to dawn than to dusk.

[180] ASFi Mediceo del Principato 3258, fo. 251, letter to Francisco de Melo, 1 July 1636; a priest in nearby Lonate wrote that it took eight hours to throw this bridge across the Ticino a little more than 10 metres above the spur that channelled water into the *naviglio*. 'Relazione del curato Francesco Comerio di Lonate', in Bertolli and Colombo, *La peste del 1630 a Busto Arsizio*, 439.

[181] Bibliotèque Nationale de France, Ms Fr 16929, *Relation de M. d'Esmery de ses negociations en Piedmont en 1635 etc.*, fo. 569.

had been tricked into attacking thinking that the bridge could not be built in time.[182] The two confederate commanders presumed that Leganés would not attack them since it was so easy to send reinforcements. But instead of reacting immediately the Duke of Savoy hesitated.

It is well established that Victor-Amadeus did not move his men into action until Créquy's lines had been assaulted for three hours.[183] He may have considered ordering a withdrawal, but this would have been politically very risky, as Cardinal Richelieu would surely take revenge on his states and annex vulnerable Savoy outright. The ambassador Hémery claims he pleaded for the duke to act and states in one letter that he had to usher troops across the bridge himself. Everyone understood that the Spaniards were certain to win from weight of numbers and a willingness to keep advancing. In retrospect, Hémery acerbically recalled the duke's hesitation. 'His diligence in building the bridge saved the army, but if he had passed the soldiers over it one hour earlier we would have beaten the enemy. He never believed that the Spaniards would attack us, however.'[184] The ambassador was never entirely certain that the commanding general was a sincere ally, which was something that undermined everyone's confidence.

Once he finally resolved to save Créquy, the duke showed considerable mettle. Victor-Amadeus's half of the army crossed the bridge battalion after battalion, starting before noon, and completed its passage four hours later. Each unit formed up for battle only once it had crossed the river. Their timely arrival allowed the tired survivors of the morning's fighting to withdraw, reform, and clean their firearms. Fresh troops were better able to withstand the musketry of their assailants. The first two regiments, Cevennes and Senantes, took up positions on the shaky southern flank next to the *naviglio*, from which the tired survivors of Florainville and Peyregourde withdrew. The Chamblay regiment relayed Créquy's hard-pressed Sault regiment around Tornavento hamlet, while the others gradually fanned out on their left.[185] Once it was fully deployed the French line was as extensive as the Spanish one.

> Aiguebonne was supported by Chamblay, and the latter by Sault. It was supported by the Lorrainers of Montchenu, and they in turn by Marolle and Ferté, then Boisdavid and finally by La Tour, which recovered the quarters [probably the parapet along the edge of the Panperduto canal]. Between these regiments and those of the enemy were waged fourteen attacks at close quarters, ebbing and flowing until the place was in our hands, all supported by cavalry charges from Boissat, Corvoux, Palluau, Venterolle, Bussy, Cauvet and Cabry.[186]

The critical position lay just south of the hamlet of Tornavento where the Spaniards and Germans of Mortara and Borso d'Este captured all the trenches

---

[182] ASFi Mediceo del Principato 3176, fo. 750–3, Letter to the Balì Cioli, 24 June 1636.

[183] In addition to Hémery's account, the captured dispatch of Mr de Maillane relates that they were under attack for three hours before reinforcements arrived. ASFi Mediceo del Principato 3180, fo. 1147, Copia di lettera di Monsù de Maillans a Monsù de Bay, 25 June 1636.

[184] Arch. Affaires Etrangères, Correspondance Politique: Sardaigne, vol. 24, letter from Hémery to Monsieur (Prince Gaston d'Orleans?), 27 June 1636.

[185] Souvigny, *Memoires*, i. 313.   [186] *Gazette de 1636*, 409.

along the top and swept the French down the slope. They discovered there a nasty surprise, in the form of *another* parapet along the retaining wall of the Panperduto canal. Two small cannon, which in archaic English are designated 'sakers' (in Italian, 'sagri'), were positioned on the valley bottom to support the French battalions during the afternoon.[187] Unfortunately for Leganés, the confederate retreat off the plateau deprived the Spanish cannon of targets.

Leganés had kept some regiments back too, and so the fight continued into the afternoon. Generals understood that the side with the most reserves enjoyed the best likelihood of victory. We are quite fortunate to have discovered several letters from Florentine sources offering first-hand descriptions of this phase of the battle along the canal. In one dispatch compiled from several sources by the Tuscan resident Pandolfini, we learn that the Spanish and German foot pushed the French off the plateau and down towards the valley floor, using their elevated position to maximum effect.[188] French reinforcements protected by the canal embankment (Chamblay's regiment, probably) directed heavy fire upon the exposed troops of the Catholic King. Mortara's Spanish infantry succeeded in driving back the French foot even from those, alternating with the German regiment of Prince Borso d'Este. The Tuscan contingent of about 500 men then relayed those two in order to keep the pressure up.[189]

The letter from the tercio commander Camillo del Monte is rich in both operational and tactical details. The Florentines were part of Gambacorta's force that had been deployed south of the Po until the last moment. They reached Abbiategrasso after an exhausting march the previous evening, before receiving word to hurry on. The officers allowed the men to rest a little at Magenta, but almost immediately came the countermanding order to march as quickly as possible throughout the night towards the battlefield. These men arrived at Tornavento already worn out by the long march and the stifling heat, made worse by the lack of food and drink, only to find that the fight was under way. The officers counted the men, and then immediately placed them into battle formation. Without any further rest del Monte marched them to the edge of the plateau to relieve the men fighting there. This haste grated on the soldiers. 'Pane!, Pane!' shouted men from the ranks behind their colonel, to his keen annoyance. Del Monte, who had fought at Lützen under Wallenstein, provides us with precious details of his tactical procedures. He first committed three companies of musketeers against the enemy dug in behind the Panperduto rampart, but they could not withstand the withering fire, so he relieved them with three more companies, followed thereafter by the rest of the shot and the pike. The close fighting pushed the French back from the parapet and down the slope towards *yet more earthworks* thrown up at the edge of the valley. The Tuscans charged down the slope with such impetus that they began

---

[187] Ibid. 409; these field pieces are mentioned also in the anonymous pro-Habsburg Italian account conserved in Bologna.

[188] AAE C.P. Sardaigne, vol. 24, letter with indecipherable date (late July) from Hémery to Cardinal Richelieu, 675.

[189] ASFi Mediceo Principato 3176, letter from Milan to the Sr. Bali Cioli, 24 June 1636, fos. 750–3.

to carry those works too, until they were forced back by weight of numbers and exposure to fire. Then they tried to prevail with the advantage of height, but were unable to inflict enough losses relative to their own, which Del Monte later estimated at 30 per cent of his tercio.[190] He made particular mention of the pair of French light cannon spewing sacks of musket balls in a lethal spray. Four or six men served these long-barrelled guns weighing about 2 tonnes. The crew draped soaked skins over the barrel repeatedly, and washed out the hot bore with wet fleece to cool it down, then wiped it dry it in order to reload. If they spaced their fire appropriately, the piece never overheated. An experienced crew could maintain a rate of fire of one shot every six minutes.[191] Since they were firing musket balls, they were not limited to their normal supply of 30 cannonballs per piece, but prolonged grapeshot fire damaged the inside of the barrels. Moreover these light projectiles were harmless beyond a range of 100 metres. Withdrawing back up the slope soon put the Tuscans out of range of those terrible weapons, for the French could not place them on the wooded hillside to fire upwards.[192]

If the Tuscan tactics reflected Spanish military doctrine, the Germans appear to have had their own methods, forged by battle experience north of the Alps. The principal difference between the Spanish and the German deployment lay in the depth of the files. The sergeant-major formed up Borso d'Este's regiment only seven to nine men deep, according to a reference taken from the Modenese prince's experience at Casale Monferrato in 1640. Musketeers fired in salvo two or three ranks at a time, aiming at the middle of the men they targeted, as soon as they reached the distance of fifty paces. These front rows then dropped to their knees to reload, while two or three rows behind them levelled their muskets to fire in turn. A regiment could deliver a volley every twenty or thirty seconds, if indeed the officers and sergeants instructed them to employ salvo fire for any length of time.[193] Both the Imperials and the Spanish also used their musketeers as a skirmishing screen placed ahead of the pike, and when threatened they retired back behind the protection of the points. This had the added benefit of reducing the number of men up close to the enemy shot, for the killing power of the bullets declined sharply beyond 100 metres.[194]

French tactical doctrine inspired by Dutch and Swedish experience emphasized close cooperation between the horse and the foot. Among the Tuscan dispatches is a captured letter to a friend from the colonel of the Maillane regiment, whose battalion numbered about 500 men.[195] The French colonel likewise committed his

---

[190] ASFi Mediceo del Principato 3180, fos. 1118–21.

[191] Manacci, *Compendio d'Instruttioni*, 14 and 59.

[192] Guthrie, *Later Thirty Years' War*, 15.

[193] Biblioteca Estense Modena, Misc. Estense Ital. 160, *Regolamento sopra il combattere dell'Infanteria in una battaglia... formato dal Maresciale di Battaglia Conte Francesco Canossa*. The same manuscript contains some specific calculations for supplying infantry and artillery with their appropriate munitions, and the effective point blank ranges for cannon of different dimensions; on aimed fire, see also White, 'Spain's Early Modern Soldiers'.

[194] Brnardic, *Imperial Armies: Infantry*, 18–20.

[195] Antoine de Porcellets, marquis de Maillane, seigneur de Saint-Paul near Avignon. François-Alexandre Aubert de la Chesnaye des Bois, *Dictionnaire de la noblesse*, xi (Paris, 1776), 436.

musketeers in batches at a time, a small party of three dozen to fight alongside a cavalry squadron, a hundred more in reserve behind the trench, and a group of fifty assigned to close with the enemy with their swords. He was unable to hold his position for very long and the Spaniards pushed his men down the slope into what he considered the last defensible posts. Maillane, engaged for fourteen hours continuously, emphasized how the outcome of the battle remained uncertain for the entire day.[196]

Over the seventeenth century, these prolonged firefights were becoming the rule rather than the exception. They could not have engaged the same men continuously, and not just because of their physical and mental exhaustion. After a while, the musket barrels would have overheated too, and the powder residue build-up around the touch-hole connecting the priming pan with the powder charge at the base of the barrel would have increased the misfires from 15 to 50 per cent.[197] Officers had to withdraw the musketeers from the firing line repeatedly so they could take their pins, scrapers, rags, and metal oils from their pouches and set to work cooling and cleaning their weapon, before returning to the danger zone.[198] At White Mountain in 1620 the initial exchange of musketry lasted only a few minutes before the opposing armies closed with their pikes and blade weapons. In the melee that followed, the larger and deeper Catholic formations pressed home their advantage over the thinner Dutch-style battalions. Chaline concludes that merely a third of each army fought close up and the entire battle lasted only two hours, inflicting losses of 500 men on each side before the Protestant collapse.[199] At Tornavento, officers engaged, withdrew, and recommitted all of the Habsburg infantry formations and most of the French ones several times over the long summer day. The firing process itself contained a mechanism that gradually separated the two adversaries. Soldiers firing continually would have exhausted their ammunition after less than a half-hour of feverish activity, and the individual men would have had to walk to the rear of the company or battalion to replenish their supply of twelve pre-measured powder capsules (the twelve apostles) hanging from their bandoliers. No document mentions pre-measured paper cartridges, only then appearing in Northern Europe. Wicks saturated in saltpetre burned at both ends at a rate of 70 cm an hour, so these would have to be replaced periodically also.[200]

The fresh French and Savoyard troops taking position along the bottom of the escarpment only gradually changed the dynamic of the battle. Du Plessis-Praslin, as the *maréchal de bataille*, placed himself at the head of the Chamblay regiment and led it up the slope in three attacks, but most of its officers were killed and wounded.[201] The Spanish attack down the slope onto the southern edge of the

---

[196] ASFi Mediceo del Principato 3180, fo. 1147.

[197] Guthrie, *Later Thirty Years' War*, 9. The author levels out the rate of misfire to about one in five shots, but of course this was not a stable rate and depended upon the number of rounds fired before cleaning.

[198] Biblioteca Estense Modena, Misc. Estense Ital. 635, Avvertimenti militari...composto per il Colonello Bartolomeo Pelliciari di Modena, *c.*1641, fo. 35.

[199] Chaline, *La bataille de la Montagne Blanche*, 161–80.

[200] Lugs, *Firearms Past and Present*, 17; Chaline, *La bataille de la Montagne Blanche*, 164.

[201] *Gazette de France*, 99 (1636).

French position took most of the pressure off the men of the Marqués de Mortara and Borso d'Este who were closing in on the canal parapet behind Tornavento hamlet. The fully armoured Duke of Savoy rode directly to this dangerous sector and rallied the French infantry as they faltered, first by upbraiding them—and their officers—for their lack of courage. Gualdo Priorato, echoing Hémery, emphasizes that the duke personally rallied them and made them face about and recover their trenches along the canal.[202] 'The Duke of Savoyes Men did upon this occasion so valiantly behave themselves, that most men are of opinion, had it not been for them, the French Army had been utterly ruined.' Victor-Amadeus proved to be the saviour of the confederate army, taking control of a reserve unit, choosing the critical spot where the enemy assault was the most relentless and sharing the danger. 'When it is really imperative for a general to face danger, he must dash into the fray with lowered head and not be sparing of his own person,' recommended Raimondo Montecuccoli.[203]

Cevennes and Senantes discharged musket-fire into the enemy formations in front of them along the valley floor and slowly forced them back. It was important to bring to bear the maximum number of musketeers, and so these fanned out in front of the pike, profiting from the absence of Spanish cavalry close by. No document indicates whether this was salvo-fire produced by rotating rows of musketeers. An infantry 'charge' consisted of the new row of marksmen moving five or six paces ahead of the previous one, to an emplacement where the captain stood. The officer remained exposed there and then strode even closer to the enemy to set the new emplacement. (Officers conducted ordered retreats in the same manner, with the new rank of marksmen five or six paces to the rear of the previous one.[204]) This was the rolling line formation, or counter-march, practised by all armies at least part of the time. Should the defending force not yield to the pressure of musketry, the attacker could then close once or twice with the pikes to decide the matter.[205] Musketeers, armed with swords and daggers too, used their firearms as clubs in close combat. Unlike the pikemen, however, they wore little armour. If these exertions failed to drive the enemy back, the two sides separated to a range the men found bearable and the musketeers resumed their firing.

Understandably, the soldiers experienced great stress in this exchange, although reloading and firing their muskets at least kept them busy.[206] The non-coms exhorted the men to open out their ranks to facilitate weapons handling, or to close up to receive a charge, while the officers shouted instructions to the drummers.[207] Battle was the moment in which leaders had to inspire confidence in others, by their conspicuous calmness under fire. Officers wore more brightly coloured clothing than the men, and Habsburg officers in particular wore the red sash

---

[202] Gualdo Priorato, *An History of the late Warres*, 357.

[203] Barker, *Military Intellectual and Battle*, 157–8.

[204] Gualdo Priorato, *Il maneggio dell'armi*, 92; see also Nosworthy, *Anatomy of Victory*, 5–6.

[205] Nosworthy, *Anatomy of Victory*, 18.

[206] Ardant du Picq, *Etudes sur le combat*, 115.

[207] Dyer, *War*, 18–20 and 166; on the importance of the drums in battle, Gualdo Priorato, *Il maneggio dell'armi*, 14–29.

around their torso for better identification.[208] Spanish sources claim that officers and men of different nationalities took pains to maintain the reputation of their compatriots relative to others. Each nobleman would also have to face the judgement of peers and relatives back home in this critical moment for the status and reputation of his house.[209] French aristocrats could hope to be mentioned not merely in dispatches to the king and to ministers, but to be singled out in print, in the *Gazette*, or in single pamphlets published in Paris or Lyon.[210] Demonstrations of courage and sang-froid before hundreds of witnesses on this day could boost their status for an entire lifetime.[211] In addition to the officers fighting with their units, other commissioned ranks left their own units in garrison or more distant posts in order to help out. Milanese aristocrats without any commission reputedly donned their armour and took their places in Leganés's array as volunteers or *venturieri*. Montecuccoli considered experienced officers and nobles spread out along the forward deployment to be important buttresses and props supporting a sagging wall under pressure.[212] These men also carried orders around the field, not trusting underlings to pass them around by hand or word of mouth.[213]

Mere soldiers, who were mostly young men in their twenties, were keenly aware of their killed and wounded comrades, which was a major source of stress.[214] Soldiers could also interpret the drumbeats of their adversaries, and sense the mounting danger on the other side of the smoke before they could see it clearly.[215] Morale is not a steady current, but an oscillating wave, writes Edward Coss. A sense of control or helplessness makes a huge difference to their levels of testosterone or the depression-inducing cortisol.[216] Soldiers in action pass through physiological phases of alarm, and hormone surges of adrenaline and noradrenaline then increase the blood flow and heartbeat, triggering a sharp spike of sugar in the blood. This mobilization of the organism only lasts a short time, however, after which men must rely on their reserves of energy. If the peril lasted any length of time, they would become subject to severe fatigue and apathy.[217] Officers feared that the men fired as quickly as they could, even without taking the time to aim, simply in order to exhaust their powder.[218] However, a soldier moving to the rear, ostensibly to obtain more ammunition, passed in full view of his comrades. Unit cohesion relied not just on obedience to one's officers, it was also based on the

[208] Brnardic, *Imperial Armies: Infantry*, 38.

[209] Angelantonio Spagnoletti, 'Onore e spirito nazionale nei soldati italiani al servizio della monarchia spagnola', in C. Donati and B. Kroener (eds), *Militari e societa civile nell'Europa dell'eta moderna, sec. XVI–XVIII* (Bologna, 2007), 211–53; the emulation among different nationalities is stressed in the Spanish account, Biblioteca Nacional Madrid, Ms 2367, Italia 1636, 50.

[210] Drévillon, *L'Impôt*, 392.

[211] Costa, *Psicologia militare*, 65 and 127.

[212] Barker, *Military Intellectual and Battle*, 85; for the Milanese volunteers, see the letter of Carlo Sirtoni, reminding the king of 'la prontezza de cotesti cavaglieri li quali hanno sacrificato la loro vita nell'incontro d'Oleggio servendo de venturieri'. Archivio Storico Civico di Milano, Dicasteri 149, letter of 18 July 1636.

[213] Sieur du Praissac, *Discours et questions militaires* (Paris, 1638), 43.

[214] Costa, *Psicologia militare*, 251.   [215] Malfoy-Noël, *L'épreuve de la bataille*, 57.

[216] Edward J. Coss, *All for the King's Shilling* (Norman, OK, 2010), 193–208.

[217] The best description is that of Malfoy-Noël, *L'Epreuve de la bataille*, 70–1.

[218] Ardant du Picq, *Etudes sur le combat*, 204.

mutual surveillance of all the men who had lived together for months or years. Even a new recruit had to prove to his comrades (who, practically speaking, were his family too) that they could rely on him to do his part in their collective trial. 'That is the place where fraternity, unity, professionalism (*sens du métier*) and mutual confidence is born.'[219] From the moment of enlistment, the soldier belonged to a company and a tercio or regiment stitched together by *personal* relations. If a soldier let his companions down, he reasoned, he deserved to be ostracized by them and lose the status he had acquired among them to that moment.[220] Soldiers knew, too, that their cohesion as a force around their standards was key to their survival. But this reasoning was continually beset by the instinct of self-preservation that could take hold in an instant and override group loyalty. Men would fight on if they expected success, and believed that death and injury would be random and confined to an unlucky minority; survivors would reap the rewards. But if they began to think that continuous combat meant death *for them*, nothing could induce them to continue.[221] Every order to approach the enemy anew was akin to rolling the die again. Even thrill-seekers testing their limits at some point begin to appraise the risk differently; the steadily increasing anxiety leads to avoidance or withdrawal.[222]

All the accounts of the battle collapse the remainder of the day's action, even though the combat had not reached its halfway point. The Thirty Years' War saw battles become rather protracted firefights at fairly long range, despite the best efforts of the officers to have the men move closer.[223] Battle paintings are not reliable guides as to the typical range of musketry, for painters employed artistic licence to stress the heroism of the winning side. At Tornavento the Spanish advance stopped along the plateau's edge or a few metres below along the Panperduto canal, but the fighting continued as a *scaramuccia*. This particular tactic does not figure often in the drillbooks, but Gualdo Priorato provides a description of it, adding that it was 'di grande osservanza' (Fig. 3.9). The musketeers alternated between reloading and moving up to the firing line. Soldiers in combat accelerated the reloading process to half a dozen sequences, standing in the rear, right foot immobile. Holding the loaded weapon on an oblique angle (so as not to shoot a comrade by accident), the musketeer paced forward carefully behind the man in front, and then reaching the front row spread out as much as he was able, and once being certain that no friendly marksman was standing in front, placed the musket on its support, aimed deliberately at an enemy soldier and took his time to fire. Then he retraced his steps to the rear without turning his back to the enemy, while another man stepped forward to take his place. This form of musketry was not executed to specific orders and each man returned to the firing line as quickly as he had reloaded—in theory! 'The more this is done individually (*sconcertatamente*), the more likely it succeeds because there is no confusion or congestion'.[224] It was

[219] Ibid. 81.   [220] Holmes, *Acts of War*, 143.
[221] Tooby and Cosmides, *Evolution of War*, 6–7.
[222] Zuckerman, *Sensation Seeking*, 67.
[223] Rogers, 'Tactics and the Face of Battle', 203–35.
[224] Gualdo Priorato, *Il maneggio delle armi*, 102–3.

Battaglia Spagnola.

Fig. 3.9. Johann Wilhelm Baur, 'Battaglia Spagnuola': Spanish musketeers fight in loose order, possibly a 'scaramuccia', but the musketeers are not employing the forked rest. The depiction is dated 1636.

confusion, stressed the author-soldier, that was the mother of all disasters. Firing in this manner could continue all day. This looser order of firing tended to increase the number of skulkers or shirkers who hung back from the firing line.[225] The interests of the soldiers were not the same as those of Leganés, Victor-Amadeus, or Créquy, for they all hoped to finish the day unharmed. Wounded men who could walk spontaneously left the ranks for the rear to find the surgeons.

The fresh confederate battalions before long brought much greater firepower to bear on the tiring soldiers of the Catholic King, in part because the compression of the area defended by the Franco-Savoyard army increased the density of their deployment. This was not without its own danger: phalanx formations risked becoming death traps if the men were too tightly pressed to use their weapons efficiently, and became a target too big and dense to miss. But for the French and Savoyards, there was no place of refuge near the battlefield whose existence undermined their will to resist, only the wide Ticino river. One Tuscan eyewitness source, unfortunately uncorroborated by others, claims that after taking the heights Leganés wheeled eighteen cannon to the edge of the plateau with the intention of

---

[225] Gervase Phillips, 'Military Morality Transformed: Weapons and Soldiers on the 19th-Century Battlefield', *Journal of Interdisciplinary History*, 41 (2011), 565–90.

destroying the bridge with their fire.[226] Due to the trees on the slope and the thick pall of smoke below they would have had no clear view of a target and would have had to withdraw. There is no agreement on the number of cannon Leganés had at his disposal but he undoubtedly held an enormous advantage. Count Rinieri also claimed that, in the initial attack, Leganés placed two cannon on each flank of his advancing first line. The priest Comerio claims the Spanish had a total of eight larger cannon against a mere two sakers for the French.[227] Maillanes complained that just three enemy guns did a lot of damage to his men and to the cavalry in particular. The engraving depicting the battle clearly shows cannon arrayed on Leganés's left flank, including atop the Panperduto levees. Pushing the French off the plateau and down the slope would have made it impossible for them to continue firing.

As the French and Savoyards completed their deployment during the afternoon, Leganés called on his last reserves, in the hope of provoking a rout among the enemy foot. The final Spanish assaults targeted the regiments of Henrichemont and Roquefeuil on the French left (northern) flank that had just relieved that of Sault in the French centre, while smaller and more discreet detachments infiltrated the river plain from the north aiming to destroy the bridge.[228] The king of Spain's troops launched two furious attacks, in which almost all the French officers became casualties (it is claimed). After some fighting at close quarters, the French repulsed the attacking Spaniards 'as far as their entrenchments'.[229] But instead of retiring from the field, the Habsburg army set to work digging in (*se loger*).[230] This is something that does not appear in any of the Spanish accounts, but figures in two of the French versions; Spanish earthworks facing the French ones seem to appear out of nowhere. In all likelihood, they were the second line of trenches on the plateau that the French had thrown up near the edge of the escarpment. It only took a few hours to pile up enough earth to constitute a protective rampart, and it is possible that the officers put to work the great militia contingent, spectators of the fighting, repairing and modifying these protective works just out of sight and beyond the musket range of the French positions along the edge of the canal below them.[231] Holding the heights also concealed the deployment of troops from the enemy below.

Towards late afternoon, after the French managed to recover some of their entrenchments above the valley floor, the action tapered off into a series of scattered exchanges of musketry and the occasional local melee. The fight continued into the evening at a range where the musketry did little harm to either side. Both armies became more circumspect in order not to lose the battle. Créquy and

[226] ASFi Mediceo del Principato 3176, letter of one Count Rinieri, 23 June, fos. 1125–6.

[227] 'Relazione del curato Francesco Comerio di Lonate', in Bertolli and Colombo, *La peste del 1630 a Busto Arsizio*, 439.

[228] ASFi Mediceo del Principato 3180, copy of the letter from Monsù de Maillans to Monsù de Bay, 25 June 1636.

[229] *Gazette de France*, 410.

[230] Bibliothèque Nationale de France, Ms Fr 16929, *Relation de M. d'Esmery de ses negociations en Piedmont en 1635 etc.*, fo. 569.

[231] *Gazette de France*, 210.

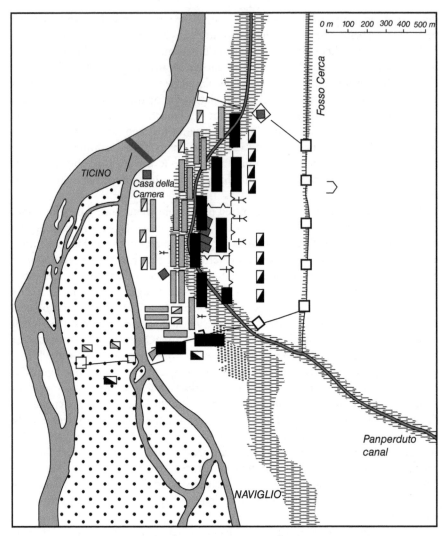

Map 6. Hypothetical positions at Tornavento, early afternoon.

Victor-Amadeus decided not to venture from their fortifications and press the attack, although their army now outnumbered their opponents.[232] A Lombard eyewitness tells us that the French remained behind the Panperduto parapet and then gained the top edge of the wooded slope at day's end. They recovered the hamlet of Tornavento in the last, nocturnal phase of the fighting.[233]

---

[232] Biblioteca Universitaria Bologna, vol. 473, Misc. H, n.15, *Relatione del fatto d'Arme*; the anonymous account describes the last phase of the fighting as 'semplici scaramuccie'.

[233] Archivio Storico Civico di Milano, Archivio Sola Busca: Serbelloni b.53, letter from Raimondo della Torre to Count Giovanni Serbelloni, 23 June 1636.

DISENGAGEMENT AND ASSESSMENT

Formations on both sides had broken and recoiled during the course of the day, under the weight of heavy casualties. The officers rallied the men and placed them back in the line, but they proved increasingly unreliable.[234] 'Of the combattants committed earlier, some are wounded, some are only interested in booty and still others are reluctant to undergo fresh peril, thinking that they have already done their duty', noted Montecuccoli. 'Moreover, they are altogether so excited that they do not understand or do not wish to understand a command.'[235] Men displayed a natural tendency to drift to the rear, especially once they felt they had done enough.[236] There may be some threshold of casualties beyond which unit morale collapses catastrophically, placed by some writers at one-third of the initial complement.[237] Clausewitz considered units that had suffered one-quarter to one-third casualties as 'a heap of burnt-out cinders'.[238] It gradually became clear to Leganés that he would not prevail against troops that were dug in, more numerous than his own and for the most part fresher. He decided to withdraw his men from the most exposed posts. Retreating from the field was very perilous, however, for it would energize the enemy and provoke them into a spirited pursuit with their superior cavalry onto the open heath. It was not so much the close fighting, or the musketry exchange at several score metres that constituted the bloodbath in battle, but the withdrawal, the flight of a beaten army, that triggered the wholesale massacres at White Mountain, Nördlingen, and Wittstock later that year.[239] Leganés himself witnessed the frenzy of his victorious Spaniards and Italians, intent on murder, chasing after the Germans and Scots as they withdrew.[240] Retreat triggers in the victors a sudden loss of fear and an irrepressible desire to destroy their adversaries before they can recover and continue the fight. Soldiers in battle undergo a roller-coaster of emotions from the exhilaration of victory to apathy to wild panic. Those chasing a beaten enemy in the flush of victory suddenly lose all their inhibitions against killing helpless victims.[241] These instincts are universal and appear in battle accounts from the earliest times in recorded history.[242] 'It is in the

---

[234] Du Praissac, *Discours et questions militaires*, 42.

[235] Barker, *Military Intellectual and Battle*, 84.

[236] S. L. A. Marshall, *Men Against Fire* (New York, 1947 [1967?]), 150.

[237] Costa, *Psicologia militare*, 173; George Raudzens, 'Firepower Limitations in Modern Military History', *Journal of the Society for Army Historical Research*, 67 (1989), 130–53.

[238] Griffith, *Forward into Battle*, 55.

[239] Anja Grothe and Bettina Jungklaus, 'Archaeological and Anthropological Examinations of a Mass Grave from the 1636 Battle at Wittstock: A Preliminary Report', in Gisela Grupe et al. (eds), *Limping Together through the Ages* (Rahden Westfalen, 2008), 127–35; on the battle and the massacre of fleeing Imperial soldiers, Steve Murdoch, Kathrin Zickermann, and Adam Marks, 'The Battle of Wittstock 1636: Conflicting Reports on a Swedish Victory in Germany', *Northern Studies*, 43 (2012), 71–109.

[240] Guthrie, *Battles of the Thirty Years War*, 272–84. At White Mountain, the combat at close quarters between the two armies inflicted only about 500 casualties on each side, but the Protestant army lost thousands of men in the ensuing panic flight. Chaline, *La bataille de la Montagne Blanche*, 181.

[241] Malfoy-Noël, *L'épreuve de la bataille*, 80–7.

[242] A recently unearthed example of it in Britain would be Towton (1461), George Goodwin, 'This Bitter Field', *History Today*, 61/5 (May 2011); on the experience of White Mountain, see Chaline, *La bataille de la Montagne Blanche*, 202.

subsequent pursuit of a broken or defeated enemy that the vast majority of the killing happens. Dogs understand this too, and you will be pursued if you run from them. From one perspective, the actual battle is a process of posturing until one side turns and runs. This posturing is critical to warfare.'[243] Centuries before Grossman, Montecuccoli noted the same effect: 'the greatest slaughter of the foe does not take place in combat, but during flight. Thus, the sole objective in establishing a battle order is to be able to disrupt, smite, rout, confuse and hound the enemy from the field. In pursuit, one can massacre him because, being disorganized and panic-stricken, he lacks the courage to defend himself.'[244]

Leganés rejoiced in his dispatch to Madrid the next day that his troops advanced with few laggards and stood 'punto a punto' from 8.00 in the morning until three hours after sundown.[245] But he understood by late afternoon or early evening on this longest day of the year that he could not ask of his men the impossible. The cavalry horses suffered terribly from a combination of heat and of the lack of water, which killed many of them.[246] Leganés decided, with the concurrence of his senior officers, that the best course was to continue the combat until nightfall and then to break off and withdraw under cover of darkness.[247] His army would retreat, regroup, and survive to fight another time. But the firing did not let up until well into the night.[248] The retreat was a model of the genre: Leganés had soldiers align hundreds of pikes in the ground behind their own entrenchments to give the impression that they were held in force, and then set hundreds of muskets alongside them, with their lit wicks glowing in the darkness. He instructed a detachment of dragoons left behind as the rearguard to prowl along the enemy line and fire all night long into the darkness.[249] Meanwhile, the tired Habsburg columns trudged southwards, to Castano and Boffalora, and then on to Abbiategrasso where an entrenched camp of their own awaited them, along the same road Gambacorta had used for his march to battle the previous night.[250] This night march at the end of a long day's hard-fought battle covered a greater distance than a normal daytime advance, losing neither baggage nor cannon! Upon reaching Abbiategrasso the following morning, officers and men at the limit of their endurance all lay down and slept.

Victor-Amadeus and Créquy too chose discretion over valour, being content to recapture the redoubts and positions they had lost.[251] The French and Savoyard officers judged their troops to be completely exhausted from the combination of prolonged musketry and repeated close action fighting. As the firing tapered off,

---

[243] Grossman, *On Combat*, 200–1.

[244] Barker, *Military Intellectual and Battle*, 82–3.

[245] AGS Estado 3344, letter in cipher of 23 June 1636.

[246] The hardship of the heat and lack of water on the horses was a widely reported detail; Alessandro Giulini, 'Un diario secentesco inedito d'un notaio milanese', *Archivio Storico Lombardo*, 57 (1930), 466–82.

[247] BNM Ms 2367, Italia 1636, 51.

[248] Hardy de Perini, *Batailles françaises*, 216.   [249] *Gazette de France*, 412.

[250] ASFi Mediceo del Principato 3176, letter from Milan to the Balì Cioli in Florence, 24 June 1636.

[251] Gualdo Priorato, *An History of the late Warres*, 357.

Victor-Amadeus, Créquy, and Hémery gathered together the principal officers in the recaptured *cascina* of Tornavento to discuss what course to take. The ambassador's account is refreshing in its frankness. 'In this meeting, if everyone had expressed their personal sentiment, our retreat would have been certain. But the fear of being accused of cowardice (*lâcheté*) finally determined us to fight again the next day and hold our position as best we could. Nevertheless we decided to pass the baggage to the other side of the river in case of ill fortune and to have the bridge unencumbered in case of retreat.' Other participants remembered the meeting differently. Victor-Amadeus claims that only he, the Piedmontese comte de Verrua, and his aides-de-camp Castelan and Roqueservières kept their heads and recommended digging in for a new fight at daybreak, only a few hours away. Créquy's son, the comte de Sault, unsettled by the impetus of the Spanish assault, lost his head and urged an immediate retreat, seconded by Du Plessis-Praslin. Créquy himself, Victor-Amadeus tells us, thought that his troops were worn out by the continual 'escarmouche' and would not be able to withstand a fresh attack. The Duke of Savoy considered it almost miraculous to have repelled the Spanish assault.[252] They finally resolved to repair their entrenchments and to await a fresh Habsburg attack the next morning. With the sunrise it slowly dawned on the confederates that they had prevailed during the previous day's fighting.[253] However, again in Hémery's words, 'the field and the dead belonged to us. It was the only benefit we had from winning this battle.'

All the accounts stress the extreme length of the encounter, about fourteen hours of continuous combat. This was the most obstinate fight in over a hundred years, Leganés wrote to Madrid, and it was no hyperbole when he claimed that even the oldest soldiers would have never seen such a thing.[254] Hémery echoed Leganés in his statement to Richelieu that professional soldiers had never seen the like of what had just taken place. He calculated the French and Savoyard ammunition expenditure as 25,000 or 30,000 pounds of gunpowder, which was almost all confined to musketry.[255] This amount represented somewhere between 12 and 14 metric tonnes of powder. Matchlock musket weights declined quickly after the onset of the Thirty Years' War, to the point where after 1630 they shortened by about 15cm and weighed just 4.6kg, with 17.5 to 18mm in the bore, firing a ball weighing about 30g.[256] On the principle that the powder charge should correspond to about half of the ball's weight, this meant that each shot required a little

---

[252] These appreciations Victor-Amadeus sent in a dispatch to his ambassador in France the marquis de Saint-Maurice, 28 June 1636 and a coded letter of 15 July 1636, ASTo Materie politiche interne: Lettere ministri, Francia, vol. 34.

[253] Decades later, Du Plessis-Praslin claimed substantially the opposite, that it was the Duke of Savoy who pressed for withdrawal, while he recommended digging in and waiting for developments. *Mémoires du Maréchal Du Plessis*, in Michaud and Poujoulat, *Mémoires pour servir à l'histoire de France*, vii (Paris, 1838), 358–60.

[254] *Relacion del Combate del exercito de su magestad*, 1636.

[255] AAE Correspondance Politique: Sardaigne, vol. 24, 675. Letter from Héméry to Cardinal Richelieu (July 1636).

[256] Peter Engerisser, 'Matchlock musket, Suhl, ca. 1630', <www.engerisser.de/Bewaffnung/weapons/Matchlockmusket.html>; Keith Roberts claims that weights were reduced by reducing the length of the barrel, as well as the diameter of the bore; Roberts, *Matchlock Musketeer*, 9.

over 15g of corned powder, or sixty-five shots per kilo.[257] This equates to 850,000 to 900,000 shots! Misfires were common enough, but did not occur at a steady rate. So let's reduce the successful discharge of the muskets by a liberal quarter-million shots, leaving 675,000. Not all the French and Savoyard infantry was engaged from the outset, and only two-thirds of them were musketeers. Let's propose a hypothetical equivalent of 6,000 musketeers responsible for the over-whelming majority of these rounds. (The cavalry with their pistols were in range of their enemy for very short periods, and the two light cannon spewing musket balls were busy only in the early afternoon.) The calculation obtained is a considerable 150 shots per individual (including misfires), so even if they had all been firing continuously all day (they were not), each man would have fired a minimum of ten rounds every hour.[258] It is possible to recalibrate some of these numbers. Reloading might have taken closer to one minute than two, since soldiers firing level or upwards didn't bother pushing a wad of paper or cloth down the barrel to hold the ball close to the powder charge: they simply banged the butt end of the weapon on the ground in order to compress the powder before aiming.[259] French and Savoyard reinforcements arrived early enough in the day to push the number of musketeers closer to 8,000, which would give us a rough average of 112 shots per musketeer for the day and eight shots per hour. Whatever the true mean, the intensity and duration of the firefight probably broke some records.

The contest of casualty claims began almost immediately after the battle, char-acterized by a huge disparity. The relation of the *Gazette* published only days after news reached Paris claimed that the Spaniards had lost 3,000 foot and be-tween 300 and 400 cavalrymen killed or mortally wounded, of whom 1,500 were left on the field, and as many others incapacitated by their injuries. Practically on the same page it added that only 700 enemy soldiers lay slain on the battlefield, while Leganés abandoned other corpses along the roads to the south.[260] A further account based on dispatches from Genoa published on 11 July inflated Spanish losses still higher, to 4,000 killed, of whom twenty were captains, but then claimed the death of twenty-two ethnic Spanish captains, 'and almost all the Neapolitans'.[261] With the number of men who would have des-

---

[257] Lugs, *Firearms Past and Present*, 17.

[258] The 18th-century British fusil, the Brown Bess, required a powder charge of 9g or 10g. I have calculated generously the reloading time at two minutes per round. Well-trained infantry was capable of better performances. This would modify the above figures by perhaps a third; see N. A. Roberts, J. W. Brown, B. Hammett, and P. D. F. Kingston, 'A Detailed Study of the Effectiveness and Capabilities of 18th-Century Musketry on the Battlefield', *Journal of Conflict Archaeology* (2008), 1–21; one Modenese source gives us an estimate of each powder charge, at half an ounce. But ounces and pounds varied from place to place. Readers will recall that a Troy ounce weighs 31.1g, an avoirdu-pois ounce 28.3g. Italian 12-ounce pounds oscillated from about 310g (Genoa, Tuscany) to about 330g (Milan, Parma). A north-Italian half-ounce charge weighed about 13g But the author was refer-ring perhaps to Imperial pounds. In the 17th century, Köln standards were often used, at 468g (a half-ounce weighs 14.6g). French ounces might have been the reference, since Prince Borso was in French service at the time Canossa was writing. Who knows which one he meant? For the reference, Biblioteca Estense Modena, Misc. Estense Ital. 160, Count Francesco Canossa, *Regolamento sopra il combattere dell'Infanteria in una battaglia*.

[259] Engerisser, 'Matchlock musket'.   [260] *Gazette de France* (1636), 411.

[261] *Gazette de France*, 100 (11 July 1636).

erted Spanish colours during the fight and the night march afterwards, the losses incurred by the enemy would have reached 6,000 men.[262] However, despite many hours of close fighting, the prisoners of note numbered only twelve, of a total number of 400, many of whom were 'found almost asleep'.[263] In his dispatches to Madrid, Leganés claimed that he had lost 1,300 men killed and 1,000 wounded, but that casualties among the officers numbered 200.[264] The separate page containing details of casualties in Leganés's dispatches seems to have gone missing. The anonymous Italian account appears to give plausible figures; 'we lost more than 1,500 dead and 1,000 wounded, among whom were a great number of officers'.[265] The same source stated that the Franco-Savoyards lost more than 1,200 killed, among whom were more than seventy officers. In his camp at Abbiategrasso, Leganés held a muster of his remaining troops, who amounted to 6,000 foot and 4,500 horse, which pretty much confirms the anonymous Italian estimate.[266] The Milanese notary Calco recorded in his diary on the following day that wagons carried more than 600 wounded soldiers into the city for treatment.[267] It is interesting that the number of wounded should be inferior to that of the dead: this would reflect the gravity of wounds inflicted by the tremendous muzzle velocities of muskets at close range, and the deadliness of larger musket balls relative to later periods.[268] Experiments using eighteenth-century muskets firing smaller bullets produced ugly wounds at 75 metres, measuring 48mm across at the entry and 55mm for the exit, which would have been fatal if inflicted on the torso, either initially from the impact and loss of blood, or else from a secondary infection.[269] Battlefield accounts were always shy about discussing the carnage everyone witnessed, and no source mentions the collection of wounded men while the fight was raging.[270]

Tuscan officials sent the Grand Duke in Florence casualty figures too. The resident Pandolfini writing two days after the battle estimated thirty men killed and as many wounded for that contingent. The entire loss for the Spanish force that day he first estimated at 500 killed, as many wounded and about a thousand men dispersed.[271] Ten days after the battle, Camillo del Monte sent a more sombre account, of forty men killed (including two captains) and another eighty wounded, and others not accounted for who totalled 163 men, or about 30 per cent of the tercio committed to battle.[272] Two more captains were completely out of commission, and required replacement. These losses among the officers would have been much worse but for the armour they were wearing. Del Monte himself was struck

[262] *Gazette de France*, 112 (1 Aug. 1636).
[263] ASFi Mediceo del Principato 3180, fo. 1147, letter of Maillane.
[264] Oltrona Visconti, *La battaglia di Tornavento*, 126.
[265] Biblioteca Universitaria Bologna, vol. 473, Misc. H, no. 15.
[266] Oltrona Visconti, *La battaglia di Tornavento*, 130.
[267] Giulini, 'Un diario secentesco'.
[268] Roberts et al., 'Detailed study of Effectiveness'.   [269] Ibid.
[270] Chaline, *La bataille de la Montagne Blanche*, 211; see also Malfoy-Noël, *L'épreuve de la bataille*, 102.
[271] ASFi Mediceo del Principato 3176, fo. 751.
[272] ASFi Mediceo del Principato 3181, fos. 418 and 470.

four times by musketry, twice on the torso and twice more on the knee, but these left nothing more than big bruises.[273]

We can approach the problem from another perspective, by comparing the strength of the Spanish army's companies reported in May with that of the same units early in August. The imprecision stems partly from the fact that some companies of the tercios present at the battle remained behind in garrison and suffered no losses at all. Yet another source of imprecision stems from the absence in August of numerous companies that existed in May, which implies that the officers had been killed and the survivors amalgamated into other units. Still, where we are able to compare single companies on both rosters, there is stark evidence of the severity of casualties. In Don Martin d'Aragon's tercio of Lombardy, the shortfall was at least 243 men, or 18 per cent of the full complement. The companies of the Spanish tercio of the Marqués de Mortara were down by only 8 per cent, but the Italians of the Spìnola tercio suffered a shortfall of no less than 26 per cent, representing more than 400 men. Many of those companies appear to have been butchered in the battle. Spìnola's own company lost 'only' 27 per cent, but four more were down by a third. Hermes Nembri's company had a shortfall of 44 per cent, Carlo Negri's slightly over half, and Gerardino Sostono's company was missing 60 per cent of its previous complement. Survivors of companies eviscerated by heavy casualties were redistributed among others, and I suspect that the losses from the battle were even higher than the compared number of soldiers suggests. The six tercios for which we can draw comparisons totalled 89 companies in May, each led by a captain. By August, twenty-four captains, or 27 per cent, were unaccounted for, and likely killed. Don Martin d'Aragon's tercio lost a third of its captains, and Antonio Arias Sotelo, who was grievously wounded himself, lost nine of his nineteen captains. The German companies of Gil de Haes and Abraham Lener, which were in the thick of the fighting, were considerably reinforced following the battle, and cannot be compared, but de Haes's regiment lost four captains that day.[274]

Cardinal Richelieu's published figures for French losses, which constitute the most accessible French source, claim that the Franco-Savoyard army lost only 400 to 500 infantry, both killed and wounded, and 120 cavalrymen, although losses among the officers numbered no fewer than eighty.[275] These figures constitute a deliberate misrepresentation. The first letters to Paris, those of the maréchal de Créquy, admitted the loss of 700 soldiers killed and wounded, and another 100 officers.[276] The *Gazette* published in Paris two weeks after the battle tabulated the officers killed, wounded, and captured for specific regiments, but ignored the losses among the rank and file. Maillane's private letter admitted to seventy-six

[273] ASFi Mediceo del Principato 3180, fo. 1119.

[274] Charles Rahlenbeck, *Gilles de Haes* (Ghent, 1854), 13.

[275] *Memoires du Cardinal de Richelieu*, in Michaud and Poujoulat, *Nouvelle collection des Memoires pour servir à l'histoire de France*, ix. 51.

[276] AAE Correspondance Politique, Sardaigne, vol. 24, letter dated 25 June from Créquy describing the combat.

killed and twenty-four badly wounded men, leaving his battalion with only 400 survivors, a casualty rate of 20 per cent.[277] The Chamblay regiment lost its lieutenant-colonel and no fewer than five of its captains killed outright, and the Florainville regiment on the valley floor similarly lost five captains killed. In the Lyonnais regiment that withstood the first shock, nine officers were presumed killed or prisoners of the Spaniards, including its colonel La Tour, presented as a prize to Leganés. These were grievous losses, for French regiments typically numbered only ten or twelve companies in all. Just among captains, the *Gazette* reported seventeen killed and another twenty wounded.[278] The cavalry suffered too, with about 120 troopers killed and wounded.[279] Years later, Hémery admitted to the loss of 110 officers and 1,200 soldiers killed and wounded in the battle itself, about half the losses of the Spanish army. The enemy was weakened by 4,000 men, he claimed (fairly plausibly if one includes men disbanding in the immediate aftermath) and the Franco-Savoyard troops were diminished by 2,000 (also plausible).[280]

Spanish and Italian sources insist that French losses were heavier than their own. The first Tuscan dispatch claimed that many French soldiers drowned in the shallow *naviglio* or the Ticino river as they tried to flee. A week later the resident Pandolfini reported that French prisoners captured in the aftermath confessed to 1,200 dead during the battle and another 300 dying of their wounds in the subsequent days.[281] The regiments of Bonne and Monsù Poitié (I cannot identify this one) were totally ruined. Another Tuscan report gave total mortality as 3,500 for both sides, and about 600 wounded Habsburg soldiers captured.[282]

Whatever the apparent precision of the casualty reports, no good source tabulated exact losses, for military administrations were not concerned about this.[283] Published accounts often record casualties among the higher officers, because many of these well-connected men frequented the court outside the campaigning season. The rank and file turned their backs on their civilian origin and did not send much information home. The best we can do is to give concordant figures as a rough estimate. George Raudzens attempted some generalizations about other battles on the basis of published statistics, but as we have seen, these are fragmentary and typically one-sided. They rarely specify how many men were killed, wounded, or prisoners.[284] Let us conclude that losses on each side in this battle were heavy, perhaps equivalent to a fifth of the number of men engaged, with a

[277] ASFi Mediceo del Principato 3180, fo. 1147.

[278] *Gazette de France*, 99 (1636), 412.

[279] *Relation de la victoire obtenue en Italie par l'armèe du Roy* (Lyon, 1636).

[280] BNF Ms Fr 16929, *Relation de M. d'Esmery*, fo. 570.

[281] ASFi Mediceo del Principato 3176, fo. 151, letter to Florence 24 June 1636; also fo. 781, letter of 2 July 1636.

[282] ASFi Mediceo del Principato 3258, fo. 251, letter from Florence to Don Francisco de Melo, 1 July 1636.

[283] Alain Guéry, 'Les comptes de la mort vague après la guerre: Pertes de guerre et conjoncture du phénomène guerre', *Histoire et Mesure*, 6 (1991), 289–312.

[284] George Raudzens, 'In Search of Better Quantification for War History: Numerical Superiority and Casualty Rates in Early Modern Europe', *War and Society*, 15 (1997), 1–30.

clear disadvantage to the Spanish, who attacked a desperate adversary defending prepared positions.

By all accounts, then, Tornavento was a bloody encounter, singular in its stubbornness. How could the soldiers, who were not fighting for religious or idealistic aims, and who never received the wages they were promised, have endured it? Perhaps the clue lies in the extraordinary ammunition expenditure of the confederate French and Savoyards, which implies that it took about 300 shots to kill or wound a single enemy soldier. The heavy losses were not inflicted in a short time. If the Spanish casualties to musketry did not far exceed 2,000 men, these would have been killed and wounded at a rate of about 150 men per hour along a kilometre or more of frontage, say two or three men a minute. Of course this is an abstraction that ignores that there were moments when the attrition would have been heavier, but that would have been offset by intervals without appreciable casualties on either side. This low *frequency* of casualties helps explain the stubbornness of the contest.

Given the minute proportion of hits, it seems that a fair proportion of the musketeers did not fire *to kill* the enemy they faced, or deliberately aimed too high. The phenomenon was first noted by S. L. A. Marshall in the American army during the Second World War, and John Keegan discusses this in his analysis of musketry effectiveness at the battle of Waterloo. In the latter case, most of the musketry missed its target—a large body of men—even at 50 metres.[285] This phenomenon has been known since the age of muskets, and until recently historians explained it as a consequence of the crudeness of the weapon, and the difficulty of controlling its recoil. But the matchlock musket was not *that* inaccurate, and the heavy firearm with its support and larger ball was more lethal at a greater range than the simple arquebus that preceded it or the fusil that replaced it. Austrian experiments on these weapons conducted in 1988 and 1989 determined that, although the muzzle velocity was remarkable, its killing zone was limited to a range of 90 to 120 metres due to the rapid loss of momentum of the round bullet to air resistance. In these tests where the 'human element' was not present, 60 per cent of the shots were on target at 100 metres.[286] But this human element is central to the art of battles. 'It would be a mistake to imagine that these soldiers were automatons and fundamentally different from soldiers of other eras, numb to the prospects of their own violent death.'[287]

The inability of the soldier to aim directly at his adversary, out of fear, confusion, and blinding smoke resulted in what Olivier Chaline calls 'un remarquable absence de précision dans le tir'.[288] Two hundred years later, when the soldier's individual firearm had a much greater range, accuracy, and rate of fire, Charles Ardant du

---

[285] Keegan, *Face of Battle*, 172.

[286] Bert S. Hall, *Weapons and Warfare in Renaissance Europe: Gunpowder, Technology and Tactics*, (Baltimore and London, 1997), 135–40; see the table provided by Peter Krenn, 'Test-Firing Selected 16th—18th Century Weapons', *Military Illustrated Past and Present*, 33 (Feb. 1991), 34–8. The immobile target measured 167 × 30 cm, about half a metre square.

[287] Hall, *Weapons and Warfare*, 150.

[288] Chaline, *La bataille de la Montagne Blanche*, 175.

Picq described the difficulty of getting the troops to fire effectively in the heat of combat. 'Volley fire supposes such self-control that if ever troops were capable of it, they would cut down battalions like scythes mow grain.' He suspected that the men deliberately aimed to miss their targets, judging from the fact that casualties were so low relative to the number of shots fired. 'C'est toujours le soldat qui commande le feu.'[289] Our writer was well aware of the studies of fire efficiency conducted in the eighteenth century, and considered that there had been no progress in a hundred years. 'In the ranks, firing at will (the only practical way), with the emotion, the smoke and the awkwardness (*gêne*), one is lucky to get, not aimed fire, but horizontal fire.' Part of the problem was that, quite apart from nervousness, and the annoyance from the loud percussion of firing in their ears, the men got in each other's way. They were eager to fire as much as possible, 'c'est-à-dire, le plus mal possible', in order to preserve themselves from the enemy's return fire. The officers were vigilant to prevent the men from firing only in order to exhaust their ammunition, which would permit them to retire from the firing line.[290] Enemy soldiers behaved identically, so that whoever fired more, hit more of the enemy.

Contemporary historians alive to this human element in combat have readjusted their assessment of tactics in the early modern and modern era in order to account for this kind of 'inefficiency'. Paddy Griffith, in his exploration of fighting tactics in the nineteenth and twentieth centuries noted how neither the British nor the French expected to defeat the enemy by shooting at them. When it happened, the firefight was 'lengthy, inconclusive and costly'. Much better to fix bayonet and charge, or else retire out of range.[291]

One of Ardant du Picq's readers was the American army sociologist Samuel Marshall, member of a Senior Observors Board studying the effectiveness of tactics and fire systems in the field in 1944–5, but he did not publish his book until after the Korean War. Marshall discovered that only a quarter of the soldiers in the front line actually fired their weapons at the enemy, something he attributed to human nature and the existence of inhibiting instincts that made it hard for men to kill. Battles were fought and often decided by small numbers of more motivated warriors, supported by deadly team weapons fired from far away. Marshall claimed that this problem had probably always been present in war, but no one had ever thought to collect the data.[292]

In addition to this legacy of psychology, which presupposes that people everywhere are endowed with identical psychic mechanisms that have evolved since prehistory, the last twenty years has seen the blossoming of other disciplines rooted in the concept of human nature. John Keegan's early work was informed by the work on aggression by Konrad Lorenz and some of his disciples, whose study of animal behaviour or ethology scientists quickly redirected toward human subjects. Keegan's subsequent work allows even greater scope for human ethology, that is, the understanding that humans are evolved animals packed with universal

---

[289] Ardant du Picq, *Etudes sur le combat*, 138–41.   [290] Ibid. 196–204.
[291] Griffith, *Forward into Battle*, 18–28; see also Earl J. Hess, *The Union Soldier in Battle: Enduring the Ordeal of Combat* (Lawrence, KS, 1997).
[292] Marshall, *Men Against Fire*.

instincts, although these always operate in specific historical contexts.[293] On the shoulders of Ardant du Picq, Marshall, and Lorenz, Dave Grossman, an officer and psychologist of the American Marines, has recently developed a far-reaching model of these inhibitions around killing, with an eye to teaching soldiers and law enforcers how to overcome them. Grossman claims that only 2 per cent of people (almost exclusively men) are 'natural-born killers', able to terminate the existence of others without remorse. One might qualify only a few of these as pathological.[294] Intraspecies violence cannot be reduced to fight or flight, he notes. Two other behavioural strategies exist in the human repertoire, namely combat posturing and submission. The former action serves to convince an opponent through sight and sound that the posturer is dangerous. Among primates and many other animals, fighting is rarely waged to the death, because submissive gestures by one of the combatants usually put an end to it.[295] Posturing, mock battle, and submission gestures are vital to the survival of the species for they prevent deaths and ensure that the males will survive their youthful ardour to be able to procreate later. Among humans, most of the participants in predatory organizations like gangs are more interested in status and display than in bloodlust, and are willing to limit damage to their enemies if it similarly reduces risk to themselves. In warfare, the drums and trumpets, battle cries, and painted shields and masks serve to intimidate opponents into retiring. Firing deliberately over the heads of the enemy serves the same purpose. This posturing is especially strong when soldiers stand face-to-face across from their enemies, for they need to be doing *something* to keep the threat at bay. Officers' direct orders helped reduce the inhibitions to kill if these leaders exerted sufficient social and professional influence over their men, but they had to remain in close proximity to their subordinates to exert this control. The cannon was a far more lethal weapon, for a team operated it under close supervision and it fired from much further away. Distance from our enemy reduces the inhibitions we have to kill them. Modern air strikes and drones practically inflict death in the abstract, which is psychologically easier for the pilots or systems engineers pushing the buttons.[296] In early modern warfare, the musket was an improvement over the pike, for soldiers could inflict casualties on the enemy from further away: indeed, the soldiers would have preferred to fire from the greatest possible range! Distance is not strictly spatial: combatants can be distant from one another by race and religion too, because such differences served to dehumanize the enemy. However, these elements were not extreme at Tornavento; all the participants were Europeans and the great majority were Roman Catholics.

Grossman claims that this reluctance to kill other men at close quarters has existed throughout history. He and S. L. A. Marshall have made some counterintuitive claims about man's behaviour in battle. Grossman calls the neglect to discuss posturing a conspiracy of silence by historians, and a combination of forgetfulness, distortion, and lies; one could make a special condemnation of poetry and literature, rich sources of self-deception![297] Grossman's claim that posturing

---

[293] Keegan, *History of Warfare*, 1993, 79–84; similarly, Dyer, *War*, 53–86.
[294] Grossman, *On Killing*, 50 and 180.
[295] Ibid. 5–6.   [296] Ibid. 10.   [297] Ibid. 36.

has always been an essential part of battle throughout human history is something that historians must examine more closely. Some anthropologists and psychologists doubt that we have such inhibitions to kill. As much as Grossman's studies illuminate the process of combat and the psychological instincts that influence the outcome, his claims have not been subject to much close scrutiny. The 'fire ratios' first noted by S. L. A. Marshall were not systematically studied by the Senior Observors Board during the Second World War, and grew out of the author's later writings.[298] There are increasing suspicions that he just made them up.[299] Nevertheless, an element of posturing at close quarters in battle may help explain the low frequency of casualties incurred during musketry exchanges, when added to the defects in accuracy of the weapons at ranges that the soldiers found more tolerable. Eyewitnesses emphasized the effectiveness of the Spanish artillery firing roundshot from far away, and of the lethality of French grapeshot unleashed close up. So the casualty figures from the bloody day at Tornavento are quite compatible with Grossman's surprising claim.

Trying to soften the blow of being repulsed with heavy losses and leaving Milan threatened by two enemy armies, Leganés reassured Madrid that Spanish arms were as formidable as they had ever been. The day's fighting would refute those Italians who warned of the demise of Spain's power.[300] Crack troops were those who would advance altogether without firing until the last possible moment, or who stood their ground before an enemy advance without flinching. In both those respects, his men demonstrated their worth at Tornavento. However, while the French infantry had bent under the strain, they did not break, and the Duke of Savoy stood by Créquy at the critical moment. Chastened by the brutal experience of 22 June, both sides would prove reluctant to repeat it.

---

[298] Robert Engen, 'Tuer pour son pays: Nouveau regard sur l'homicidologie', *Revue Militaire Canadienne*, 9 (2009), 120–8.

[299] Robert Engen, *Canadians under Fire: Infantry Effectiveness in the Second World War* (Montreal and Kingston, 2009), 11–27.

[300] Estado 3344, letter of the Marqués de Leganés, 25 June 1636.

4

'The War Becomes Cruel'

AFTERMATH OF CARNAGE

The French and Savoyard soldiers, physically and psychologically spent, cooked their meal and stared into the campfire, discussing the day's ordeal and expecting to undergo more of the same after sunrise.[1] The sights and sounds they had just experienced occasioned an emotional arousal that talking helped contain—something we call 'debriefing' today.[2] Victor-Amadeus ordered some men to work on their entrenchments, despite the fact that both the officers and the ranks were at the limit of their physical strength.[3] Confusion and disorientation rendered some of them effectively useless for days afterwards. Everyone had good reason to be worried. The Habsburg army, they believed, was well dug in on the heights above them and (for all they knew) received reinforcements during the night. Should the battle recommence the following day, the Spaniards held the high ground. Leganés might well renew his assault, knowing that the French cavalry could not charge on the wooded slope traversed by the canal. If on the other hand the French and Savoyards attacked from the edge of the plateau, they would still be unable to deploy their horse to good effect, while enemy soldiers were well dug-in and supported by abundant artillery firing grapeshot at close range. Neither prospect inspired confidence. Victor-Amadeus therefore issued the order to strengthen the bridge in order to transfer baggage carts and cannon to the western bank, to facilitate retreat should the Spanish force them out of their positions during the second round.[4] French officers beseeched Victor-Amadeus to cross the river as well in order to 'conserver sa personne', but he refused, considering, as did Hémery, that he could be more easily accused of cowardice if he complied with the suggestion.[5] Everyone remained unaware that the skilful Spanish army had entirely withdrawn.

Yet the French and Savoyards had it easy. Leganés's tired men withdrew from the fight only to undertake an extenuating night march of some twenty-seven

---

[1] Louis Crocq, *Les traumatismes psychiques de guerre* (Paris, 1999), 73–4.

[2] Dave Grossman, *On Combat* (Mascoutah, IL, 2004), 303.

[3] Archives des Affaires Etrangères, Correspondance Politique Sardaigne, vol. 24, letter from Hémery, (illegible) July (end of the month); *Gazette de France*, 102 (1636).

[4] ASFi Mediceo del Principato 3258, letter to Don Francisco de Melo, 1 July 1636. The Tuscans received this information from their spy placed in Victor-Amadeus's entourage, who dispatched a letter to Florence on 23 July.

[5] BNF Ms Fr 16929, *Relation de M. d'Esmery de ses negociations en Piedmont en 1635 etc.*, fo. 570.

kilometres (as the crow flies) from Castano to Boffalora and then to Abbiategrasso to the south—almost the equivalent of two days' march on campaign. Camillo del Monte complained that he spent six days and nights without sleeping or relaxing, like his soldiers tormented by the oppressive heat.[6] One minor functionary in the camp the next day sought to have someone reply to an urgent message from General Serbelloni in Milan, but he could not rouse anyone from their beds.[7]

Concern for collecting the wounded and burying the dead manifested itself only the next day. Between 2,000 and 3,000 men died during the hot, long day of 22 June. A comparable number of men lay wounded more or less grievously. The Spanish evacuated some 600 wounded men in forty cartloads to Milan the next day, where if they survived the forty-kilometre ride in the heat, they would fortunately find medical treatment comparable to the best in Europe. Military hospitals were very much a novelty in the period, and Spanish military hospitals in particular ranked among the best anywhere, but none existed yet in Northern Italy.[8] Large city hospitals were a more than adequate substitute. In relatively hygienic environments—for the seventeenth century—surgeons applied themselves to the difficult task of tending to wounds under optimal conditions. The Ospedale Maggiore was 'the fairest pallace in Milan...fitter to be the Court of some Kings then to keep Almes men in', wrote an English traveller, who had never encountered its equivalent (Fig. 4.1).[9] The great institution, the largest landowner in the entire duchy, rose prior to 1500 adjacent to the medieval rampart and to the canal that served as a moat before the city's expansion. A banker's huge legacy in 1626 permitted it to expand and eliminate the practice of laying patients in gurneys in the corridors while awaiting better accommodations. There were about fifteen smaller hospitals in the city, but this one was intended to provide medical care for people who might be cured. Fevers were treated on the ground floor, while attendants carried people with wounds upstairs to be treated by increasingly specialized surgeons. The personnel would have been fairly young, since the great plague of 1630 wiped out the previous generation of medical caregivers in a single terrible sweep. Regimental surgeons busy the day before just behind the battlefield converged on the city to assist the wounded under better conditions.[10] The great hospital took in about 500 patients a month, and possessed over a thousand beds. Still, the influx of hundreds of wounded soldiers overwhelmed the doctors, surgeons, barbers, nurses, and sundry other assistants working there. Fortunately again, it was easy to draw upon the numerous medical personnel of the great city. The hospital

---

[6] ASF Mediceo del Principato 3181, letter of 24 June 1636, fo. 415.

[7] Archivio Storico Civico di Milano, Archivio Sola Busca: Serbelloni b.53, letter from Raimondo della Torre at Abbiategrasso, 23 June 1636.

[8] Cristina Borreguero Beltràn, 'El coste humano de la guerra: mortandad, enfermedad y desercìon en los ejercitos de la Epoca Moderna', in Fidel Gomez Ochoa and Daniel Macias Fernandez (eds), *El Combatiente a lo largo de la historia: imaginario, percepcìon, representacìon* (Santander, 2012), 57–82.

[9] John Raymond, *An Itinerary contayning a voyage made through Italy in the years 1646 and 1647* (London, 1648), 244–5.

[10] On regimental surgeons of the period, Eric Gruber von Arni, *Justice to the Maimed Soldier: Nursing, Medical Care and Welfare for Sick and Wounded Soldiers and their Families during the English Civil Wars and Interregnum, 1642–1660* (Aldershot and Burlington, 2001), 63.

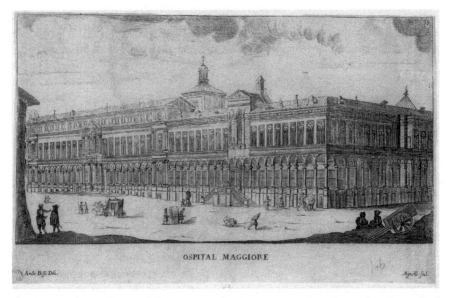

OSPITAL MAGGIORE

Fig. 4.1. Andrea Biffi, Ospedale Maggiore of Milan. More a palace than a place for medical treatment, wrote an English traveller. In 1636 the facilities of this great institution were on par with the best in Europe.

possessed a well-stocked medical dispensary, copious stores of food and wine, ample kitchens, and a refectory. The principal shortcoming, apart from the shortage of facilities for bathing patients (a mere ten wooden tubs served this purpose), was a lack of ready cash.[11] The Tuscan resident Pandolfini appeared the next day to distribute coins to the attendants to cover the expenditures of men belonging to the Grand Duke's tercio.[12] Wounded men lay in great beds designed for two or three patients, lining each side of the great corridor. The large windows aligned above the beds were not entirely sufficient to remove the odours emanating from the hygienic facilities in little alcoves nearby. This 'impurity of the air' gave rise to what were known as hospital fevers that delayed or counteracted the healing process.[13] Numerous attendants fed the patients, changed the sheets, and tended the wounds, while friars confessed them and distributed sacraments. Professional nurses helped cup the wounds, administered bleedings and purges, and held men down while surgeons operated.[14]

[11] Giorgio Cosmacini, *La Ca'Granda dei Milanesi: Storia dell'Ospedale Maggiore* (Rome and Bari, 1999), 101–14 and 131.

[12] ASF Mediceo del Principato 3180, letter of 24 June 1636, fo. 1119.

[13] Giorgio Cosmacini, *La carità e la cura: L'Ospedale Maggiore di Milano nell'età moderna* (Milan, 1992), 71–2.

[14] Gruber von Arni, *Justice to the Maimed Soldier*, 3–13; see 180–5 for details on tending wounds and maintaining hygiene; hospitals for sick and wounded soldiers also existed in Pavìa and Novara, and perhaps anywhere hosting a large garrison. That of Novara housed 100 beds in 1637, ASNo Comune di Novara parte antica 1875, Memoriali, 19 Oct. 1637.

Men wounded by swords enjoyed the best prospects for quick recovery, for attackers tended to inflict them with the sharpened edge in a cutting gesture, which was most often superficial, rather than impaling the victim with the point. Most wounds were inflicted by the musketry. A heavy arquebus ball could penetrate a breastplate 3 to 4mm thick at 30 metres. Men struck in the head, the thorax, and the abdomen at closer range would not likely survive, since the balls caused bone fractures and the cavity quickly became infected with dirt and fragments of cloth-ing.[15] In the century before Tornavento, surgeons made great progress in the treat-ment of gunshot wounds but they would still only be able to save a fraction of victims relative to today. The mid-sixteenth-century French army surgeon, Ambroise Paré wrote a widely disseminated manual on how to treat these wounds (Fig. 4.2, Fig. 4.3). The surgeon first had to feel for bone fragments, bits of clothing, and armour with his fingers, more sensitive than other instruments, then withdraw them from the cavity with pincers shaped like a crane's beak. For fractured bones protruding from the wound, he designed a clipper very reminiscent of a garden branch-cutter that was quicker and less painful than a saw. The surgeon possessed a panoply of instruments he drew from his tool-box as he proceeded, like sounding-rods of different dimensions to locate hard-to-reach bullets, which he dislodged with the most appropriate-shaped pair of pincers. The wound he then 'disinfected' with a mixture of rose-oil and terebenthine, injected by syringe three or four times an hour. An ointment of egg white applied to the surface preceded the final bandaging procedure. Bone-fractures complicated the entire process, which had to be trepanned and cauterized. Patients (who endured this without any kind of anaesthesia—the word patient derives from *patir*, to suffer) were especially terrorized by the glowing-hot cauterizing iron, so Paré developed a combination of vitriol, boiling sulphur, and similar substances that might have the same effect.

Inflammation could easily trigger the gangrene process, in which the flesh around the wound began to rot and putrify healthy flesh adjacent to it, giving off the abominable stench of decomposition. The first procedure was to cut away the dead flesh with a razor or knife, and then cauterize the tissue. If that didn't work, the surgeon had to amputate, ensuring first that the infected part was completely dead. It was the surgeon's skill that determined how much of the limb would have to come off. The assistant would make a tight ligature just above the place he would intervene, and then he would quickly sever the flesh around the bone with a razor or curved knife in order to limit the pain and the terror to the patient, using the saw only to cut through the bone. After completing the amputation, the sur-geon pressed cautering irons against the bleeding tissue and into the bone cavity too. The process concluded by applying a mixture of egg whites and rose oil, soaking the bandages in the same concoction, and enveloping the wound in them

---

[15] Olivier Chaline, *La bataille de la Montagne Blanche (8 novembre 1620)* (Paris, 1999), 186–8; for another lurid description of the procedures of army surgeons in the aftermath of battle, see Lorraine White, 'The Experience of Spain's Early Modern Soldiers: Combat, welfare and violence', *War in History*, 9 (2002), 22.

Fig. 4.2. Polino, Wounds of the soldier Bastiano Diano Molinaro, *c.*1630; a musket ball hit this victim in the shoulder and exited in the chest below the throat.

for four or five days before changing them.[16] By the seventeenth century, a firearm wound did not automatically entail a death sentence, especially if one could benefit from the services of skilled surgeons in a proper hospital. A Lombard source congratulated the surgeons for their skill in quickly putting the officers back on their feet, but the leaders were the lucky ones.[17]

French and Savoyard soldiers had no equivalent to the great Milanese hospital, although Casale Monferrato's surgeons, over a hundred kilometres away, had a lot

[16] Ambroise Paré, *La manière de traicter les playes faictes tant par hacquebutes, que par fleches: et les accidentz d'icelles, comme fractures et caries des os, gangrene et mortification: avec les pourtraictz des instruments necessaires pour leur curation* (Paris, 1552), 3–62.

[17] 'Relazione del curato Francesco Comerio di Lonate', in Franco Bertolli and Umberto Colombo (eds), *La peste del 1630 a Busto Arsizio* (Busto Arsizio, 1990), 440.

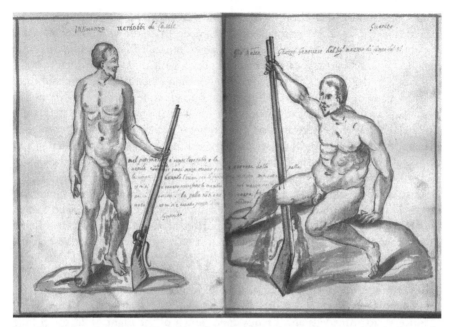

Fig. 4.3. Polino: Innocenzo Verdobbi of Casale received a musket wound in the lower abdomen, breaking the pubic bone. The ball was never located or extracted, but the victim healed notwithstanding.

of expertise treating battlefield wounds.[18] Barely two months previous, King Louis XIII gave the order to establish in Pinerolo a hospital for his army in Italy, under the direction of six religious of the order of La Charité, but nothing would have been ready in the aftermath of the battle, and the great fortress lay even further away.[19] Victor-Amadeus similarly had made no provision for treating large numbers of wounded men and penned an urgent letter the day after the battle to his treasurer in Turin to find the means to take care of them.[20] Attendants carried French and Savoyard wounded across the bridge to Oleggio, while other cases were carted back to Fontaneto or to Gattinara, the rear base twenty-five kilometres away.

Typical of the era, nobody speaks of the plight of wounded soldiers left on the battlefield, crying out for help. There was no quick collection of the wounded after the fighting, given that it ceased only after nightfall. Hours after daybreak, none of the confederate troops ventured out of their positions to have a look. Two or three

[18] Giovanni Carbonelli, 'La Cronaca chirurgica dell'assedio di Casale (1628–1629) di Horatio Polino, chirurgo', *Bollettino Storico-Bibliografico Subalpino*, 9 (1904), 153–71. My gratitude to Giovanni Cerino Badone for bringing this article and the Polino manuscript to my attention.

[19] Archives du Service Historique de la Défense, A1 27, no. 259, letter to the Général de la Charité, 18 Apr. 1636.

[20] ASTo Materie politiche interne: Lettere del duca Vittorio Amedeo, vol. 56; letter to Mr le Président du Faure, 23 June 1636.

hundred wounded Habsburg soldiers, who lay inside the perimeter of the entrenchments, remained prisoners of the French. An unknown number of others lay suffering in the heath atop the plateau, or on the valley floor leading up to the parapets. Soldiers did not carry a first-aid pouch with them with which to wash and bandage the wounds of injured comrades. Blood loss, dehydration, and fever claimed many of the wounded, while unlucky others would have been despatched by soldiers and army attendants looting the cadavers the next day.[21] Soldiers could easily empathize with the wounded men crying out, next to disfigured corpses of men and horses, for most of those who survived the day without a mishap would have heard many musket balls pass close by. But memorialists chose not to talk of such things.[22] The odour of the battle would have lingered along with the cries, the acrid stench of powder mixed with that of blood and the excrement of men and horses.[23] The ceasefire did not eliminate the stress on the survivors, who had to endure the sight, sound, and smell of the horrors of war at close quarters. I know of no text suggesting that the psychological damage of the experience scarred the participants, but we can expect it existed. The Spanish military hospital at Mechelen near Antwerp began to diagnose a kind of post-traumatic stress disorder in the 1640s, a *mal de corazon*, and officials recommended that such broken soldiers be sent home.[24]

Since Victor-Amadeus and Créquy spent much of the night of 22 to 23 June preparing for a new onslaught, only after sunrise did they issue cavalry patrols to gather intelligence. 'If we had enough good spies in order to learn the direction of the enemy retreat, we would have had them all, and their cannon too,' wrote Du Plessis-Praslin (the most aggressive of the French generals) in a jubilant letter to the cardinal in Paris.[25] Decades later, he claimed in his memoirs that the immediate spoils consisted of 2,000 prisoners and all the cannon, but he had surely misremembered it.[26] 'If we had fresh troops', echoed Créquy, 'we would have followed them, but in the morning we didn't know where they were.'[27] One lucky patrol encountered a convoy of fourteen baggage wagons on the road, and captured some of them.[28] Within a day or two, the confederate commanders learnt of Leganés's safe retreat to Abbiategrasso.

Similarly, the Spanish staff sought to assess the position and the state of the French army now that they had broken contact. Leganés was especially anxious to know if the Duke of Rohan was marching westwards to join up with Créquy, or if

[21] Dorothée Malfoy-Noël, *L'épreuve de la bataille (1700–1714)* (Montpellier, 2007), 94–8.

[22] Ibid. 111.

[23] Richard Holmes, *Acts of War*, 2nd edn (London, 2003), 178.

[24] Geoffrey Parker, *Global Crisis: War, Climate Change and Catastrophe in the 17th Century* (New Haven and London, 2013), 591; Borreguero Beltràn, 'El coste humano de la guerra'; Napoleonic surgeons labelled the same diagnosis, the 'syndrome du vent du boulet', Crocq, *Traumatismes psychiques*, 36.

[25] AAE Correspondance Politique: Sardaigne, vol. 24, letter from Du Plessis-Praslin to Cardinal Richelieu, 24 June 1636.

[26] *Memoires du Maréchal Du Plessis* (Paris, 1838), 360.

[27] AAE Correspondance Politique: Sardaigne, vol. 24, letter from Mr de Créquy, 25 June 1636.

[28] Bologna Biblioteca Universitaria, vol. 473 Misc. H, no. 15, Relatione del fatto d'Arme seguito fra l'Esercito spagnolo e francese.

the contingent of the Duke of Parma had marched out of the Monferrato.[29] Rumours of all kinds flourished about which side had won the battle, while scores, perhaps hundreds, of survivors penned letters home to tell of their experience. Prince Borso d'Este (who had missed the fight) wrote to his nephew Duke Francesco of Modena from Cremona on his way back to the army on 24 June, to relay news he picked up from his peers. It was not true that the French were beaten, he warned, and the news that Créquy was killed and the Duke of Savoy wounded had not been confirmed.[30] Duke Carlo Gonzaga, France's reluctant ally, took care to multiply his sources in order to have a more balanced view. One Lodovico Porri wrote him from the camp at Oleggio just as the battle was beginning, noting that while Créquy's force was badly outnumbered the bridge was finished.[31] The Chancellor Antonio Ronquillo penned him a triumphal letter in Spanish two days later, announcing that, although Leganés had to withdraw from the field at night, the Habsburg army escaped without being harried after giving a fine account of itself. French casualties were above 6,000 men, he crowed, and Créquy was killed. On 25 June the duke's correspondent Sigismondo Vecchi delivered a more balanced assessment, noting that the losses were very high on both sides, but the Spanish army had suffered disproportionately from fighting on open ground. He suggests that about 3,000 men were wounded, a far higher number than the numbers being broadcast by both sides. Vecchi reported that many people in Milan thought that the Habsburg army would soon be ready to fight again.[32] The duke had a reasonably accurate picture of what had just transpired when he received his ambassador's letter from Paris, wherein it was broadcast at the French court that Tornavento was a great victory, followed by the capture of large numbers of prisoners, the baggage and the artillery of the defeated army. Victor-Amadeus had performed better than was anticipated, and the confederate army was marching unopposed on Milan.[33]

One of the first pretexts for renewing contact between the belligerent armies concerned the recovery of the bodies of the officers and the exchange of prisoners. Suspension of fighting to avoid unnecessary carnage seems to be an innate human quality, attested everywhere.[34] In the decades-long struggle between Catholics and Protestants in the Low Countries, European armies elaborated rules designed to alleviate some of the horrors of war, many of which resemble mere courtesies, but others constituted harbingers of humanitarianism.[35] Within ten days of the fight, both sides had released their prisoners, some of whom were mortally wounded,

[29] ASF Mediceo del Principato 3176, letter of 24 June 1636, fo. 753.
[30] ASMo, Casa e Stato: Carteggi fra Principi Estensi 209, letter of 24 June 1636.
[31] ASMn, Archivio Gonzaga 1761, lettere da Milano, 22 June 1636.
[32] ASMn, Archivio Gonzaga 1761, lettere da Milano, Don Antonio Ronquillo, 24 June, and Sigismondo Vecchi, 25 June 1636.
[33] ASMn, Archivio Gonzaga 678, lettere di Francia, Lodovico Priandi, 2 July 1636.
[34] Marco Costa, *Psicologia militare* (Milan, 2003), 83–99.
[35] Catherine Denys, 'Quelques réflexions sur la régulation de la violence de guerre dans les Pays-Bas méridionaux aux XVIIe et XVIIIe siècles', in Jean-François Chanet and Christian Windler (eds), *Les Ressources des faibles: Neutralités, sauvegardes, accommodements en temps de guerre (XVIe–XVIIIe siècle)* (Rennes, 2009), 205–19.

like Don Luigi Caetano. By the seventeenth century, prisoners had become the property of the sovereign, not of the individual soldiers capturing them. Once the soldiers and junior officers had no claim to compensation, prisoners might have been seen as an encumbrance destined for slaughter, for prisoners required guards and precious food. Not so. Quick exchange of prisoners became commonplace in the war between Spain and the Netherlands and in 1636 it appears to have been routine in Italy too. We have politely worded letters from Victor-Amadeus directed to Leganés in March and April just subsequent to the sharp encounter outside Vespolate, reassuring the Spanish general that those men still in Savoyard captivity were well-treated, just as he expected Savoyards to be adequately cared for if taken by the Spaniards. In surprisingly courteous terms, he protested the ill-treatment of some of these captives at the hands of the Governor of Novara.[36] Reciprocity clearly governed the mercy shown to men captured by the enemy. Killing them would have invited reprisals, and the prospect of death at the hands of captors was a disincentive to surrender.[37] 'Nowadays, prisoners are not dragged through the streets in triumphal processions, are not thrown into irons, or held as slaves. They have no reason to be reduced to desperation or believe that they are doomed to die. When they see that fighting no longer offers any prospect of victory, they will yield to a sense of futility,' wrote Montecuccoli, who enjoined victors to be magnanimous.[38] It is never mentioned if released prisoners were compelled to swear not to re-enlist for the duration of the campaign, but their officers were keen to have them back in order to collect information about the condition of the enemy. Another courtesy provided to the foe was to return to them the officers slain in battle. A few cartloads of eminent cadavers were collected during the battle itself, delivered to their families and buried in pomp in dynastic chapels.[39] Leganés paid special attention to recovering the corpse of Gherardo Gambacorta, which had not been identified; officials feared that the French incinerated his remains together with many others in a great funeral pyre erected outside Fontaneto.[40] Victor-Amadeus eventually delivered up a cadaver that Leganés draped with a brocade shroud before conducting it to Milan for solemn burial, for which all the officers and local nobility assembled. His brother commemorated his memory soon after in a sumptuous ceremony in Naples.[41] The Tuscan colonel Camillo del Monte waited until 1 July before sending the son of Captain Balbi to retrieve his father's corpse from the French camp in order to give it a burial befitting a Florentine

[36] ASTo Materie politiche dell'Interno: Registro di lettere alla Corte 38, letters of 30 Mar. and 4 Apr. 1636.

[37] Fritz Redlich, *De Praeda Militari: Looting and Booty 1500–1815* (Wiesbaden, 1956), 30; Geoffrey Parker, 'The Etiquette of Atrocity: The Laws of War in Early Modern Europe', in *Empire, War and Faith in Early Modern Europe* (Harmondsworth, 2002), 160.

[38] Thomas M. Barker, *The Military Intellectual and Battle* (Albany, NY, 1975), 167.

[39] *Gazette de France*, 99 (1636).

[40] ASF Mediceo del Principato 3176, letter of 2 July 1636, fo. 781. Count Rinieri reported the day after the battle that Gambacorta's cadaver had been collected immediately and sent to Milan along with the wounded officers, mentioning Gil de Haes by name, ASFi 3180, fo. 1130, letter of 23 June.

[41] Raffaele Maria Filamondo, *Il Genio bellicoso di Napoli: Memorie istoriche d'alcuni capitani celebri napoletani c'han militato per la fede, per lo re, per la patria nel secolo corrente* (Naples, 1694), i. 321.

aristocrat.[42] Nine days! This raises the question of whether or not armies quickly buried the dead.

TO THE VICTORS THE SPOILS

One immediate consequence of battle stress was the terrible insensitivity of the soldiers towards the civilian population nearby, exposed to the intense desire of the victors to compensate themselves for the peril they had undergone.[43] Once it became clear the Spanish troops had withdrawn, parties of French soldiers emerged from their entrenchments in search of booty from whatever source.[44] Wars between kings in the medieval tradition did not differentiate between combatants and civilian subjects, who could be spoliated at will in order to inflict pain on their lord. Easy booty helped attract new soldiers, whose pay otherwise arrived only fitfully. The central treasuries did not pay the French and Savoyard troops in any meaningful way, despite the promise of pay to recruits upon their enlistment. The finance minister Bullion was a personal enemy of Hémery and considered that the French army in Italy should be content to live from 'contributions' levied on the populations in its path. The soldiers were supposed to be paid in eight 'musters', but few received more than three. Soldiers were, however, fed to the best of the army's ability to supply bread and whatever meat on the hoof the troops could obtain for themselves. Food was never lacking in the theatre, Hémery reported to Paris.[45] So while these troops were not threatened with starvation, they had ample incentive to make the enemy pay for their upkeep.[46]

Over the course of the sixteenth century warlords alive to the needs of discipline did their best to codify the right of plunder without depriving their soldiers of it entirely.[47] Soldiers also wished the safe possession of booty to be recognized, in order to forestall other soldiers from robbing them in turn. In some armies the officers claimed a 10 per cent share of whatever booty the men seized on routine forays.[48] In open villages or isolated habitations, experienced soldiers adopted a formal tactic; four or five musketeers first reconnoitred each farm, moving cautiously from building to building sniffing out the most likely places for ambush, while another party lay close by in case of resistance. No soldier was permitted to break off from his detachment in order to get the best pickings for himself.[49] Small parties often belonged to the same 'chambrées' of men who messed together and

[42] ASF Mediceo del Principato 3181, letter of 2 July 1636, fo. 470.

[43] Costa, *Psicologia militare*, 196; on the feeling of vulnerability as a consequence of suffering heavy casualties, 251.

[44] Ibid. 54; Giorgio Basta emphasized how difficult it was to prevent soldiers from seeking booty, even during the heat of combat, *Le gouvernement de la cavalerie legere* (Rouen, 1616), 37.

[45] AAE Correspondance Politique: Sardaigne, vol. 24, letter of 2 July 1636.

[46] David Parrott, *Richelieu's Army* (Cambridge, 2001), 172–6, 266, and 346.

[47] Redlich, *De Praeda Militari*, 3–9.

[48] Biblioteca Estense Modena, Misc. Estense Ital. 635, Avvertimenti militari...composto per il Colonnello Bartolomeo Pellicari di Modena, fo. 19ᵛ.

[49] Ibid., fo. 50ʳ.

shared their booty as a matter of strict principle.[50] These foraging detachments seized local inhabitants to serve as guides, bound and prodded towards a likely target. Civilian prisoners could inform them as to the enemy's movements or give details on the status of particular households.[51] Notables taken hostage served to keep the remaining inhabitants in line.

The French had liberally plundered Lonato and the district just beyond Tornavento in the week leading up to the battle. Now they were bent on systematic rapine. John Keegan, referring to irregular soldiers, reminds us that 'over their habits of loot, pillage, rape, murder, kidnap, extortion and systematic vandalism, civilized employers chose to draw a veil'.[52] But here it was the professional soldiers who were red in tooth and claw. The predatory cruelty of victorious soldiers directed against unarmed civilians was part and parcel of war in Italy, as in Germany.[53] Peasants expecting this fled in their many thousands to castles or indeed to Milan. 'All the frightened peasants (*contadini*) brought everything into the city, day and night coming and going as if to a continual fair, and it is certain that a hundred thousand cartloads of belongings, that is, furnishings, grain and wine were brought into the city, such that it's not possible to describe it completely', wrote the canon Giovanni Battista Lupi of Busto Arsizio, who swore at the beginning of his chronicle not to tell tales or spread lies.[54] The *Gazette de France* likewise boasted that a thousand carts carried the possessions of frightened peasants into Milan, to keep them from the clutches of the French, and from the newly arrived friendly Germans too. Many noblemen withdrew their most precious belongings into neutral Venetian territory not far away.[55] People who could not escape the district fled into churches, the consecrated spaces they hoped the soldiers would not defile (Fig. 4.4).

Spreading terror in enemy territory with fire and sword, and giving the district over to wholesale destruction was an accepted stratagem of warfare in the seventeenth century, straight out of the textbook of Raimondo Montecuccoli, first published in 1670 but penned decades earlier.[56] In the aftermath of their recent ordeal, the soldiers far surpassed the officers' recommendations.[57] There were important differences between their behaviour after the battle compared to the plunder and the foraging conducted during the campaign leading up to it. This fresh rapine

---

[50] George Satterfield, *Princes, Posts and Partisans: The Army of Louis XIV and Partisan Warfare in the Netherlands, 1673–1678* (Leiden and Boston, 2003), 193.

[51] Basta, *Le gouvernement de la cavallerie légère*, 44.

[52] John Keegan, *A History of Warfare* (New York, 1993), 5.

[53] Costa, *Psicologia militare*, 219; Otto Ulbricht, 'The Experience of Violence during the Thirty Years' War: A Look at the Civilian Victims', in J. Canning, H. Lehmann, and J, Winter (eds), *Power, Violence and Mass Death in Pre-Modern and Modern Times* (Burlington, VT, and Aldershot, 2004), 97–129.

[54] Giovanni Battista Lupi, 'Storia della peste avvenuta nel borgo di Busto Arsizio, 1630', in Bertolli and Colombo, *La peste del 1630 a Busto Arsizio*, 206. Lupi's chronicle continues from 1632 until 1642.

[55] *Gazette de France*, 105 (1636). It cites a dispatch dated 26 June; the report condemning the rapacity of the Germans is confirmed by the Milanese notary Calco in an entry dated 28 June.

[56] Costa, *Psicologia militare*, 122.

[57] Ibid. 219.

Fig. 4.4. Jacques Callot, Soldiers burn a church and sack a convent. The soldiers, says the inscription, 'plunder and burn everything, casting down the altars and mocking the respect due to divine things'. Soldiers on the left seize a nun, and lead a priest away as a hostage on the right.

unmistakably resembles the wholesale destruction visited upon Germany.[58] Quentin Outram contrasts it with the 'instrumental' plundering by soldiers aimed to keep the military machine working, which depended upon threats but not on mortal violence. The villagers accepted passively this state of affairs because the soldiers were not wantonly destructive. This was the case in Germany during the first phase of the war before 1630 and in England too during the Civil War, where soldiers and civilians understood that they lived in a shared 'imagined community' and that peace would soon return. On the other hand, with the internationalization of the German war following 1631 and especially with the arrival of the Croat dragoons, gratuitous destruction taught populations that there were no such things as 'friendly' troops.[59]

We possess multiple eyewitness accounts of this grim rapine, principally from the clergy, who for the most part were not subjected to bodily harm. A Capuchin brother (the most austere branch of the Franciscans) dispatched from Milan to plead for the respect of religious communities in the path of the coalition army noted on 23 June that French soldiers arrived at Lonate just next to the battlefield around midday, 'saying that they wanted to eat and drink'.[60] The army's rations consisted principally in bread: any delicacies they acquired by scrounging for it.[61] The next day, the soldiers returned to the monastery of Santa Maria in Lonate to carry away the nuns' bread, wine, and the silver and gilt sacred vessels too. At

[58] Jean-Michel Boehler, 'La guerre au quotidien dans les villages du Saint-Empire au XVIIe siècle', in Christian Desplat (ed.), *Les villageois face à la guerre, XIVe–XVIIIe siècle* (Toulouse, 2002), 65–88.

[59] Quentin Outram, 'The Demographic Impact of Early Modern Warfare', *Social Science History*, 26 (2002), 245–72.

[60] Franco Bertolli, 'L'invasione franco-sabauda del 1636 nel Novarese e nel Milanese', in Guido Amoretti (ed.), *Il Ticino: Strutture, storia e società nel territorio tra Oleggio e Lonate Pozzolo* (Gavirate, 1989), 51–70, 57.

[61] Keith Roberts, *Matchlock Musketeer 1588–1688* (New York and Oxford, 2002), 31 and 45.

Cardano, not far away, the French sacked the monastery of these same Capuchin begging friars. 'The French soldiers were very diligent in finding in the house of poor priests and villagers (*paesani*) everything that was hidden: if it was worth anything they took it away, and if not, they broke it or trampled it.' Victor-Amadeus placed guards around the monasteries and convents in Lonate only on 26 June in order to place them off limits to the looters. He also used the monastic presence as a pretext to forbid setting the large village aflame.[62] In addition to stealing the stocks of food, the soldiers pastured their horses in the fields of ripening grain. The parish priest Comerio estimated that two-thirds of the standing grain in Lonate's district was lost in this fashion.

The diligent local historian Franco Bertolli has cast his net wider in order to flesh out the reports of damage compiled by ecclesiastics in the aftermath of the invasion. Priests placed their emphasis on the religious objects carried away by the French soldiers, most of whom were certainly Catholics. Some of the French and even many Savoyard troops were Calvinists specially motivated to spoliate churches and to destroy what they considered sacrilegious or idolatrous pomp, but we might recall Frank Tallett's observation that armies tended to dechristianize the soldiers in them, whose mixed confessional backgrounds and irregular lifestyle rendered them insensitive to religious taboos.[63] At Cavagliano, north-east of Novara, the soldiers took away the baldaquin, the ornate canopy carried over the consecrated host when it was brought to the infirm and the dying. In the Novarese town of Bellinzago, the soldiers carried off all the relics from the church, no doubt for their pricey silver and crystal display coffers. Across the Ticino in the archdiocese of Milan, whose prelate ordered the clergy to make an inventory of the damage almost immediately, the scope of the French and Savoyard assault on the churches is striking. At Nosate, just south of the battlefield, the soldiers carried off the contents of the church and the presbytery, but for good measure burned the confessional, a crucifix, the balustrade of the altar, the books and parish registers, and the very doors of the edifice. From a nearby shrine the soldiers made off with a silver statue of the Virgin and a collection of picturesque silver ex-votos, cast in the shape of the object which had benefited from a miracle—'a silver baby, a pair of eyeglasses, a pair of silver breasts'. At Magnago the soldiers stole from the parish priest forty pieces of maiolica, his clothing, riding tack, wine, and other furnishings worth 800 lire, then threw down the church roof tiles smashing them on the ground. Finally they burned the hedge around his garden. Everywhere the churches were targets. At Ferno, another large village near Lonate, the soldiers carried away the parish registers, which had no commercial value, although they might have expected local inhabitants to purchase them back because authorities relied on them to establish official papers, legitimate births, marriage eligibility, and the like. At Besnate the soldiers stole few furnishings and left a pair of altar painting masterpieces, but they removed from the statue of the Virgin Mary all her clothes,

---

[62] 'Relazione del curato Francesco Comerio di Lonate', in Bertolli and Colombo, *La peste del 1630 a Busto Arsizio*, 440.

[63] Frank Tallett, *War and Society in Early Modern Europe* (London and New York, 1992), 128.

her coral jewelry, her silver crown, and a diamond ring that adorned her finger. At Somma, a small town of over 2,000 inhabitants the soldiers burst into the collegiate church where much of the population took refuge, raped some women there, and made off with the silver ornaments, the paintings, and other decorations, and destroyed the organ, which could not be removed. They trampled the relics, threw out the consecrated oils in the stables, and made off with the eucharist.[64]

This kind of plunder went far beyond the instrumental collection of foodstuffs and fodder for the army and inflicted severe and lasting hardship on everyone. At Momo south of Fontaneto, the soldiers broke into all the houses and carried off the entire furnishings of the parish church—right down to the altar cloths—while the frightened inhabitants hid in the woods nearby. Other people fled from their open villages or farmhouses into walled towns under French control like Oleggio where the local authorities might serve as a buffer. It is worth mentioning in this context that Habsburg troops acted similarly, often enough forcing the closure and reconsecration of churches in friendly territory while in winter quarters.[65] French soldiers contesting villages against rebels in France did not respect churches either.[66]

Reports of what the soldiers did to churches implied they did as much or worse to private houses, loading up whatever could be carried off into peasant carts or on harnesses fixed to their horses. 'All these places had not seen armies or even soldiers for many years', wrote a well-informed chronicler in Casale Monferrato. 'They had houses full of beautiful and expensive things, such that the French [soldiers] grew rich from the fat booty and the fine linen, copper cookware, tin [plates] etc.'[67] Mattresses they emptied of their feathers in order to use the cover as a capacious sack. While the soldiers might have spurned the wooden household objects of little value, they were especially attracted by the fine clothing and jewellery that even peasants possessed, or the sturdy footwear. Officers prized the chests filled with linens and other bedding, the pewter and crockery items stored on kitchen shelves.[68] Soldiers smashed what they could not carry off, like the barrels full of wine, in order to take away the iron hoops as scrap metal. Anything of value they seized they hoped to sell to army sutlers, officers, and other hangers-on in camp who intended to make a profit by buying them at knockdown prices and reselling them at a distance.[69] At Fontaneto, the soldiers razed 142 houses inside the

---

[64] Archivio Diocesano Milano, Visite Pastorali, Dairago, vol. 21; 'De invasione francorum in plebe Daijraghi, anno 1636'. The document contains twenty-seven pages of lists of religious objects stolen or destroyed by French troops in the district 5 or 6 km distant from Tornavento.

[65] Alessandro Buono, *Esercito, istituzioni, territorio: Alloggiamenti militari e case herme nello stato di Milano, secoli XVI e XVII* (Florence, 2009), 79 n. 49.

[66] Laurent Coste, 'Les malheurs de la Fronde en Entre-deux-Mers', in A. Corvisier and Jean Jacquart (eds), *Les malheurs de la guerre: De la guerre à l'ancienne à la guerre réglée* (Paris, 1996), 131–45.

[67] Giuseppe Giorcelli, 'Annali Casalesi (1632–1661) di Gian Domenico Bremio, speciaro di Casale Monferrato', *Rivista di Storia, Arte, Archaeologia della provincia di Alessandria*, 18 (1909), 381–436.

[68] Ruth Mohrmann, 'Everyday Life in War and Peace', in K. Bussmann and H. Schilling (eds), *1648: War and Peace in Europe* (Munster and Osnabruck, 1998), 319–28.

[69] Brian Sandberg, '"The Magazine of all their pillaging": Armies as Sites of Second-Hand Exchanges during the French Wars of Religion', in Laurence Fontaine (ed.), *Alternative Exchanges: Second-Hand Circulations from the 16th Century to the Present* (New York and Oxford, 2008), 76–96; this impatience was customary for soldiers, Reinhard Baumann, *I Lanzichenecchi: La loro storia e cultura dal tardo medioevo alla Guerra dei Trent'anni* (Turin, 1996), 185; also Redlich, *De Praeda Militari*, 51–2.

fortified perimeter immediately upon capturing the town, not to enhance its defensibility, but likely to make space for the vital supply carts, their haulage teams, and forage supplies.

What made the damage so considerable was that peasants had freshly harvested the wheat and stacked it in sheaves convenient to carry. They had also just finished the season for feeding silkworms and possessed considerable quantities of cocoons to unwind: indeed this constituted one of the principal sources of Lombard rural income.[70] One might object that local authorities exaggerated these accounts of damage in order to obtain reductions in their taxes, as in Germany. But Hémery boasted of this damage in a letter he wrote on 26 June to the king's brother and heir, Gaston d'Orléans. 'Yesterday we gave orders to burn the standing grain as far as the gates of Novara, and we are carrying this out both in direction of Novara and toward Milan too.' The troops had orders to kill any peasants who ventured out to bring in the harvest. 'The guards of Monsieur de Savoy have begun this execution [i.e. the confiscation of goods] and the rest of the cavalry will take their turn.'[71]

Almost as galling as the French marauding were the expectations of German troops still arriving as Habsburg reinforcements. Leganés's German auxiliaries with their women and children in tow certainly had a more predatory understanding than the Spaniards or Italians as to what was permitted towards civilians, even those they were ostensibly protecting. Used to collecting extortionate 'contributions' from civilians on both sides, and from wholesale looting whenever possible back home, they were not about to change their ways now that they were in the employ of the king of Spain. Veteran soldiery knew that they were indispensable, and that their officers would probably not inflict severe penalties on their thieving out of fear of losing them.[72] In the jurisdiction of Vimercate, closer to Milan, the German cavalry were claiming 'contributions' of a scudo (7 lire) per day each in addition to the food and drink for themselves, their women and children, their grooms and horses.[73] Ronald Asch suggests that the women in the baggage train egged the soldiers on. The younger men used their bellicosity and their ability to bring back plunder as ways to enhance their status in the eyes of the women, who provided multiple services to them.[74] The beleaguered population was learning that the Germans were hardly 'friendly' troops.[75]

There have always been limitations on war's violence in ways that make conquest more efficient, and some of these inhibitions are, if not innate to humans universally, then at least occur around the world and throughout time.[76] Men waged war

[70] Bertolli, 'L'invasione franco-sabauda del 1636', 65–9.

[71] AAE Correspondance Politique: Sardaigne, vol. 24, letter of 26 June 1636.

[72] On the leeway given to early modern soldiers, Sabina Loriga, *Soldats: Un laboratoire disciplinaire: l'armée piémontaise au XVIIIe siècle* (Paris, 1991), 148.

[73] Alessandro Giulini, 'Un diario secentesco inedito d'un notaio milanese', *Archivio Storico Lombardo*, 57 (1930), 478–9. The notary Calco thought it worth noting on 7 July that the thieving by the Germans was falling off.

[74] Ronald G Asch, ' "Wo der soldat hinkömbt, da ist alles sein": Military Violence and Atrocities in the Thirty Years' War Re-examined', *German History*, 18 (2000), 291–309.

[75] Quentin Outram, 'The Demographic Impact of Early Modern Warfare', *Social Science History*, 26 (2002), 245–72.

[76] Costa, *Psicologia militare*, 83–99.

in the framework of international rules known to both the soldiers and the civilians, wherein non-belligerents could not be massacred without provocation.[77] In Lombardy both the soldiers and their victims were South European Catholics, so priests were diligent in lecturing the French and Savoyard officers on their duties in this regard. The archbishop of Milan hurried two Capuchin fathers to Victor-Amadeus in order to remind him of his Christian obligations.[78] The population understood that churches were refuges and that soldiers were not to mistreat them while they stood on consecrated ground. Chroniclers dwelled on exceptions to the rule. Soldiers' aggressive behaviour against defenceless civilians was always subject to moderation by reason and calculation, it would appear, because instances of negotiation emerge from the same sources.[79] Both Créquy and Victor-Amadeus operated under the assumption that conquered areas might soon pass to French or Savoyard sovereignty. Moderation was also a reasonable policy because the other side would have no reason to commit atrocities in order to even the score. No doubt thousands of people died as a direct result of the Franco-Savoyard incursion into the State of Milan, but paradoxically the soldiers killed few inhabitants directly, with their weapons. Along the Ticino river zone, priests reported only small numbers of civilians killed by soldiers, rarely more than two or three at a time, and we do not know if the latter were provoked (Fig. 4.5). Even in Germany, soldiers who held all the power towards enemy civilians routinely negotiated with them.[80]

Notwithstanding the restraint exercised by the soldiery towards unarmed civilians, war inflicted wholesale destruction on the countryside in the path of invasion, in ways that took years, sometimes decades, to recover fully. Troops of both sides deployed across one of the richest agricultural economies in Europe at the height of the harvest season. Both the Franco-Savoyards and the Germans frightened the peasants into abandoning the standing crops in the fields, and prevented them from sowing the secondary cereal crops that helped the poor in city and country make ends meet.[81] The troops seized draught animals (rare horses and precious mules, indispensable oxen, numerous cows, even humble donkeys) and dragooned peasants into hauling army supplies without pay. Cows and oxen frequently finished in the soup pots of the soldiers, who enjoyed a meat-rich diet at the expense of civilians both friendly and enemy.[82] Peasants who still possessed large livestock lost the vital stocks of hay, oats, and spelt necessary for their subsistence because it was just too bulky to transport to safety.

[77] Barbara Donagan, *War in England, 1642–1649* (Oxford and New York, 2008), 130–41; see also Parker, 'Etiquette of Atrocity'.

[78] The French *maréchal de camp* Count Du Plessis-Praslin claims the two Capuchins approached the duke with an offer to halt their invasion in exchange for 500,000 scudi, and lets it be understood that the duke would have preferred to stop the invasion on his own, not for the money, but rather to prevent his French ally from becoming too powerful. *Memoires du Maréchal Du Plessis*, 358–9.

[79] Keegan, *History of Warfare*, 81–4.

[80] Ulbricht, 'Experience of Violence'.

[81] Archivio Storico Civico di Milano, Dicasteri 149, letter from Carlo Sirtoni to the king of 19 July 1636.

[82] For a contemporary example, Gregory Hanlon, *The Hero of Italy* (Oxford, 2014), 136; ASPr Comune di Parma 1738, Truppe francesi 1636.

Fig. 4.5. Jacques Callot, Soldiers sack a village, *c.*1630. The troops make off with the carts and livestock, and set fire to some houses after killing some of the inhabitants. Soldiers, perhaps militia, are barricaded around a church serving as a strongpoint.

And of this wholesale rapine and destruction, people died in large numbers. Franco Bertolli is one of the rare historians of the Thirty Years' War to have taken the trouble to examine the parish registers to measure the impact of the occupation of villages by a hostile army. At Oleggio, the base for French troops, where five parishioners died on average every month, priests interred sixty-nine in July, eighty-seven in August after the French had left, sixty-seven in September, forty-four in October, ten in November, and nineteen in December. Similarly at Bellinzago in the Novarese, behind the theatre of skirmishing, where twenty-five people died on average every year, and where 130 individuals died during the plague years of 1630 and 1631, the five last months of 1636 pushed 152 people into their graves.[83] Mortality on this scale conforms entirely to the German experience but no one has ever studied it in Italy. My own research on the demographic impact of the occupation of the duchy of Parma by Habsburg troops gives identical results. In Castel San Giovanni, a town which the Habsburg forces occupied for most of 1636, at least half of the population died, as determined from the burial register. Mortality spiked even in the fortified cities where enemy soldiers never penetrated, as a result of the crowding and poor accommodation for the refugees.[84] Study of the Milanese parish registers will one day likely confirm this and provide a rough idea of the number of victims.

---

[83] Bertolli, 'L'invasione franco-sabauda del 1636'.

[84] Gregory Hanlon, 'Wartime Mortality in Italy's Thirty Years War: The Duchy of Parma 1635–1637', *Histoire, Economie et Société* (2012), 3–22; a systematic study will not be easy, even where the parish registers have survived. The Catholic Church in Italy cut short the Mormon project to microfilm these (enabling scholars around the world to have easy access to them), on the grounds that the Mormons were using Catholic records for religious purposes of their own. Fair enough. However, the old registers are still dispersed across thousands of different churches. One hopes that one day soon an association will form to photograph these and display the records online. What a huge progress this would be for the demographic, economic, social, and cultural history of Italy!

Counting burials presents no special difficulty. It is more problematic to determine what these unfortunate victims died from. An analysis of sex ratios of infants
presented to baptism will tell us if parents deliberately killed newborn boys or girls
in order to conserve resources for their toddlers, as we have found for both rural
and urban Italy and France during this and later periods.[85] Soldiers were especially
keen to seize food stocks from the inhabitants, who suffered severe malnutrition
until the next harvest. Studies on hunger indicate that an inadequate supply of
bread without additional proteins forces the body to break down its own proteins
in order to supplement an inappropriate diet. Insufficient or inadequate food com-
promises the immune system and increases the risk of infection. The soldiers themselves brought new sources of infection with them, and destabilized the summary
sanitary equilibrium. Destruction of wine stocks forced people to drink polluted
water. The typhus infections and e-coli dysentery that flourished in army camps
spread to civilians wherever the soldiers took up quarters.[86]

Historians have rarely examined the many ways soldiers inflicted destruction on
the rural economy. While the rules of war condemned killing unarmed men and
women, the code did authorize burning the houses and farms of inhabitants who
fled in order to avoid the soldiers' exactions, something that occurred even in
England where such destruction was less widespread than on the continent.
Germans still applied the rule in France during the advance of 1914.[87] The damage
inflicted on the duchy of Parma by Habsburg soldiers later in 1636 finds an echo
in the papers of the Magistrato Camerale, the tribunal governing the administration of public property, which it leased, usually on long-term contracts, to a myriad
of individuals. These victims addressed petitions to the magistrates describing the
damage and pleaded for some kind of compensation. Typically the soldiers seized
the grain and fodder stores, and passed them on to their camp; soldiers prodded
away most of the animals too. They commonly (but not universally) burned the
farm buildings along with the furnishings inside. French and Savoyard soldiers
burned or otherwise ruined many houses in dozens of villages across the district,
but rarely all of them. Antoine de Ville, who wrote a guidebook for this kind of
small-scale war, deplored this detestable modern practice of setting everything on
fire. 'C'est une coutume brutale, contre les sentiments naturels, qui nous incom-
mode autant qu'il endommage l'ennemi.'[88] Even when they did not put the buildings to the torch, soldiers often wrecked houses by wrenching out door and window
frames, and smashing roof tiles on the ground.[89] Short of destroying the houses,
the soldiers stripped them of whatever scrap metal they could find, like the locks,

---

[85] Gregory Hanlon. 'L'infanticidio di coppie sposate in Toscana nella prima età moderna', *Quaderni
Storici*, 38 (2003), 453–98; and Laura Hynes, 'Routine Infanticide by Married Couples? An
Assessment of Baptismal Records from Seventeenth-Century Parma', *Journal of Early Modern History*,
15 (2011), 507–30.

[86] W. Gregory Monahan, *Year of Sorrows: The Great Famine of 1709 in Lyon* (Columbus, OH,
1993), 150–3; also Quentin Outram, 'The Socioeconomic Relations of Warfare and the Military
Mortality Crises of the Thirty Years' War', *Medical History*, 45 (2001), 151–84.

[87] Pierre Miquel, *La bataille de la Marne* (Paris, 2003), 155–7.

[88] Antoine de Ville, *De la charge des gouverneurs des places* (Paris, 1674; 1st publ. 1639), 494.

[89] Stephen Porter, *Destruction in the English Civil Wars* (Dover, NH, 1994), 32–3 and 59.

shutter and door hinges, window fittings, grates—and even nails, pried individually from planks. Their penchant for destroying barrels in order to remove the hoops proved especially damaging, for a large barrel cost the equivalent of months of income for a peasant family. Soldiers made a clean sweep of sheds, barns, and mills for the hammers, chains, iron rods, tools, and whatever other metal paraphernalia they could find. Soldiers on their knees in the grass hunted for spent musket balls that would be reused or recycled. Armies required a considerable amount of scrap metal on campaign, melted down and hammered into horseshoes by cavalry blacksmiths, or transformed into triggers and matchlocks by armourers repairing firearms.[90]

Wherever soldiers established a bivouac, they needed to rip out hedges, chop down vines, fruit, and mulberry trees to create sightlines and a field of fire (Fig. 4.6). The invaders used wooden stakes supporting plants for their kindling.[91] They often chopped up household furniture to feed their campfires, rather than send vulnerable details off to collect firewood. This kind of damage, which entailed no special hostility towards civilians, would require years to repair (Fig. 4.7). The same documents reveal how war demolished the commercial edifice of rich Northern Italy: rural and urban entrepreneurs invested their earnings and borrowed substantial sums to lease mills or distribute salt to country households, purchased rights to distribute water to the farms adjacent to rivers or signed leases to manage village taverns and inns. The suspension of travel and the flight of the rural population inflicted a sharp loss of revenue that ruined many country entrepreneurs as well as the city merchants and nobles who lent them money. Milan was on a rebound after the plague of 1630 wiped out half the population: it remained an active commercial centre that channelled North Italian manufactures towards Germany and, indirectly, towards France too.[92] It was imperative that Leganés should halt the enemy advance that destroyed fixed rural and industrial capital on a vast scale.

The soldiers were not everywhere so destructive, and it seems that towns were much better treated than villages, as was the case elsewhere in Europe.[93] Small towns inherited a medieval defensive infrastructure last used a century previous during the momentous wars of Italy (1494–1559), similarly pitting France against the House of Austria. Tumbledown ramparts could be patched up and made notionally stronger by palisades and ditches, and a few towers, guarded by watchmen.[94] Troops on the rampage, if they were numerous enough, usually made short work of such feeble defences. A few hundred horse and foot with some carts loaded

[90] Sandberg, 'The Magazine of all their pillaging'.

[91] I draw these indications from petitions (*memoriali*) submitted to Parma's Magistrato Camerale in 1636 and 1637. ASPr Magistrato Camerale Parma: Memoriali 23 and 24. They concern almost exclusively claims for compensation by leaseholders of government property, and make only passing reference to the damage to their private assets.

[92] Stefano D'Amico, 'Rebirth of a City: Immigration and Trade in Milan, 1630–1659', *Sixteenth Century Journal*, 32 (2001), 697–721.

[93] Denys, 'Quelques réflexions', 208.

[94] Martial Gantelet, 'Reguler la guerre aux frontières des Pays-Bas espagnols: La naissance empirique du droit des gens (Metz, 1635–1659)', in Chanet and Windler, *Les ressources des faibles*, 221–40.

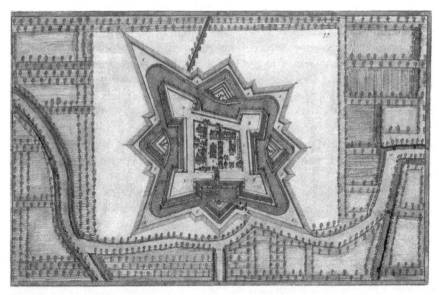

Fig. 4.6. Anonymous, Village of Poviglio and its fortifications, *c*.1640: Soldiers routinely cut down the mulberry trees on the ramparts and for hundreds of metres outside the walls, to harvest the wood and to create effective sightlines. The loss of the leaves, which were fed to silkworms, was a huge blow to the rural economy, and took years to make good.

Fig. 4.7. Pieter van Laer, Soldiers looting an Italian farm, *c*.1640, Galleria Spada, Rome. The cavalier will probably not shoot the peasant, but he does want the laden donkey. Other soldiers set fire to the house and its outbuildings.

with explosive devices and tools for demolishing walls were sufficient to overwhelm most small towns or walled villages.[95] On 19 June a force of 150 cavalry and 100 infantry stormed into Busto Arsizio, home to almost 3,000 people. The bulk of the population there took refuge in the churches that they understood to be places where the French would not torment them. The soldiers gave assurances that no harm would come to persons if the inhabitants paid 50 scudi, which happened twice and they sacked only three houses.[96] In the town of Gallerate invaders burned thirty houses, presumably owned by people who fled with their possessions.[97] A few intrepid priests and magistrates sought out the officers of these parties and purchased safe-conducts that were more lucrative than disorderly plundering.

If it is obvious that the soldiers were not actively slaughtering civilians wholesale, our evidence concerning rape is more ambiguous. War is always fought by men (the few combative women are statistically insignificant), and sexual violence on the women of conquered territories is as old as war itself.[98] Certainly the threat of rape was always in the air. Rohan's invasion of the Valsassina valley near Lake Como allegedly inflicted rape on a large scale on both lay women and nuns, but our source for this claim did not live nearby and it would have constituted hearsay, like the report of the Milanese notary Calco to the same effect, who wrote that the nuns had been 'shamed' (*svergognati*). The nuns in their convents in Lonate and Busto Arsizio feared for the loss of their virginity (*pudicità*) as the soldiers ransacked their dwellings and storehouses. When referring to nuns, these terms probably mean that they were violated simply by being thrust into public view. The notary Giulio Cesare Lomeni of Gallarate reported that French troops on the rampage before the battle on 17 June raped women in churches without specifying where exactly it occurred.[99] The priest of Lonate specified the same day that soldiers had plundered all the churches of the district, committing 'carnal sins' in some of them. At Cardano the soldiers reportedly sequestered one young (unnamed) noblewoman and raped her over a period of several days. In the town of Somma after the battle, the soldiers stormed into the principal collegiate church and raped women therein and battered others. The clergy could not cover these events with a cloak of complicit silence, for canon law required the clergy to report these actions, which polluted the consecrated space. Priests could not celebrate mass there until senior clerics carried out the appropriate purification rituals.[100] How common was rape at the hands of soldiers? Both lay and ecclesiastical authorities considered it a serious crime, worthy of the galleys for the perpetrator. I have reported here all the allusions to it occurring in the sources, and I would not

---

[95] Ville, *De la charge des gouverneurs*, 398–9 and 479–82.

[96] Lupi, 'Storia della peste avvenuta nel borgo di Busto Arsizio', pp. 203 and 205; see also Giulini, 'Un diario secentesco', 476.

[97] Bertolli, 'L'invasione franco-sabauda del 1636'; Bertolli provides numbers and proportions of the houses burned in different localities, 65.

[98] Costa, *Psicologia militare*, 70.

[99] 'Memorie del notaio gallaratese Giulio Cesare Lomeni', in Bertolli and Colombo, *La peste del 1630 a Busto Arsizio*, 401.

[100] Bertolli, 'L'invasione franco-sabauda del 1636', 64.

assume that the absence of explicit evidence of it implies that it must have been too common to report.[101] 'The individual propensity to rape might be distributed in any population on a bell-curve, just like other distributed characteristics', writes Lionel Tiger, who underlines the emotional maleness of soldiers.[102]

Even the earliest attempts to regulate plunder warned the soldiery against raping women, and promised dire punishment for the perpetrators.[103] The Chevalier de Ville recommended that offensive warfare should lay waste to enemy territory and confiscate whatever necessary to continue the war, but he sternly recommended treating churches, women and the personal security of non-combatants as something sacred.[104] Gualdo Priorato, in a publication the following year, recommended that princes and generals should keep their soldiers in hand and not allow them to commit violence and extortion on the subjects of enemy princes in their clutches, because it was not conducive to good supply and it fostered an ardent desire for vengeance in the victims.[105] In Lombardy, however, the soldiers and their superiors imprudently paid little attention to these warnings. The principal danger came not from divine retribution, but from the reciprocity that guides all human interaction, the fierce desire to get even. An atrocity might impose a mute passivity on the victims in the short term, but the perpetrators knew that they could not surrender or expect mercy from those same civilians once they were at a disadvantage.[106]

At first, the helpless population blamed the Spaniards for their hardships:

> for an opinion was spread abroad, and it was firmly believed by the people, that the Spaniards would not give the French battaile in open field, but be sure to destroy them by temporizing, which was known to be their best course. But the common people being ignorant of State Interests, and hard to be made understand reason [sic], though never so apparent, did greatly exclaim against and complaine of the Souldiers, who had hitherto made great brags, and canted it in the Piazzas, and in their quarters, where they behaved themselves stoutly against the Battery of dishes, but occasion now being offered, they could not find the way to defend those to whom they were so much beholding.[107]

If the aim of the atrocities was to force the population into sullen helplessness, it did not succeed. 'Victory amplifies and increases the authority of the winner, who easily obtains everything merely by asking. His soldiers are ready to fight and he is obeyed by every officer. The vanquished party has discontented and insubordinate soldiers, and is deserted by his friends.' If that were so, then Tornavento was no victory. Letters dispatched from both armies quickly made it clear that this

---

[101] For a more negative view of the behaviour of soldiers, Asch, 'Wo der soldat hinkömbt'.

[102] Lionel Tiger, Men in Groups (New York, 1969), 165.

[103] Redlich, De Praeda Militari, 36.

[104] Bernard Peschot, 'Les 'Lettres de feu': la petite guerre et les contributions paysannes au XVIIe siècle', in Desplat, Les villageois face à la guerre, 129–42.

[105] Galeazzo Gualdo Priorato, Il guerriero prudente e politico, ed. Angelo Tamborra (Naples, 2002; 1st publ. 1640), 59.

[106] Dave Grossman, On Killing (Boston and London, 1995), 207.

[107] Galeazzo Gualdo Priorato, An History of the late warres and other state affaires of the best part of Christendome (London, 1648; 1st publ. 1641), 359.

Reverse copy

Fig. 4.8. Jacques Callot, Rounding up deserters and robbers from their forest lairs, *c.*1630: Habsburg troops and local militias killed and captured a large number of enemy soldiers on their looting forays.

great *scaramuccia* stopped the invasion cold.[108] Only four days after the battle French marauders around Cardano were put to flight by a militia detachment of a hundred horse and infantry musketeers, who reportedly killed several, took five prisoners, and recovered the stolen booty.[109] The militia also repulsed French soldiers assaulting the castle of Cerago, after killing a number of them. The same day, two companies of German dragoons and a company of foot ambushed a French detachment in Gallarate, killing about eighty of them and captured others who were sent to Milan as prisoners. On 27 June a detachment of French trying to enter Busto Arsizio was frightened off after a lookout gave the alarm; militiamen gave chase to the outnumbered assailants. Small French parties needed surprise in order to enjoy success, but the population around them began to organize a more effective defence (Fig. 4.8). In the subsequent weeks, professional soldiers and militiamen killed many more French and Savoyard marauders and delivered others to Milan as trophies.[110] The principal organizers of this militia response were leading Lombard feudatories, who took charge of districts where they owned lands and valuable infrastructure: Count Lampugnano around Gallarate, Count Marliani further north at Varese, Count Borromeo in Arona and Lake Maggiore, Count Montecastelli across the Ticino towards Vercelli.[111] Victor-Amadeus, in a letter to his brother-in-law King Louis XIII asked for reinforcements, in part for the 'irreparable disorders flowing from the marauding (*picorée*) of the soldiers, because those

[108] ASPr Archivio Gonzaga di Guastalla, 29 June and 3 July 1636. Duke Ferrante Gonzaga of Guastalla replying to his uncle's letter of 24 June sent from Abbiategrasso.
[109] Lupi, 'Storia della peste avvenuta nel borgo di Busto Arsizio', 206.
[110] Giulini, 'Un diario secentesco', 479.
[111] ASMn Archivio Gonzaga 1761, letter from Sigismondo Vecchi in Milan to Duke Charles, 9 July 1636.

Fig. 4.9. Jacques Callot, Peasants killing soldiers, c.1630. Villagers ambush and kill small groups of foraging soldiers, outnumbered and taken by surprise.

who go do not come back... everyone is against us, both the district and the peasants, due to the ill treatment they receive at the hands of our soldiers' (Fig. 4.9).[112]

In the aftermath of the battle, Milan itself mobilized as never before. Francisco de Melo hurried to the city and ordered that two city gates be bricked up to prevent them from being surprised at night. His first instructions aimed to strengthen the great castle by stocking it with provisions enough to sustain a six-month siege. Workers dug out a covered way, a sheltered ledge around the outside edge of the moat, from where musketeers could snipe at approaching besiegers. Demolition crews hurriedly pulled down city houses constructed too close to the citadel. Then he ordered repairs to the city walls themselves, and appointed militiamen to serve as sentries. Canon were hauled onto bastions, and drawbridges were constructed at each functioning city gate.[113] Provisions poured into the city in case the invading army should blockade it. Authorities mustered about 8,000 townsmen and peasants in the district for the defence of the city, and distributed 6,000 muskets to them from the great magazine in the citadel. Another 4,000 country militiamen marched towards Lecco to reinforce Paolo Sormani's professional troops in their entrenchments blocking Rohan.[114] Cardinal Monti joined the parade on 28 June by marching processionally to the great cathedral, where he blessed the tombs and

---

[112] AAE Correspondance Politique: Sardaigne, vol. 24, letter of 25 June 1636.

[113] GianDomenico Oltrona Visconti, *La battaglia di Tornavento* (Gallarate, 1970), 40.

[114] Davide Maffi, 'Le milizie dello Stato di Milano (1615–1700): Un tentativo di controllo sociale', in J. J. Ruiz Ibañez (ed.), *Las milicias del Rey de España (siglos XVI y XVII)* (Madrid, 2010), 245–67; and by the same author, 'Un bastione incerto? L'Esercito di Lombardia tra Filippo IV e Carlo II (1630–1700)', in E. Garcia Hernan and D. Maffi (eds), *Guerra y sociedad en la Monarquia Hispanica* (Madrid, 2006), i. 501–36.

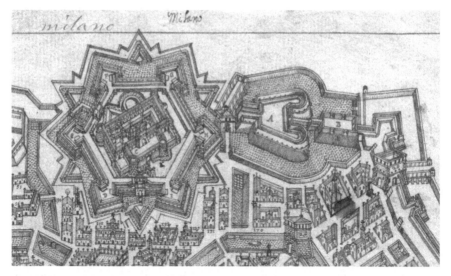

Fig. 4.10. Anonymous, City of Milan, *c.*1640 (detail): the great citadel's well-supplied Spanish garrison kept all of Lombardy under Madrid's firm control.

praised the sacrifice of the dead.[115] Social elites understood how the danger increased their leverage with the king of Spain, who needed their help: six leading aristocrats of Milan disbursed money to raise 2,000 new professional soldiers, and the city provided 2,000 horses to mount them.[116] Hémery noted this enthusiasm in his dispatches home. The distinct danger, he thought, was that the reinforced Spanish army would soon return to Tornavento and stage a rematch.[117]

LETHAL INDECISION

The Franco-Savoyard army sat immobile in its trenches, fearing that if it advanced towards Milan, the enemy would intercept its supply from Piedmont. Worse, if the Habsburg army seized the western bridgehead on the opposite bank, they would not be able to retreat. Meanwhile, they spent day after day in the oppressive heat of Northern Italy, perfecting their defensive works and reinforcing the bridge in order to better enable their heavy cannon and artillery baggage wagons to cross the river.[118]

French and Savoyard administrative sources tell us little about the hard realities of campaigning, which hardly changed before the twentieth century.[119] No source

---

[115] Giulini, 'Un diario secentesco', 478.

[116] Gianvittorio Signorotto, *Milano Spagnola: Guerra, istituzioni, uomini di governo (1635–1660)* (Milan, 2001), 55.

[117] AAE Correspondance Politique: Sardaigne, vol. 24, letter to Monsieur (Gaston d'Orléans) 26 June.

[118] Bertolli, 'L'invasione franco-sabauda del 1636', 59.

[119] Marc Russon and Hervé Martin, *Vivre sous la tente au Moyen-Age (Ve–XVe siècle)* (Rennes, 2010), 227–31.

discusses the burial of the dead. Today, workers occasionally uncover by accident mass graves dating from the period. It was customary for soldiers or civilians to bury soldiers close to where they had fallen, after stripping the cadavers of any clothes they could sell or recycle. At Wittstock in Brandenburg where a bloody battle took place less than four months after Tornavento, archaeologists dug up the remains of about 130 cadavers, piled above each other in neat rows laid out in a sand pit.[120] Archaeologists hunted more actively for the victims of the indecisive slaughter at Lützen on 16 November 1632. In one lucky discovery, they uncovered up to 175 skeletons in a single mass grave, which they excavated as a single chunk of earth weighing 55 tonnes and trucked off to a laboratory for analysis. At Lützen the survivors marched away from the scene of carnage almost immediately. Burial details sent out from the garrison of Weissenfels, assisted by the inhabitants of Lützen itself, laid the men out in a trench in two rows, feet touching. These German graves are interesting finds, for soldiers' bones reveal something about their age (all males between 17 and 40), their height (from 156 to 182cm, with a mean of 170 cm), and diet. Close examination can identify the kinds of wounds that killed the victims, how old they were, whether or not they were well fed, and from a strontium isotope analysis, researchers can determine the ethnic origin of the victim.[121] The methodical burial of soldiers in those German battles was helped immeasurably by the lateness of the campaign season, which lowered temperatures enough to eliminate insects.

At Tornavento, cadavers lay uncollected for at least several days after the combat, and likely much longer. Perhaps men buried the bodies falling within the fortified perimeter, or carried them to another location for interment, but several sources speak of the terrible odour from the hundreds of cadavers strewn about. The stench of the decomposing bodies of both men and horses must have been unbearable, and terribly stress-inducing, for the dangers of 'corrupted air' were well known. Montecuccoli recommended quick burial of the dead for both moral and practical reasons, not only as an act of sacred piety to the fallen, and as a benefit to the survivors, but also because unburied bodies would infest the air with sickness.[122] 'There were so many putrefying bodies remaining, that an infinity of flies were attracted by the stench, which kept the soldiery in constant torment', wrote Girolamo Brusoni, on the strength of witnesses' recollections.[123] Whether officers systematically appointed burial details to clear the site of decaying men and animals is not something I have ever encountered in the sources. There is a lone reference to burning corpses in a funeral pyre at Fontaneto distant from the battlefield. These were likely the remains of the unlucky wounded who had been evacuated there.

---

[120] David Crossland, 'Mass Grave Sheds Light on Europe's Bloody History', *Spiegel Online*, 31 July 2007; Anja Grothe and Bettina Jungklaus, 'Archaeological and Anthropological Examinations of a Mass Grave from the 1636 Battle at Wittstock: A Preliminary Report', in G. Grupe et al. (eds), *Limping Together through the Ages* (Rahden Westfalen, 2008), 127–35.

[121] Christoph Seidler, 'Mass Grave Begins Revealing Soldiers' Secrets', *Spiegel Online*, 27 Apr. 2012.

[122] Barker, *Military Intellectual and Battle*, 164.

[123] Girolamo Brusoni, *Delle Historie memorabili, contiene le Guerre d'Italia de'nostri tempi* (Venice, 1656), 39.

Civilians could not be pressed into performing this labour (unless officers drew on camp followers), for the French and Savoyards chased them away. It is by no means certain that armies methodically buried their dead. A decade later, as the French were lifting their futile siege of Cremona, they established a makeshift hospital for several hundred sick and wounded men in the Parman town of Colorno. The local priest claims that attendants simply tossed the bodies into the river—sometimes before the unfortunate wretches were completely dead.[124] French armies in Catalonia during the 1670s displayed a similar indifference to the proximity of unburied dead who lay for days in the military hospital in Perpignan next to sick men.[125]

The priest Giovanni Battista Lupi, who lived near the battlefield, confirms that the historian Brusoni was well-informed. 'On Monday 7 July, Monsù Chirichi with his army moved from the post of Tornavento, chased away (*discacciato*) by the great sickness of the flies, and by the excessive heat which made the soldiers ill.' He attributed the departure of the French to divine intervention, for God 'permitted the great swarm of flies and the abundance of "tafani", which chased them from the State, just like God punished Pharaoh with mosquitoes, frogs and thunderbolts'. These insects, known in English as horse flies, encompassed some eighty species in Italy, in eleven genuses. Some of these species were vectors of viruses and bacteria, because they flew from one victim to another to complete their meal. They would congregate wherever armies, with their thousands of horses, would feed them. Since the Middle Ages it has been known that these insects could sense blood from sixty kilometres away. They would land on an injured or killed soldier within seconds of his fall and begin a feeding frenzy on the corpse. Females lay their eggs on the inert bodies, and on any moist spot like the nose, mouth, eyes, navel, and anus. Within four to six hours on a hot day, the eggs hatch into thousands of maggots.[126] 'The worms and flies which abound from the nourishment they find in the carcasses will cease to be troublesome if they are removed to a sufficient distance from the camp', wrote the first physician to address these matters, but he was only stating common knowledge.[127]

There are four stages in a body's decomposition, beginning with autolysis or self-digestion, where the enzymes present in living cells break down the cell's own walls unchecked and release the liquid inside. This then seeps between the layers of skin and loosens them, so that when people lift the cadavers by the arms and hands, the skin simply slides off, something called 'gloving'.[128] The liquid released from the cells makes contact with the bacteria in the intestines, or the mouth, becoming

[124] Cristina Trombella, *La 'Memoria di Colorno' (1612–1674) di Don Costantino Canivetti: Parte Prima 1612–1658*, Tesi di Laurea, Università degli Studi di Parma, Facoltà di Magistero 1997–8, 19 Oct. 1648.

[125] Alain Ayats, 'Armées et santé en Roussillon au cours de la guerre de Hollande (1672–1678)', in J. M. Goger and N. Marty (eds), *Cadre de vie, équipement, santé dans les sociétés mediterranéennes* (Perpignan, 2006), 119–35.

[126] Bill Bass and Jon Jefferson, *Death's Acre: Inside the Forensic Lab, the Body Farm, Where the Dead Do Tell Tales* (New York, 2003), 102–5.

[127] Luca Antonio Porzio, *The Soldier's Vade Mecum* (London, 1747; 1st publ. 1685), 25.

[128] Mary Roach, *Stiff: The Curious Life of Human Cadavers* (New York and London, 2003), 65.

food for the bacteria, which multiplies as a result of this sudden rush of resources. The bacteria metabolism produces a waste product in intestinal gas, which builds up to the point where the belly bloats. The mouth can bloat too, pushing out the tongue. Bloat continues until something gives way, and occasionally the torso will rip open under the pressure, exposing the intestines. This bloating phase continues for about a week, faster if the weather is hot—like at Tornavento. Meanwhile, the maggots feed and multiply. They dislike sunlight, so burrow under clothes, or under the skin where they feast on the subcutaneous fat, making a faint popping and hissing sound. Thousands of maggots feeding on a cadaver attract in their turn flies and other insects to the corpse, such as wasps, who feed both on the flesh and on the flies and maggots too. Carrion beetles then arrive for their share. Putrefaction also makes the corpse really interesting for animals such as foxes, which emerge from their burrows at night, and dogs, which accompanied the army or were abandoned by country dwellers as the troops advanced. These nibble on hands and feet, which before long can be detached and consumed elsewhere. The brain liquefies very quickly, pouring out the ears or the mouth, and other organs just collapse into the ground, oozing out a waxy substance. After two weeks, in hot weather, the abdomen collapses, the hair falls off in a mat, the skull is reduced to bone, and the vertebrae become increasingly visible.[129]

Human cadavers decompose in measurable ways, known as 'accumulated degree days' (ADD), where the average daily temperature is the key variable. Advanced decay is reached at about 400 ADDs (twenty days where the average temperature is 20°C) for a 68kg human cadaver. At Tornavento the smaller cadavers and the hotter weather, probably reaching well above 30°C for most of each day, accelerated the process. The state of advanced decay would have been reached in about sixteen days, compatible with Bill Bass's estimate of about two weeks for the skeletonization to occur. The liquids leach into the soil and change its composition by saturating it with potassium, calcium, magnesium, phosphorus, ammonium, sulphates, and other chemicals.[130] This soup and its sweet, cloying odour, a cross between rotting fruit and rotting meat, impregnates shoes that trod the sodden soil around the cadaver. It takes ages for it to disappear.[131] Small wonder that soldiers preferred to ignore the cadavers around them and wandered off to plunder the district instead. Those assigned to the ghastly task of interring the rotting corpses would not have been able to put it out of their mind very quickly. Would the burial details have touched the horses? Likely hundreds of them lay where they had fallen in the desperate cavalry charges or died of thirst on the plateau.

---

[129] These lurid paragraphs, necessary in order to underscore war's grim reality, resume the studies of two writers, the founder of the Tennessee 'Body Farm' Bill Bass, who first decided to study the decomposition of human remains in a scientific manner beginning in the 1980s, and an irreverent journalist with a gift for description, Mary Roach. See Bass, *Death's Acre*, 99–133; and Roach, *Stiff*, 62–70.

[130] David O. Carter and Mark Tibbett: 'Cadaver Decomposition and Soil: Processes', in *Soil Analysis in Forensic Taphonomy: Chemical and Biological Effects of Buried Human Remains* (Boca Raton, FLA, 2008), 29–52.

[131] Roach, *Stiff*, 70.

Having located and consumed thousands of human and animal cadavers, the flies and wasps migrated to targets still living. The females in particular suck blood from a variety of vertebrates, lacerating the skin as they do so. Their attacks cause much torment to their victims by reducing their appetite and causing blood loss. On humans the painful bite could cause allergic reactions or worse. The same fly passes from a victim with infected blood to insert it into a healthy host.[132] Not surprisingly, men fell sick in large numbers in the aftermath of the battle from a variety of ailments. The curate of Lonate Pozzolo, who lived nearby, recorded how, after two weeks of staying put in the camp, the French were driven off by a combination of the flies feeding off the decomposing cadavers, and a growing lack of supplies and fodder.[133] Lupi's manuscript chronicle cites the saying repeated almost verbatim by Brusoni twenty years later. 'Throughout the state they say that the flies and the horseflies achieved more than the Governor of Milan.'[134] In nearby Milan, academicians composed both erudite and sneering verse mocking the torments of the men by the flies, sometimes equated to wasps, although wasps may indeed have multiplied too.[135]

Not mentioned by anyone was the fact that the stomach-churning sight and stench of decomposing flesh was compounded by the smell of excrement around the entrenchments, where soldiers customarily relieved themselves.[136] The need for some emplacement for men to excrete was part of campaign lore since Antiquity, but one will search in vain for any reference to it in the early seventeenth century. Count Montecuccoli stressed the necessity of keeping the camp clean of filth, by burying it, and moving camp once the air had become corrupt, but the passage does not mention excrement specifically (Fig. 4.11).[137] No trace of latrines appears in the very detailed text by John Cruso on the creation of camps (more than a little inspired by the Huguenot Sieur du Praissac). The author specifies that men must bury the wastes of butchered animals in appointed pits at some distance from the camp. Cruso identifies a long list of specialized quarters for the commanders, the sutlers, the artillery, the infantry, and the horse, but makes no mention of human and animal wastes. Cavalrymen were instructed to arrange their horse so that they could sleep by its head and better see to its feeding.[138]

The casual attitude of soldiers—and their officers—towards excrement would eventually kill more men than battle, but on this important problem, there are few explicit sources. The great painting by Pieter Snayers of the siege of Valenza depicts the French soldiers squatting with their backs against the parapet of their earth-

---

132 See also Wikipedia article, at: <http://it.wikipedia.org/wiki/Tabanidae>.

133 'Relazione del curato Francesco Comerio di Lonate', 440–1.

134 Lupi, 'Storia della peste avvenuta nel borgo di Busto Arsizio', 207–8.

135 Fr. Guglielmo Plati da Mondaino, *Le Vespeide dell'Academico Caliginoso, allude alla strage fatta nel campo de Franchi dallo Vespe Silvestre nelle trinciere di Tornavento* (Milan, 1636); Pier Francesco Minozzi, *Il Politico Trionfante, ovvero l'Ill.mo ed Ecc.mo Sgr. Il Signor Don Diego Felippez de Guzman Marchese de Leganés* (Milan, 1637).

136 Malfoy-Noël, *L'épreuve de la bataille*, 59. The French historian emphasizes that this tormented French armies during hot Italian summers, especially.

137 *Memoires de Montecuculi, generalissime des troupes de l'Empereur* (Amsterdam, 1752), 111.

138 John Cruso, *Castrametation, or the measuring out of the quarters for the encamping of an army* (London, 1642).

Fig. 4.11. Balthasar Moncornet, Le chieur. A gardener finds a secluded place to ease himself. People outdoors did not seek use latrines. This was true of armies also, with catastrophic consequences when they remained immobile for any length of time.

works, calmly defecating. Commanders became more sensitive to the problem by the century's close, but in the meantime, habit ruled. French garrison soldiers in Roussillon in the 1670s slept on straw that was almost never changed, despite being contaminated with faeces and other microbes. Newly arrived marshal Noailles began his tenure with a general clean-up designed to reduce mortality in 1676, in which public latrines played a part.[139] A Spanish military manual of 1684 recommended establishing latrines some 100 paces from the front or rear parapet not far from the sutlers' tents, and advised posting sentinels to prevent men from

[139] Ayats, 'Armées et santé', 132.

relieving themselves too close to camp.[140] The very first book designed to educate soldiers on camp hygiene was that of the Neapolitan physician Luca Antonio Porzio (1637–1715), who accompanied the Imperial army in Hungary in the 1680s. He published his observations and recommendations in Latin in 1685. 'It is often very hard, if not impossible to preserve cleanliness where there are vast multitudes of people', he warned. It was an eccentricity of Turkish soldiers to dig latrines and keep them apart from the camp. 'The Turks, in order to preserve the cleanliness in their camps, interr the excrements of the men in ditches. Our soldiers do not resemble them in this, since they often ease Nature beside the very Tents of their Generals.'[141] 'The carcasses of animals and the excrements of men should be buried in ditches, by which means the flies will not have such a number of nests to deposit their eggs in. By this means the air will be rendered more pure and the soldiers not be indisposed to a noxious and ungrateful smell. These things are well known, but they are not less important for that.'[142] The Turks dug field latrines, surrounded by a rectangular tent open to the sky, with proper benches for the men.[143] European soldiers *ought* to wash and cleanse themselves, and take proper repose, wrote Porzio. There are numerous references in his writing to the indifference of soldiers to the smell of decomposing men and animals, for they often resisted the burial details that would have protected them.[144]

The heat, of course, made this situation almost unbearable. Men could find some protection from the heat in their two-man shelters or huts, which were more comfortable than tents. Soldiers quickly put these together from poles covered with branches, and then made them more comfortable with straw laid out on the ground.[145] Shelters from the heat, these were crawling with insects, considered a lesser evil. Detachments of soldiers stripped the woods of branches and undergrowth in their search for materials, and they felled trees as well to fuel their campfires and to buttress the bridge and the fortifications. Vaclav Matoušek has calculated that seventy or eighty gabions assembled to fortify a single redoubt would have required 240 trees and stripped the natural cover for 500 to 700 square metres.[146]

Soldiers compounded the sanitary problem by rarely changing their clothes or taking them off to sleep while on campaign, in part so that they might repel sur-

[140] Hugo O'Donnell y Duque de Estrada, 'El reposo del ejército: Estudio del campamento temporal del tempo de los Austrias', in Garcia Hernan and Maffi, *Guerra y sociedad*, 381–99; O'Donnell cites Francisco Davila Orejòn Gaston, *Politica y Mecanica Militar para Sargento Major de Tercio* (Brussels, 1684); on the elaboration of rules for camp hygiene in the Spanish army after 1660, Borreguero Beltràn, 'El coste humano de la guerra', 60.

[141] For convenience I have used the first English edn published sixty years later, Luca Antonio Porzio, *The Soldier's Vade Mecum* (London, 1747), 128.

[142] Ibid. 25.

[143] Andrew Wheatcroft, *The Enemy at the Gate: Habsburgs, Ottomans and the Battle for Europe* (New York, 2008), 16.

[144] Porzio, *The Soldier's Vade Mecum*, 25.

[145] Sieur du Praissac, *Discours et questions militaires* (Paris, 1638), 30–3; see also Vladimir Brnardic, *Imperial Armies of the Thirty Years' War: Infantry and Artillery* (Oxford and New York, 2009), 23. The author claims with some plausibility that one could generally smell the camp before it could be seen.

[146] Vaclav Matoušek, 'Building a Model of a Field Fortification of the Thirty Years' War near Olbramov (Czech Republic)', *Journal of Conflict Archaeology* (2005), 114–32.

prise attacks on their quarters.[147] Sleeping unclothed in proper beds was a luxury of garrison soldiers. Soldiers who sleep many nights with their clothes on risk contracting diseases, starting with sores that attract vermin, Porzio noted. Smoke might destroy some species of lice and other vermin, but insects were a nuisance that soldiers learned to live with. Safe drinking water was also a luxury. Troops posted to the plateau suffered from the same lack of water as the Habsburg men and horses the day of the battle. The Ticino and a couple of mill-races on the valley bottom might have served, but they required a long walk to reach, and so clean water would have been at a premium, not likely used to wash clothes. The army was thus ripe for the two diseases that bore off countless soldiers living in camps, like the refugees living in cities in similar unsanitary conditions, the 'bloody flux' (e-coli bacillary dysentery) and typhus, spread by lice. The first of these brought symptoms like sustained fever, abdominal distension, coughing, spot rashes, diarrhea, and delirium. Lice spread typhus in conditions of crowding and poor sanitation. Those cases began with sudden fever, headaches, pain in the joints, and the eruption of red spots in the first week. In both cases, the men might be incapacitated for weeks before they either recovered or died. For typhus, the rate of mortality for infected men was between 10 and 40 per cent. When typhus was added to an e-coli infection, the result was always fatal.[148] The remedies were pitifully inadequate; Porzio recommended chewing tormentil wood to stem the bloody flux. Soldiers also extinguished a red-hot iron in water or wine, or ate boiled quinces if they were available. Wormwood applied to the stomach or held in the hand was judged a standard remedy for fevers. Soldiers also ingested broths made from willow bark and leaves, or consumed rhubarb or grated oak bark infused in white wine.[149] The Neapolitan physician also thought that soldiers' normal diet in the field was deficient in several ways. 'If the bread in camps is much worse than what it is in cities, heavier and less baked, it often happens that it resembles dough more than bread.'[150] Soldiers customarily purchased their foods ready-cooked from sutlers who catered to their tastes, instead of eating more substantial fare from a regimental kitchen, for 'soldiers do not care to eat healthy food, even at the risk of their health'.[151]

The seventeenth century probably marked a low point in European hygiene, after the syphilis epidemic of the previous century forced the closure of the urban bath-houses prostitutes haunted. The Counter-Reformation clergy's disapproval of human sensuality and fear of sexual contact pushed social elites and peasants alike into garb designed for modesty. Bathing was a novelty for most people in town and country. The flies and the lice that accompanied the army fed off tired bodies weakened by the heat.[152] Dysentery and diarrhoea were a familiar presence in

---

[147] Biblioteca Estense Modena, Misc. Estense Ital. 635, Avvertimenti militari...per il colonello Bartolomeo Pelliciari, fo. 29ʳ.

[148] Padraig Lenihan, 'Unhappy Campers: Dundalk (1689) and After', *Journal of Conflict Archaeology* (2007), 196–216.

[149] Porzio, *The Soldier's Vade Mecum*, 145–75; see also Gruber von Arni, *Justice to the maimed soldier*, 176–8.

[150] Porzio, *The Soldier's Vade Mecum*, 8.

[151] Ibid. 48.   [152] Holmes, *Acts of War*, 111.

army camps of that period and long after, before the revolution of Pasteur. For a suggestive extrapolation of what happened at Tornavento, let's multiply the daily stool of 15,000 people by about twenty days of almost continuous occupation of the camp, before and after the battle, and we arrive at a total of 300,000 bowel evacuations—without counting the horses! Within three days of the battle, Victor-Amadeus begged Louis XIII for substantial reinforcements, 'for our troops diminish daily from the sickness caused by the excessive heat' as well as by the indiscipline of marauders. The next day, 26 June, Hémery claimed that some 3,000 to 4,000 troops had fallen sick and that only 8,000 men were fit to fight, for 'the heat kills'.[153] About a week later, a priest coming from their camp informed Leganés that, from the day of the battle, quartermasters distributed some 5,000 fewer rations among the troops.[154] Heat waves could dissolve an army just as easily as heavy rains, and the exposed camp was inadequate shelter.[155] Historians sometimes cite the estimations of Patrick Landier who claims that about a quarter of the French soldiery died every year—a total of 600,000 men for almost twenty-five years of war (1635–59).[156] Jacques Dupâquier claims that perhaps only 10 per cent of these died from combat. These are guesstimates almost impossible to verify, because armies saw men come and go continually and did not keep records of the deaths of individual soldiers.[157] We have no good idea what military mortality was during the Thirty Years' War, but it is certain that battle claimed a minority of the total number of victims. Soldiers dying of disease in hospital in Roussillon were six times as numerous as those killed in combat in the 1670s.[158]

The immobility of the confederate army was owed in part to the necessity of awaiting reinforcements enabling it to resume the invasion. An additional challenge was to link up with the army of Rohan, which had advanced as far as Lecco two weeks before the battle. It withdrew a few days later after Spanish and Italian professional troops and a great host of militiamen dug in across its path. Rohan's numbers were too small to venture across the Lombard plain in search of his allies and with each passing day many of his soldiers presented themselves to Spanish authorities in order to receive a passport to leave the theatre.[159] For days, Victor-Amadeus and Créquy awaited news of Rohan's progress. Confederate leaders still clung to the illusion that the subjects of the king of Spain were ripe for revolt. 'When Mr de Rohan joins us after six or seven days' march, we can make camp at Bufalore and make Milan rise up.'[160] Rohan received fresh exhortations from Victor-Amadeus to march on 5 July, three days after the duke wrote it. The Duke

---

[153] AAE Correspondance Politique: Sardaigne, vol. 24, letters 25 and 26 June, 1636.

[154] ASF Mediceo del Principato 3176, letter from Camillo del Monte, 7 July 1636.

[155] Russon and Martin, *Vivre sous la tente*, 231.

[156] Patrick Landier, '1643: Etude quantitative d'une année de violence, en France pendant la Guerre de Trente Ans', *Histoire, Economie et Société*, 1 (1982), 187–212.

[157] Borreguero Beltràn, 'El coste humano de la guerra', 58–9.

[158] Ayats, 'Armées et santé', 120.

[159] ASMn Archivio Gonzaga 1761, letter of Sigismondo Vecchi in Milan to Duke Charles, 9 July 1636.

[160] AAE Correspondance Politique: Sardaigne, vol. 24, letter from Héméry to Monsieur, 26 June 1636.

of Savoy was disinclined to venture far from the Ticino river since his supply line was so tenuous, and so proposed to the Huguenot general a circuitous route around the Alpine lakes. He recommended marching across the marshy north end of Lake Como and through the town of Gravedona (already sacked in search of food), then follow a narrow track along the lakeshore south to the valley of the Cavargna river. That provided easy marching across a broad valley to Porlezza and Lake Lugano, but then the mountains reduced the roadway to a narrow lakeside path. Lugano was Swiss territory, but immediately thereafter the road led into very hilly country and the path south to Varese passed through at least one narrow defile. Examining small-scale historical maps and modern satellite images, the proposed route of over ninety kilometres seems feasible, but French troops on the narrow path would have been vulnerable first to amphibious Spanish-Italian troops, and then to Lombard militia detachments hovering overtop the column. There were several bottlenecks where a small determined force might interrupt their march for a while. 'Don't worry about your provisions', Victor-Amadeus wrote optimistically, 'you will only need enough for eight days, and you can easily have a supply of biscuit follow you.' Victor-Amadeus was proposing to rescue the little Alpine army, not to meet it in a triumphant march of conquest. Rohan dared not leave the valley, knowing that it would throw off the Swiss Grison yoke as soon as he left, and so he replied that the proposed march path was unfeasible.[161] The population of the Valtellina remained deeply pro-Habsburg and fed information to Milan on the state of the Franco-Grison army. There was nothing Rohan could do to realize the ambitious plan he had proposed the previous winter, for his army was one of those that Richelieu starved (literally) in order to provide for the others. Several of his French regiments mutinied for lack of pay in June, and his Swiss regiments imitated them after they were owed an entire year's pay. Rohan mortgaged his own estates to provide operating funds for his men, and tried raising more in the nearby Venetian Republic. He knew he did not have the strength to go forward.[162]

The weight of the campaign now rested squarely on the shoulders of the Duke of Savoy, who sent for smaller detachments across the Po to join him. Several thousand French troops abandoned in the Monferrato by the Duke of Parma, and another 2,000 Piedmontese garrison troops near Asti marched eastward to strengthen the invasion army.[163] Fresh French troops were destined for the duke's own contingent, and he drew up plans to recruit a new regiment in Savoy.[164] Despite the extra effectives, Victor-Amadeus did not have enough men to blockade a large town, and the army's pitiful complement of cannon was no match for

[161] Sandro Massera, 'La spedizione del Duca Henri de Rohan in Valtellina (1635–1637)', in S. Massera (ed.), *La Spedizione del Duca di Rohan in Valtellina: Storia e memorie nell'età della Guerra dei Trent'Anni* (Milan, 1999), 21–108; ASTo Materie Politiche dell'Interno: Registro di lettere alla Corte, vol. 38. Letter from Victor-Amadeus to Rohan, 2 July 1636.

[162] Pierre and Solange Deyon, *Henri de Rohan, Huguenot de plume et d'épée, 1579–1638* (Paris, 2000), 175; see also the *Memoires du Cardinal de Richelieu*, 51.

[163] ASTo Materie Politiche dell'Interno: Registro di lettere alla Corte 38, letter from Victor-Amadeus to Cardinal Richelieu, 25 June 1636.

[164] ASTo Materie politiche interne: Lettere del duca Vittorio Amedeo, vol. 56, letters of 10 and 20 July 1636.

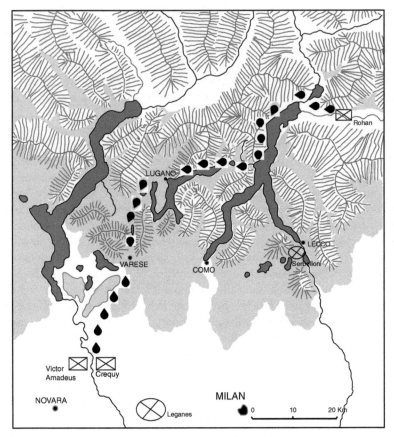

Map 7. Proposed march to unite with Rohan's army, July 1636.

the citadel and city of Milan. In an undated letter to Louis XIII not long after the battle, the duke denied that he was listening to Spanish peace proposals. But the present state of things could not continue long, he warned, for the army was falling apart from lack of pay.

Victor-Amadeus's predicament was to conduct a successful campaign in such a way that its results did not render his state and the status of his house more vulnerable than before. Voices in the French royal council, which he attributed to Créquy's influence, greatly diminished his role in the recent battle. Victor-Amadeus sent the first full dispatch describing the battle back to Fontainebleau, whose receipt lifted the spirits of the grateful cardinal. A franker, but still praiseworthy report followed from the ambassador Hémery.[165] Créquy's letter followed them shortly, focusing on the fateful conference during the night after the battle. His version (which made the rounds of the court, embellished still more by the

---

[165] ASTo Materie politiche interne: Lettere ministri, Francia, vol. 34, letter from Victor-Amadeus to the Marquis de Saint-Maurice, his ambassador in France, 9 July 1636.

emissary comte de Palluau) minimized the role of the Duke of Savoy. Victor-Amadeus's ambassador the Marquis de Saint-Maurice submitted an 'official' relation of the battle for publication in the *Gazette*, but the version that appeared was that of Hémery, which barely mentioned Savoyard participation.[166] This *Gazette*, which was very much a public relations instrument for Richelieu's policies, consented to insert supplementary information in a later issue, mentioning the Count of Verrua. Victor-Amadeus tried to even the score with a letter to Cardinal Richelieu emphasizing his firmness the night after the battle, and berated the shortcomings of his French colleagues. 'It was a miracle that we emerged from the battle with the upper hand.' Du Plessis-Praslin he conceded was courageous. Créquy was brave too, 'mais peu judicieux et sans conduite'. Those who had experience like Monsieur de Créquy didn't have the necessary firmness (*solidité*) and let themselves be led by Du Plessis-Praslin who had a quick mind, but lacked experience. As for the comte de Sault, 'ils ne l'ont jamais eu en réputation de soldat'. The others, apart from his aides-de-camp Roqueservières and Castelan, were mere followers, he added in another letter. 'I don't listen to their opinions, and I decided to do the opposite of what they said. I told them that they could do whatever they wanted.' Mutual backbiting among the generals was a serious problem, for it underscored their indecision in the aftermath of the battle and the sense they all had that the campaign was slipping away from them.[167]

Three weeks after the fight, Hémery tallied the French forces available as 14,000 infantry and 2,500 cavalry in the field and ten regiments in garrison (perhaps another 4,000 men) and 3,000 infantry for the Duke of Savoy (exclusive of the duke's garrisons in his own duchy and at least 1,500 horse).[168] This calculation ignored French troops (perhaps 2,000 men) stranded in the duchy of Parma and still others in Mantua, not to mention the men under the command of the Duke of Rohan, perhaps another 4,000 subjects of Louis XIII, all redoubtable veterans. Another 4,000 foot assembled in Provence awaited embarkation to rescue the duchy of Parma by sea. If one were to add the Swiss Grisons, Piedmontese, Parmans, and Mantuans, whose engagement in the cause was questionable, the confederates would still come out ahead with well over 40,000 professional soldiers in the theatre.[169] This was considerably more than France could realistically maintain. Victor-Amadeus mobilized 150,000 livres on his own credit to supply the army in the field.[170] Hémery's correspondence confirms that the army had

[166] ASTo Materie politiche interne: Lettere ministri, Francia, mazzo 34, 15 July 1636.

[167] ASTo Materie politiche interne: Lettere ministri, Francia, mazzo 34, letters to the Marquis de Saint-Maurice, 28 June and 15 July 1636.

[168] AAE Correspondance Politique: Sardaigne, vol. 24, letter from Hémery to Cardinal Richelieu, 15 July 1636.

[169] Parrott, *Richelieu's Army*, 193–200.

[170] Archivio di Stato Torino, Materie Militari, mazza 1, no. 30: *Giornaliere della guerra fatta da S.A.R. e truppe confederate contro il Duca di Mantova e dello Stato di Milano.* 'Memoria in forma d'Istruzione al Marchese di S. Morizio, ambasciatore di S.A.R. in Francia, in giustificazione contro le doglianze de'Francesi per la supposta inazione dell'armata, e di non essersi potuto portar soccorso a Parma', n.d.

received only one pay or 'montre' since the beginning of the year.[171] 'We need cavalry and infantry reinforcements to replace those who were killed or fell sick', he begged. The army consisted for the most part of poorly disciplined new recruits, many of whom deserted daily despite the measures taken to prevent it. 'I placed a provost's lieutenant and some archers along the roads to stop it, but the multitude of paths renders these measures useless.' He pleaded for the dispatch of veteran soldiers (*des vieux corps*) to maintain and stiffen those who remained under the colours.[172] In addition to ambushing enemy marauders, Spanish commanders adopted a sensible policy of giving French deserters a scudo coin and a passport for their trouble and sending them on their way east into Venetian territory.[173] Desertion concerned the youngest recruits and the most recent formations in particular. Young recruits, volunteer sons of good family, adventurers, mercenaries of disparate religious and ethnic backgrounds, former prisoners and deserters from the enemy, vagabonds pressed into service, flocked into the new regiments, whose number rose continuously. As David Parrott notes, it was easy enough to enrol new men into these armies, but quite another to keep them under the colours.[174] Same refrain from the Marques de Leganés, who complained that everyone was hiring soldiers now, and on the slightest pretext soldiers quit his service to join some other army.[175] This constant depletion of forces in the field—on both sides—was another structural constant of campaigning, and there was no remedy for it.

As they waited for developments, the French and Savoyard soldiers literally shat themselves out of their strong position astride the Ticino river and their only source of water. In the short term, the only solution was to spread out the encampment. The makeshift huts (*barracche*) soon stretched eight kilometres along the river valley, making it impossible to defend the army from an attack.[176] On 2 and 3 July, after leaving the earthworks garrisoned on both sides of the river, Créquy moved most of his troops out of their overextended lodgings in the valley and onto the open heath by the Panperduto ditch and dug in there, still suspecting that Leganés would return to give battle.[177] Extending over two kilometres in length, the new trenches were still too vast to defend easily, but at least the men escaped the stench of unburied bodies.[178]

---

[171] AAE Correspondance Politique: Sardaigne, vol. 24, letter from Héméry to Cardinal Richelieu, 2 July 1636.

[172] AAE Correspondance Politique: Sardaigne, vol. 24, letter from Héméry to Cardinal Richelieu, 3 July 1636.

[173] Galeazzo Gualdo Priorato, *Historia delle guerre dal Conte Galeazzo Gualdo Priorato* (Venice, 1646), 347.

[174] André Corvisier, 'Renouveau militaire et misères de la guerre, 1635–1659', *Histoire militaire de la France 1: Des origines à 1715* (Paris, 1992), 352–82; Bernard Masson, 'Un aspect de la discipline dans les armées de Louis XIII: La lutte contre la désertion du soldat 1635–1643', *Revue Historique des Armées*, 162 (1986), 12–23; David Parrott, 'Strategy and Tactics in the Thirty Years' War: The "Military Revolution"', *Militärgeschichtliche Mitteilungen*, 38 (1985), 7–25.

[175] AGS Estado 3344, 45, 26 May 1636.

[176] Lupi, 'Storia della peste avvenuta nel borgo di Busto Arsizio', 207.

[177] 'Relazione del curato Francesco Comerio di Lonate', 440–1.

[178] Bertolli, 'L'invasione Franco-sabauda del 1636', 57–8.

The Tornavento crossing could not be properly fortified on both sides of the river and held with a modest force. The invaders needed a better crossing place upriver at Sestri and Castelletto where they could build two forts and lodge 3,000 men, enough to delay even the strongest Habsburg flying columns until help arrived. Ideally the army would advance north to Varese closer to the Alps, and build a fort there while they waited for Rohan to join them. Three weeks sitting in the same position resulted in a forage crisis too, since cavalry patrols needed to advance ever further to find the hay and the cereals they needed for the horses' subsistence. So on 7 July, prompted by what the *Gazette* called a 'plague' infesting their camp, the coalition army formed up into three great formations, and marched north towards Sesto.[179] The cavalry reconnaissance and an infantry support force with four cannon large and small, accompanied by some artillery wagons, started out just a few hours after dawn. The main contingent, or 'battle', followed behind with the wagons, the rest of the artillery, and a great number of horses. The third squadron, after dismantling the bridge across the Ticino and burning the huts that had sheltered the men, formed the rearguard. Each of the three corps kept a compact formation in order to prevent watchful Habsburg skirmishers picking off the stragglers.[180] By the late afternoon the entire force had evacuated Tornavento. The cavalry reached Sesto at dusk, and the foot spent the night not far behind at Somma, which they sacked.[181] Immediately upon their departure, the civilians from surrounding villages converged on the former camp and collected the flotsam and jetsam left behind, in the form of hardware, muskets, crockery, hauling equipment, and other munitions deemed an impediment to an army on the march.[182]

From their new position, Franco-Savoyard troops extended their destructive forays northward towards the Alpine foothills, triggering another wholesale flight of the rural population.[183] A French detachment moved on Varese in order to tempt Rohan to advance in their direction. Meanwhile, at Sestri the Franco-Savoyard army reassembled its bridge across the Ticino and fortified it at both ends with earthworks, while the commanders considered their next move. The ports of Arona and Angera, facing each other across Lake Maggiore, became prime targets now that they were in easy reach. The seizure of the castles dominating them would permit the allies to close off the boat traffic into the Ticino and hence to Milan.

Leganés dispatched Ferrante Bolognini, the Milanese ambassador to Modena, to strengthen the antiquated fortifications of both places in the immediate aftermath of the battle at Tornavento, with the aid of a small detachment of professional soldiers sent to stiffen the militia.[184] On 14 July the French embarked 100 musketeers on a large boat armed with four cannon, and sailed it into the middle of the lake between the two ports to prevent any communication between them.

[179] *Gazette de France*, 117 (1636).

[180] Satterfield, *Princes, Posts and Partisans*, 193.

[181] 'Relazione del curato Francesco Comerio di Lonate', 441.

[182] Lupi, 'Storia della peste avvenuta nel borgo di Busto Arsizio', 207.

[183] Giulini, 'Un diario secentesco', 479.

[184] Archivio Comunale Pavia, MS II 59, Gabrio Busca, Descrizione delle fortezze di frontiera dello Stato di Milano, *c*.1600, fo. 35, for descriptions of the antiquated fortifications of both castles. Neither could have withstood more than a few days' bombardment.

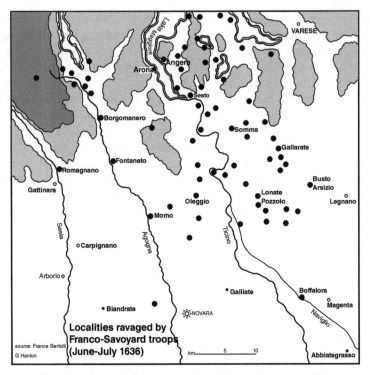

Map 8. Localities ravaged around the Ticino, June–July 1636.

Small Spanish boats filled with musketeers approached them and the two floating detachments exchanged fire on the lake, while a Spanish battery of cannon along the shore tried vainly to score a direct hit. Outgunned, the French craft retreated downstream to Sesto. Meanwhile, a detachment of about 4,000 men commanded by Créquy's son, the comte de Sault, invested the castle at Angera and began to plant batteries and sap the approaches. Soon, however, upon receiving news that Leganés had crossed to the west bank of the Ticino, they decided to interrupt their siege and withdraw, while the garrison chased after them and inflicted about sixty casualties.[185] The coalition soldiery meanwhile rampaged throughout the district between Varese and Lake Maggiore, as they had further south. One report claims they burned between half and three-quarters of the houses in the villages they overran and defiled the churches for good measure. At Cadrezzate they pried open the tombs inside the church 'to see if goods were hidden there'.[186]

Notwithstanding the change of scenery and a new supply of booty, large numbers of French soldiers continued to die of sickness in their new quarters. Some regiments cut to ribbons at Tornavento and then depleted further by sickness and ambush became mere shadows of their former selves. The average company com-

---

[185] ASMo, Ambasciatori Milano 107, fasc. 21, letter from Fra Ferrante Bolognini, 20 July 1636.
[186] Bertolli, 'L'invasione franco-sabauda del 1636', 65–7.

plement in the Florainville infantry regiment by the end of the campaign was only fourteen men.[187] Victor-Amadeus disbanded the regiment of Bonne and dispatched the remnants of the understrength regiment of Aiguebonne to garrison duty in Pinerolo.[188] The lack of pay pushed more men to desert, as the Spanish army began to swell.

THE INVADERS OUTFLANKED

Leganés's successful nocturnal retreat to Abbiategrasso on 23 June left his troops half-dead from exhaustion, hunger, and thirst.[189] In the safety of his entrenched camp, in fertile and comfortable territory, the general conducted a general muster of his forces in order to determine his strength. These amounted to 6,000 infantry and 4,500 cavalry, which confirmed the disproportionate weight of the battle on the foot.[190] These losses would have included a large number of men who drifted unhurt off the battlefield, or separated from their units at night during the withdrawal. Many of them would return to the colours not long after. A truly beaten army would have come apart from desertion and panic, allowing the victor to follow up their momentary advantage and seize the cities.[191] 'One must not be terrified by defeat,' wrote Montecuccoli speaking from personal experience, 'for Mars is impartial; one must not despair but rather turn about and meet *fortuna* face to face.'[192] There were nevertheless a few signs of discouragement. Grand Duke Ferdinando II of Tuscany decided to transform his duchy's participation from an active expeditionary corps to a strictly monetary subsidy to Spain. Many of the officers, completely discouraged after the fight, announced their intention to go home.[193] Camillo dal Monte (who was ill) retired to Florence and left the overall command to the cavalry leader Cosimo Ricciardi. Tuscan troops remaining in Lombardy then passed onto the Spanish payroll.[194] We have no way of knowing how many Tuscan soldiers decided to return home. The Grand Duke promised a half-pay subsidy to those who wished to retire.[195] He continued to offer Leganés suggestions for promotion of specific officers remaining in service.[196]

The withdrawal of the demoralized Florentines was more than offset by the gradual recovery of the Spanish army around Abbiategrasso in the subsequent weeks. A vanguard of dragoons placed in Castelletto, a kilometre to the east of the town, threw up defensive works along the *naviglio*, while a tercio of infantry and

---

[187] Parrott, *Richelieu's Army*, 49.

[188] AAE Correspondance Politique, Sardaigne, vol.24, letter from Héméry, 3 July 1636.

[189] Brusoni, *Delle Historie memorabili, contiene le Guerre d'Italia de'nostri tempi*, 39.

[190] ASFi Mediceo del Principato 3180, fo. 1119, letter from Milan to the Balì Cioli, 24 June 1636.

[191] Gabriel Perjés, 'Army Provisioning, Logistics and Strategy in the Second Half of the Seventeenth Century', *Acta Historica Academiae Scientiarum Hungaricae*, 16 (1970), 1–51.

[192] Barker, *Military Intellectual and Battle*, 171.

[193] ASF Mediceo del Principato 3180, fo. 1120, letter of 24 June 1636.

[194] ASF Mediceo del Principato 3258, fo. 253, letter of 1 July 1636.

[195] ASF Mediceo del Principato 3180, fo. 605, letters of 1 and 8 July 1636.

[196] ASF Mediceo del Principato 141, Minute di lettere, 7 Sept. 1636.

most of the cavalry camped behind them in support. In and around Abbiategrasso, which was a substantial walled town, Leganés posted the remainder of his foot, who dug more entrenchments.[197] As the threat of an advance by the Duke of Rohan receded, Leganés judged it opportune to shift the Spanish tercio of Juan de Garay from the Adda river entrenchments westward to the Ticino. It occupied Tornavento two days after Victor-Amadeus abandoned the position, and immediately set about removing the obstruction placed at the mouth of the *naviglio*. No boats were able to descend from Lake Maggiore right away, but at least the flowing water brought relief to the parched fields and pastures around Milan. More reinforcements soon joined Leganés, while all summer long Milanese noblemen created new companies of soldiers intent on defending the territory from spoliation. Cardinal Trivulzio, who had already raised a tercio posted to cover the Po river frontier with Parma, added new companies to it. Priests blessed their banners in a public ceremony at the beginning of August.[198] A muster of the field army on the morning of 2 July at Abbiategrasso gave a total of about 12,000 men, of which one-third was cavalry. Mere days later, with the transfer of Della Gatta's men from across the Po, the Habsburg field army surpassed 15,000 horse and foot, 'bravissimi e impazienti'.[199] Leganés expected a further 8,000 Neapolitans, Germans, and Spaniards in the coming weeks.[200] On 11 July, galleys from the Naples flotilla disembarked another 2,000 infantry without hindrance, for the French fleet off the Provençal coast took no initiatives (Fig. 4.12).[201] Both the Italian anonymous account and the official version published in Madrid claimed that the Catholic King's army was in good spirits and looked forward to a rematch in the near future, confident that their undisciplined adversaries were increasingly fearful of another encounter in the field.[202]

Flush with reinforcements, Leganés spread his men out across a series of entrenched camps along the *naviglio* from Abbiategrasso to Robecco about six kilometres to the north, in order to block the advance of French raiding parties and deprive the enemy camp of fodder. 'Now the Court is here in Robecco', wrote Cesare Alfieri to General Serbelloni on 6 July, 'a village completely burgled where the houses are all empty and there are no facilities (*commodità*), and we have begun to sleep on the ground without any straw. And so we find ourselves

[197] ASF Mediceo del Principato 3176, letter from Camillo del Monte, 2 July 1636.
[198] Giulini, 'Un diario secentesco', 479.
[199] ASFi Mediceo del Principato 3176, letter from Milan, 7 July 1636.
[200] ASF Mediceo del Principato 3181, letter from Camillo del Monte, 2 July 1636.
[201] *Gazette de France*, 113 (1636). The French source claimed that the troops disembarked here, 2,000 foot and 400 horse, elicited pity from the onlookers. This may not be mere propaganda, for Leganés assigned two depleted Neapolitan tercios, those of Tiberio Brancaccio and Michele Pignatelli, entirely to garrison duty. An additional 2,000 foot remained aboard the galleys, destined to reinforce the Habsburg army in Spain. Maffi estimates that almost 4,000 foot and 2,000 horse were recruited in Germany for the Italian theatre in 1636, *Il baluardo della corona* (Florence, 2007), 147.
[202] Biblioteca Universitaria Bologna, vol. 473, Misc. H, no. 15; Relatione del fatto d'Arme seguito fra l'Esercito spagnolo e francese nella selva di Soma; this finds an echo in Tuscan dispatches as well, ASFi 3258, letter from Florence to Don Francisco de Melo, 12 July 1636.

Fig. 4.12. Johann Wilhelm Baur, Soldiers landing in port. The arrival in a Mediterranean port of Spanish reinforcements, *c.*1640. The troop ships were escorted by galleys, of which the Spanish enjoyed a large superiority. The great French fleet off Provence proved totally incapable of interdicting enemy seaborne relief. (Courtesy of Brown University.)

merrily...'[203] After another muster at Magenta on 5 July, Leganés threw a bridge of boats across the Ticino to funnel reinforcements to Novara less than fifteen kilometres away. By 19 July he assembled a great army at Galliate, just outside the city.[204] This deployment away from Milan frightened the inhabitants of the metropolis, who were still adding to their defences, but it marked a clear turning point in the campaign.[205]

Philip IV and Olivares could not manage developments in Italy or Flanders in any direct way, for dispatches took at least two weeks to arrive from these key bastions of the empire and sometimes much longer.[206] Madrid learnt of the battle of Tornavento only on 17 July, and the first reaction to Leganés's official dispatch was bombastic satisfaction, although private channels of information resonated more pessimistically. The king and his minister hoped that the German and Neapolitan

---

[203] Archivio Storico Civico di Milano, Archivio Sola Busca: Serbelloni b. 53, letter of Cesare Alfieri to Count Giovanni Serbelloni, 6 July 1636; also ASFi Mediceo del Principato 3176, letter of 7 July 1636.

[204] 'Relazione del curato Francesco Comerio di Lonate', 441.

[205] Archivio Storico Civico di Milano, Dicasteri 149, letter from Carlo Sirtoni to the king, 19 July 1636.

[206] AGS Estado 3833; letters from Milan dated 16 May 1635 took five weeks to reach Madrid.

reinforcements on their way would suffice to stabilize the theatre, and pondered measures to raise more troops in Spain; these included devaluating the coinage still further, and squeezing the nobles and churchmen for contributions from their own pockets.[207] Five hundred Spaniards embarked on galleys in Barcelona, including General Don Felipe de Silva who would assume the overall command of the cavalry. Galleys conveyed more troops from Naples, whom the Milanese preferred to the Germans for their better discipline towards civilians.[208] The southern kingdom sent about 10,000 soldiers to Northern Italy every year until 1640.[209] We possess a state of the Catholic King's field army early in August, that is, excluding the garrisons. It numbered over 15,000 infantry and almost 6,000 cavalry, exclusive of the forces still blocking the Alpine valleys across from the Duke of Rohan (two Spanish and two Lombard tercios), those hemming in the Duke of Parma, and still others posted to the Ligurian Riviera. Leganés's mobile force was comprised of five Spanish tercios, four Neapolitan, two Lombard, and one Florentine tercio, plus five German regiments of foot totalling 4,000 men. The horse included over 3,000 Italian and Spanish troopers and several German regiments numbering over 2,500 men. Even better, additional reinforcements from Spain were on their way. By the end of the summer, Leganés could deploy at least 35,000 professional soldiers, an increase of about 50 per cent relative to a year previous, plus about half that number of mobile militiamen.[210] The number dispatched to join his army was significantly larger than the total of men who figured on the roster, since Habsburg soldiers deserted in large numbers, like the French. Maffi estimates that about a third of the Catholic King's soldiers deserted every year, perhaps lower among the Spaniards and higher among the Neapolitans.[211] The ability of Spain to funnel men and supplies to Italy and to maintain such high numbers despite the wastage through sickness and desertion forces admiration. The pessimistic Hémery wrote to Cardinal Richelieu on 27 June, 'I have often written that the Spaniards are not as weak as we thought.' He reflected the prevailing gloom of the allied command when he wrote that the Spanish army was far from destroyed, and that with their reinforcements they would be ready for a second battle in ten or twelve days.[212] Leganés reverted instead to his more cautious approach, aiming to force the invasion to recede by choking off its provisions with little loss to his own army.[213]

Even worse than the dwindling French effectives, Victor-Amadeus worried about his tenuous supply line across the foot of the Alps from Piedmont. Almost from the immediate aftermath of the battle, cavalry patrols from Mortara and Novara hunted the vulnerable convoys west of the Ticino. Early modern armies, like modern ones, could not advance without having secure lines of supply to

[207] ASF Mediceo del Principato 4961, Lettere da Spagna, letter of 19 July 1636.
[208] Archivio Storico Civico di Milano, Dicasteri 149, letter of 18 July 1636.
[209] Maffi, *Il baluardo della corona*, 96.
[210] Luis Ribot Garcia, 'Milano, piazza d'armi della monarchia spagnola', in F. Motta (ed.), *'Millain the great'* (Milan, 1989), 349–63.
[211] Maffi, *Il baluardo della corona*, 132–4.
[212] AAE Correspondance politique: Sardaigne, vol. 24, letter to Gaston d'Orléans 26 June 1636.
[213] Gualdo Priorato, *An History of the late warres*, 359.

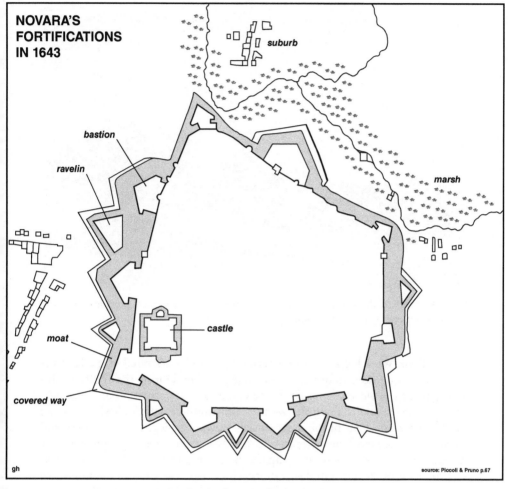

NOVARA'S FORTIFICATIONS IN 1643

suburb

bastion

ravelin

marsh

moat

castle

covered way

gh

source: Piccoli & Pruno p.67

Map 9. The fortress of Novara in 1643.

their rear. Enemy strongholds within reach of their supply magazines would have to be captured. This was easy for the castles, whose walls and towers could not withstand a long bombardment from heavy canon. Novara was different: it was the 'antemurale del Ticino', the forward bulwark blocking the secure control over the river and its vital traffic (Map 9).[214] The city of 4,000 or 5,000 inhabitants lay just over fifteen kilometres south of the invaders' main supply road to Oleggio—two or three hours' canter for cavalry.[215] At the beginning of the seventeenth century, its fortifications were completely inadequate to withstand a

---

[214] Paola Piccoli and Simona Pruno, *Il Castello e le mura di Novara: Storia e progetti per una città fortezza tra il XVI e il XVII secolo* (Novara, 2010), 43.
[215] Gualdo Priorato, *Historia delle guerre*, 338.

Fig. 4.13. Stefano della Bella, Baggage train, *c.*1630: Cavalry soldiers provide a necessary escort in case enemy partisans should appear.

serious siege. Work began on its modernization, and accelerated in the 1620s as international tensions underscored its strategic value. During the 1630s, engineers ignored the old castle inside the new walls and concentrated on building a series of new bastions along the western and southern approaches, with some ravelins between them in the moat to slow down a besieger. The northern and eastern sides retained the sixteenth-century aspect, but they were protected by marshy stream beds close to the ramparts. By the summer of 1636 work on these sections had just begun, and the moat lacked a covered way in front of it to allow the garrison to fire on approachers.[216] Even as an imperfect fortress, Novara presented a serious obstacle to an invading army, for it would require weeks of undisturbed siege to breach its walls. Troops camped on the soggy land surrounding the fortress would surely succumb in large numbers to malaria and dysentery. The city was home to four large companies of militia, well-armed and serving on alternating days, who stood watch at night.[217] Leganés also took care to provide the city with a large garrison of professional troops, and furnished it with as much grain and forage as he could collect from the vulnerable countryside around it. So much grain had been stocked in the army magazines that town magistrates feared there was no longer enough for the civilian population.[218] Leganés reinforced Novara with eleven more cavalry companies after the end of

---

[216] Ibid. 53–67.
[217] ASNo Comune di Novara, parte antica 1221: Milizia urbana, 27 July 1635.
[218] ASNo Comune di Novara, parte antica 1875, Memoriali, 20 Feb. 1637.

June. Town officials patiently purchased houses abandoned in the aftermath of the plague in order to house the soldiers, but suddenly they were overwhelmed with the new arrivals.[219] Space for troopers was so tight that four entire companies of Count Schlick's fearsome German regiment took up residence outside the Cathedral in a cloister belonging to the diocesan administration. This desperate measure brought the urban worthies entrusted with military lodgings to the edge of excommunication.[220] Novara's cavalry made the invasion's slender supply corridor extremely vulnerable, notwithstanding the large Franco-Savoyard detachments left in towns like Romagnano, Fontaneto, and Oleggio whose task it was to escort the wagons. Hémery recommended entrenching no fewer than 3,000 foot and 600 horse between Fonaneto and Oleggio to protect the wagons' passage, but these would have to be subtracted from the dwindling numbers of men across the Ticino river.[221] Every day or two, columns of wagons and their armed escorts scurried from one fortified post to another, hoping to avoid strong Spanish patrols en route (Fig. 4.13). On 8 July a strong Spanish contingent of 300 horse and 300 foot swarmed the district around the Piedmontese border city of Vercelli, burning some houses, rounding up the livestock, and herding it across the shallow Sesia river.[222]

A week later, Leganés increased the pressure considerably. First a contingent of 800 horse, an equal force of musketeers, and an unspecified number of militiamen marched on Romagnano where they cut the cables holding the bridge across the Sesia in place and tried to burn the bridge itself. Then they crossed the river into Piedmont to set fire to some mills outside nearby Gattinara, a larger town better fortified.[223] On 16 July, a stronger force of 4,000 horse and foot under Lucio Boccapianola tried to seize Gattinara itself, whose well-stocked storehouses served as a forward magazine for the army.[224] These were repulsed by several thousand men under Guido Villa who were providentially passing by, aided by 600 horse dispatched in the nick of time from Ghemme, across the Sesia river. Purportedly the town's inhabitants hurraughed 'Viva Savoia!' as the two forces skirmished around the walls.[225] In their withdrawal, the Habsburg cavalry, who included companies from the regiment of Count Schlick, set fire to five or six Piedmontese villages, 'and killed infants in their cradles'.[226]

[219] Buono, *Esercito, istituzioni, territorio*, 154–70.

[220] ASNo Comune di Novara, parte antica 1875, memoriali, letter from the city regents to the military governor, 30 Sept. 1636.

[221] AAE Correspondance Politique, Sardaigne, vol. 24, letter from Hémery to Monsieur, 26 July 1636.

[222] *Gazette de France*, 121 (1636); for the same event from the Spanish perspective, ASFi Mediceo del Principato 3176, letter from Milan 7 July 1636.

[223] ASTo Materie politiche interne: Lettere ministri, Francia m. 34, letter to the Marquis de Saint-Maurice, 14 July 1636.

[224] Alexandre de Saluces, *Histoire militaire du Piémont* (Turin, 1818), iv. 27.

[225] ASTo Materie politiche interne: Lettere ministri, Francia, vol. 34: letter of Duchess Christine to the ambassador in France, 17 July 1636.

[226] Biblioteca Palatina Parma, Ms Parmense 462, Da Libri della chiesa di Corticelle (copy by Affò); the parish priest of Corticelle qualified Schlick's troops quartered on his village as 'uomini piuttosto barbari e feroci, che umani, perchè uccidevano le persone senza motivo, devastono senza maniera il paese, e guastavano le case come demoni'.

The war is becoming cruel, now that the Spaniards rape and pillage the state of the Duke of Savoy, wrote Hémery to Cardinal Richelieu without a trace of irony. 'Every day there is a skirmish, and the sutlers make themselves scarce.' He urged Victor-Amadeus to reply in kind to teach the enemy a lesson.[227] Same refrain a week later: 'All the territory as far as Vercelli is unsafe and the enemy makes raids where they burn everything, or throw up fortifications in strategic locations.'[228] Almost as soon as Victor-Amadeus left the Tornavento position, Juan de Garay's tercio reoccupied it and set about reinforcing the fortifications on both sides of the river, 'and to hinder the French from getting it again so easily as they had done'.[229]

This war was fought with spades and picks, which could be wielded by militiamen and professional soldiers alike. The multiplication of earthen defensive works further constricted the foraging territory that fed the coalition army. Similar powerful works barred the way out of the Valtellina to Rohan. 'Italy is not like Germany', lamented Hémery in another plaintive letter to Richelieu, 'there is nowhere to go that is not fortified'.[230] For days, the confederate commanders at Sesto discussed one option, then another, without being able to formulate a firm resolution.[231] On 16 July Victor-Amadeus and Créquy, fearing for their supplies and the vulnerability of Piedmontese towns, decided they could no longer hold the Ticino river position. The army demolished its entrenchments at Sesto, loaded its gear into the wagons and set out towards the west to Borgomanero, at the very foot of the Alps. Having given up trying to capture the towns on the southern edge of Lake Maggiore, Franco-Savoyard patrols plundered the hilly region just south of Lake Orta after 20 July. At Soriso where they arrived on 22 July they reportedly killed about fifteen people and burned almost all the houses. Nearby the militia repulsed one of these French raids, and credited their little victory to the Virgin Mary of their local sanctuary. The reflux of the invasion army was unavoidable, in order to protect Piedmont from enemy incursions. From Sesto to Borgomanero, and then back towards Romagnano on the Sesia river frontier, Victor-Amadeus and Créquy marched their army, now reduced to about 10,500 foot and 2,500 horse, with the methodical order laid out in the textbooks (Fig. 4.14). They first evacuated their wounded and the sick from Oleggio, and deposited their heavy guns in fortified Fontaneto.

Leganés with his main force just east of Novara shadowed them cautiously, and then approached the confederate camp from the south, at Carpignano, about seven kilometres away. Victor-Amadeus formed up his army in battle array to face them, while the convoy of guns and their impedimenta under heavy cavalry escort withdrew from Fontaneto.[232] According to the *Gazette*, Victor-Amadeus then marched his army just out of range of the Spaniards and offered them a fresh battle. For eight hours, the two armies stood arrayed and ready for a contest, but Leganés refused to close with the invaders.[233] By now, the soldiers and officers in

[227] AAE Correspondance Politique: Sardaigne, vol. 24, letter 15 July 1636.
[228] AAE Correspondance Politique: Sardaigne, vol. 24, letter 23 July 1636.
[229] Gualdo Priorato, *An History of the late warres*, 359.
[230] AAE Correspondance Politique: Sardaigne, vol. 24, letter of 23 July.
[231] ASMn Archivio Gonzaga 1761, letter from Lodovico Porri at Sesto to Duke Charles, 12 July 1636.
[232] *Memoires du Comte de Souvigny, lieutenant-général des armées du roi*, 313.
[233] *Gazette de France*, 128 (1636).

Fig. 4.14. Stefano della Bella, Army on the march. The engraving depicts the progress of the 'battle', or the largest of three components of a field army en route to its destination. The cannon in the middle ground is drawn by sixteen horses.

aboth armies had come to respect the fighting qualities of their adversary. Moving past Gattinara, the Franco-Savoyard army camped between Trino and Casale Monferrato, where it assembled a new boat bridge across the Po that would permit them to move troops rapidly to whichever portion of the frontier was threatened. But this was a defensive posture.[234] Obliging the allies by attacking them at Carpignano would not have accomplished anything strategic for Spain, for apart from the mopping up, the invasion of Lombardy was over.

Don Martin d'Aragon advanced on Fontaneto with a few cannon and after bombarding the place for three days, allowed the French garrison of 400 men to march away with its arms and baggage on 7 August. He then led another contingent towards Vercelli, intending to lay waste to the Sesia river border area and threaten the fortress of Breme, in which Victor-Amadeus had laid up large quantities of provisions. Gattinara was stormed again on 6 August with a larger force. The little French garrison of 200 men surrendered the place, which had no modern fortifications, without much resistance. Habsburg troops purportedly drew from it 30,000 sacks of grain and whatever else was worth taking. They reportedly (in French accounts) raped and killed the nuns and set their convent alight along with the town, 'not leaving one stone on top of another'.[235] Habsburg troops disarmed the French rank and file and dismissed them, keeping only the commanding lieutenant-colonel to exchange against the nephew of General Serbelloni, who was one of Rohan's prisoners.[236]

The threat against Milan from Rohan by now had completely disappeared. A plague epidemic broke out in the Lombard Alps and by 26 July it had killed or incapacitated a third of his remaining army. Rohan himself fell sick with it in

---

[234] *Memoires du Comte de Souvigny,* 313.

[235] Lupi, 'Storia della peste avvenuta nel borgo di Busto Arsizio', 208; see also *Gazette de France,* 128 (1636).

[236] ASMo: Casa e Stato, Carteggi fra Principi Estensi 209; letter of Prince Borso d'Este to Duke Francesco of Modena, 6 Aug. 1636.

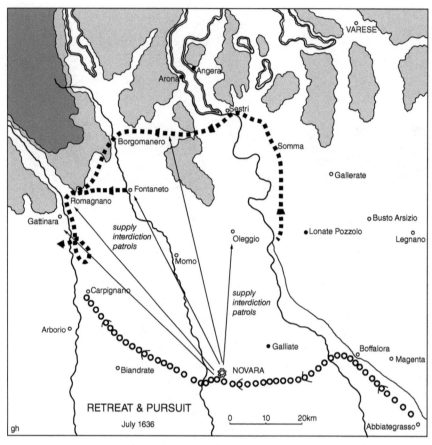

Map 10. Franco-Savoyard retreat and Habsburg pursuit, July 1636.

Sondrio and hovered close to death for a month. As talks for a general peace seemed to be making little progress in Cologne, his Swiss Grison allies began extending peace feelers towards Spain and Austria.[237] Now that he had some numerical superiority, it was Leganés's turn to carry the war into enemy territory. It was imperative that he should fodder his horses at Savoyard expense and deprive the enemy of those same resources. The Habsburg army shifted its centre of gravity from Novara to Alessandria south of the Po and a strong force sacked the district around Asti and the nearby Monferrato, with the intention of inflicting as much damage as possible on it. The hilly district with its tiny settlements and a multitude of castles would have soaked up too many men in minute garrisons if the invasion continued, and so he halted the advance after a few days. 'The Spanish army advanced beyond the Tanaro as far as Croce Bianca near Asti, where they halted for several days', wrote a chronicler in nearby Casale, 'and their soldiers sacked the

---

[237] Massera, 'La spedizione del Duca Henri de Rohan in Valtellina', 76–80.

villages of Grana, Castagnole and Montemagno, where they respected no church, or women, or old men, carrying off the sacred ornaments from the altar, raping both virgins and married women, killing poor elderly people with acts of true barbarism. Then Leganés withdrew.'[238] At Montegrosso, a fortified village a dozen kilometres south of Asti, the French garrison and its militia helpers put up such a stout defence that when Borso d'Este's German soldiers finally broke through the breach, they massacred the entire garrison and many civilians too; 'there was such obstinacy among the defenders, that most of them paid for it with their lives, since we wished to waste no time'. This event, whose existence figures in the Spanish sources too, might have been the most significant atrocity of the war.[239] The ducal council of Milan complained to Leganés after German troops got out of hand again at Castignoli, in the Monferrato, for it feared the French would retaliate against Lombard communities to even the score.[240]

Having secured the western border of the duchy of Milan, Leganés then dispatched Don Martin and Gil de Haes towards Piacenza with orders to similarly devastate the district and to force the obstinate Duke Odoardo of Parma to withdraw from the war. Don Vincenzo Gonzaga, freshly promoted lieutenant-general of the Milanese cavalry, and entrusted with a separate command, was instructed to do his worst. By winter, he was forced to organize special food convoys from Modenese territory to prevent his own troops from dying of hunger.[241]

The entire military balance had swung away from Cardinal Richelieu by the early summer of 1636. If Aquitaine had risen up in revolt the previous year, now it was Poitou, the Angoumois, and Saintonge in the west, which required the urgent dispatch of cavalry to repress the peasant rebels who would not pay their taxes.[242] The galley squadrons of Naples and Sicily, guided by disgruntled French pilots, expertly navigated the coastal waters of eastern Provence and carried relief to the Hispano-Italian garrisons based there.[243]

Leganés was perhaps unaware that momentous events were unfolding in northern France, where a surprise invasion of Picardy by a reinforced Army of Flanders captured a few modest French fortresses. The fall of little Corbie on the Somme river on 15 August opened the floodgates to a general inundation of rich northern France by Habsburg troops in the direction of Paris, by an army twice as large as the one operating in Lombardy.[244] The unexpected breakthrough (which could

---

[238] Giuseppe Giorcelli, 'Annali Casalesi (1632–1661) di Gian Domenico Bremio, speciaro di Casale Monferrato', *Rivista di Storia, Arte, Archaeologia della provincia di Alessandria*, 18 (1909), 381–436, under 1637.

[239] Gualdo Priorato, *An History of the late warres*, 361; the incident is reported in the *Gazette de France*, 149 (1636); for the Spanish admission to the massacre, AGS Estado 3344, no. 205; also Ghilini, *Annali di Alessandria* (Alessandria, 1903), 125.

[240] ASMn Archivio Gonzaga, Lettere di Milano, Alberto Prata to Duke Charles, 18 Nov. 1636.

[241] ASPr Archivio Gonzaga di Guastalla 63, letter from Duke Ferrante Gonzaga to the military governor of Reggio Emilia, 20 Jan. 1637.

[242] Archives du Service Historique de la Défense (Vincennes), A28, no. 150, 26 June 1636.

[243] Archives du Service Historique de la Défense (Vincennes), A28, no. 166, Relation de l'état des iles Ste-Marguerite et de l'armée des Espagnols.

[244] This assessment comes from the work of J. P. A. Bazy, *Etat militaire de la monarchie espagnole sous le règne de Philippe IV* (Poitiers, 1864), 53.

not be properly exploited because no supply preparations had been made for a considerable advance) evaporated all the French resources destined for other theatres. Louis XIII and Cardinal Richelieu decreed an obligatory conscription of much of the French nobility (the arrière-ban) and mobilized Paris and its hinterland to meet the emergency. They immediately shelved their plans to reinforce the Italian theatre with men and money, so young Duke Odoardo was on his own. Therefore the campaign of 1636 ended in a complete debacle for the confederate cause, months before cold weather forced the troops into winter quarters. French armies eventually recovered Corbie in November 1636, while the North Germans and Scots in Swedish pay won an unexpected victory at Wittstock in Brandenburg and avoided final elimination from the war.[245]

Duke Victor-Amadeus was widely thought to emerge the winner, paradoxically. Spain continued to try to entice him away from the French cause, by forwarding dispatches to him from his brother Prince Tommaso. 'Diverse were therefore the discourses, and divers the opinions hereupon.' The malicious Du Plessis-Praslin many years later recalled that two Capuchins arrived in camp from Milan two days after the battle offering the duke 500,000 crowns in order to halt his invasion; 'a few days later' the army withdrew from Spanish territory and went into winter quarters on 15 August, incontrovertible proof that Victor-Amadeus did not wish to conquer territory for the benefit of French arms. He could not resign himself to relinquishing Pinerolo and its adjoining territory that would leave him vulnerable to betrayal from his ally.[246] The duke's purported lethargy and obstruction had made it impossible for the French to capture the weak fortress of Valenza the year before. Now his zeal and energy had made it impossible for the Spanish to defeat the French in an open battle;

> if he had been worsted or put to the rout, he would have been much blamed for the conduct of his affaires, and on the contrary he should purchase much glory by the victory; and that he could not well do less, lest he should too openly declare himself opposite to the intentions of the French. But those who better understood the reasons of State, by rightly weighing this affaire, found, that as the Duke of Savoy liked not the French should get footing so far in Italy, by gaining the strong holds of the State of Milan, and increase their dominions by having such places to retreat unto; so likewise it did not stand with his interest that the Spaniards should extend themselves beyond their bounds, and hereupon it was probably judged, that the Duke intended to keep the French army in force and vigour, to counterpoise the Spanish power.[247]

Victor-Amadeus held to the French alliance for the time being, now that he appeared to have a better hand.[248] He resolved his predicament with more apparent success than either Créquy or Leganés.

[245] Steve Murdoch, Katherin Zickerman, and Adam Marks, 'The Battle of Wittstock, 1636', *Northern Studies*, 43 (2012), 71–109.
[246] Du Plessis-Praslin, *Memoires du Maréchal Du Plessis*, 361.
[247] Gualdo Priorato, *An History of the late warres*, 360.
[248] AGS Estado 3344, no. 223, Dispatch from Don Francisco de Melo from Genoa, 29 Sept. 1636.

Conclusion
The Resilience of Spanish Italy

The importance of the battle of Tornavento became clear in the minds of observers and participants only gradually. A decisive French victory would have forced Serbelloni to retire from Lecco, leaving Rohan a free hand to advance into the plain, harvesting all the food he needed and repaying his soldiers for their patience with the rich pickings of Lombardy. Energized by success, the Franco-Savoyard army might have captured the city of Milan (if not the citadel) by blockading the place for a few weeks. If the Habsburg army was sufficiently battered to the point where he had to disperse it into many garrisons, Leganés might not have been able to break the great city's encirclement.

In the event, Spanish strategy after the battle, defensive and risk-averse, aimed to close off the border to Franco-Savoyard incursions and to forage cavalry on enemy territory as much as possible. French initiatives in Italy were no longer possible once the Army of Flanders threatened Paris, so Leganés could relax. The crisis past, a sense of routine returned to the Habsburg army, while the principal officers thought of advancing their careers against the claims of their rivals. Borso d'Este turned down the offer to become general of cavalry to replace Gambacorta, hoping instead to be nominated 'Sergente Generale di Battaglia' of all the Imperial regiments in Italy and of any other German corps raised in the pay of Spain; he became Leganés's 'German' lieutenant. In the meantime he expected his nephew the Duke of Modena would send enough money to make up the heavy losses his regiment suffered. Prince Rinaldo d'Este, all of 18 years old, arrived in camp just after the battle to begin his military career under the wardship of Prince Borso. Younger brother and close confidant of Duke Francesco, Rinaldo became a tercio commander of Italian infantry in a few short years. In the callowness of youth, he ardently wished to see a fine battle (*bella fazione*) before the campaign of 1636 was over.[1] Other officers reverted to their normal fractious behaviour in order to maintain their status among restless and ambitious peers, typical alpha males. Leganés came to be plagued by refusals of his higher officers to obey their immediate superiors.[2] Mutual insults between the Burgundian baron de Batteville and the Bolognese aristocrat Cornelio Malvezzi escalated into a duel staged by a number of the officers and discussed by all. The two principals fought each other on horseback

[1] Archivio di Stato Modena (ASMo): Casa e Stato, Carteggi fra Principi Estensi, 209; Lettere del Principe Borso. See letters of 12 Aug. and 13 Sept.
[2] Davide Maffi, *Il baluardo della corona*, (Florence, 2007), 215.

with swords, and after exchanging 'valorosamente' a few strokes the duel ended when the baron received a slight wound in his arm. Borso d'Este and Prince Rinaldo, who served as arbiters, halted the affair and congratulated the officers for behaving as true gentlemen (*veri cavaglieri*). The two belligerents embraced each other and swore to be good friends as before.

Leganés seized his opportunity to push the smaller confederate allies out of the war. The Franco-Savoyard retreat into Piedmont allowed Spanish troops to unfurl over the Piacentino, with the aim of forcing Duke Odoardo to make peace. After being routed by Don Martin d'Aragon in a brief battle before the town of Rottofreno (15 August), demoralized Parman and French troops surrendered key strongpoints to the invaders.[3] Prince Doria's autonomous force of Spaniards, Germans, and feudal militiamen blocked the arrival of French reinforcements in Parma through the mountainous Genoese Republic to the south. Only the two large cities held out, but their modest garrisons of foreign soldiery feared the sullenness of the suffering population who resented their vain duke's foolish war. Habsburg forces feasted on the rich countryside and extracted millions of lire in contributions. Gil de Haes herded some 1,000 precious cows and oxen across the river into the State of Milan, to compensate for Lombard losses to the French.[4]

French preparations to rescue Odoardo's landlocked duchy with a seaborne expeditionary force stalled over July and August because Richelieu was unwilling to lay out clear lines of authority among the different commanders.[5] When this force finally moved, it proved unable to isolate and capture some fortified islands off the French Riviera that would have played havoc with their supplies had they been left undisturbed. A great French fleet of armed sailing vessels sat useless in harbour, for the Spanish superiority in galleys enabled the latter to ferry reinforcements to any threatened point. The dispersal of the Habsburg army into winter quarters in November permitted Leganés to dispatch reinforcements to the coast.[6] French reports claimed that 6,000 or 7,000 thousand soldiers and 2,000 Moorish captives built up the island fortifications by bearing stones on their backs like ants.[7] Small naval actions in September proved inconclusive, so in December the French fleet withdrew to Toulon. When it finally re-emerged ready with their rescue troops in February (Spanish galleys could not operate in winter), it was too late: the Duke of Parma had surrendered on 4 February 1637.

Duke Odoardo, cut off from French assistance, and increasingly mistrustful of his own subjects, refused to negotiate until December 1636 when his whole duchy cried out for peace. Spain laid plans to annex Piacenza and transfer Parma to direct papal rule, thus dispossessing the Farnese dynasty entirely. This measure, which

---

[3] ASMo: Ambasciatori Milano 107, fasc. 23; report of Sigismondo Coccapani, Aug. 1636.

[4] Charles Rahlenbeck, *Gilles de Haes* (Ghent, 1854), 13.

[5] Archives du Service Historique de la Défense (ASHD Vincennes), A1 33, no. 166, Relation de l'état des iles Sainte Margherite et de l'Armée des Espagnols, n.d.; the entire microfilm reel pertains to preparations in Provence and the operations along the Riviera.

[6] E. Delahaye, 'Une campagne de l'armée navale sous Louis XIII: La reprise des iles de Lérins et le secours de Parme (1636–1637)', *La Revue Maritime*, 115 (1929), 13–37; see also R. C. Anderson, 'The Thirty Years' War in the Mediterranean', *The Mariner's Mirror*, 56 (1969), 435–51.

[7] ASHD Vincennes: A1 33, no. 166.

would have upset the stable status quo giving Spain ascendancy but not crushing superiority over native dynasties in the peninsula, provoked an outcry among Italian princes, who encouraged Odoardo to negotiate for better terms. Leganés and de Melo, who had considerable leeway to negotiate, were willing to leave Odoardo all of his hereditary lands (including the fiefs in the kingdom of Naples) in exchange for a quick capitulation. By the first days of 1637 hostilities fell off and in late February the Habsburg troops withdrew from the shattered duchy.[8]

Leganés and de Melo applied their diplomatic talents next to restore peaceful relations with the Swiss Grisons, who opened peace talks with Spain in October. The Swiss finally turned on Rohan on the grounds that he could not deliver the money he promised. Rohan withdrew from the Valtellina and his regiments disbanded for lack of money and supplies. The ensuing treaty of 17 January 1637 marked the definitive end of the Valtellina crisis and within two years Spain reached an agreement to raise regiments of Grisons for its army in Italy.[9] The death of Duke Charles of Mantua on 24 September the same year removed another lukewarm ally from the French camp. Qualified by one of his loyal subjects in Casale Monferrato as a 'good prince, but neither a good captain nor a good soldier', the duke was predeceased by his warrior son the duc de Rethel, and left only an 8-year-old child in the wardship of his actively pro-Spanish mother, Maria Gonzaga.[10] Within months Spain and Mantua reached a durable accord by which the Catholic King promised to return Monferrato towns lost to France and Savoy if ever it should capture them. The exit of Mantua from the coalition removed the last nuisance to the east of Milan and enabled Leganés to concentrate his forces entirely along the Piedmontese frontier.

With French resources concentrated on barring the northern road to Paris and with preventing Spanish forays along the Pyrenees border, Créquy and Victor-Amadeus managed as best they could against Leganés's limited offensive in 1637. The Duke of Savoy battered don Martin d'Aragon's little army that blundered into him at Mombaldone in southern Piedmont, a minor success. It was still widely believed that Victor Amadeus was content to tread water, and did not wish to make any conquests against Spain.[11] But the duke died (some say of poison) on 7 October, falling sick along with many of his officers after a banquet in Vercelli from which French officers emerged unscathed. This left the duchy in the hands of Duchess Christine and her 2-year-old son Charles Emanuel II. She was an ambitious, incautious, controversial figure trusted by few. In order to undercut her authority, Richelieu broadcast believeable rumours that the heir was born of an adulterous relation. Princes Tommaso and Cardinal Maurizio called on their supporters to resist French hegemonic ambitions, and the duchy slid into a three-year

---

[8] For an overview of the campaign in Emilia, see my *The Hero of Italy* (Oxford, 2014), chs 4 and 5.

[9] Sandro Massera, 'La spedizione del Duca Henri de Rohan in Valtellina (1635–1637)', in Massera (ed.), *La Spedizione del Duca di Rohan in Valtellina* (Milan, 1999), 21–108; a dispatch from Milan echoes these talks held in Innsbruck, AGS Estado 3839, 24 Dec. 1636.

[10] Giuseppe Giorcelli, 'Annali Casalesi (1632–1661) di Gian Domenico Bremio, speciaro di Casale Monferrato', *Rivista di Storia, Arte, Archeologia della Provincia di Alessandria*, 18 (1909), 391.

[11] Ibid. 390.

civil war. Breme fell to Spanish besiegers during a brief late-winter siege in 1638, and a cannonball killed Créquy when he approached to save the place. Early in July Leganés captured the key Piedmontese border fortress of Vercelli, and in the aftermath of its fall many towns in the duchy invited Spanish troops to rescue them from French control.[12] He refused to part with 8,000 veterans earmarked for Catalonia where the French were beginning to mark progress, and launched instead an all-out offensive against both Turin and Casale Monferrato in 1640 with the assistance of Prince Tommaso. He failed to eject Duchess Christina from the powerful citadel of Turin, and so to compensate, he undertook a siege of Casale Monferrato. The French marshal Harcourt frustrated that project too with a determined assault on the siege lines that forced the Spaniards to withdraw without their artillery. Not long after, the defection of Prince Tommaso to Richelieu's camp swung the balance of forces in Italy to French advantage. Recalled to Spain at the end of 1641, Leganés led the demoralized and undersupplied army in Catalonia where the French trounced him at Lerida. He served long enough in the Spanish theatre to take his revenge on the French at Lerida again in 1646.[13] Spanish fortunes improved slowly as France drifted into the Fronde civil war in 1648, during the minority of Louis XIV when the great kingdom was governed by the unpopular Italian Cardinal Mazarin and his finance minister Hémery.[14]

Spain's unexpected resilience in the 1630s was the consequence of the great project of the chief minister Olivares, whose ambitious and controversial Union of Arms policy assigned quotas of troops, ships, and money on each of the autonomous kingdoms and duchies making up the Spanish Empire in Europe. Castile and Naples had been carrying a heavy load for decades and could no longer support the burden. Perhaps no more than 4,000 recruits left Spain every year to defend its overseas possessions in the decades after 1620.[15] After a spurt of energy in 1635 and 1636, the Spanish bureaucracy began to allow military enterprisers of all sorts find the soldiers to defend the Iberian Peninsula. Conscripts, feudal levies, town contingents, and a variety of other motley organizations complemented the few experienced tercios available. The best troops were in Italy and the Low Countries.[16] Milan and Brussels spent heavily themselves to fend off French conquest. Olivares was willing to establish an *honest peace* with France in 1636 and 1637, in order to prevent Dutch inroads into far-off Brazil, but Pinerolo was the sticking point. Its retention allowed Richelieu an easy corridor into Italy.[17] In the

---

[12] Jacques Lovie, 'Les fières heures de Madame Royale, duchesse de Savoie (1606–1663)', *Bulletin de l'Académie Delphinale*, 5 (1984), 21–35. This Piedmontese civil war is long overdue for closer study.

[13] Francisco Arroyo Martin, 'El marqués de Leganés: Apuntes biograficos', *Espacio, Tiempo y Forma, serie IV: Historia Moderna*, 15 (2002), 166–70.

[14] For a close study of France's pressure on Italian princes during the era, see Anna Blum, *La Diplomatie de la France en Italie du Nord au temps de Richelieu et de Mazarin* (Paris, 2014).

[15] I. A. A. Thompson, 'El soldado del Imperio: Una aproximaciòn al perfil del recluta español en el Siglo de Oro', *Manuscrits*, 21 (2003), 17–38.

[16] Luis A. Ribot Garcia, 'Les types d'armées en Espagne au début des temps modernes', in P. Contamine (ed.), *Guerre et concurrence entre les Etats européens du XIVe au XVIIIe siècle* (Paris, 1998), 43–81; and by the same author, 'El reclutamiento militar en España a mediados del siglo XVII. La "composicion" de la milicias de Castilla', *Cuadernos de Investigacion Historica*, 9 (1986), 63–89.

[17] Bély, *Les relations internationales en Europe, XVIIe–XVIIIe siècles* (Paris, 1992), 127.

meantime, Olivares hoped that Prince Gaston d'Orleans and his noble collaborators would finally succeed in assassinating the French cardinal-minister, as they were plotting to do.

But the other Habsburg kingdoms felt sacrificed (Portugal was losing its overseas colonies to Dutch fleets) or else violated in their liberties (Aragon, Catalonia, Sicily). Faced with incipient rebellion in Catalonia late in the summer of 1640, Olivares opted for repression without compromise, and turned to Portugal to find new men and money to carry it out. This spurred the Portuguese nobility to designate a king from among their number, and they rose in rebellion too.[18] Revolts in both Portugal and Catalonia in 1640 marked the onset of the real, irreversible decline of the Spanish empire. Spanish resources suddenly focused on recovering the lost Iberian kingdoms, leaving little for other theatres. After a revolt in Sicily (1647) and Naples (1648), Lombardy carried the weight of perennial war against France and Savoy without much help.[19] The southern kingdoms submitted to the Catholic King soon after, because the nobility held firm in its loyalty. An enterprising Governor of Milan and veteran of Tornavento, the Marqués de Caracena, restored enough confidence among the Lombards to keep the French on the defensive. Spanish and Italian forces inflicted devastation on the Duke of Modena when he incautiously joined the French in 1647, and Caracena captured Casale Monferrato in 1652, the culmination of Habsburg progress.[20] Cardinal Mazarin outlasted the plots of his adversaries, and once he restored calm to France, the war continued throughout the 1650s, but with diminishing intensity due to mutual exhaustion. French attempts to acquire key Spanish fortresses (Alessandria, Pavia) failed in the face of stiff resistance by the local population. The French only captured the smallest and weakest fortresses (Valenza, Mortara) and proved unable to recover the Piedmontese strongpoints held by Spain, like powerful Vercelli. So when peace finally came in 1659, it was on the basis of the status quo ante in Italy. Habsburg Spain relinquished very little territory elsewhere after a quarter-century of full-scale war against Bourbon France.[21]

The Spanish system in Italy proved remarkably viable and resilient under enormous stress. But the monarchy's accumulated debt and lack of political direction in the second half of the century left the great empire prostrate and unable to withstand its powerful French neighbour under Louis XIV. Italian aristocrats from most of the peninsula who had contributed so generously to support the Catholic King turned elsewhere, and increasingly turned away from military careers altogether. Spain continued to decline, while French power increased exponentially. Louis and

[18] Robert Stradling, *Europe and the Decline of Spain* (London, 1981), 95.

[19] The leading specialist of the Spanish war effort in Northern Italy is Davide Maffi. Among his many publications, see 'Un bastione incerto? L'Esercito di Lombardia tra Filippo IV e Carlo II (1630–1700)', in E. Garcia Hernan and D. Maffi (eds), *Guerra y sociedad en la Monarquia Hispanica* (Madrid, 2006), i. 501–36; on the great revolt of Naples, Alain Hugon, *Naples insurgée (1647–1648): De l'évènement à la mémoire* (Rennes, 2011).

[20] For a well-researched overview, see Gianvittorio Signorotto, *Milano Spagnola*, 2nd edn (Milan, 2001).

[21] Stradling, *Europe and Decline of Spain*, 125–6; for an overview, Gregory Hanlon, *The Twilight of a Military Tradition* (New York and London, 1998), 128–34.

his ministers quickly disengaged from Italian politics, however, and left the land almost undisturbed for over a generation. The Spanish system endured by default, but without the ability to instil fear in anyone. Into the vacuum stepped the Austrian Holy Roman Emperor, quickly replacing the Spanish predominance with a German one after 1690, setting the stage for a new, German era in Italian history.

Sources and Bibliography

ARCHIVAL SOURCES

Bibliothèque Nationale de France
Ms fr 16929: Relation d'Hemery sur les negociations en Piemont, fos. 528–604

Archives des Affaires Etrangères, Paris
Correspondance Politique: Sardaigne, vol. 24

Service Historique de la Defense, Vincennes
Serie A1 27
Serie A1 28
Serie A1 31
Serie A1 33

Biblioteca Nacional (Madrid)
Ms. 2367, pp. 27–58: Italia 1636

Archivo General Simancas
Estado 3343, 3344, 3345

Bologna: Biblioteca Universitaria
Vol. 473, Misc. H, no. 15: Relatione del fatto d'Arme seguito fra l'Esercito spagnolo e francese nella selva di Soma di là del Ticino e Tornavento e Ca' della Camera, il 22 giugno, 1636
Vol. 9E 27: Lettera a Don Martin D'Aragona 29 Nov. 1636

Archivio di Stato di Firenze
Mediceo del Principato 141, Minute di Lettere, 1636
Mediceo del Principato 3176, Lettere al Granduca, 1636
Mediceo del Principato 3180, Lettere di ministri, 1636
Mediceo del Principato 3181, Lettere da Camillo del Monte, 1636
Mediceo del Principato 3258, Lettere al Don Francisco de Melo, 1636
Mediceo del Principato 4961, Lettere dall'ambasciatore in Spagna, 1636
Miscellanea Medicea 183: Narrazione della guerra del Monferrato, cc. 318–47

Archivio di Stato di Milano
Miscellanea Mappe e Disegni, arruotolate 110: Topografia per l'irrigazione delle Brughiere di Somma 1777

Archivio Storico Civico di Milano
Archivio Sola Busca: Serbelloni b.53, Co: Giovanni Serbelloni, 1636
Dicasteri 149, Lettere da Carlo Sirtoni al Re, 1636

Archivio Diocesano Milano
Visite Pastorali, Dairago vol. 21, De invasione francorum in plebo Daijraghi, Anno 1636

Biblioteca Estense Modena
Misc. Estense Ital. 160, Regolamento sopra il combattere dell'Infanteria in una battaglia, e ragguaglio dell'Artiglieria di campagna formato dal Maresciale di Battaglia Co: Francesco Canossa, *c.*1645
Misc. Estense Ital. 635, Avvertimenti militari di quello che vole havere un buon soldato di pratica et un buon caporale et un sargente et un Alfiero et un Capitano … composto per il Colonello Bartolomeo Pelliciari di Modena, 1641
Ms. Sorbelli 1410, Vite e morti di personnaggi illustri, *c.*1650

Archivio di Stato di Modena
Casa e Stato, Carteggi fra Principi Estensi 209, Lettere del Principe Borso
Ambasciatori Milano 107, fasc. 21, 1636, lettere del Fra Ferrante Attendolo Bolognini

Archivio di Stato di Mantova
Archivio Gonzaga 678: Lettere di Francia 1636
Archivio Gonzaga 1761: Residente a Milano 1635–1636

Archivio di Stato Novara
Comune di Novara, parte Antica 1221, Milizia Urbana
Comune di Novara, parte Antica 1823, Corrispondenze 1635
Comune di Novara, parte Antica 1875, Memoriali, 1636–1637
Manoscritti Biblioteca Civica 119: Libro di Ricordanze del monastero dell'Abbazia Vallombrosa

Biblioteca Palatina Parma
Ms Parmense 462, Miscellanea di Storia Parmense (copia Affò)
Ms Parmense 737, L'Heroe d'Italia, da Ippolito Calandrini
Ms Parmense 1673, Ettore Lodi, Istoria di Casalmaggiore
Ms Parmense 3711, Piante e disegni con la penna di alcune città d'Italia, *c.*1650

Archivio di Stato Parma
Governo Farnesiano, Milizie 33, Esercizio della militia a piedi, n.d. (*c.*1630)
Magistrato Camerale di Parma, Memoriali 23 and 24, 1636–1637
Archivio Comunale Parma 331, Minute delle Ordinazioni, 1634–1637
Archivio Gonzaga di Guastalla, vol. 63: Lettere 1636–1637

Archivio Comunale Pavìa
MS II 59, Gabrio Busca, Descrizione delle fortezze di frontiera dello Stato di Milano, sec. XVII (*c.*1600)

Archivio di Stato di Torino
Materie militari, mazza 1, no. 30: Giornaliere della guerra fatta da S.A.R. e truppe confederate contro il Duca di Mantova e dello Stato di Milano (1636)
Materie militari, mazza 1, no. 30: Memoria in forma d'Istruzione al marchese di S. Morizio, ambasciatore di SAR in Francia, in giustificazione contro le doglianze de' Francesi per la supposta inazione dell'armata

Biblioteca dell'Archivio di Stato, Corte: Ms Racc. Mongiardino, vol. 53, Relazione del paese...delli Grisoni, 1620–1638

Biblioteca dell'Archivio di Stato, Corte: Ms Racc. Mongiardino, vol. 54, Relazioni dei fatti occorsi in Lombardia...dal 1630 al 1638

Materie politiche interne: Lettere ministri Francia, 34

Materie politiche interne: Registro di lettere alla Corte, 38

Materie politiche interne: Lettere del duca Vittorio Amedeo, vol. 56, 1635–1636

Archivio di Stato di Varese
Catasto MT 1722: Tornavento

PRINTED SOURCES

Basta, Giorgio, *Le gouvernement de la cavalerie legere*, Rouen, 1627.

Bremio, GianDomenico, 'Annali Casalesi (1632–1661) di GianDomenico Bremio speciaro di Casale Monferrato', ed. Dott. Giuseppe Giorcelli, *Rivista Storica Alessandrina*, 18 (1909), 381–436.

Brusoni, Girolamo, *Delle Historie memorabili, contiene le Guerre d'Italia de' nostri tempi*, Venice, 1656.

Capriata, Pietro Giovanni, *Movimenti d'armi successi in Italia*, Genoa, 1649.

Carbonelli, Giovanni (ed.), 'La Cronaca chirugica dell'assedio di Casale (1628–1629) di Horatio Polino, chirurgo', *Bollettino Storico-bibliografico subalpino*, 9 (1904), 157–71.

Chorier, Nicolas, *Histoire de la vie de Charles de Créquy de Blanchefort, duc de Lesdiguières*, Grenoble, 1684.

Comerio, Francesco, 'Relazione di Francesco Comerio, curato a Lonate', in Franco Bertolli and Umberto Colombo (eds), *La peste del 1630 a Busto Arsizio*, Busto Arsizio, 1990, 438–41.

Cruso, John, *Castrametation, or the measuring out of the quarters for the encamping of an army*, London, 1642.

Filamondo, P. fra Raffaele Maria, *Il Genio bellicoso di Napoli: Memorie istoriche d'alcuni capitani celebri Napoletani c'han militato per la fede, per lo re, per la patria nel secolo corrente*, 2 vols, Naples, 1694.

Fossati, Giovanni Francesco, *Memorie historiche delle guerre d'Italia del secolo presente descritte dall'abbate Fossati*, Bologna, 1641.

Gazette de France, Paris, 1636.

Ghilini, Girolamo, *Annali di Alessandria*, ed. A. Bossola, Alessandria, 1903.

Giulini, Alessandro, 'Un diario secentesco inedito d'un notaio milanese', *Archivio Storico Lombardo*, 57 (1930), 466–82.

Gualdo Priorato, Galeazzo, *Il guerriero prudente, e politico*, Venice and Bologna, 1641.

Gualdo Priorato, Galeazzo, *Historia universale del conte Galeazzo Gualdo Priorato, delle guerre successe nell'Europa dall'anno 1630 sino all'anno 1640*, Genoa, 1642.

Gualdo Priorato, Galeazzo, *Il maneggio delle armi*, Bologna, 1642.

Gualdo Priorato, Galeazzo, *Successe dall'anno 1630 sino all'anno 1636*, Venice, 1646.

Gualdo Priorato, Galeazzo, *An History of the late warres and other state affaires of the best part of Christendom*, London, 1648 (first published 1641).

Leti, Giovanni, *L'Italia regnante, o overo nova descritione dello stato presente di tutti principati e republiche d'Italia*, 4 vols, Genoa, 1675–76.

Lodi, Ettore, *Memorie istoriche di Casalmaggiore*, ed. E. Cirani, Cremona, 1992.

Lomeni, Giulio Cesare, 'Memorie del notaio gallaretese Giulio Cesare Lomeni', in Franco Bertolli and Umberto Colombo (eds), *La peste del 1630 a Busto Arsizio*, Busto Arsizio, 1990, 401–2.

Lostelneau, Sieur de, *Le Mareschal de bataille*, Paris, 1647.

Lupi, Giovan Battista, 'Storia della peste avvenuta nel borgo di Busto Arsizio, 1630 (1632–1642)', in Franco Bertolli and Umberto Colombo (eds), *La peste del 1630 a Busto Arsizio*, Busto Arsizio, 1990, 99–217.

Manacci, Marcello, *Compendio d'Instruttioni per gli bombardieri*, Parma, 1640.

Mercure François, Paris, 1635–7.

Minozzi, Pier Francesco, *Il Politico trionfante, . . . panegirico*, Milan, 1637.

Montecuccoli, Raimondo, *Memoires de Montecuculi, generalissime des troupes de l'Empereur, divisé en trois livres*, Amsterdam, 1752.

Montecuccoli, Raimondo, 'Concerning Battle', in Thomas Barker, *The Military Intellectual and Battle: Raimondo Montecuccoli and the Thirty Years War*, Albany, NY, 1975, 73–173.

Montglat, François de Paule de Clermont, marquis de, *Memoires*, in A. Petitot and Monmerqué, *Collection des memoires relatifs à l'histoire de France, depuis l'avènement de Henri IV jusqu'à La Paix de Paris conclue en 1763*, xl–li, Paris, 1829.

Pallavicino, Ferrante, *Successi del mondo dell'anno 1636*, Venice, 1638.

Paré, Ambroise, *La maniere de traicter les playes faictes tant par hacquebutes, que par fleches: et les accidents d'icelles, comme fractures et caries des os, gangrene et mortification: avec les pourtraictz des instrumentz necessaires pour leur curation. Et la methode de curer les combustions principalement faictes par la pouldre à canon*, Paris, 1552.

Plati, Guglielmo, *Le Vespeide dell'Academico Caliginoso, allude alla strage fatta nel campo de'Franchi dalle vespe silvestre nelle trinciere di Tornavento*, Milan, 1636.

Plessis-Praslin, César de Choiseul, *Mémoires*, in Joseph François Michaud and Jean-Joseph François Poujoulat, *Mémoires pour servir à l'histoire de France*, Paris, 1838, vii.

Praissac, sieur du, *Discours et questions militaires*, final edn, Paris, 1638.

Raymond, John, *An Itinerary contayning a voyage made through Italy in the years 1646 and 1647*, London, 1648.

Relacion del combate del exercito de su majestad, con los de Francia y Saboya en 22 de Iunio, Madrid, 1636.

Relation de la victoire obtenue en Italie par l'armee du Roy, Lyon, 1636.

Richelieu, Armand Jean du Plessis, cardinal de, *Memoires*, in A. Petitot and Monmerqué, *Collection des memoires relatifs à l'histoire de France, depuis l'avènement de Henri IV jusqu'à La Paix de Paris conclue en 1763*, xxii–xxx (numbered I–IX in text), Paris, 1827.

Royal Encampment of his Majesties forces on Hounslow Heath 1686, London, 1686.

Siri, Vittorio. *Memorie recondite di Vittorio Siri dall'anno 1601 fino al 1640*, Lyon, 1677–9.

Souvigny, Jean de Gagnieres, comte de, *Vie, memoires et histoire de messire Jean de Gangieres*, 2 vols, Paris, 1906.

Stanchi, Bernardino, 'Narrazione dell'assedio di Valenza nel 1635, fatta da Bernardino Stanchi, sotto nome di Randiberno Caston', in *Memorie Storiche Valenzane*, ed. Francesco Gasparolo, Casale Monferrato, 1923, reprinted Bologna, 1986, 258–96.

Trombella, Cristina (ed.), *La 'Memoria di Colorno' (1612–1674) di Don Costantino Canivetti: Parte Prima 1612–1658*, Tesi di Laurea, Università degli Studi di Parma, Facoltà di Magistero, 1997–8.

Valdes, Francisco de, *The sergeant major*, London, 1590.

Ville, Antoine de, *De la charge des gouverneurs des places*, Paris, 1674 (first published 1639).

STUDIES

Albi de la Cuesta, Julio, *De Pavia a Rocroi: Los tercios de infanteria española en los siglos XVI y XVII*, Madrid, 1999.

Alfani, Guido, 'Plague in Seventeenth-Century Europe and the Decline of Italy: An Epidemiological Analysis', *European Review of Economic History* (2013), 1–23.

Alvarez-Ossorio Alvarino, Antonio, 'The State of Milan and the Spanish Monarchy', in T. J. Dandelet and J. A. Marino (eds), *Spain in Italy: Politics, Society and Religion 1500–1700*, Leiden and Boston, 2007, 99–133.

Amoretti, Guido, *Il Ducato di Savoia dal 1559 al 1713*, ii. *Dal 1610 al 1659*, Turin, 1985.

Anderson, Raymond C., 'The Thirty Years' War in the Mediterranean', *The Mariner's Mirror*, 56 (1969), 435–51.

Andretta, Stefano, *La Repubblica inquieta: Venezia nel Seicento tra Italia e Europa*, Rome, 2000.

Ardant du Picq, Charles, *Etudes sur le combat: Combat antique et combat moderne*, Paris, 2004 (1904 edn).

Arfaioli, Maurizio, *The Black Bands of Giovanni: Infantry and Diplomacy during the Italian Wars (1526–1528)*, Pisa, 2005.

Arnett, Jeffrey, 'Still Crazy After All These Years: Reckless Behavior among Young Adults aged 23–27', *Personality and Individual Differences*, 12 (1991), 1305–13.

Arroyo Martin, Fernando, 'El marqués de Leganés: Apuntes biograficos', *Espacio, Tiempo y Forma, serie IV, Historia Moderna*, 15 (2002), 145–85 (online).

Asch, Ronald G., ' "Wo der soldat hinkoembt, da ist alles sein": Military Violence and Atrocities in the Thirty Years War Re-examined', *German History*, 18 (2000), 291–309.

Audoin-Rouzeau, Stéphane, *Combattre: Une anthropologie historique de la guerre moderne (XIXe–XXIe siècle)*, Paris, 2008.

Ayats, Alain, 'Armées et santé en Roussillon au cours de la guerre de Hollande (1672–1678)', in J.-M. Goger and N. Marty (eds), *Cadre de vie, équipement, santé dans les sociétés mediterranéennes*, Perpignan, 2006, 119–35.

Azan, Paul, *Un tacticien du XVIIe siècle*, Paris, 1904.

Barker, Thomas M., *The Military Intellectual and Battle: Raimondo Montecuccoli and the Thirty Years War*, Albany, NY, 1975.

Bass, Bill, and Jefferson, Jefferson, *Death's Acre: Inside the Legendary 'Body Farm'*, New York, 2003.

Baxter, Douglas Clark, *Servants of the Sword: French Intendants of the Army, 1630–1670*, Urbana, IL, 1976.

Bazy, Jean-Pierre Antoine, *Etat militaire de la monarchie espagnole sous le règne de Philippe IV*, Poitiers, 1864.

Bély, Lucien, *Les relations internationales en Europe, XVIIe–XVIIIe siècles*, Paris, 1992.

Bély, Lucien, Bérenger, Jean, and Corvisier, André, *Guerre et paix dans l'Europe du XVIIe siècle*, 2 vols, Paris, 1991.

Benavides, Jose Ignacio, *Milicia y diplomacia en el reinado de Felipe IV: El marques de Caracena*, Leon, 2012.

Benigno, Roberto, 'Ripensare la crisi del '600', *Storica*, 5 (1996), 7–52.

Bennett, Martyn, *The Civil Wars Experienced: Britain and Ireland*, London, 2000.

Bercé, Yves-Marie, 'Les guerres dans l'Italie au XVIIe siècle', *L'Italie au XVIIe siècle*, Paris, 1989.

Bercé, Yves-Marie, 'Rohan et la Valtelline', in L. Bély (ed.), *L'Europe des traités de Westphalie: Esprit de la diplomatie et diplomatie de l'esprit*, Paris, 2000, 321–35.

Bérenger, Jean, 'Le Conflit Franco-Espagnol et la guerre du Nord', in Y.-M. Bercé, J. Bérenger, A. Corvisier, and L. Bély (eds), *Guerre et paix dans l'Europe du XVII siècle*, 2nd edn, Paris, 1991, i. 309–40.

Bérenger, Jean, 'La collaboration militaire austro-espagnol au XVIe–XVIIe siècles', in A. Molinié and A. Merle (eds), *L'Espagne et ses guerres: De la fin de la Reconquête aux guerres de la Indépendance*, Paris, 2004, 11–33.

Bertolli, Franco, 'L'invasione franco-sabauda del 1636 nel Novarese e nel Milanese', in Guido Amoretti (ed.), *Il Ticino: Strutture, storia e società nel territorio tra Oleggio e Lonate Pozzolo*, Gavirate, 1989, 51–70.

Bianchi, Alessandro, 'Una rivalità di lungo periodo: I rapporti politico-diplomatici tra gli Este e i Gonzaga', in Elena Fumagalli and Giovanni Vittorio Signorotto (eds), *La Corte estense nel primo Seicento: Diplomazia e mecenatismo artistico*, Rome, 2012, 349–67.

Bianchi, Paola, 'La riorganizzazione militare del Ducato di Savoia e i rapporti del Piemonte con la Francia e la Spagna', in Enrique Garcia Hernan and Davide Maffi (eds), *Guerra y Sociedad en la Monarquìa Hispanica: Politica, Estrategia y cultura en la Europa moderna (1500–1700)*, Madrid, 2006, 189–216.

Bianchi, Paola, *Sotto diverse bandiere: L'internazionale militare nello Stato sabaudo d'antico regime*, Milan, 2012.

Bianchi, Paola, Maffi, Davide, and Stumpo, Enrico, *Italiani al servizio straniero in età moderna*, Milan, 2008.

Black, Jeremy, *European Warfare 1494–1660*, London, 2002.

Black, Jeremy, *Rethinking Military History*, London, 2004.

Black, Jeremy, *War in European History, 1494–1660*, Washington, DC, 2006.

Blackmore, David, *Arms and Armour of the English Civil Wars*, London, 1990.

Blier, Gérard, *Les grandes batailles de l'histoire de France*, Paris, 2009.

Blomac, Nicole de, 'Le cheval de guerre entre le dire et le faire: Quelques variations sur le discours équestre adapté à la réalité militaire', in Daniel Roche and Daniel Reytier (eds), *Le cheval de guerre du XVe au XXe siècle*, Paris, 2002, 55–65.

Blum, Anna, *La diplomatie de la France en Italie du Nord au temps de Richelieu et de Mazarin*, Paris, 2014.

Boehler, Jean-Michel, 'Les conséquences à long terme des guerres du XVIIe siècle en Alsace: Pour l'élaboration d'un "modèle rhénan"', in André Corvisier and Jean Jacquart (eds), *Les malheurs de la guerre: De la guerre à l'ancienne à la guerre réglée*, Paris, 1996, 201–17.

Boehler, Jean-Michel, 'La guerre au quotidien dans les villages du Saint-Empire au XVIIe siècle', in C. Desplat (ed.), *Les villageois face à la guerre, XIVe–XVIIIe siècle*, Toulouse, 2002, 65–88.

Bonsall, James, 'The Study of Small Finds at the 1644 Battle of Cheriton', *Journal of Conflict Archaeology*, 3 (2007), 29–52.

Borreguero Beltràn, Cristina, 'El coste humano de la guerra: mortandad, enfermedad y deserciòn en los ejercitos de la Epoca Moderna', in Fidel Gomez Ochoa and Daniel Macias Fernandez (eds), *El Combatiente a lo largo de la historia: Imaginario, percepciòn, representaciòn*, Santander, 2012, 57–82.

Brambilla, Elena, and Muto, Giovanni (eds), *La Lombardia spagnola: Nuovi indirizzi di ricerca*, Milan, 1997.

Brancaccio, Nicola, *L'Esercito del vecchio Piemonte: gli ordinamenti, parte 1: Dal 1560 al 1814*, Rome, 1923.

Brnardic, Vladimir, *Imperial Armies of the Thirty Years War (1): Infantry and Artillery*, Oxford and New York, 2009.

Brnardic, Vladimir, *Imperial Armies of the Thirty Years War: Cavalry*, Oxford and New York, 2010.

Brzezinksi, Richard, *Lützen 1632: Climax of the Thirty Years War*, Oxford and New York, 2001.

Buono, Alessandro, *Esercito, Istituzioni, Territorio: Alloggiamenti militari e case herme nello Stato di Milano, secoli XVI e XVII*, Florence, 2009.

Buono, Alessandro, 'Guerra, Elites locali e monarchia nella Lombardia del Seicento: Per un'interpretazione in chiave di compromesso di interessi', *Società e Storia*, 123 (2009), 3–30.

Caferro, William P., 'Warfare and Economy in Renaissance Italy, 1350–1450', *Journal of Interdisciplinary History*, 39 (2008), 167–209.

Carbonelli, Giovanni, 'La Cronaca chirurgica dell'assedio di Casale (1628–1629) di Horatio Polino, chirurgo', *Bollettino Storico-bibliografico Subalpino*, 9 (1904), 157–71.

Carignani, Giuseppe, *Le Truppe napoletane durante la guerra de' Trent'Anni*, Florence, 1888.

Carter, David O., and Tibbett, Mark, 'Cadaver Decomposition and Soil: Processes', in M. Tibbett and D. O. Carter, *Soil Analysis in Forensic Taphonomy: Chemical and Biological Effects of Buried Human Remains*, Boca Raton, FLA, 2008, 29–52.

Cerino Badone, Giovanni, 'Le Seconde Guerre d'Italia (1588–1659)', unpublished doctoral dissertation, Università degli studi del Piemonte Orientale, 2011.

Chaboche, Robert, 'Les soldats français de la Guerre de Trente Ans: Une tentative d'approche', *Revue d'Histoire Moderne et Contemporaine*, 20 (1973), 10–24.

Chaboche, Robert, 'Le recrutement des sergents et des caporaux de l'armée française au XVIIe siècle', *Recrutement, mentalités, sociétés: Actes du colloque international d'histoire militaire*, Montpellier, 1974, 25–43.

Chagniot, Jean, 'Mobilité sociale et armée', *Dix-Septième Siècle*, 31 (1979), 37–49.

Chagniot, Jean, *Guerre et société à l'époque moderne*, Paris, 2001.

Chaline, Olivier, *La bataille de la Montagne Blanche (8 novembre 1620): Un mystique chez les guerriers*, Paris, 1999.

Chauviré, Fréderic, 'Le problème de l'allure dans les charges de cavalerie du XVIe au XVIIIe siècle', *Revue Historique des Armées*, 249 (2007), 16–27.

Chauviré, Fréderic, *Histoire de la Cavalerie*, Paris, 2013.

Choppin, Henri, *Les origines de la cavalerie française: Organisation régimentaire de Richelieu, la cavalerie Weimarienne, le régiment de Gassion*, Paris and Nancy, 1905.

Claretta, Gaudenzio, *Storia della Reggenza di Cristina di Francia, duchessa di Savoia*, i, Turin, 1868.

Contreras Gay, Jose, 'Aportacion al estudio de los sistemas de reclutamiento militar en la Espana moderna', *Anuario de Historia Contemporanea*, 8, 1981, 7–45.

Contreras Gay, Jose, 'El siglo XVII y su importancia en el cambio de los sistemas de reclutamientos durante el Antiguo Regimen', *Studia Historica: Historia Moderna*, 14 (1996), 141–54.

Cornette, Joël, *Le roi de guerre: Essai sur la souveraineté dans la France du Grand Siècle*, Paris, 1993.

Cornette, Joël, 'La révolution militaire et l'état moderne', *Revue d'Histoire Moderne et Contemporaine*, 41 (1994), 696–709.

Corvisier, André, 'Le moral des combattants, panique et enthousiasme', *Revue d'Histoire de l'Armée* (1977), 7–32.

Corvisier, André, 'Renouveau militaire et misères de la guerre 1635–1659', in Philippe Contamine (ed.), *Histoire militaire de la France*, i. *Des origines à 1715*, Paris, 1992.

Cosmacini, Giorgio, *La carità e la cura: l'Ospedale maggiore di Milano nell'età moderna*, Milan, 1992.

Cosmacini, Giorgio, *La Ca'granda dei milanesi. Storia dell'ospedale maggiore*, Rome, 1999.

Coss, Edward J., *All for the King's Shilling: The British Soldier under Wellington, 1808–1814*, Norman, OK, 2010.

Costa, Marco, *Psicologia militare: Elementi di psicologia per gli appartenenti alle forze armate*, Milan, 2003.

Coste, Laurent, 'Les malheurs de la Fronde en Entre-deux-Mers', in André Corvisier and Jean Jacquart (eds), *Les malheurs de la guerre: De la guerre à l'ancienne à la guerre réglée*, Paris, 1996, 131–45.

Cozzi, Gaetano, 'La Repubblica di Venezia e il Regno di Francia tra Cinquecento e Seicento: Fiducia e sfiducia', in Alberto Tenenti (ed.), *Venezia e Parigi*, Milan, 1989, 113–44.

Cristini, Luca, and Pogliani, Giuseppe, *La battaglia di Tornavento del 1636 e la guerra dei Trent'Anni in Italia*, Milan, 2011.

Crocq, Louis, *Les traumatismes de guerre*, Paris, 1999.

Crossland, David, 'Mass Grave Sheds Light on Europe's Bloody History', *Spiegel Online*, 31 July 2007.

Croxton, Derek, 'A Territorial Imperative: The Military Revolution, Strategy and Peacemaking in the Thirty Years War', *War in History*, 5 (1998), 253–79.

D'Amico, Stefano, 'Rebirth of a City: Immigration and Trade in Milan, 1630–1659', *Sixteenth Century Journal*, 32 (2001), 697–722.

D'Amico, Stefano, *Spanish Milan: A City within the Empire 1535–1706*, Basingstoke and New York, 2012.

De Consoli, Claudio, *Al soldo del duca: L'amministrazione delle armate sabaude (1560–1630)*, Turin, 1999.

De Moor, J. A., 'Experience and Experiment: Some Reflections upon the Military Developments in 16th and 17th Century Western Europe', in Marco van der Hoeven (ed.), *Exercise of the Arms: Warfare in the Netherlands (1568–1648)*, Leiden, 1997, 17–32.

Del Negro, Piero, *Guida alla storia militare italiana*, Milan, 1997.

Delahaye, E., 'Une campagne de l'armée navale sous Louis XIII: La reprise des Iles de Lérins et le secours de Parme (1636–1637)', *La Revue Maritime*, 115 (1929), 13–37.

Denys, Catherine, 'Quelques réflexions sur la régulation de la violence de guerre dans les Pays-Bas méridionaux aux XVIIe et XVIIIe siècles', in Jean-François Chanet and Christian Windler (eds), *Les Ressources des faibles: Neutralités, sauvegardes, accommodements en temps de guerre (XVIe–XVIIIe siècle)*, Rennes, 2009, 205–20.

Deyon, Pierre, and Deyon, Solange, *Henri de Rohan, huguenot de plume et d'épée 1579–1638*, Paris, 2000.

Dominguez Nafria, Juan Carlos, *El Real y Supremo Consejo de Guerra (siglos XVI–XVIII)*, Madrid, 2001.

Donagan, Barbara, *War in England 1642–1649*, Oxford and New York, 2008.

Donati, Claudio (ed.), *Alle frontiere della Lombardia: Politica, guerra e religione nell'età moderna*, Milan, 2006.

Donati, Claudio, 'The Profession of Arms and the Nobility in Spanish Italy: Some Considerations', in T. J. Dandelet and J. A. Marino (eds), *Spain in Italy: Politics, Society and Religion 1500–1700*, Leiden, 2007, 314–24.

Drévillon, Hervé, 'Vices et vertus du noble exercice de l'escrime au XVIIe siècle', in *A quoi joue-t-on? Pratiques et usages des jeux et des jouets à travers les ages*, Montbrison, 1999, 469–82.

Drévillon, Hervé, ' "Publier nos playes et valeurs": Le fait d'armes et sa notoriété pendant la guerre de Trente Ans (1635–1648)', in J. Pontet and M. Figeac (eds), *La noblesse de la fin du XVIe au debut du XXe siècle, un modèle social?*, Anglet, 2002, i. 289–308.

Drévillon, Hervé, *L'impôt du sang: Le métier des armes sous Louis XIV*, Paris, 2005.

Drévillon, Hervé, *Batailles: Scènes de guerre de la Table ronde aux Tranchées*, Paris, 2007.

Duby, Georges, *The Legend of Bouvines: War, Religion and Culture in the Middle Ages*, Berkeley and Los Angeles, 1990 (first published 1973).

Dugatkin, Lee Alan, *Cooperation among Animals: An Evolutionary Perspective*, Oxford, 1997.

Dyer, Gwynne, *War*, 2nd edn, Toronto, 2004.

Edwards, Peter, 'Les chevaux et les guerres civiles anglaises au milieu du XVIIe siècle', in Daniel Roche and Daniel Reytier (eds), *Le cheval et la guerre du XVe au XXe siècle*, Paris, 2002, 243–9.

Elliott, John H., *Richelieu and Olivares*, Cambridge and New York, 1984.

Elliott, John H., 'Managing Decline: Olivares and the Grand Strategy of Imperial Spain', in P. Kennedy (ed.), *Grand Strategies in War and Peace*, New Haven, 1991, 87–104.

Elliott, John H., 'Staying in Power: The Count-Duke of Olivares', in J. H. Elliott and L.W. B. Brockliss (eds), *The World of the Favourite*, New Haven & London, 1999, 112–22.

Engen, Robert, *Canadians under Fire: Infantry Effectiveness in the Second World War*, Montreal and Kingston, 2009.

Engen, Robert, 'Tuer pour son pays: Nouveau regard sur l'homicidologie', *Revue Militaire Canadienne*, 9 (2009), 120–8.

Engerisser, Peter, 'Matchlock musket, Suhl appr. 1630', <www.engerisser.de/Bewaffnung/weapons/Matchlockmusket.html>.

Engerisser, Peter, and Hrnčiřik, Pavel, *Nördlingen 1634: Die Schlacht bei Nördlingen: Wendepunkt des Dreissigjähringen Krieges*, Weissenstadt, 2009.

Epino Lopez, Antonio, 'La historiografia hispana sobre la guerra en la epoca de los Austrias: Un bilance, 1991–2000', *Manuscrits*, 21 (2003), 161–91.

Externbrink, Sven, 'Le coeur du monde et la liberté d'Italie: Aspects de la politique italienne de Richelieu 1624–1642', *Revue d'Histoire Diplomatique*, 114 (2000), 181–208.

Externbrink, Sven, 'L'Espagne, le duc de Savoie et les "portes": La politique italienne de Richelieu et Louis XIII', in Giuliano Ferretti (ed.), *De Paris à Turin: Christine de France, duchesse de Savoie*, Paris, 2014, 15–24.

Fagniez, Gustave, *Le Père Joseph et Richelieu (1577–1638)*, 2 vols, Paris, 1894.

Ferretti, Giuliano, 'Au nom du droit (de conquête): La politique italienne de la France au XVIIe siècle', *La Pierre et l'Ecrit: Revue d'Histoire et du Patrimoine en Dauphiné*, 23 (2012), 101–25.

Ferretti, Giuliano, 'La politique italienne de la France et le duché de Savoie au temps de Richelieu', *XVIIe Siècle*, 262 (2014), 7–20.

Foa, Salvatore, *Vittorio Amedeo I*, Turin, 1930.

Foucault, Michel, *Surveiller et Punir*, Paris, 1975.

Frezet, Jean, *Histoire de la maison de Savoie*, 3 vols, Turin, 1826–7.

Frigo, Daniela, 'Negozi, alleanze e conflitti: La dinastia estense e la diplomazia del Seicento', in Elena Fumagalli and Gianvittorio Signorotto (eds), *La Corte estense nel primo Seicento: Diplomazia e mecenatismo artistico*, Rome, 2012, 51–92.

Gaber, Stéphane, *La Lorraine meurtrie*, 2nd edn, Nancy, 1991.

Gal, Stéphane, *Lesdiguières: Prince des Alpes et connetable de France*, Grenoble, 2007.

Gal, Stéphane, *Charles-Emanuel I de Savoie: La politique du précipice*, Paris, 2012.

Gantelet, Martial, 'Réguler la guerre aux frontières des Pays-Bas espagnols: La naissance empirique du droit des gens (Metz, 1635–1659)', in Jean-François Chanet and Christian Windler (eds), *Les Ressources des faibles: Neutralités, sauvegardes, accommodements en temps de guerre (XVIe–XVIIIe siècle)*, Rennes, 2009, 221–40.

Gat, Azar, 'The Causes of War in Natural and Historical Evolution', in H. Høgh-Olesen (ed.), *Human Morality and Sociality: Evolutionary and Comparative Perspectives*, Basingstoke and New York, 2010, 160–90.

Ghiglieri, Michael P., *The Dark Side of Man: Tracing the Origins of Male Violence*, Cambridge, MA, 2000.

Giannini, Massimo Carlo, 'Risorse del principe e risorse dei sudditi: Fisco, clero e comunità di fronte al problema della difesa comune nello Stato di Milano (1618–1660)', *Annali di Storia Moderna e Contemporanea*, 6 (2000), 173–225.

Glete, Jan, *War and the State in Early Modern Europe: Spain, the Dutch Republic and Sweden as Fiscal-Military States 1500–1600*, London and New York, 2002.

Gonzalez de Leon, Fernando, ' "Doctors of the Military Discipline": Military Expertise and the Paradigm of the Spanish Soldier in the Early Modern Period', *Sixteenth Century Journal*, 27 (1996), 61–85.

Gonzalez de Leon, Fernando, 'Spanish Military Power and the Military Revolution', in G. Mortimer (ed.), *Early Modern Military History, 1450–1815*, Basingstoke and New York, 2004, 25–42.

Gonzalez de Leon, Fernando, *The Road to Rocroi*, Boston and Leiden, 2009.

Goodwin, George, 'Towton 1461: This Bitter Field', *History Today*, 61/5 (2011), 37–41.

Gregory, Charles, 'The End of Richelieu: Noble Conspiracy and Spanish Treason in Louis XIII's France, 1636–1642', D.Phil. dissertation, Oxford University, 2012.

Griffith, Paddy, *Forward into Battle: Fighting Tactics from Waterloo to the Near Future*, Swindon, and Novato, CA, 1991.

Grossman, Dave, *On Killing: The Psychological Cost of Learning to Kill in War and Society*, Boston, 1995.

Grossman, Dave, *On Combat: The Psychology and Physiology of Deadly Conflict in War and in Peace*, Mascoutah, IL, 2004.

Grothe, Anja, and Bettina Jungklaus, 'Archaeological and Anthropological Examinations of a Mass Grave from the 1636 Battle at Wittstock: A Preliminary Report', *Limping Together through the Ages: joint afflictions and bone infections*, Gisela Grupe, George McGlynn & Joris Peters eds, Rahden Westfalen, 2008, 127–35.

Gruber von Arni, Eric. *Justice to the Maimed Soldier. Nursing, medical care and welfare for sick and wounded soldiers and their families during the English Civil Wars and interregnum, 1642–1660*, Aldershot UK & Burlington VT, 2001.

Guéry, Alain. 'Les comptes de la mort vague après la guerre. Pertes de guerre et conjoncture du phenomène guerre, XVIIe-XIXe siècle', *Histoire et Mesure*, 6 (1991), 289–312.

Guthrie, William P., *Battles of the Thirty Years War: From White Mountain to Nordlingen*, Westport, CT, and London, 2002.

Guthrie, William P., *The Later Thirty Years War*, Westport, CT, and London, 2003.

Gutmann, Myron P., 'Putting Crises in Perspective: The Impact of War on Civilian Populations in the Seventeenth Century', *Annales de Démographie Historique* (1977), 101–28.

Haas, J., *The Anthropology of War*, Cambridge, 1990.

Haehl, Madeleine, *Les affaires étrangères au temps de Richelieu: Le secrétariat d'Etat, les agents diplomatiques (1624–1642)*, Brussels, 2006.

Hall, Bert S., *Weapons and Warfare in Renaissance Europe: Gunpowder, Technology and Tactics*, Baltimore and London, 1997.

Hanlon, Gregory, *The Twilight of a Military Tradition: Italian Aristocrats and European Conflicts, 1560–1800*, London and New York, 1998.

Hanlon, Gregory, *Early Modern Italy 1550–1800: Three Seasons in European History*, Basingstoke and New York, 2000.

Hanlon, Gregory, 'L'infanticidio di coppie sposate in Toscana nella prima età moderna', *Quaderni Storici*, 38 (2003), 453–98.

Hanlon, Gregory, 'Wartime Mortality in Italy's Thirty Years War: The Duchy of Parma 1635–1637', *Histoire, économie et société*, 31 (2012), 3–22.

Hanlon, Gregory, *The Hero of Italy: The Duke of Parma, his Soldiers and his Subjects in the Thirty Years' War*, Oxford and New York, 2014.

Hardy de Perini, Edouard, *Batailles françaises*, Paris, 1894–1906, iii. 204–20.

Helfferich, Tryntje, and Sonnino, Paul, 'Civilians in the Thirty Years War', in L. S. Frey and M. L. Frey (eds), *Daily Lives of Civilians in Wartime Europe, 1618–1900*, Westport, CT, and London, 2007, 23–58.

Henninger, Laurent, *Rocroi, 1643*, Paris, 1993.

Henriksen, Rune, 'Warriors in Combat: What Makes People Actively Fight in Combat?', *Journal of Strategic Studies*, 30 (2007), 187–223.

Hess, Earl J., *The Union Soldier in Battle: Enduring the Ordeal of Combat*, Lawrence, KS, 1997.

Hildesheimer, Françoise, *Richelieu: Une certaine idée de l'état*, Paris, 1985.

Hildesheimer, Françoise, 'Guerre et paix selon Richelieu', in Lucien Bély (ed.), *L'Europe des traités de Westphalie: Esprit de la diplomatie et diplomatie de l'esprit*, Paris, 2000, 31–54.

Holmes, Richard, *Acts of War: The Behaviour of Men in Battle*, 2nd edn, London, 2003.

Horodowich, Elizabeth, 'War and Society: The New Cultural History?', *Sixteenth-Century Journal*, 40 (2009), 209–12.

Hughes, B. P., *Firepower: Weapons Effectiveness on the Battlefield, 1630–1850*, New York, 1974.

Hugon, Alain, 'Des Habsbourg aux Bourbons: Le combat espagnol pour la conservation de l'hégémonie européenne, milieu XVIe–fin XVIIe siècle', *Bulletin de la Société d'Histoire Moderne et Contemporaine*, 3–4 (2000), 34–55.

Humbert, Jacques, *Le Maréchal de Créquy, gendre de Lesdiguières, 1573–1638*, Paris, 1962.

Hynes, Laura, 'Routine Infanticide by Married Couples? An Assessment of Baptismal Records from Seventeenth-Century Parma', *Journal of Early Modern History*, 15 (2011), 507–30.

Israel, Jonathan, 'Olivares, the Cardinal-Infante and Spain's Strategy in the Low Countries (1635–1643): The Road to Rocroi', in Richard Kagan and Geoffrey Parker (eds), *Spain, Europe and the Atlantic World: Essays in Honour of John H. Elliott*, Cambridge, 1995, 267–95.

James, Alan, *The Navy and Government in Early Modern France*, Woodbridge and Rochester, NY, 2004.

January, Peter, and Knapton, Michael, 'The Demands Made on Venetian Terraferma Society for Defence in the Early Seventeenth Century', *Ateneo Veneto*, 194 (2007), 25–115.

Kamen, Henry, *Spain's Road to Empire: The Making of a World Power, 1492–1763*, London, 2002.

Keegan, John, *The Face of Battle*, Harmondsworth and New York, 1978.

Keegan, John, *A History of Warfare*, New York, 1993.

Keegan, John, 'Towards a Theory of Combat Motivation', in P. Addison and A. Calder (eds), *A Time to Kill*, London, 1997, 3–11.

Keelay, L. H., *War Before Civilization: The Myth of the Peaceful Savage*, Oxford, 1996.

Kellett, A., *Combat Motivation: The Behavior of Soldiers in Battle*, Boston, 1982.

Kleinschmidt, Harald, 'Using the Gun: Manual Drill and the Proliferation of Portable Firearms', *Journal of Military History*, 63 (1999), 601–29.

Krenn, Peter, 'Test-Firing Selected 16th–18th Century Weapons', *Military Illustrated, Past and Present*, 33 (Feb. 1991), 39–48.

Kroener, Bernhard R., 'Conditions de vie et origine sociale du personnel militaire subalterne au cours de la Guerre de Trente Ans', *Francia*, 15 (1987), 321–50.

Kroener, Bernhard R., 'Le Maraudeur: A propos des groupes marginaux de la société militaire au debut de l'époque moderne', in *Nouveaux regards sur la guerre de Trente Ans*, Centre d'Etudes d'Histoire de la Defense, Vincennes, 1998, 167–79.

Kroener, Bernhard R., 'The Soldiers are Very Poor, Bare, Naked, Exhausted: The Living Conditions and Organizational Structure of Military Society during the Thirty Years' War', in K. Bussmann and H. Schilling (eds), *1648: War and Peace in Europe*, Munster and Osnabruck, 1998, 285–91.

Landier, Patrick, '1643: Etude quantitative d'une année de violence, en France pendant la Guerre de Trente Ans', *Histoire: Economie et Société*, 1 (1982), 187–212.

LeBlanc, Steven A., 'Why Warfare? Lessons from the Past', *Daedalus*, 136 (2007), 13–21.

Le Blanc, S. A., and Register, K. E., *Constant Battles: The Myth of the Noble, Peaceful Savage*, New York, 2003.

Leman, Auguste, *Richelieu et Olivares, leurs négociations secrètes de 1636 à 1642 pour le retablissement de la paix*, Lille, 1938.

Lenihan, Padraig, 'Unhappy Campers: Dundalk (1689) and After', *Journal of Conflict Archaeology*, 3 (2007), 197–216.

Lloyd Moote, A., *Louis XIII, the Just*, Berkeley, CA, 1989.

Loriga, Sabina, *Soldats: Un laboratoire disciplinaire. L'armée piémontaise au XVIIIe siècle*, Paris, 1991.

Louis, Gérard, *La Guerre de Dix Ans, 1634–1644*, Besançon, 1998.

Lovie, Jacques, 'Les fières heures de Madame Royale, duchesse de Savoie (1606–1663)', *Bulletin de l'Académie Delphinale*, 5 (1984), 21–35.

Lugs, Jaroslav, *Firearms Past and Present: A Complete Review of Firearms Systems and their Histories*, i, London, 1973 (first published 1956).

Lynn, John, 'Recalculating French Army Growth during the Grand Siècle, 1610–1715', *French Historical Studies*, 18 (1994), 881–906.

Lynn, John, *Giant of the Grand Siecle: The French Army 1610–1715*, Cambridge, 1997.

Lynn, John, *Battle: A History of Combat and Culture*, Boulder, CO, 2003.

McPherson, James M., *For Cause and Comrades: Why Men Fought in the Civil War*, New York and Oxford, 1997.

Maffi, Davide, 'Guerra ed economia: Spese belliche e appaltatori militari nella Lombardia spagnola (1635–1660)', *Storia Economica*, 3 (2000), 489–527.

Maffi, Davide, 'Confesionalismo y Razòn de Estado en la edad moderna: El caso de la Valtellina (1637–1639)', *Hispania Sacra*, 57 (2005), 467–89.

Maffi, Davide, 'Il potere delle armi: La monarchia spagnola e i suoi eserciti (1635–1700). Una rivisitazione del mito della decadenza', *Rivista Storica Italiana*, 118 (2006), 394–445.

Maffi, Davide, 'Un bastione incerto? L'esercito di Lombardia tra Filippo IV e Carlo II (1630–1700)', in Enrique Garcia Hernan and Davide Maffi (eds), *Guerra y Sociedad en la Monarquia Hispanica*, Madrid, 2006, i. 501–36.

Maffi, Davide, *Il baluardo della corona: Guerra, esercito, finanze e società nella Lombardia seicentesca (1630–1660)*, Florence, 2007.

Maffi, Davide, 'Le milizie dello Stato di Milano (1615–1700): Un tentativo di controllo sociale', in Jose Javier Ruiz Ibañez (ed.), *Las milicias del Rey de Espana (siglos XVI y XVII)*, Madrid, 2010, 245–67.

Magni, Cesare, *Il Tramonto del Feudo Lombardo*, Milan, 1937.

Malacarne, Giancarlo, *I Gonzaga di Mantova, una stirpe per una capitale europea*, v. *Morte di una dinastia 1628–1708*, Modena, 2008.

Malfoy-Noël, Dorothée, *L'épreuve de la bataille (1700–1714)*, Montpellier, [2007].

Marshall, S. L. A., *Men Against Fire*, New York, 1947 [1967?].

Martin, Philippe, *Une guerre de Trente Ans en Lorraine 1631–1661*, Metz, 2002.

Martin Gomez, Pablo, *El Ejército español en la guerra de los 30 años*, Madrid, 2006.

Martinez Ruiz, Enrique, 'Los ejercitos hispanicos en el siglo XVII', in J. Alcala-Zamora (ed.), *Calderon de la Barca y la Espana del Barroco*, Madrid, 2001, 17–25.

Martinez-Ruiz, Enrique, 'La eclosion de la historia militar', *Studia Historica: Historia Moderna*, 25 (2003), 17–25.

Martinez-Ruiz, Enrique, *Los soldados del Rey*, Madrid, 2008.

Massera, Sandro, 'La spedizione del Duca Henri de Rohan in Valtellina (1635–1637)', in S. Massera (ed.), *La Spedizione del Duca di Rohan in Valtellina: Storia e memorie nell'età della Guerra dei Trent'Anni*, Milan, 1999, 21–108.

Masson, Bernard, 'Un aspect de la discipline des armées de Louis XIII: La lutte contre la désertion du soldat, 1635–1643', *Revue Historique des Armées*, 162 (1986), 12–23.

Matoušek, Vaclav, 'Building a Model of a Field Fortification of the Thirty Years' War Near Olbramov (Czech Republic)', *Journal of Conflict Archaeology*, 1 (2005), 115–32.

Meier, David A., 'An Appeal for Historiographical Renaissance: Lost Lives and the Thirty Years War', *The Historian*, 67 (2005), 254–74.

Ménager, Daniel, 'Le récit de bataille', *Ecritures de l'histoire (XIVe–XVIe siècles)*, Geneva, 2005.

Merlin, Pierpaolo, et al., *Il Piemonte Sabaudo: Stato e territori in età moderna*, Turin, 1994.

Mesa, Eduardo de, *Nordlingen 1634: Victoria decisiva de los tercios*, Madrid, 2003.

Meuvret, Jean, 'Louis XIV et l'Italie', *XVIIe siècle* (1960), 84–102.

Miller, W., *The Mystery of Courage*, Cambridge, 2000.

Mohrmann, Ruth E., 'Everyday Life in War and Peace', in K. Bussmann and H. Schilling (eds), *1648: War and Peace in Europe*, Munster and Osnabruck, 1998, 319–28.

Monahan, W. Gregory, *Year of Sorrows: The Great Famine of 1709 in Lyon*, Columbia, OH, 1993.

Mortimer, Geoffrey, *Eyewitness Accounts of the Thirty Years War, 1618–1648*, Basingstoke and New York, 2002.

Mortimer, Geoff, 'Individual Experience and Perception of the Thirty Years War in Eyewitness Personal Accounts', *German History*, 20 (2002), 141–60.

Mortimer, Geoff, 'War by Contract, Credit and Contributions: The Thirty Years War', in G. Mortimer (ed.), *Early Modern Military History*, Basingstoke, 2004, 101–17.

Mozzarelli, Cesare, 'Dall'antispagnolismo al revisionismo', in A. Musi (ed.), *Alle origini di una nazione: Antispagnolismo e identità italiana*, Milan, 2003.

Mozzarelli, Cesare, *Antico regime e modernità*, Rome, 2008.

Muir, Rory, *Tactics and the Experience of Battle in the Age of Napoleon*, New Haven and London, 1998.

Mun, Gabriel de, *Richelieu et la maison de Savoie: L'ambassade de Particelli d'Hemery en Piémont*, Paris, 1907.

Murdoch, Steve, and Grosjean, Alexia, *Alexander Leslie and the Scottish Generals of the Thirty Years' War 1618–1648*, London, 2014.

Murdoch, Steve, Zickermann, Katherin, and Marks, Adam, 'The Battle of Wittstock 1636', *Northern Studies*, 43 (2012), 71–109.

Musi, Aurelio, 'The Kingdom of Naples in the Spanish Imperial System', in T. J. Dandelet and J. A. Marino (eds), *Spain in Italy: Politics, Society and Religion 1500–1700*, Leiden and Boston, 2007, 73–98.

Muto, Giovanni, 'Il governo dell'Hacienda nella Lombardia spagnola', in Gianvittorio Signorotto and Paolo Pissavino (eds), *Lombardia Borromaica Lombardia Spagnola 1554–1659*, Rome, 1995, 303–69.

Muto, Giovanni, "Pouvoirs et territoires dans l'Italie espagnole', *Revue d'histoire Moderne et Contemporaine*, 45 (1998), 42–65.

Muto, Giovanni, 'Noble Presence and Stratification in the Territories of Spanish Italy', in T. J. Dandelet and J. A. Marino (eds), *Spain in Italy: Politics, Society and Religion 1500–1700*, Leiden and Boston, 2007, 251–98.

Negro, Piero del, 'La Storia militare nell'Italia moderna nello specchio della storiografia del Novecento', *Cheiron*, 22 (1995), 11–33.

Nosworthy, Brent, *The Anatomy of Victory: Battle Tactics 1689–1763*, New York, 1990.

Nosworthy, Brent, *With Musket, Cannon and Sword: Battle Tactics of Napoleon and his Enemies*, New York, 1996.

Ochoa Brun, Miguel Angel, 'La diplomatie espagnole dans la première moitié du XVIIe siècle', in Lucien Bély (ed.), *L'Europe des traités de Westphalie: Esprit de la diplomatie et diplomatie de l'esprit*, Paris, 2000, 537–54.

O'Donnell y Duque de Estrada, Hugo, 'El reposo del ejèrcito: Estudio del campamento temporal del tempo de los Austrias', in Enrique Garcia Hernan and Davide Maffi (eds), *Guerra y sociedad en la Monarquìa Hispanica: Politica, estrategia y cultura en la Europa moderna (1500–1700)*, Madrid, 2006, 381–99.

Oltrona Visconti, GianDomenico, *La battaglia di Tornavento*, Gallarate, 1970.

Oresko, Robert, 'The House of Savoy in Search for a Royal Crown in the Seventeenth Century', in R. Oresko, G. C. Gibbs, and H. M. Scott (eds), *Royal and Republican Sovereignty in early modern Europe: Essays in Memory of Ragnhild Hatton*, Cambridge and New York, 1997, 272–350.

Oresko, Robert, 'The House of Savoy and the Thirty Years War', in K. Bussmann and H. Schilling (eds), *1648: War and Peace in Europe*, Munster and Osnabruck, 1998, i. 142–53.

Oresko, Robert and Parrott, David. 'Reichsitalien and the Thirty Years' War', in K. Bussmann and H. Schilling (eds), *1648: War and Peace in Europe*, Munster and Osnabruck, 1998, i. 141–2.

Osborne, Toby, *Dynasty and Diplomacy in the Court of Savoy: Political Culture and the Thirty Years' War*, Cambridge and New York, 2002.

O'Siochru, M., 'Atrocity, Codes of Conduct and the Irish in the British Civil Wars 1641–1653', *Past and Present*, 195 (2007), 55–86.

Ostoni, Marco, *Il tesoro del Re: Uomini e istituzioni della finanza pubblica milanese fra Cinque e Seicento*, Naples, 2010.

Outram, Quentin, 'The Socioeconomic Relations of Warfare and the Military Mortality Crises of the Thirty Years' War', *Medical History*, 45 (2001), 151–84.

Outram, Quentin, 'The Demographic Impact of Early Modern Warfare', *Social Science History*, 26 (2002), 245–72.

Pagès, Georges, 'Autour du "grand orage": Richelieu et Marillac: deux politiques', *Revue Historique*, 179 (1937), 63–97.

Panella, Antonio, 'Una lega italiana durante la guerra dei Trent'Anni', *Archivio Storico Italiano*, 94 (1936), 3–36.

Pardo Molero, Juan Francisco, 'Hijos del dios Marte: Historias de soldados y espiritu de cuerpo en los ejercitos de la monarquia hispanica', *Mediterranea: Ricerche Storiche*, 20 (2010), 61–86.

Paret, Peter, 'The Annales School and the History of War', *Journal of Military History*, 73 (2009), 1289–94.

Parker, Geoffrey, *European Soldiers 1550–1650*, Cambridge and New York, 1977.

Parker, Geoffrey, 'The Etiquette of Atrocity: The More Things Change, the More they Stay the Same', *MHQ: Quarterly Journal of Military History*, 1993; reprinted in Parker, *Empire, War and Faith in Early Modern Europe*, London, 2002, 143–68.

Parker, Geoffrey, *Global Crisis: War, Climate Change and Catastrophe in the Seventeenth Century*, New Haven and London, 2013.

Parker, Geoffrey, et al., *The Thirty Years War*, London, 1984.

Parrott, David, 'The Causes of the Franco-Spanish War of 1635–1659', in J. Black (ed.), *The Origins of War in Early Modern Europe*, Edinburgh, 1978, 72–111.

Parrott, David, 'Strategy and Tactics in the Thirty Years' War: The Military Revolution Revisited', *Militargeschichtliche Mitteilungen*, 38/2 (1985), 7–25.

Parrott, David, 'French Military Organization in the 1630s: The Failure of Richelieu's Ministry', *Seventeenth Century French Studies*, 9 (1987), 151–67.

Parrott, David, 'A "prince souverain" and the French Crown: Charles de Nevers 1580–1637', in R. Oresko, G. C. Gibbs, and H. M. Scott (eds), *Royal and Republican Sovereignty in Early Modern Europe: Essays in Memory of Ragnhild Hatton*, Cambridge, 1997, 149–87.

Parrott, David, 'The Role of Fortifications in the Defence of States: The Farnese and the Security of Parma and Piacenza', in A. Bilotto, P. del Negro, and C. Mozzarelli (eds), *I Farnese: Corti, guerra e nobiltà in Antico Regime*, Rome, 1997, 509–60.

Parrott, David, *Richelieu's Army: War, Government and Society in France, 1624–1642*, Cambridge, 2001.

Parrott, David, 'Cultures of Combat in the Ancien Régime: Linear Warfare, Noble Values and Entrepreneurship', *International History Review*, 27 (2005), 518–33.

Parrott, David, 'France's Wars Against the Habsburgs 1624–1659: The Politics of Military Failure', in Enrique Garcia Hernan and Davide Maffi (eds), *Guerra y sociedad en la Monarquìa Hispanica: Politica, estrategia y cultura en la Europa moderna (1500–1700)*, Madrid, 2006, 31–48.

Parrott, David, 'The Utility of Fortifications in Early Modern Europe: Italian Princes and their Citadels', *War in History*, 7 (2007), 127–53.

Parrott, David, 'Italian Soldiers in French Service, 1500–1700: The Collapse of a Military Tradition', in Paolo Bianchi and Davide Maffi (eds), *Italiani al servizio straniero in età moderna*, Milan, 2008, 15–40.

Parrott, David, *The Business of War: Military Enterprise and Military Revolution in Early Modern Europe*, Cambridge and New York, 2012.

Patrucco, C. E., 'L'Antifrancesimo in Piemonte sotto il regno di Vittorio Amedeo I', *Bollettino Storico-Bibliografico Subalpino*, 2–3 (1896), 158–74.

Pedretti, Sara, 'Ai confini occidentali dello Stato di Milano: L'impiego delle milizie rurali nella guerra del Seicento', in C. Donati (ed.), *Alle frontiere della Lombardia: Politica, guerra e religione nell'età moderna*, Milan, 2006, 177–200.

Pepper, Simon, 'Aspects of Operational Art: Communications, Cannon and Small War', in Frank Tallett and D. J. B. Trim (eds), *European Warfare 1350–1750*, Cambridge and New York, 2010, 181–202.

Perjés, Geza, 'Army Provisioning, Logistics and Strategy in the Second Half of the 17th Century', *Acta Historica Academiae Scientiarum Hungaricae*, 16 (1970), 1–51.

Peschot, Bernard, 'Les "lettres de feu": La petite guerre et les contributions paysannes au XVIIe siècle', in C. Desplat (ed.), *Les villageois face à la guerre, XIVe–XVIIIe siècle*, Toulouse, 2002, 129–42.

Pezzolo, Luciano, 'La "Revoluzione militare": Una prospettiva italiana 1400–1700', in A. Dattero and S. Levati (eds), *Militari in età moderna: La centralità di un tema di confine*, Milan, 2006, 15–64.

Pezzolo, Luciano, 'Professione militare e famiglia in Italia tra tardo medioevo e prima età moderna', unpublished paper 2009.

Phillips, Gervase, ' "Of nimble service": Technology, Equestrianism and the Cavalry Arm of Early Modern European Armies', *War and Society*, 20 (2002), 1–21.

Phillips, Gervase, 'Military Morality Transformed: Weapons and Soldiers on the Nineteenth-Century Battlefield', *Journal of Interdisciplinary History*, 41 (2011), 565–90.

Picaud, Sandrine, 'La "guerre de partis" au XVIIe siècle en Europe', *Stratégique* (2007), 101–46.

Piccoli, Paola, and Pruno, Simona, *Il Castello e le mura di Novara: Storia e progetti per una città fortezza tra il XVI e il XVII secolo*, Novara, 2010.

Picouet, Pierre, *Les Tercios espagnoles 1600–1660*, Paris, 2011.

Picouet, Pierre, 'Bataille de Tornavento 22/06/1636: Victoire Franco-Savoyarde (Tactique)', <http://uk.oocities.com/aow1617/TornaventoFr.html>.

Pillorget, Réné. 'Populations civiles et troupes dans le Saint-Empire au cours de la Guerre de Trente Ans', in V. Barrie-Curien (ed.), *Guerre et pouvoir en Europe au XVIIe siècle*, Paris, 1991, 151–74.

Pinker, Steven, *The Better Angels of our Nature: The Decline of Violence and its Causes*, London and New York, 2011.

Porter, Stephen, *Destruction in the English Civil Wars*, Dover, NH, 1994.

Prove, R., 'La nouvelle histoire militaire de l'époque moderne en Allemagne', *Revue Historique des Armées*, 257 (2009), 14–26.

Quazza, Guido, 'Giulio Mazzarini mediatore fra Vittorio Amedeo I e il Richelieu (1635–1636)', *Bollettino Storico-Bibliografico Subalpino*, 48 (1950), 53–84.

Quazza, Guido, *Guerra Civile in Piemonte 1637–1642: Nuove ricerche*, Turin, 1960.

Quazza, Romolo, 'Il periodo italiano della guerra di Trent'Anni', *Rivista Storica Italiana*, 50 (1933), 64–89.

Rahlenbeck, Charles, *Gilles de Haes*, Ghent, 1854.

Raudzens, George, 'Firepower Limitations in Modern Military History', *Journal of the Society for Army Historical Research*, 67 (1989), 130–53.

Raudzens, George, 'In Search of Better Quantification for War History: Numerical Superiority and Casualty Rates in Early Modern Europe', *War and Society*, 15 (1997), 1–30.

Redlich, Fritz, *De Praeda Militari: Looting and Booty 1500–1815*, Wiesbaden, 1956.

Ribot Garcia, Luis A., 'El reclutamiento militar en la Espana a mediados del siglo XVII', *Cuadernos de Investigacion Historica*, 9 (1986), 63–89.

Ribot Garcia, Luis A., 'Milano piazza d'armi della Monarchia Spagnola', in F. Motta (ed.), *Millain the Great: Milano nelle brume del Seicento*, Milan, 1989, 349–63.

Ribot Garcia, Luis A., 'Las provincias italianas y la defensa de la Monarquia', in A. Musi (ed.), *Nel sistema imperiale l'Italia spagnola*, Naples, 1994, 67–92.

Ribot Garcia, Luis A., 'Les types d'armée en Espagne au début des temps modernes', in Philippe Contamine (ed.), *Guerre et concurrence entre les Etats européens du XIVe au XVIIIe siècles*, Paris, 1998, 43–81.

Ricotti, Ercole, *Storia della monarchia piemontese*, v, Florence, 1865.

Rizzo, Mario, 'I Cespiti di un maggiorente lombardo del Seicento: Ercole Teodoro Trivulzio e la milizia forese', *Archivio Storico Lombardo*, 120 (1990), 463–77.

Rizzo, Mario, 'Istituzioni militari e strutture socio-economiche in una città di antico regime: La milizia urbana a Pavia nell'età moderna', in C. Donati (ed.), *Eserciti e carriere militari nell'Italia moderna*, Milan, 1998, 63–89.

Rizzo, Mario, ' "Ottima gente da guerra": Cremonesi al servizio della strategia imperiale', in G. Politi (ed.), *Storia di Cremona: L'Età degli Asburgo di Spagna (1535–1707)*, Cremona, 2006, 126–45.

Rizzo, Mario, ' "Rivoluzione dei consumi", "State building" e "rivoluzione militare": La domanda e l'offerta di servizi strategici nella Lombardia Spagnola, 1535–1659', in I. Lopane and E. Ritrovato (eds), *Tra Vecchi e nuovi equilibri: Domanda e offerta di servizi in Italia in età moderna e contemporanea*, Bari, 2007, 447–74.

Roach, Mary, *Stiff: The Curious Lives of Human Cadavers*, New York, 2003.

Roberts, Keith, *Matchlock Musketeer 1588–1688*, Oxford, 2002.

Roberts, Keith, *Pike and Shot Tactics 1590–1660*, Oxford, 2010.

Roberts, N. A., Brown, J. W., Hammett, B., and Kingston, P. D. F., 'A Detailed Study of the Effectiveness and Capabilities of 18th-Century Musketry on the Battlefield', *Journal of Conflict Archaeology*, 4 (2008), 1–21.

Robinson, Gavin, 'Equine Battering Rams? A Reassessment of Cavalry Charges in the English Civil War', *Journal of Military History*, 75 (2011), 719–31.

Roche, Daniel, *Humeurs vagabondes: De la circulation des hommes et de l'utilité des voyages*, Paris, 2003.

Roche, Daniel, and Reytier, Daniel (eds), *Le cheval et la guerre du XVe au XXe siècle*, Paris, 2002.

Rogers, Clifford J., 'Tactics and the Face of Battle', in Frank Tallett and D. J. B. Trim (eds), *European Warfare 1350–1750*, Cambridge and New York, 2010, 203–35.

Rosen, Stephen Peter, *War and Human Nature*, Princeton, 2005.

Rosso, Claudio, *Il Piemonte sabaudo: Stato e territori in età moderna*, Turin, 1994, 199–236.

Russon, Marc, and Martin, Hervé, *Vivre sous la tente au Moyen-Age (Ve–XVe siècle)*, Rennes, 2010.

Sallmann, Jean-Michel, 'Le cheval, la pique et le canon: Le rôle tactique de la cavalerie du XIVe au XVIIe siècle', in Daniel Roche and Daniel Reytier (eds), *Le cheval et la guerre du XVe au XXe siècle*, Paris, 2002, 253–67.

Saluces, Alexandre de, *Histoire militaire du Piémont*, iv, Turin, 1818.

Salva, Miguel, *Coleccion de documentos ineditos para la historia de España*, xxiii, Madrid, 1853.

Sanchez Martin, Juan Luis, 'Identificaciòn de los llamados maestres de campo del Senado', *Estudios Historiobelicos*, 22 (Oct. 2004), 54–7.

Sandberg, Brian, 'The Magazine of All their Pillaging: Armies as Sites of Second-Hand Exchanges during the French Wars of Religion', in L. Fontaine (ed.), *Alternative Exchanges: Second-Hand Circulations from the 16th Century to the Present*, New York and Oxford, 2008, 76–96.

Sandberg, Brian, *Warrior Pursuits: Noble Culture and Civil Conflict in Early Modern France*, Baltimore, 2010.

Satterfield, George, *Princes, Posts and Partisans: The Army of Louis XIV and Partisan Warfare in the Netherlands 1673–1678*, Leiden, 2003.

Schaub, Jean-Frederic, 'La crise hispanique de 1640: Le modèle des "revolutions périphériques" en question', *Annales: Histoire, Sciences Sociales* (1994), 219–40.

Seidler, Christoph, 'Mass Grave Begins Revealing Soldiers' Secrets', *Der Spiegel Online*, 27 Apr. 2012.

Séré, Daniel, *La Paix des Pyrénées: Vingt-quatre ans de négociations entre la France et l'Espagne (1635–1659)*, Paris, 2006.

Showalter, Dennis, 'A Modest Plea for Drums and Trumpets', *Military Affairs*, 39 (Apr. 1975), 71–4.

Shy, John, 'History, and the History of War: The 2008 George C. Marshall Lecture in Military History', *Journal of Military History*, 72 (2008), 1033–46.

Signorotto, Giovanni Vittorio, *Milano Spagnola: Guerra, istituzioni e uomini di governo (1635–1660)*, 2nd edn, Milan, 2001.

Signorotto, Giovanni Vittorio, 'Modena e il mito della sovranità eroica', in Elena Fumagalli and Gianvittorio Signorotto (eds), *La Corte estense nel primo Seicento: Diplomazia e mecenatismo artistico*, Rome, 2012, 11–50.

Signorotto, Giovanni Vittorio, 'Milan et l'ennemi savoyard dans la première moitié du XVIIe siècle', in Giuliano Ferretti (ed.), *De Paris à Turin: Christine de France, duchesse de Savoie*, Paris, 2014, 35–58.

Sodini, Carla, 'L'Italie et la Guerre de Trente Ans', *Nouveaux regards sur la Guerre de Trente Ans*, Centre d'Etudes d'Histoire de la Defense, Vincennes, 1998, 37–56.

Spagnoletti, Angelantonio, *Principi italiani e Spagna nell'età barocca*, Milan, 1996.

Spagnoletti, Angelantonio, *Le dinastie italiane nell'epoca moderna*, Bologna, 2003.

Spagnoletti, Angelantonio, 'Onore e spirito nazionale nei soldati italiani al servizio della monarchia spagnola', in C. Donati and B. Kroener (eds), *Militari e società civile nell'Europa dell'età moderna*, Bologna, 2007, 211–53.

Stevenin, Michel, 'Une fatalité: Les devastations des gens de guerre dans l'Est de la France (1620–1660). L'exemple de la Champagne', in André Corvisier and Jean Jacquart (eds), *Les malheurs de la guerre*, i. *De la guerre à l'ancienne à la guerre réglée*, Paris, 1996, 161–79.

Stradling, Robert A., 'Spain's Military Failure and the Supply of Horses, 1600–1660', *History*, 69 (1984), 208–21.

Stradling, Robert A., 'Olivares and the Origins of the Franco-Spanish War, 1627–1635', *English Historical Review*, 101 (1986), 68–94.

Susane, Louis, *Histoire de l'Ancienne infanterie française*, iv, Paris, 1852.

Susane, Louis, *Histoire de l'Infanterie française*, iii, Paris, 1876.

Tallett, Frank, *War and Society in Early Modern Europe, 1495–1715*, London, 1992.

Thompson, I. A. A., 'El soldato del Imperio: Una aproximación al perfil del recluta español en el Siglo de Oro', *Manuscrits*, 21 (2003), 17–38.

Tibbett, M., and Carter, D. O., *Soil Analysis in Forensic Taphonomy: Chemical and Biological Effects of Buried Human Remains*, Boca Raton, FLA, 2008.

Tiger, Lionel, *Men in Groups*, New York, 1969.

Tlusty, B. Ann, *The Martial Ethic in Early Modern Germany*, London and New York, 2011.

Tooby, John, and Cosmides, Leda, *The Evolution of War and its Cognitive Foundations*, Institute for Evolutionary Studies Technical Report, 88–1, 1988, <www.cep.ucsb.edu/papers/Evolofwar.pdf>.

Ulbricht, Otto, 'The Experience of Violence during the Thirty Years War: A Look at the Civilian Victims', in J. Canning, H. Lehmann, and J. Winter (eds), *Power, Violence and Mass Death in Pre-Modern and Modern Times*, Aldershot, 2004, 97–127.

Vignal Souleyreau, Marie-Catherine, *Richelieu et la Lorraine*, Paris, 2004.

Waal, Frans B. M. de, 'Morality and its Relation to Primate Social Instincts', in H. Høgh-Olesen (ed.), *Human Morality and Sociality: Evolutionary and Comparative Perspectives*, Basingstoke and New York, 2010, 31–57.

Wanklyn, Malcolm, *Decisive Battles of the English Civil Wars: Myth and Reality*, Barnsley, 2006.

Westbrook, S., 'The Potential for Military Disintegration', in S. C. Sarkesian (ed.), *Combat Effectiveness: Cohesion, Stress and the Volunteer Military*, Beverly Hills, CA, 1980, 244–78.

Wheatcroft, Andrew, *The Enemy at the Gate: Habsburgs, Ottomans and the Battle for Europe*, New York, 2008.

White, Lorraine, 'Spain's Early Modern Soldiers: Origins, Motivations and Loyalty', *War and Society*, 19 (2001), 19–46.

White, Lorraine, 'The Experience of Spain's Early Modern Soldiers: Combat, Welfare and Violence', *War in History*, 9 (2002), 1–38.

Wilson, Peter H., 'New Perspectives on the Thirty Years War', *German History*, 23 (2005), 237–61.

Wilson, Peter H., 'Defining Military Culture', *Journal of Military History*, 72 (2008), 11–41.

Wilson, Peter H., *Europe's Tragedy: A History of the Thirty Years War*, Harmondsworth, 2009.

Zeller, Gaston, 'Bresse, Turin et Pignerol', *Revue Historique*, 193 (1942–3), 97–110.

Zuckerman, Marvin, *Sensation Seeking and Risky Behavior*, Washington, DC, 2007.

Index